Environment and Industry in Developing Countries

The views expressed in this publication are those of the authors and do not necessarily reflect the views of the Secretariat of the United Nations Industrial Development Organization. The description and classifications of countries and territories used, and the arrangements of the material, do not imply the expression of any opinion whatsoever on the part of the Secretariat concerning the legal status of any country, territory, city or area, of its authorities, concerning the delimitation of its frontiers or boundaries, or regarding its economic system or degree of development. Designations such as 'developed', 'industrialized' and 'developing' are intended for statistical convenience and do not necessarily express a judgment about the stage reached by a particular country or area in the development process. Mention of firm names and commercial products does not imply the endorsement of the United Nations Industrial Development Organization.

Environment and Industry in Developing Countries

Assessing the Adoption of Environmentally Sound Technology

Ralph A. Luken

former Economist, Environmental Protection Agency, USA and former Senior Environmental Adviser, United Nations Industrial Development Organization (UNIDO), Vienna, Austria

and

Frank Van Rompaey

United Nations Industrial Development Organization (UNIDO), Vienna, Austria

With a foreword by Mr Kandeh K. Yumkella, Director-General, UNIDO

Edward Elgar

Cheltenham, UK • Northampton, MA, USA

United Nations Industrial Development Organization

Published by
Edward Elgar Publishing Limited
Glensanda House
Montpellier Parade
Cheltenham
Glos GL50 1UA
UK

Edward Elgar Publishing, Inc.
William Pratt House
9 Dewey Court
Northampton
Massachusetts 01060
USA

A catalogue record for this book
is available from the British Library

Library of Congress Cataloguing in Publication Data
Luken, Ralph Andrew.
  Environment and industry in developing countries : assessing the adoption of environmentally sound technology / by Ralph A. Luken, Frank Van Rompaey.
    p. cm.
  Includes bibiographical references and index.
  1. Industrial management—Environmental aspects—Developing countries. 2. Technology—Environmental aspects—Developing countries. 3. Environmental management—Developing countries. I. Van Rompaey, Frank, 1964– II. Title.

HD30.255.L85 2007
338.9′27091724—dc22
                                                         2006034042

ISBN 978 1 84542 183 0

Printed and bound in Great Britain by MPG Books Ltd, Bodmin, Cornwall

Contents

List of abbreviations   vi
Foreword   by Mr Kandeh K. Yumkella, Director-General, UNIDO   x
Preface   xi

 1   Introduction   1
 2   Decoupling of environmental pressure from industrial growth,
     1990–2002   7
 3   Heuristic model of EST adoption   28
 4   Brazil   52
 5   China   81
 6   India   113
 7   Kenya   143
 8   Thailand   172
 9   Tunisia   203
10   Viet Nam   231
11   Zimbabwe   261
12   Eight-country assessment of factors influencing EST adoption   288
13   Findings, policy implications and programme proposals   318

Index   333

Abbreviations

GENERAL

BAT	best available technology
BOD	biochemical oxygen demand
CETP	common effluent treatment plant
CIP	competitive industrial performance
COD	chemical oxygen demand
CP	cleaner production
CPI	consumer price index
CPT	cleaner production technology
CT	cleaner technology
CTs	clean techniques and technologies
EG	environmental governance
EIA	environmental impact assessment
EMS	environmental management system
EOP	end of pipe
EST	environmentally sound technology
ETP	effluent treatment plant
EU	European Union
EUI	energy-use intensity
FAO	Food and Agriculture Organization
FDI	foreign direct investment
FTZ	free trade zone
GDP	gross domestic product
GNI	gross national income
GNP	gross national product
IEA	International Energy Agency
IMF	International Monetary Fund
ISIC	international standard industrial classification
ISO	International Organization for Standardization
MFN	most favoured nation
MVA	manufacturing value added
NGOs	non-governmental organizations
ODA	overseas development assistance
PATs	pollutant abatement technologies

PPP	purchasing power parity
R&D	research and development
S&T	science and technology
SMEs	small and medium enterprises
SOE	state owned enterprises
TC	technological capabilities
TI	technology import
TMP	tariff on manufactured products
TOE	tons of oil equivalent
TRI	trade restrictiveness index
UNDP	United Nations Development Programme
UNEP	United Nations Environment Programme
UNIDO	United Nations Industrial Development Organization
WTO	World Trade Organization

SPECIFIC

Brazil

BRACELPA	Brazilian Association of Pulp and Paper Manufacturers
CNTL	Centro Nacional de Tecnologias Limpas Brazil
CONAMA	National Council of the Environment
IBAMA	The Brazilian Environmental Institute
MMA	Ministry of Environment

China

CNCPC	China National Cleaner Production Centre
EPB	Environmental Protection Bureau
SEPA	State Environmental Protection Agency
TVE	town and village enterprise

India

CPCB	Central Pollution Control Board
CTS	Centre for Technology Studies
MOEF	Ministry of Environment and Forests
NCPC	National Cleaner Production Centre
SPCB	State Pollution Control Board
SSI	small scale industry

Kenya

EPC	export Promotion Council
EPZ	export processing zone
EPZA	Export Processing Zones Authority
KES	Kenyan shillings
KIRDI	Kenyan Industrial Research and Development Institute
KNCPC	Kenya National Cleaner Production Centre
NEMA	National Environment Management Authority

Thailand

ASEAN	Association of South East Asian Nations
DANCED	Danish Cooperation for Environment and Development
DIW	Department of Industrial Works
IEAT	Industrial Estate Authority of Thailand
MOI	Ministry of Industry
MOSTE	Ministry of Science, Technology and Environment
PCD	Pollution Control Department
TEI	Thailand Environmental Institute
THTI	Thailand Textile Institute

Tunisia

ANPE	National Environmental Protection Agency
API	Industry Promotion Agency
CETTEX	Technical Centre for Textiles
CITET	Tunis International Centre for Environmental Technology
ETE	Euro-Tunisie-Entreprise Programme
MEAT	Ministry of the Environment and Land Use Planning
ONAS	National Sewerage Company
PMN	Industrial Upgrading Programme
SONEDE	National Water Supply and Exploitation Society

Viet Nam

ASEAN	Association of South East Asian Nations
MONRE	Ministry of Natural Resources and Environment
VEPA	Viet Nam Environment Protection Agency
VNCPC	Viet Nam National Cleaner Production Centre
VND	Vietnamese Dong

Zimbabwe

ESAP	Economic Structural Adjustment Programme
MET	Ministry of Environment and Tourism
SIRDC	Scientific and Industrial Research and Development Centre
ZNCPC	Zimbabwe National Cleaner Production Centre

Foreword by the Director-General of UNIDO

Technological change is key to achieving sustainable development. It is the essential basis for economic growth – the *sine qua non* for poverty reduction – and for the preservation of environmental quality.

UNIDO fully appreciates the importance of firm-level technological change for initiating a path of sustainable development. It works actively with the relevant national and international stakeholders to foster productivity growth in developing countries and in economies in transition. Growth in productivity results from producing goods more efficiently, producing goods of better quality and producing new goods. All these involve innovation and technological change.

In broad terms, technological change can be defined as any change in the way in which inputs are transformed into outputs. Undertaking such a change requires information, knowledge and skills on the part of the firm as well as a conducive business environment. Understanding this change process and its determinants is obviously crucial for stimulating the growth of higher-value production in developing countries. Moreover, an improved understanding of this process is instrumental in defining how public policy can shape technological change in more environmentally benign directions. While recent studies of technological change in developing countries have greatly advanced our insight into this process, more theoretical and empirical work is still needed – particularly in terms of its environmental aspects.

It is for this reason that UNIDO has undertaken this research to determine the factors that govern, in various circumstances, the adoption of environmentally sound technology (EST), which includes a variety of cleaner technology measures and pollution control solutions. This research aims to contribute to the debate on this subject and to further the understanding of how environmentally sound technological change can best be encouraged in developing countries. It underscores once more UNIDO's commitment to sustainable industrial development and builds upon the insights gained from its years of technical cooperation in technology transfer and the promotion of cleaner production. The results of this research will feed into the Organization's policy advisory services and technical cooperation interventions.

Preface

This book is an outcome of a research project we initiated as part of UNIDO's preparatory activities for the World Summit on Sustainable Development (Johannesburg, 2002). Our objective was to gain a better understanding of what motivates industry in developing countries to adopt environmentally sound technology (EST).

We started the research by formulating a heuristic model of EST adoption derived from a review of the literature on technology diffusion and technological capabilities, and of empirical studies of EST adoption in developing countries. On the basis of this model we prepared a semi-structured questionnaire to be used in interviewing plant managers and key informants in three industrial sub-sectors in eight countries. We then contracted country teams to carry out the survey in each country in late 2001 and early 2002 and to provide background data on the country and the sub-sector investigated. On the basis of their findings, we wrote country chapters, analysed the survey data and identified policy implications and programme proposals that could accelerate the adoption of EST.

We would like to acknowledge the assistance of the team leaders and associated organizations in each of the eight countries: Mr Celso Foelkel and Centro Nacional de Technologias Limpas of Brazil; Mr Wan Nianqinq and the China Cleaner Production Centre and the Chinese Academy of Environmental Sciences; Mr Guyar Alam and the Centre for Technology Studies of India; Ms Jane Nyakang'O and the Kenya National Cleaner Production Centre; Ms Patcharin Worathanakul and the Thailand Environmental Institute; Mr Rachid Nafti and the Centre International des Technologies de l'Environnement de Tunis; Mr Nhan Tran Van and the Institute for Environmental Science and Technology of the Hanoi University of Technology; and Ms Sharon Gomez and the Environment and Remote Sensing Institute of the Scientific and Industrial Research and Development Centre of Zimbabwe. We would also like to acknowledge the provision of independent reviews of each of the eight country chapters by Mr Ronaldo Seroa da Motta (Brazil), Mr Kuang Shi Jun (China), Mr Shashi Jain (India), Mr Charles Orina (Kenya), Mr Virat Tandaechanurat (Thailand), Ms Faten Ben Aicha (Tunisia), Mr Bertrand Collegnon (Viet Nam) and Mr Morris Chidavaenzi (Zimbabwe). We, however, bear sole responsibility for the present text.

We would also like to express our thanks to several other groups of individuals. We were assisted by several UNIDO interns and research assistants, in particular, Mr Praved Krishnapilla, Mr Fernando Castellanos Silveria, Ms Mariana Vilpoux and Ms Katja Zigova. We were advised on sub-sector technical matters by Ms Rosely Viegas-Assumpcao (UNIDO/pulp and paper), Mr James Gallup (US EPA/textiles), Mr Yuan-Hoi Lee (UNIDO/ textiles), Mr Neil McCubbin (independent expert/pulp and paper), Mr John Peter Moll (UNIDO/textiles) and Mr Ferenc Schmel (UNIDO/leather processing). We received survey guidance from Tim Forsyth (London School of Economics), information assistance from Donna Coleman (UNIDO) and Elizabeth Mayer (UNIDO), and editorial assistance from Ms Barbara Bohle, Ms Maria Fermie (UNIDO), Ms Lesley Parker and Mr Malachy Scullion.

Finally, we would like to acknowledge our gratitude to UNIDO management for providing the financial support for the country teams and reviewers, for providing logistical support and for allowing us the working time to write this book.

1. Introduction

INDUSTRY AND THE ENVIRONMENT

Developing countries, in spite of common perceptions to the contrary, have achieved major improvements in the environmental performance of their industry since the Rio Conference of 1992. They have performed better than developed countries in reducing energy-use and water-pollutant intensities between 1990 and about 2002; they cut the energy intensity of their production by 27 per cent, compared to only 8 per cent by developed countries, and the water-pollutant intensity by 49 per cent, compared to only 29 per cent by developed countries (see Chapter 2). These globally aggregated achievements are confirmed by developing-country case studies that show that numerous manufacturing plants in many developing countries, such as Bangladesh, China, Indonesia and Mexico, are in compliance with environmental norms (World Bank, 2000).

The improved environmental performance is not surprising for several reasons. First, environmentally sound technology (EST), particularly pollutant abatement technologies (PATs), are now readily available and well known, given their long development history – 50 years for air pollution and 150 years for water pollution (Anderson, 2001). Second, the costs of these technologies are low for many manufacturing sub-sectors compared to overall production costs. The costs of pollution control are on average about 2 per cent of production costs and around 15 per cent of one-time investment costs (OECD, 1993). Third, there is an increased understanding on the part of industry in developing countries of the importance of using cleaner technologies (CTs) in combination with PATs to achieve environmental compliance. Environmentally, CTs do not lead to the transfer of pollutants from one environmental medium to another, whereas PATs often do, as in the case of water pollution where PATs create secondary air-pollution and solid-waste problems; economically, CTs are generally productivity-enhancing and cost-lowering technological options, whereas PATs are only an added cost of production.

But in spite of this remarkable progress, there is still a large gap between the current environmental performance of industry in developing and developed countries. The energy-use intensity of industry remains almost three times higher in developing than in developed countries, water-use intensity more than 11 times higher, water-pollutant intensity six times higher and carbon dioxide intensity four times higher (see Chapter 2). And with the accelerating industrialization of developing countries this gap could grow, if not necessarily in the intensity of energy use and pollutant release, certainly in the absolute amount of energy that will be used and the levels of pollution reached. The developing countries' share of global manufacturing value added (MVA) has already grown significantly, from 16.9 per cent to 25.5 per cent between 1990 and 2005, while the developed countries' share decreased from 78.6 to 70.3 per cent during the same period (UNIDO, 2005). Clearly it is essential that developing countries gain a better understanding of the factors motivating improved industrial environmental behaviour and of what they can do to strengthen these factors.

In light of the major environmental achievements that have been made in industry in developing countries and given, at the same time, the urgent need to take this further, it is surprising how little is actually known about the factors that have motivated industry in developing countries to comply with environmental standards and, more particularly, to adopt EST. Admittedly some investigations have been undertaken into these factors, most of them conducted directly by the World Bank or externally funded by the Bank. However, as seen in the literature review in Chapter 3, only a few studies have examined, directly or indirectly, the factors that have influenced plant-level decisions on the adoption of EST under the specific conditions faced in developing countries. Most of the recent studies on plant-level behaviour in developing countries have focused on factors determining environmental performance rather than technology choice because of the concern for reducing environmental pressure. Moreover these studies investigated only one or two countries, one or two sub-sectors and a limited set of factors affecting plant-level behaviour, making it difficult to generalize about what has accelerated the adoption of EST in developing countries.

The United Nations Industrial Development Organization (UNIDO), as the specialized United Nations agency promoting industrial development in developing and transitional economics, is keenly aware of the need to enhance the capacity of developing-country institutions to assist their industry in improving its environmental performance. UNIDO is actively supporting implementation of Agenda 21, approved by the United Nations Conference on Environment and Development (1992), and the Johannesburg Plan of Implementation, approved by the World Summit on Sustainable Development (2002). Both action plans implicitly recognize the need to close the gap in resource use and pollutant intensities between developed and developing countries and call for urgent action to be taken to promote, facilitate and, as appropriate, finance the development, transfer and diffusion of EST and the corresponding know-how to and among developing countries (United Nations, 1992 and 2002). In supporting these two action plans, UNIDO recognized that successful technical assistance programmes to accelerate the adoption of EST in developing countries must be based on a sound empirical understanding of the multitude and relative importance of factors that influence EST adoption in these countries. To improve its understanding as well as that of the larger community of bilateral and multilateral organizations undertaking technical cooperation programmes in developing countries, UNIDO undertook a study in late 2001–early 2002 on the determinants of EST adoption by 98 plants in three manufacturing sub-sectors located in eight developing countries. The findings of this study are reported in this book.

This study was designed to identify the factors that determine the adoption of CTs as well as PATs. The aim was to document and assess the relative importance of factors that were broadly classified as contextual, that is, part of the plant's external environment, and those classified as plant-specific. Examples of contextual factors are buyer and environmental regulatory pressures; examples of plant-specific factors are environmental commitment and technological capabilities.

DEFINITION OF ENVIRONMENTALLY SOUND TECHNOLOGY (EST)

EST is often divided into two categories, abatement and prevention technologies. Abatement technologies, conventionally referred to as PATs, reduce the discharge of pollutants at the end of the production process. PATs collect pollutants, separating or neutralizing them in various ways (usually with specially built treatment installations). In contrast, prevention technology, often referred to as CTs, minimizes the generation of pollutants (and the utilization of some inputs such as water or fuel) throughout the production process. CTs are hence defined as manufacturing processes or product technologies that reduce both pollutant generation and the use of production inputs (raw materials, water and energy) in comparison to the technologies they replace. Although reducing the need for more costly abatement technologies, they require modifications in production processes, sometimes disrupting ongoing production activities.

OVERVIEW OF CHAPTERS 2 TO 13

Chapter 2

The differences in trends in the decoupling of environmental pressure from industrial growth in developed and developing countries, which is the under-lying reason for undertaking this study, are compared in this chapter. First, the Organization for Economic Cooperation and Development (OECD) approach to estimating decoupling of economic growth from environmental pressure is described. Then global trends in decoupling for energy use, water use, organic matter effluent and carbon dioxide emission (CO_2) are compared between 1990 and 2002. A brief description of the three factors that have influenced these trends – scale, sub-sectoral composition and technological configuration – concludes the chapter.

In Appendix 2A in Chapter 2 selected evidence is provided on the potential of CTs to reduce industrial pollutants in the three sub-sectors covered in this study: textiles; pulp and paper; and leather processing. The annex consists of a generic description of CT options with examples of CT applications in country-specific situations.

Chapter 3

The heuristic model that guided this investigation of factors determining the adoption of EST in developing countries is presented in this chapter. First, the literature on technology diffusion and technological capabilities is briefly reviewed, followed by a more detailed review of empirical studies of EST adoption in developing countries. The heuristic model, derived from this literature, is then described. Finally, the three modes of investigation identified in the heuristic model and applied in the research are introduced: assessment of policy effectiveness in the eight countries in this study; plant managers' and key informants' perceptions of factors that influenced EST adoption (perceived factors); and a statistical analysis of underlying factors that the country survey teams observed as influencing EST adoption (observed factors).

Chapters 4 to 11

Chapters 4 to 12 present eight country case studies that provide the background information needed for the three modes of investigation. In each country a local team carried out a survey of the factors influencing the adoption of EST in a particular sub-sector during the late 1990s/early 2000s: pulp and paper in Brazil, China, India and Viet Nam; leather processing in Kenya and Zimbabwe; and textiles in Thailand and Tunisia. Using semi-structured questionnaires provided by UNIDO, they interviewed plant managers and key informants, the latter including employees of environmental regulatory agencies, technology centres, NGOs, business associations and chemical and equipment suppliers. Each team also provided background data on the country and on the selected sub-sector.

Each chapter describes the national economic and environmental context in which plants made their EST adoption decisions; the country's environmental, economic and technology policies; production in the selected sub-sector and characteristics of the plants investigated; and key informants and international donors, all of whom influenced the adoption of EST.

The environmental, economic and technology policies reviewed in each chapter are those most related to the adoption of EST:

- The environmental policies reviewed are those aimed at reducing pollutant discharge from industry into the environment: industry-related environmental legislation, institutional arrangements and policy instruments, basically, those measures concerned with industrial environmental management. A global comparison is then presented of the effectiveness of each country's environmental management policy.
- The economic policies reviewed, in addition to macroeconomic performance, are those that most directly affect technological modernization – industrial, trade and resource pricing policies – and the associated institutional arrangements, since more modern technology is usually cleaner technology. A global comparison is given of the effectiveness of each set of policies.
- The technology policies reviewed are those that have the potential to increase the adoption of EST, particularly CTs, by directing the technological infrastructure to support plant-level adoption of more productive technologies and to train workers to operate these technologies. This includes technology policies and programmes and associated institutional arrangements aimed at increasing productivity in the manufacturing sector, with special reference to the sub-sector investigated in each country. A global comparison is presented of the effectiveness of each country's technological capability.

Chapter 12

The findings from the three different modes of investigation used to identify the factors that influenced EST adoption in the eight countries are presented in Chapter 12. The first mode of investigation examines the relationship between the three policy regimes that created the incentive structure brought to bear on plant-level behaviour via government, markets and civil society and the actual levels of resource-use and pollutant intensities that might be attributed to these policies. The second describes the perceptions of 98 plant managers and 91 key informants about the relative importance of government, markets and civil society as external drivers for EST adoption. The third uses statistical techniques to analyse the factors observed by the survey teams as having influenced plant-level behaviour at the 98 plants in the eight countries.

Chapter 13

A summary of the findings in Chapters 2 to 12, policy implications derived from these findings, and proposals for government programmes that build on these implications are presented in Chapter 13. These programme proposals are examples of how governments can increase the ability of and incentives for the manufacturing sector to adopt EST, by using the potential for several policy regimes to influence plant managers' decisions.

REFERENCES

Anderson, D. (2001), 'Technical progress and pollution abatement: an economic view of selected technologies and practices', *Environment and Development Economics*, **6** (3), 275–81.
OECD (1993), *Environmental Policies and Industrial Competitiveness*, Paris: Organization for Economic Cooperation and Development (OECD).
UNIDO (2005), *International Yearbook of Industrial Statistics 2005*, Cheltenham, UK and Northampton, MA, US: Edward Elgar Publishing.
United Nations (1992), 'Agenda 21', United Nations, New York (available on: http://www.un.org/esa/sustdev/documents/agenda21).
United Nations (2002), 'Johannesburg plan of implementation', United Nations, New York (available on: http://www.un.org/esa/sustdev/documents/WSSD).
World Bank (2000), *Greening Industry: New Roles for Communities, Markets and Governments*, Oxford, UK: Oxford University Press.

2. Decoupling of environmental pressure from industrial growth, 1990–2002

INTRODUCTION

The differences in trends in the decoupling of environmental pressure from industrial growth in developed and developing countries between 1990 and 2002, the time period for this study, are compared in this chapter. First, the OECD approach to estimating decoupling of economic growth from environmental pressure is described. Then global trends in decoupling for energy use, water use, organic matter effluent reported as biochemical oxygen demand (BOD) and carbon dioxide (CO_2) emission are compared. Finally, factors are presented that have contributed to these differences in the trends in decoupling, all of which suggest that significant decoupling resulted from the adoption of EST.

ESTIMATING DECOUPLING

Concept

The concept of decoupling, as defined by the OECD (2002), refers to the relative growth rates of environmental pressure and the economic activity with which it is causally linked. Decoupling occurs when the growth rate of an environmentally relevant variable, such as energy use, is less than the growth rate of the economically relevant variable, such as industrial output, over the same period of time.[1] Relative decoupling is said to occur when the growth rate of the environmentally relevant variable is positive but less than the growth rate of MVA. For the most part, however, the fundamental concern is not the relative but the absolute change in the environmental variable, since decoupling could occur but yet not be sufficient to keep an economic activity within the limits of environmental standards. If MVA displays a positive growth, then 'absolute decoupling' is said to occur when the growth rate of an

7

environmentally relevant variable is zero or negative, that is, pressure on the environment is either stable or falling.

The numerator of a decoupling indicator can be both inputs into the production process (withdrawals from the environment) and non-product outputs (releases into the environment). Environmental withdrawals can be disaggregated into five categories: energy, water, other natural resources, recycled material, and land; however, only two categories used by the manufacturing sector, energy and water, are taken into account in this chapter because of data limitations. Environmental releases can be disaggregated into two categories, pollutant discharge (via air and water) and waste disposal/by-products, but only two types of pollutant discharge, BOD effluent and CO_2 emission, are taken into account here, and no waste disposal/by-products, again because of data limitations.

Finally, the denominator of the decoupling indicator is either an economic measure or population. The denominator used for this analysis is MVA at constant 1995 prices. MVA data are available from both the World Bank (2004) and UNIDO (2005); UNIDO data are used for the calculations in this study because they include sub-sector estimates of value added as well as estimates for the manufacturing sector.

In undertaking the analysis for this chapter, a search was carried out for internally consistent global data on environmental withdrawals by and releases from the manufacturing sector (ISIC 3). While manufacturing-related environmental data are relatively robust, though still limited, for most developed countries, this is not the case for developing countries. Here the data are fragmented and of uneven quality, there being no international organization systematically collecting and vetting resource use or pollutant release data for the manufacturing sector in these countries. The United Nations Environment Programme focuses its data-collecting efforts on environmental quality (ambient conditions) and not on its precursors, pollutant releases that affect environmental quality (UNEP, 2005). The only exceptions to this bleak picture are energy use and associated CO_2 emission data, available from the International Energy Agency (IEA) and the United Nations Framework Convention on Climate Change Secretariat; BOD effluent data, available from the World Bank (WB); and water withdrawal data, available from the Food and Agricultural Organization (FAO).

GLOBAL TRENDS IN DECOUPLING

Estimates of changes in eco-intensity and decoupling in four parameters, energy use, water use, BOD effluent and CO_2 emission, are presented below, eco-intensity in Table 2.1 and decoupling in Table 2.2, for the manufactur-

Table 2.1   Intensity estimates, 1990–about 2002

Country group	Energy-use intensity			Water-use intensity			BOD-effluent intensity			CO$_2$ emission intensity		
	# of countries / # of countries in group	toe/10^6 US$ of MVA		# of countries / # of countries in group	10^3 m^3/10^6 US$ of MVA		# of countries / # of countries in group	tons/10^6 US$ of MVA		# of countries / # of countries in group	tons/10^6 US$ of MVA	
		1990	2002		1990	2000		1990	2001		1990	2002
Industrialized countries	25/25	200	190	7/25	25	22	24/25	1	0.5	25/25	420	310
Transition economies	7/22	1380	580	13/22	360	690	10/22	7	5	7/22	3260	1270
Developing countries	53/100	780	590	37/100	190	250	57/100	6	3	57/100	2120	1290
Least developed countries	8/47	700	640	7/47	100	90	14/47	15	10	12/47	1470	1330

Abbreviations: bio-chemical oxygen demand (BOD); carbon dioxide (CO$_2$); and manufacturing value added (MVA) in constant 1995 US dollars.

Sources: IEA (2005a) for energy use; FAO (2005) for water use; World Bank (2004) for BOD effluent; IEA for CO$_2$ emission (2005b); and UNIDO (2005) for MVA.

Table 2.2 *Summary of global decoupling analysis 1990–about 2002*

Country group	Energy use (1990–2002)		Water use (1990–2000)		BOD effluent (1990–2000)		CO$_2$ emission (1990–2002)	
	Relative	Absolute	Relative	Absolute	Relative	Absolute	Relative	Absolute
Developed countries	−5	12	−12	−2	−50	−18	−26	−9
Transition economies	−58	−47	NA	−1	−30	−40	−61	−50
Developing countries	−24	43	NA	146	−50	−5	−39	20
Least developed countries	−9	75	−10	41	−33	31	−10	75

Notes: Relative decoupling is the percentage change in resource/pollutant intensities presented in Table 2.1 For example, energy-use intensity for the developed country group decreased from 200 to 190 toe/10^{6}US$ of MVA, a 5 per cent decrease. Absolute decoupling is the percentage change in energy use. For example, energy use increased in the developed country group from 848 10^6 toe to 951 10^6 toe, a 12 per cent increase. NA is not applicable. See endnote 1.

Abbreviations: biochemical oxygen demand (BOD); carbon dioxide (CO$_2$); and manufacturing value added (MVA) in constant 1995 US dollars.

Sources: IEA (2005a) for energy use; FAO (2005) for water use; World Bank (2004) for BOD effluent; IEA for CO$_2$ emission (2005b); and UNIDO (2005) for MVA.

ing sector in all the countries for which data were reported or calculated; estimates are summarized for four country groups, namely, developed countries, transition economies, developing countries and least developed countries.[2] These are the groupings used by the United Nations, based on the composition of selected economic and social statistics (UNSTAT, 2005).

Energy Use

The changes in the level of the energy-use intensity presented by country group in Table 2.1 are measured in tons of oil equivalent (toe) per million US dollars of MVA. Energy-use intensity decreased in all four country groups between 1990 and 2002. Most remarkable was the decrease in energy-use intensity in the transition economies. As of 2002, energy intensity in the developed countries was more than three times that of developed countries.

The decoupling estimates for energy use presented in Table 2.2 show that over the 13-year period there was relative decoupling in all four country groups, with absolute decoupling occurring in only one group, transition economies.

Water Use

The changes in water-use intensity presented in Table 2.1 are measured in cubic metres of water withdrawal per million US dollars of MVA. Water-use intensity decreased in two country groups, developed countries and least-developed countries, and increased in the other two country groups, transition economies and developing countries. As of 2000, water-use intensity was comparatively low (i.e. water use was highly efficient) in both least-developed countries and industrialized countries, comparatively high in developing economies (i.e. the efficiency of water use was low) and very high in transition economies.

The decoupling estimates for water use presented in Table 2.2 show that there was relative decoupling in developed and least-developed countries. Absolute decoupling occurred only in developed countries and transition economies.

BOD Effluent

The changes in BOD-effluent intensity presented in Table 2.1 are measured as tons of BOD effluent per million US dollars of MVA. BOD-effluent intensity decreased in all four country groups. Most remarkable was the decrease in BOD intensity in the developed countries. In 2001 BOD intensity was lowest in the developed countries, followed by the developing countries. The least-developed countries, even though their BOD intensity was less in 2001 than in 1990, had a BOD intensity of almost four times that of the developed countries.

The decoupling estimates for BOD-effluent intensity presented in Table 2.2 show that relative decoupling occurred in all four country groups and absolute decoupling in three, developed countries, transition economies and developing countries.

CO_2 Emission

Changes in CO_2-emission intensity presented in Table 2.1 are measured in tons of CO_2 emissions per million US dollars of MVA. CO_2-emission intensity decreased in all four country groups, but barely so for least-developed countries. Most remarkable was the decrease in CO_2-emission intensity in transition economies. In 2002, CO_2-emission intensity among the four country groups still differed by a factor of four; it was lowest in developed countries and comparatively and equally high in the three other country groups.

The decoupling estimates for CO_2 emission presented in Table 2.2 show that all four country groups experienced relative decoupling, while absolute decoupling occurred in only developed countries and transition economies.

FACTORS AFFECTING DECOUPLING

The complexity of factors that link environmental pressure to economic activity (in this study manufacturing) can be summarized under the headings of scale, composition and technological configuration (EC, 1990, and OECD, 1997). The scale of production has the potential to affect environmental pressure because pollutant generation and discharge are by-products of production. With ever-increasing levels of industrial output, the scale of production would have a negative effect (increased pollutant generation) on environmental pressure unless there were changes in sub-sector composition and technological configuration. Changes in sub-sector composition could have a positive or negative effect on environmental pressure: a positive effect (decreased pollutant generation) if the share of industrial output produced by less pollutant-intensive sub-sectors increases as a percentage of total industrial output, and, conversely, a negative effect if the share produced by more pollutant-intensive sub-sectors increases as a percentage of total industrial output. Technological configuration refers to the method of production, including the utilization of CTs as part of the production process or the addition of PATs at the end of the production process.

Effect of Scale

Globally, MVA increased by 30 per cent over the period 1990 to 2002 (Table 2.3). It increased significantly for the developing countries and least-developed countries, but declined for the transition economies.[3] This positive increase in MVA suggests that both resource use and pollutant discharge might have increased over the period, but this did not occur in some country groups for some parameters, that is, those with negative absolute decoupling.

Effect of Shifts in Sub-sector Composition

Changes in sub-sector composition can refer to both broad sectoral shifts (agriculture, industry and service) and narrow sectoral shifts (sub-sector composition within the manufacturing sector) (Arrow et al., 1995). The focus here is on the effects of narrow sub-sectoral shifts, sometimes referred to as the structural change effect. These effects can be either positive or negative depending on whether the share of resource-intensive sub-sectors (significant users of material, water and energy) in the overall production increases or decreases over time.

Table 2.3   Changes in MVA by country groups, 1990–2002

Country group	1990 MVA (1995 US$ billion)	Percentage of 1990 global MVA	2002 MVA (1995 US$ billion)	Percentage of 2002 global MVA	Percentage change, 1990 to 2002
Developed countries	4200	78.6	5100	73.3	21
Transition economies	310	4.3	220	3.2	−29
Developing countries	810	16.9	1600	23.2	98
Least developed countries	20	0.2	30	0.3	50
Total	5340	100	6950	100	30

Source: UNIDO (2005).

Table 2.4   Share of MVA in most resource-intensive sub-sectors,
            1990 and 2002*

Country groups	1990 (%)	2002 (%)
Developed countries	25.6	21.7
Transition economies	25.2	23.1
Developing countries	33.8	35.5
Least developed countries	20.4	17.4

Note: * Paper and products (ISIC 341), Industrial chemicals (ISIC 351), Petroleum refining (ISIC 353), Other non-metallic minerals (ISIC 369), Iron and steel (ISIC 371) and Non-ferrous metals (ISIC 372).

Source: UNIDO (2005).

As seen in Table 2.4, MVA in the more resource-intensive manufacturing sub-sectors as a percentage of total manufacturing production declined in three of the four country groups between 1990 and 2002 but increased in the developing-country group. These changes in sub-sector composition would have contributed to absolute decoupling in two country groups, developed countries and transition economies, where absolute decoupling occurred significantly for most parameters, and would have made absolute decoupling in developing countries more difficult to the extent that there would have been a greater challenge to reduce resource use and pollutant loadings. Of course among developing countries there were exceptions, such as Indonesia and Thailand, where there had been a significant shift from heavy to light industries in the previous two decades.

Another type of change in sector composition, the percentage of production accounted for by small and medium-sized enterprises (SMEs), can also affect resource use and pollutant loadings. Production in small as compared to large plants in the same sub-sector is usually more resource- and pollutant-intensive per unit of output, and small plants are generally less compliant with environmental regulations than large ones (World Bank, 2000 and UNDP/UNIDO, 2000). Unfortunately there are no globally consistent data documenting changes in SMEs' share of industrial output over the previous 20 years. At best there are only limited data available for a few countries at different points in time.

Effect of Technological Configuration

What has been, and what could have been, the relative contribution of PATs and CTs to the reductions in resource and pollutant loadings by industry as described in the previous section on decoupling? Unfortunately this important question is difficult to answer as only a few studies, limited to industrialized countries, have explicitly addressed it. Information on capital investments in PATs has been collected but it is insufficient and does not span a long time period. Only the United States has systematically accumulated such data (between 1970 and 2000). A few other OECD countries have collected similar information, but only recently and on an irregular basis. Furthermore, none of these surveys includes information on how much of the investment in the production process technologies can be considered CTs.

Most of the reduction in pollutant loadings between 1970 and 2000 was attributable to PAT investments, according to the available literature. Kemp and Arundel (1998), summarizing the work of others on selected European countries in the 1980s, found that PATs, as compared to CTs, accounted for the largest share of EST investments (80 per cent and more). Similarly, de Bruyn (1997) found that the larger share of sulphur dioxide emission reductions in Europe was attributable to the use of PATs. Johnstone (1997) found that a comparable investment pattern prevailed in the United States during the period 1970 to 2000, with a gradual shift to more CT investments in the late 1980s and early 1990s. CT investments, when measured as a percentage of total EST investment, increased from 17 to 30 per cent for reducing water pollutants and from 27 to 48 per cent for reducing air pollutants. The only exception to the dominant role of PATs was the reduction of SO_2 emissions in the United States in the 1990s (Schmalensee et al., 1998). In this case, PATs (scrubbers) accounted for 45 per cent of the total emission reduction, while CTs (switching to low-sulphur fuel) accounted for the remaining 55 per cent. Apart from this exception, PATs appear to have been the dominant technology choice for pollutant abatement. Based on the above, it is suggested that PATs accounted for approximately 80 per cent of the water-pollutant reductions, and between 50 and 80 per cent of the air-pollutant reductions achieved over the past 20 years, with CTs accounting for the remainder.

This estimate is consistent with engineering data on the pollutant removal efficiencies of PATs and CTs. Wastewater effluent guidelines set by industrialized countries for most industrial sub-sectors in the 1970s required removal efficiencies equivalent to those achieved by PATs for secondary treatment. Secondary treatment, applied to textile wastewater, for example, was estimated to remove between 70 and 95 per cent of the BOD, between 50 and 70 per cent of the chemical oxygen demand (COD) and between 85 and 95 per cent of the total suspended solids (US EPA, 1978). In contrast, the reduction of pollutant generation by the most widely used CT options in the textile sub-sector was estimated to prevent the generation of between 10 and 30 per cent of conventional pollutants (UNIDO, 1995). Thus, in line with the estimate above, application of PATs is thought to have accounted for between 70 and 90 per cent, and CTs between 10 and 30 per cent, of the reduction of conventional water pollutants over the past 20 years.

Appendix 2A to this chapter offers additional information to those readers interested in the potential of CTs to reduce pollutant discharge in the three sub-sectors investigated in this study.

Relative Effect of Scale, Sub-sector Composition and Technological Configuration

As suggested above, scale, sub-sector composition and technological configuration can have countervailing effects on environmental pressure. For example, an increase in the scale of industrial output (increased MVA) can be offset by changes in sub-sector composition and, more likely, by changes in technology configuration, primarily the use of PATs. Given the empirical difficulties, only a few studies have investigated this issue. Hettige et al. (2000) found, in a 13-country study, that scale effect was only partially offset by the sub-sector composition effect. Copeland and Taylor (2003) found that the technology configuration effect exceeded the scale and sub-sector composition effects, resulting in improved environmental performance, at least for sulphur dioxide emissions.

SUMMARY

There are limited globally consistent data from which one can analyse trends in decoupling – mainly only for energy use, water use, BOD effluent and CO_2 emission – between 1990 and about 2002. Not surprisingly, in the developed country group relative decoupling occurred in all four parameters and absolute decoupling in three of the four parameters (Table 2.2), the only exception in the latter being their increase in energy use. Relative and absolute decoupling occurred in three of the four parameters in transition economies, water use being the exception. Most surprising was the extent of decoupling in the developing countries, where relative decoupling occurred in three of the four parameters and absolute decoupling in one parameter (BOD). While the degree of decoupling for least-developed-countries was not as great as for developing countries, except for water withdrawal, there was relative decoupling in all four parameters. However, there was no absolute decoupling in this group in any parameter.

While the relative decoupling achievements of the developing countries and the fact that there was relative decoupling in least-developed countries are encouraging, there is clearly a need for more to be done to reduce the continuing increase of environmental pressure from the growth of industrial output in these countries. A comparison between developed and developing countries shows that energy-use intensity is three times higher, water-use intensity is more than ten times higher, BOD-effluent intensity is six times higher and CO2-emission intensity is over four times higher in developing than in developed countries. A comparison between the developed and least-developed countries shows even more extreme differences, except in the case of water-use intensity.

Environmental pressure is coupled to industrial activity by a complexity of factors that can be summarized under the three headings of scale, sub-sector composition and technological configuration. The significant increase in the scale of industrial output over the period 1990 to 2002 enhanced the likelihood of an increase in environmental pressure, which, however, did not happen for some environmental variables in some country groups. Shifts in sub-sector composition in the manufacturing sector towards less resource- and pollutant-intensive sub-sectors occurred in developed countries, transition economies and least-developed-countries, but shifts to more resource- and pollutant-intensive sub-sectors occurred in developing countries. Data were not available to document the changes in technological configurations in terms of EST utilization between 1990 and 2002, but the use of PATs is thought to have accounted for most of the reduction in environmental pressure. If so, then the question of interest is what motivated industry, particularly in developing and least-developed countries, to adopt EST. This book provides an answer to this question.

APPENDIX 2A   CT APPLICATIONS IN THE THREE SUB-SECTORS

Introduction

EST is often divided into two categories, abatement and prevention technologies. Abatement technologies, conventionally referred to as pollution abatement technologies (PATs), reduce the discharge of pollutants at the end of the production process. PATs collect pollutants, separating or neutralizing them in various ways (usually with specially built treatment installations). In contrast, prevention technology, often referred to as cleaner process techniques and technologies (CTs), minimizes the generation of pollutants (and the utilization of some inputs such as water or fuel) throughout the production process. CTs are hence defined as manufacturing processes or product technologies that reduce both pollutant generation and the use of production inputs (raw materials, water and energy) in comparison to the technologies they replace. Although reducing the need for more costly abatement technologies, they require modifications in production processes, sometimes disrupting ongoing production activities.

The cleaner production (CP) strategy for use of these technologies is a hierarchical approach to pollutant abatement practices that assigns priority in use to CTs over PATs as follows:

- source reduction (prevents generation of wastes) (CTs);
- on-site recycling (CTs and PATs);
- treatment (PATs);
- safe disposal (PATs).

The strategy requires that only after prevention techniques and technologies have been fully adopted should recycling options be used, and only after wastes are recycled, as far as possible on site, should treatment of the residues and safe land disposal be considered. Off-site recycling is generally not considered as a CT option by those advocating the CP approach because it is not internal to plant operations (US EPA, 1992).

The CTs identified by the CP strategy are often classified into eight categories, as illustrated in Figure 2A.1 and described thus:

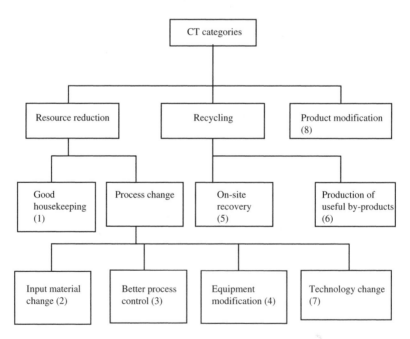

Source: UNIDO (1995).

Figure 2A.1   CT categories

- *Good housekeeping (1)*: appropriate provision to prevent leaks and spills (such as preventive maintenance schedules and frequent equipment inspections) and to enforce the existing working instructions (through proper supervision, training, etc.). Examples include repair of all leaks, keeping taps closed when not in use, and avoiding spillage.
- *Input material change (2)*: substitution of input materials by less toxic or renewable materials, or by adjunct materials with a longer service life. Examples include changing from acetic to formic acid in textile dyeing and using alkaline-based water degreasers instead of organic solvent for cleaning metal parts.
- *Better process control (3)*: modification of working procedures, machine instructions, and process record-keeping in order to run the processes at higher efficiency and lower waste and pollutant generation. Examples include adopting better firing practices in downdraught kilns and maintaining process parameters (temperature, pressure etc.) as close as possible to the desired level, using a limited number of basic instruments.
- *Equipment modification (4)*: modification of the existing productive equipment and utilities – for instance, by introducing measuring and controlling devices – in order to run the processes at higher efficiency and lower waste and pollutant generation rates. Examples include installing drip hangers to recover drag out from plating operations and using storage tanks of appropriate capacity to avoid overflows.
- *On-site recovery and reuse (5)*: reuse of waste materials in the same process or for another useful application on the site. Examples include reusing rinse solvents from formulation equipment in the same make-up of the next batch of the same product and reusing moulding sand for the preparation of new moulds.
- *Production of useful by-products (6)*: modification of the waste generation process in order to transform wastes into materials that can be reused or recycled for another application outside the company. Examples include recovery of short fibre in pulp making to make paperboard and converting rice husk ash into white ash for filling teeth.
- *Technology modification (7)*: replacement of the technology, processing sequence and/or synthesis pathway in order to minimize waste and pollutant generation during production. Examples include applying static rinse instead of continuous rinse in electroplating, using low dye-liquor jet dyers instead of 'kier' dyers, and applying electrostatic spraying techniques to minimize paint over-spray.
- *Product reformulation or modification (8)*: modification of the product characteristics to minimize the environmental impact of the product

during or after its use (disposal) or to minimize the environmental impact of production. Examples include eliminating excessive product packaging and the manufacture of liquid dyes instead of powder dyes for the textile sub-sector.

Some of these eight categories are more frequently the source of CT options than others. For example, a CP assessment in ten sub-sectors in the Netherlands yielded 164 CT options, distributed as follows: good housekeeping (28 per cent), input material change (22 per cent), technology change (39 per cent), on-site recycling (10 per cent) and product redesign (1 per cent) (Dieleman, 1991). Another example, this time from a developing country (India), showed a significant variation in the categories of CT options implemented among three different sub-sectors (pulp and paper, pesticides, and textile). In the case of the pulp and paper sub-sector, four CT categories had approximately an equal share of and accounted for most of the total number of options: technology change (21 per cent), good housekeeping (20 per cent), better process control (20 per cent) and on-site recycling (17 per cent). Most of the feasible options in the pesticides formulation sub-sector fell under the categories of good housekeeping (38 per cent), on-site recycling (30 per cent) and equipment modification (20 per cent). In the case of the textile sub-sector, two CT categories, on-site recycling (26 per cent) and better process controls (24 per cent), accounted for half of the feasible CT options. Two other categories, good housekeeping (17 per cent) and input material change (16 per cent), accounted for another third of the options (UNIDO, 1995).

Textile Sub-sector: CT Applications

A state-owned integrated textile mill in Ho Chi Minh City, Viet Nam, has an installed capacity of 20 000 000 metres of fabric, equivalent to 5000 tons per year. However, the current capacity is less than 2000 tons. It produces more than 20 different types of products ranging from synthetic fibres to natural fabrics. Its effluent has a high organic/inorganic pollution load with colour from un-exhausted dyestuffs. A factory CP team, assisted by the Viet Nam National Cleaner Production Centre, undertook a CP audit of a dyeing unit for towels. The team identified 45 CT options, of which 33 were found to be feasible. The unit has so far implemented 19 CT options, with a total investment of US$4400 and with direct cost savings of US$40 000 per annum. Some of the options are documented in Table 2A.1. The major environmental benefits have been a 25 per cent reduction in wastewater volume and significant reduction in water effluent and gaseous emissions.

Table 2A.1   CT options identified for use in a textile mill in Viet Nam

CT options	Environmental benefits	Investment (US$)	Annual savings (US$)	Remarks
1. Maximum possible (9 times) recycle of sodium hydroxide (CT 5)	Reduced wastewater volume and pollution load	nil	7200	Can be further reduced
2. Accurate weighing of dyestuffs and chemicals, installation of precision electronic balance (CT 3)	Reduced organic pollution load	1000	1400	
3. Optimization of cloth: liquor ratio from 1:15 to 1:10 (CT 3)	Reduced wastewater volume and pollution load	nil	11 400	To sustain training of operator is necessary
4. Combined bleaching and scouring process (CT 4)	Reduced wastewater volume	nil	15 000	Processing time also reduced
5. Installation of water flow meter and level indicators (CT 3)	Reduced black soot from flue gases	400	NQ	

Note: (CT X) refers to CT category in Figure 2A.1; NQ is not qualified.

Source: UNIDO (2006).

CT Application: Pulp and Paper Sub-sector

A state-owned pulp and paper mill located in Henan Province, China, produces about 18 000 tons of pulp and 30 000 tons of paper annually. The raw
material input is non-wood fibre (wheat straw). The mill has a black liquor
recovery system but no effluent treatment plant (ETP). A factory CP team,
assisted by the China National Cleaner Production Centre, identified 13 CT
options, mainly for the pulping process as documented in Table 2A.2. Of
these, three dealt with managerial issues (8, 9 and 10), two dealt with reuse
and recycling (12 and 13), two dealt with raw materials handling (1 and 4),
and six dealt with pulping and bleaching operations (2, 3, 5, 6, 7 and 11).
Six of these options were non- or low-cost and implemented at the time of
writing the report on the demonstration project. Implementation of the
options resulted in savings in water, steam and straw amounting to
US$363 000 per annum. The pollution load of COD was reduced by
approximately 5 per cent (UNIDO, 2006).

CT Application: Leather Processing Sub-sector

A leather tannery in Nairobi, Kenya has an installed capacity to process 8000
to 9000 pieces of hides and skins per day but was operating at only 50 per
cent capacity. It was processing hides and skins to the wet blue stage at a processing rate of 5.5 tons per day with a daily water consumption of 160 m^3.
The tannery was using excessive amounts of water and chemicals that were
discharged without any attempt to recycle or reuse them. A factory CP
team, assisted by the Kenya National Cleaner Production Centre, focused
on the liming and de-hairing processes, identifying over 30 CT options.
Implementation of most of these options resulted in savings in water
and chemical consumption of approximately US$70 000 per year, enhanced
the public image of the tannery and improved the morale of the staff
(Table 2A.3).

Conclusions

The numerous CTs available and utilized in a wide range of countries and
manufacturing sub-sectors suggest that there is considerable scope for
increasing the use of CTs in developing countries. The plant-level case
studies from the three developing countries (taken from the UNIDO CP
database) illustrate the potential of CTs to improve environmental performance. They show impressive improvements in the use of energy and
water, but also pollutant reductions, often achieved with relatively small
investments and in many cases also resulting in significant cost savings.

Table 2A.2   CT options identified for use in a pulp and paper mill in China

CT options	Unit operation	Environmental benefits	Investment	Annual savings (US$)	Remarks
1. Wet preparation (CT 1)	Raw material handling	Indirect effect	High	nil	Rejected
2. Cooking with caustic soda and sodium bisulphide (CT 7)	Pulping	Reduced consumption of alkali	High	nil	Rejected
3. Oxygen bleaching (CT 7)	Bleaching	Reduced discharge of oxidizing agent	High	nil	Rejected
4. Stricter control of raw material purchasing and sorting (CT 2)	Raw material preparation	Reduced ash and rejects	nil	216 000	Implemented; reduced steam and energy use by 5 to 10 percent
5. Three-stage bleaching method (CT 7)	Bleaching	Reduced pollutants in effluent	High	nil	Rejected
6. Increased concentration by press washing (CT 4)	Bleaching	Reduced water use and wastewater discharge	nil	nil	Plan to implement
7. Perfect digesting with micro-computer control system (CT 4)	Pulping	Reduced BOD (5%), COD (8%) and TSS (6%)	7500	35 000	Plan to implement; increased production efficiency and energy savings
8. Better practice and supervision (CT 1)	All units	Indirect savings of water – 42 000 tons/year	nil	7000	Implemented
9. Strengthening of personnel training (CT 1)	All units	Indirect	nil	nil	Implemented

Table 2A.2   (continued)

CT options	Unit operation	Environmental benefits	Investment	Annual savings (US$)	Remarks
10. Stricter control of washing (CT 3)	All units	Indirect savings of water – 150 000 tons/year	nil	2400	Implemented
11. Trial removal of silica (CT 4)	Pulping	Reduced BOD, COD and TSS	96 000	28 000	Experiment completed; increased alkali recovery
12. Recycling of white water (CT 5)	Paper-making	Reduced waste water discharge	nil	nil	Implemented
13. Washing pulp with condensed water of alkali recovery (CT 5)	Washing	Indirect savings of water – 720 000 tons/year	45 000	116 000	Implemented

Note: (CT X) refers to CT category in Figure 2A.1.

Source: UNIDO (2006).

The full extent of the potential application of CTs, both in terms of different types and of the number of enterprises systematically pursuing CP programmes, is unknown, however. The small amount of literature published on this topic suggests that most CT options implemented to date are of a lower order of technological complexity, building on good housekeeping, input material changes, and better process controls. Indeed, an evaluation of the technology upgrading and transfer efforts of eight UNIDO/UNEP National Cleaner Production Centres found that about 75 per cent of the CT options implemented by plants were primarily of a lower order of technological complexity and required little investment (Luken et al., 2003a). A review of eight international donor-funded CP programmes in developing countries also found that most plants that have participated in CP projects have yet to implement more complex CT options (Luken et al., 2003b).

In summary, PATs must be used more extensively to significantly reduce the currently high level of pollutant discharge in developing countries, not to mention the anticipated future levels associated with increased industrial

Table 2A.3   CT options identified for use in a leather tannery in Kenya

CT options	Environmental benefits	Investment	Annual savings (US$)
1. Simple recycling of lime and sulphide liquors after screening with 1 mm screen (CT 5)		14 000	42 750
2. Chrome fixation increased from the current 70 to 90 per cent through use of short floats, increased temperature, extended tanning time, basification and reduction in neutral salts, and use of dicarboxylic acids (CT 3)		20 000	27 000
3. Installation of a hair-saving screen machine (CT 4)		2000	
4. Segregation of incompatible chemicals in store (CT 1)			
5. Processing of fresh skins to reduce quantity of salt in waste water and amount of lime loss (CT 2)			
6. Installation of hair-saving machine (CT 7)		50 000	

Note: (CT X) refers to CT category in Figure 2C.1.

Source: UNIDO (2006).

output. CTs, which have to date been only marginally exploited in developing countries, however, could minimize significantly the use of PATs by reducing the volume of waste to be treated and thus reduce the cost of their installation.

NOTES

1. The term 'decoupling' is not used when growth of an environmental parameter is greater than the growth of an economic parameter.
2. The United Nations system has no established convention for the designation of 'developed' and 'developing' countries or areas. In common practice, Japan in Asia, Canada and

the United States in northern America, Australia and New Zealand in Oceania and Europe are considered 'developed' regions or areas. In international trade statistics, the Southern African Customs Union is also treated as a developed region and Israel as a developed country; countries emerging from the former Yugoslavia are treated as developing countries; and countries of eastern Europe and the former USSR countries in Europe are not included under either developed or developing regions. As agreed by the United Nations General Assembly, on the recommendation of the Committee for Development Policy, it was decided that 45 countries could be included in the list of the least developed countries. The classification of countries in Tables 2.1 and 2.2 is consistent with the common practice and General Assembly recommendation.

3. For transition economies, there was a decline in MVA during the 1990s, but most of them had recovered by the year 2000. For example, in the Czech Republic, industrial output declined by about 30 per cent in the mid-1990s but had recovered to the 1990 level by 2000.

REFERENCES

Arrow, K. et al. (1995), 'Economic growth, carrying capacity, and the environment', *Science*, **268**, 520–21.

Copeland, B. and M.S. Taylor (2003), *Trade and Environment: Theory and Evidence*, Princeton, NJ: Princeton University Press.

De Bruyn, S. (1997), 'Explaining the environmental Kuznets curve: structural change and international environmental agreement', *Environment and Development Economics*, **2** (4), 485–503.

Dieleman, H. (1991), 'Choosing for prevention is winning', in *Prepare Manual and Experiences*, Part II A, The Hague, The Netherlands: Ministry of Economic Affairs.

EC (1990), 'Task Force Report on the Environment and the Internal Market, "1992": The Environmental Dimension', Brussels: European Commission.

EC (2002), 'European Competitiveness Report 2002' [SEC (2002) 528], Brussels: European Commission.

FAO (2005), 'AQUASTAT: FAOSTAT', Rome: Food and Agriculture Organization of the United Nations (available on: http://www.fao.org).

Hettige, H., M. Mani and D. Wheeler (2000), 'Industrial pollution in economic development: the environmental Kuznets curve revisited', *Journal of Development Economics*, **62** (2), 445–76.

IEA (2005a), 'Online Data Services', IEA Energy Information Centre, International Energy Agency, Paris: International Energy Agency (available on: www.iea.org).

IEA (2005b), 'CO$_2$ emissions from fuel combustion 1973–2003', Paris: International Energy Agency.

Johnstone, N. (1997), 'Globalization, technology and the environment', in OECD, Environment Directorate, *Globalization and Environment: Proceedings of the Vienna Workshop*, ENV/EPOC/GEEI (97), Paris: Organization for Economic Cooperation and Development, pp. 163–203.

Kemp, R. and A. Arundel (1998), 'Survey indicators for environmental innovation', Idea paper series (available on: http://www.step.no/old/Projectarea/idea/Idea8.pdf).

Luken, R., J. Navratil and N. Hogsted (2003a), 'Technology transfer the UNIDO/UNEP national cleaner production centres programme', *International Journal of Environmental Technology and Management*, **3** (2), 107–17.

Luken, R., R. Stevenson and R. van Berkel (eds) (2003b), 'CP programmes and projects', *Journal of Cleaner Production*, **12** (3), 185–31.

OECD (1997), *Globalization and the Environment: Proceedings of the Vienna Workshop*, ENV/EPOC/GEEI (97) 5, Paris: Organization for Economic Cooperation and Development.

OECD (2002), 'Indicators to measure decoupling of environmental pressure from economic growth', SG/SD (2002)1/Final, Paris: Organization for Economic Cooperation and Development.

Schmalensee, R., P.L. Joskow, D.A. Ellerman, J.P. Montero and E.A. Bailey (1998), 'An interim evaluation of sulfur dioxide emissions trading', *Journal of Economic Perspectives*, **12** (3), 53–69.

UNDP/UNIDO (2000), 'Industrial Policy and the Environment in Pakistan', NC/PAK/97/108, Vienna: UNIDO.

United Nations Environment Programme (UNEP), the Organization for Economic Cooperation and Development (OECD), the International Energy Agency (IEA) and the Intergovernmental Panel on Climate Change (IPCC) (1995), 'IPCC Guidelines for National Greenhouse Gas Inventories: Reference Manual', Chapter 1 (Energy) and Chapter 2 (Industrial Processes), London: Intergovernmental Panel on Climate Change.

UNEP (2005), 'Global Environmental Monitoring System', Nairobi: United Nations Environment Programme (available on: http://www.unep.org).

UNIDO (1995), 'From Wastes to Profits: The Indian Experience', ID/SER.0/19, Vienna: UNIDO.

UNIDO (2005), *International Yearbook of Industrial Statistics 2005*, Cheltenham, UK and Northampton, MA, US: Edward Elgar Publishing.

UNIDO (2006), 'NCPC database', Vienna: UNIDO (available on: http://www.unido.org/ncpc, verified 15 March, 2006).

UNSTAT (2005), 'Methods and Classifications: composition of Macro Geographical (Continental) Regions, Geographical Sub-regions, and Selected Economic and Other Groupings', United Nations Statistics Division (UNSTAT) (available on: http://unstats.un.org).

US EPA (1978), 'Environmental pollution control in the textile processing industry', Washington: United States Environmental Protection Agency.

US EPA (1992), *Facility Pollution Prevention Guide*, Washington: United States Environmental Protection Agency.

World Bank (2000), *Greening Industry: New Roles for Communities, Markets and Governments*, Oxford, UK: Oxford University Press.

World Bank (2004), *World Bank Development Indicators (WDI) 2004*, CD-ROM version, Washington, DC: The World Bank.

3. Heuristic model of EST adoption

INTRODUCTION

This investigation of the factors determining the adoption of EST in developing countries was guided by a heuristic model derived from a review of two fields of literature: literature on technology diffusion and technological capabilities, briefly reviewed in the first part of this chapter, and empirical studies of environmentally sound technology (EST) adoption in developing countries, which are reviewed here in more detail. The heuristic model of EST adoption is then presented, followed by a description of its three modes of investigation: assessment of policy effectiveness, plant managers' and key informants' perceptions of drivers for EST adoption (perceived factors), and statistical analysis of factors that the country survey teams for this study observed as influencing EST adoption (observed factors).

LITERATURE REVIEW

Literature on Technology Diffusion and Technology Capabilities

The literature on technology diffusion and that on technological capabilities form, respectively, two different strands in the field of innovation studies. Given the vastness of the literature on technology diffusion, this review has focused particularly on studies that relate the general insights on the determinants of technology diffusion to the specific case of EST. The literature on technological capabilities is more restricted in size than that on technology diffusion. Given the pervasiveness of market failures related to technology change in developing countries, it has paid particular attention to firm-level technological change in developing countries.

The literature on technology diffusion, which examines the factors that affect the adoption of a new technology by potential users over time, is well established (for an overview see Kemp, 1997 and Montalvo and Kemp, 2004). Despite this, relatively little has been done to apply the general insights that have been gained to specific situations in developing countries nor to the specific case of EST adoption.[1]

Blackman (1999) provides a summary of the theoretical and empirical literature and draws several implications for the diffusion of energy-efficient technologies. He points out that nearly all the factors that determine whether and how fast firms adopt a new technology are likely to reflect systemic differences between developed and developing countries. He argues that there is sufficient empirical evidence to verify theoretical claims that firm-specific characteristics affect the adoption of new technology, that is, that new technologies are adopted fastest by firms that are large, have well-trained staff, incur high regulatory costs when using an existing technology, have infrastructure complementary to the new technology, are in fast-growing industries, invest more in research and development (R&D), pay relatively low prices for inputs used intensively by the new technology, incur low search costs and have relatively old existing capital stock. In terms of technology characteristics *per se*, profitable, small-scale and simple innovations are adopted most quickly. Although dissemination of information on a particular technology is thought to be the key to its diffusion, there is limited empirical evidence to support this claim. Blackman suggests that this might be because it is difficult to measure information flows.

Kemp (1997) also draws on the extensive literature on technology diffusion and relates it directly to EST adoption. He provides a schematic representation of the determinants of EST adoption that assigns these to one of three main categories: system of information transfer; characteristics of the technology; and adoption environment. The system of information transfer is characterized as channels of information, including the supply and credibility of information. Characteristics of the technology include both economic and technical characteristics, such as the financial costs and benefits of the technology, its economic life span, its performance relative to other technologies and its effects on product quality. The adoption environment generally captures aspects that affect a firm's incentives for technology adoption and includes the influence that governmental policies have on a firm's price and cost structure as well as characteristics of product and factor markets, such as the fierceness of competition and conditions for obtaining loans.

The literature on technological capabilities within the field of innovation studies also provides insights into the determinants of EST adoption (UNIDO, 2002). This body of work, inspired by evolutionary economics, examines how firms in developing countries actually adopt newer technology. The literature is largely empirical and qualitative in nature, and departs from the standard economics assumption that developing countries actually have the skills and knowledge needed to incorporate more advanced technologies. Technological capabilities are defined as the skills (technical, managerial or organizational) that allow firms to adopt equipment and information efficiently (Lall and Latsch, 1999). Human technical skills are seen as an essential tool that enables firms operating with imperfect knowledge of technological alternatives to source information on new technology and to subsequently adapt and master it (Romijn, 2001; Lall and Pietrobelli, 2002). The degree of uncertainty and difficulty experienced by developing country firms in applying the technology varies according to the technology but is determined by three factors: the initial capabilities of the enterprise; the support it can draw upon from its environment; and the novelty of the technology relative to its existing stock of knowledge. In analysing how firms use newer technology, scholars from this school of thought adopt a systemic approach, looking at the interplay between incentives and institutions (defined essentially in terms of organizations) and the interactive learning processes between agents.

This systemic approach to firm-level technology change in the literature on technology capabilities is similar to the approach adopted in the literature on 'national innovation systems' (Freeman, 1987; Lundvall, 1992; Lundvall et al., 2002).[2] However, the literature on technological capabilities applies those insights in the context of developing countries, where frontier innovation is not as important as other forms of technological effort, such as technology adoption and incremental innovation. Greater emphasis is therefore given to market and institutional failures in technology change and learning because they are more pervasive and stringent in developing than in developed countries (Lall and Pietrobelli, 2002). The way in which intermediary institutions can help to overcome technology-related market failures is also treated in this literature.

Empirical Studies of EST Adoption in Developing Countries

Only a limited number of empirical studies have had an explicit focus on the adoption of EST in developing countries. The absence of such studies is explained by the fact that regulatory pressure in developing countries is generally weak, due to limited monitoring and enforcement capacities, and thus it is assumed there would be limited adoption of EST. As confirmed by several studies, however, some plants in developing countries actually do comply with environmental regulations, using EST to do so (e.g. World Bank, 2000). In fact pollutant discharge levels at some plants are significantly lower than required to meet environmental standards. This runs counter to conventional views on industrial environmental regulation that assume that regulatory pressure is the principal determinant of plant-level environmental behaviour.

In an effort to explain this anomalous situation, empirical studies have identified a number of other factors in developing countries that influence plants to reduce pollutant discharge. Most of the reviewed studies can be grouped into three categories. One group looks at the effects of EST usage on environmental performance, and one at the adoption of EST, the focus of this investigation, both taking into account contextual and plant-specific factors, while a third group, limited in number, investigates the effects of only contextual factors on the adoption of CTs.

The first group of studies defines environmental performance in various ways, such as pollutant loadings, investments in PATs and self-assessments of environmental performance. Insights emanate mainly from studies conducted in the context of World Bank research on the economics of industrial pollution control in developing countries (World Bank, 2000), but also from related surveys funded by the World Bank. These studies empirically confirm that plants' decisions on pollution control are not solely driven by environmental regulation. Other contextual factors, such as societal and market pressure to abate pollution, determine their environmental behaviour. In addition, the studies point to a host of plant-specific factors that affect environmental behaviour.

This first group generally uses a variant of a cost minimization model, in which a representative plant determines its pollutant discharge based on the interplay of two schedules, namely, a marginal abatement cost schedule and an expected marginal penalty schedule. Theoretical determinants of the former include plant size, multi-division status, the specific sub-sector, process technology vintage, human resources, and experience with environmental management systems. The expected marginal penalty schedule, which reflects the cost of pollution, increasing with emissions per unit of output, is assumed to be determined by, *inter alia*, the plant's experience with regulatory inspections and enforcement of standards, the strength of informal regulatory activity in local communities, pressure from financial and product markets (in particular trade links with OECD countries for the latter) and ownership (multinational, state versus private ownership, and publicly traded versus family-owned).

Several contextual factors are identified in this group of studies as causing differences in plants' environmental performance. Hettige et al. (1996) found that community action, often termed 'informal regulation', clearly has an effect. The influence of this factor is similarly underscored in Aden et al. (1999). They measured community pressures on plants, based on plant managers' perceptions rather than by using standard proxies, such as local income and/or educational levels. There is also evidence to suggest that local communities, in an attempt to influence the enforcement of regulations, use either the political process or negotiate directly with plants. A further potential contextual pressure on plants to improve their environmental performance, pointed to by the World Bank (2000), is that of markets (buyers and investors). Aden and Rock (1999) provide some evidence that buyer pressure has indeed succeeded in influencing the environmental performance of manufacturing plants in Indonesia. In contrast, though, Dasgupta et al. (2000) found no evidence of the influence of buyer pressure from developed (i.e. OECD) country markets. Aden and Rock (1999) also provide evidence that financial incentives, such as tax breaks or duty-free imports, influence plants' investments in PATs, another contextual factor that needs to be considered when explaining plant-level environmental behaviour.

Regarding plant-specific characteristics, these research studies consistently show that pollutant intensity is negatively associated with the scale and productive efficiency of plants and the vintage of their technology (Hettige et al., 1996, and Aden et al., 1999). The studies also underscore the role of ownership, in particular that public ownership is associated with higher levels of pollutant intensity (Hettige et al., 1996). However, none of the studies that examined the determinants of actual environmental performance provide evidence for the often-argued positive influence of foreign ownership on the environmental performance of plants, once other plant characteristics, such as size, have been taken into account.

Dasgupta et al. (2000) add adoption of an environmental management system to the list of decisive plant-specific characteristics that affect environmental performance. Observing, on the one hand, the great range in both level and type of environmental management in Mexican plants and recognizing, on the other hand, that certain approaches to environmental management are more effective than others, the authors found that the observed differences exist because of the varying levels of information available to plant managers. Effective environmental regulation in Mexico, as in most developing countries, is a fairly recent phenomenon and one with which both regulators and plant managers are grappling. Consequently, the authors point out, there is considerable uncertainty about the relative effectiveness of alternative approaches to environmental regulation and plant-level environmental management. Under such conditions it cannot be assumed that the speed and magnitude of plant managers' responses to regulatory incentives are fixed parameters. Indeed, plant managers require specific information if they are to respond effectively. This type of information is, as the authors note, often scarce in developing countries.

Both contextual and plant-specific factors relating to environmental management are examined by Seroa da Motta (2006) in his investigation of the determinants of various aspects of environmental management in 325 large and medium-sized firms in Brazil in 1997. The author constructs three dependent variables for use in the statistical analysis:

(a) an environmental practice index that combines PATs, CTs, training and other measures; (b) environmental performance defined in terms of environmental investments as a percentage of total investments; and (c) environmental performance defined in terms of environmental operating costs as a percentage of total operating costs. Explanatory variables for the three EST models include both contextual and plant-specific factors based on actual observations or plant management's stated motivations. His model based only on actual observations found that the more important determinants relate to two plant-specific factors, size and foreign capital, and to one contextual variable, sanctions from environmental regulators, while his model based on both observations and stated motivations found the more important determinants to be the same two plant-specific factors noted above as well as other plant-specific factors, primarily reduction in production costs.

The second group of studies explicitly examines the factors that influence the adoption of EST rather than environmental performance *per se*, looking exclusively at abatement technologies (PATs) and prevention technologies (CTs). Adeoti (2002) investigates determinants of EST adoption in 122 firms in the food and beverage and textiles sub-sectors of Nigeria. The author constructs three dependent variables to use in his statistical analysis. When PATs and CTs together are the dependent variable, then one contextual variable, that is, environmental policy, is the major driver of EST adoption, while another contextual variable, policy implementation strategy, and two plant-specific variables, ownership structure (i.e. foreign equity) and size, are of some importance. When adoption of PATs alone is the dependent variable, environmental policy is a significant but not a major driver of adoption. In this case other variables are highly significant, namely, two plant-specific variables, size and internal capability for innovation (measured by the percentage of technical personnel in a firm's workforce). When adoption of CTs alone is the dependent variable, environmental policy is barely a significant variable, whereas three plant-specific variables, size, internal capability (even more so here than for abatement technology alone) and firm ownership, are highly significant.

Montalvo (2002) uses a behavioural model to identify factors determining plant managers' willingness to innovate in CTs, based on a survey of the perceptions of 97 plant managers working in the export processing zones in northern Mexico. He found that their technological and organizational capabilities are the most important determinants of their willingness to innovate in such technologies. Their attitudes to the economic and environmental risks of technological innovation are less important determinants, with economic risk being much more important than environmental risk. Social pressure is perceived to be the least important determinant of the willingness to innovate; within the social component, community pressure is viewed as most important and regulatory pressure as least important.

Wang and Wheeler (2000) specifically examine the relative importance of CT and PAT adjustments in plants' responses to a pollution levy. Econometric analysis of plant-level data from around 3000 Chinese plants reveals that process-integrated adjustments were made at plants in response to a pollution levy. The relative importance of the type of adjustment differs according to the type of pollution. The air pollutant levy's impact was through the increased use of CTs (process adjustment), while the water pollutant levy's impact was through greater use of PATs because there were limited opportunities for making process-related adjustments to abate water pollution.

Blackman and Kildegaard (2003) examine the determinants of the use of CTs in a cluster comprising 145 leather tanneries in Leon, Mexico. Their findings underscore the importance of a tannery's human capital and stock of technical information. They identify private-sector trade associations and input suppliers as major sources of technical information on CTs. At the same time they found that neither tannery size nor top-down regulatory pressure correlate with adoption. Their findings on size contradict those of Adeoti. In their earlier study, Blackman and Bannister (1998) found that trade associations had a strong influence on the adoption of propane, a CT that can be used by traditional Mexican brick-makers.

The third group of studies examines only the effects of contextual factors and considers only the adoption of CTs. PATs were not included because information could only be found on process technologies. Wheeler and Martin (1991) examine the adoption of CTs (thermo-mechanical pulping) in wood pulp production in 60 countries.[3] This research found that open economies surpassed closed economies by a wide margin in their adoption of CTs. Reppelin-Hill (1999) also found that the adoption of the electric arc furnace in 30 steel-producing countries, investigated over a 25-year period, was diffused faster in countries with more open trade policy regimes.

As is evident from this literature review, only a few studies have examined, directly or indirectly, the factors that influence plant-level decisions on the adoption of EST under the specific conditions faced in developing countries. Most of the recent studies on plant-level behaviour in developing countries have focused only on factors determining environmental performance because of the concern for reducing environmental pressure. The factors actually affecting the adoption of EST, both PATs and CTs, by plants in developing countries thus remain a largely uncharted terrain.

THE HEURISTIC MODEL OF EST ADOPTION

Drawing on the literature reviewed above, primarily research by the World Bank (2000) and related studies funded by the Bank, the heuristic model that guided and structured this investigation is, not surprisingly, similar to the World Bank's 'new model' of pollution control. This 'new model' for understanding the precursors of improved environmental performance posits a tripartite influence of government, markets and civil society on the adoption of EST. The heuristic model used in this study does likewise but differs from the 'new model' of pollution control in several ways and is best described as 'an expanded model of EST adoption'. It differs in (a) its more explicit and more extended inclusion of contextual variables; (b) its more expanded set of institutional participants that influence plant-level behaviour, now extended to intermediary technical support agencies, international donors and business associations; (c) its more expanded set of plant-level characteristics, reflecting the findings in the literature on technological capabilities; and (d) its focus on the adoption of EST, with its distinction between PATs and CTs. The specific nature of these differences will become more apparent when this heuristic model is described below.

The model reflects the view that a plant's decision to adopt EST is a function of many factors, both contextual and plant-specific (Figure 3.1). The contextual factors comprise the incentives that plants are presented with to adopt EST. Broadly speaking, incentive structures are created by policy regimes, with incentives being transmitted to firms through the institutions of a country. In this case, three policy regimes are of relevance: environmental, economic and technology. Environmental policy largely sets the 'price of pollution', defines the mandate of environmental regulatory agencies and legitimizes the role of civil society in exerting pressure on plant managers to comply with environmental regulations. Economic policy defines the conditions in factor and product markets and creates the public organizations that complement factor markets. Technology policy promotes technological change through supply-side measures such as the creation and promotion of technology support organizations and demand-side measures that largely coincide with the economic incentives created by economic policy.

The institutions that transmit the incentives for EST adoption are classified in Figure 3.1 as government, markets and civil society. The institutional category of government includes the public organizations that implement environmental policies (notably, environmental regulatory agencies) and those that complement their activities (international donors and technology support organizations). The market (factor as well as

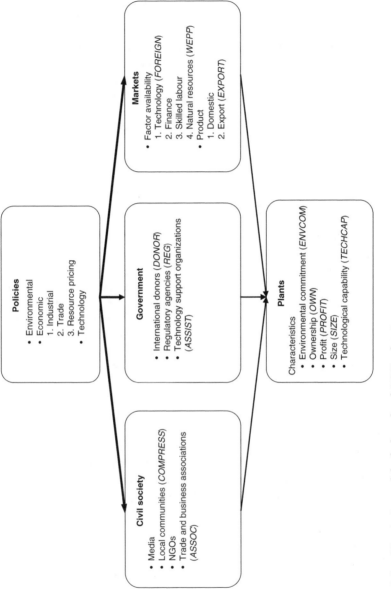

Figure 3.1   Heuristic model of plant-level EST adoption

product markets) is central in generating incentives for EST adoption. The signals emanating from the market are manifold, ranging from conditions in factor markets (technology availability, access to financing, trained labour and availability and prices of natural resources) and conditions in product markets (size and nature of demand in domestic and export markets) to economic growth prospects (at broad macro economic and sectoral levels). The civil society group is a broad-ranging institutional category encompassing local communities (which exert either direct pressure on plants for improved environmental performance or indirect pressure through the regulatory channel), NGOs, the media, and trade and business associations, the latter two formally representing the business community in public and societal matters.

The plant-specific factors, those that determine a plant's capacity to respond to the incentive structure, are largely those highlighted in the diffusion literature and the empirical investigations as important determinants of EST adoption. These are, *inter alia*, a plant's environmental commitment, ownership structure, profitability, size, and technological capabilities.

A plant manager's decision to adopt EST is considered to depend to a large extent on the perceived costs and benefits of utilizing a new technology in comparison with other technologies, including the existing one. Potential benefits, such as compliance with environmental standards, savings on resource use, efficiency and productivity gains, higher product quality and savings on pollution taxes, will be weighed against investment costs, the price of non-compliance with environmental regulation and community outrage. However, rather than being the outcome of an optimization process, in which a plant maximizes a well-defined profit function, a plant's decision on technology adoption is the result of satisfying economic behaviour. The satisfying principle states that plant managers try to attain an acceptable rather than an optimal level of profit, given the problems of information gathering and cognitive limitations (van den Bergh, 2003). As evolutionary theory points out, habits and routines are often used by plant managers for dealing with the complexity and uncertainty of technology choice. These plant routines, however, are modified over time as new information is collected, experience is accumulated and the experiences of other plants are copied (Ruttan, 2002). With respect to manufacturing plants in developing countries, Dasgupta et al. (2000) observed that plants operate with incomplete information and thus need to experiment with new production options to improve environmental performance. This requires information, which plants do not have, and explains, according to the authors, the observed differences in plant-level environmental responses.

THREE MODES OF INVESTIGATION

In seeking to identify the factors that influence EST adoption, under the guidance of our heuristic model, this study has followed three modes of investigation in the eight case countries: (a) an assessment of the effectiveness of the three policy regimes that constitute the incentive structure which the institutional network of governments, markets and civil society bring to bear on plant-level environmental behaviour; (b) a qualitative analysis of the perceptions of 98 plant managers and 91 key informants, who are participants in the organizations that constitute a plant's institutional environment, of the contextual factors determining EST adoption and (c) a statistical analysis of the factors observed by the survey teams to have influenced plant-level behaviour at the 98 plants in the eight countries. The three modes of investigation are described in the following sections; their findings will be presented in Chapter 12.

Assessment of the Effectiveness of Government Policies

The effect on EST adoption of government policies, such as industrial, trade, and resource pricing, has been documented in several studies, ably summarized in World Bank (2000) and briefly described in the literature review above. However, a rigorous statistical analysis of their effect would have required a survey of a much larger number of countries than the eight included in this study. Wheeler and Martin (1991), for example, investigated the effects of policies on CT use (thermo-mechanical pulping) in wood pulp production in 60 countries, and Reppelin-Hill (1999) investigated their effects on CT use (electric arc furnace) in steel production in 30 countries. Such a rigorous analysis would also have required countrywide information on the utilization of EST, information that is not available for any country in the world. At most, as described in Chapter 2, there is only limited information on a few specific types of PATs and for only a few countries; in fact the two investigations of CT use cited above are the only two such studies known to have been carried out.

The role of government policies in EST adoption is, however, a central part of the heuristic model; this study has found what appears to be a meaningful way to make some assessment of the effectiveness of three policy regimes – environmental, economic (comprising industrial, trade and resource pricing policies) and technology – in each of the eight countries by comparing their effectiveness in these countries with that in most countries in the world. Given the absence of a global data set on EST utilization, the effectiveness of these policies, as measured by the indices described in Table 3.1, is assessed by relating them to country-level data on resource-use and

Table 3.1 Environmental, economic and technology policy ranking and indices or scores for eight countries

Environmental governance (EG)

Country	2001 Rank	2001 Index	1990 Rank	1990 Index
Tunisia	27	0.757	25	0.729
Thailand	32	0.691	34	0.656
China	36	0.656	57	0.504
Brazil	39	0.624	42	0.620
India	43	0.602	59	0.476
Viet Nam	59	0.521	–	–
Zimbabwe	60	0.501	46	0.562
Kenya	64	0.423	62	0.444

Competitive industrial performance (CIP)

Country	2000 Rank	2000 Index	1990 Rank	1990 Index
Thailand	23	0.386	32	0.281
China	24	0.379	26	0.323
Brazil	31	0.324	27	0.321
India	40	0.275	36	0.262
Tunisia	46	0.241	49	0.213
Zimbabwe	55	0.213	42	0.239
Viet Nam	67	0.186	–	–
Kenya	80	0.134	66	0.175

Technology import (TI)

Country	2001 Rank	2001 Index	1990 Rank	1990 Index
Thailand	38	0.023	30	0.028
Tunisia	41	0.019	37	0.021
Brazil	55	0.010	53	0.006
China	66	0.005	68	0.002

Energy-use intensity (EUI)

Country	2002 Rank	2002 Score	1990 Rank	1990 Score
Tunisia	33	340	52	504
Thailand	35	351	32	304
Brazil	47	434	37	339
China	66	670	87	2243

Technological capabilities (TC)

Country	2000 Rank	2000 Index	1990 Rank	1990 Index
Thailand	68	0.342	80	0.278
Brazil	72	0.330	77	0.280
China	85	0.306	97	0.306
Tunisia	92	0.288	98	0.227

Table 3.1 (continued)

Technology import (TI)						Energy-use intensity (EUI)						Technological capabilities (TC)				
Country	2001		1990			Country	2002		1990			Country	2000		1990	
	Rank	Index	Rank	Index			Rank	Score	Rank	Score			Rank	Index	Rank	Index
Viet Nam	69	0.004	61	0.004		Zimbabwe	72	900	71	1123		Zimbabwe	96	0.279	89	0.248
Zimbabwe	72	0.002	46	0.008		Viet Nam	73	912	68	903		Viet Nam	107	0.239	118	0.164
Kenya	74	0.002	64	0.003		India	84	1280	83	1829		India	111	0.225	116	0.164
India	84	0.001	75	0.001		Kenya	86	1520	79	1608		Kenya	116	0.204	114	0.177

Note: All policy rankings are based on index values that integrate several variables except for energy-use intensity, which is an absolute value or score, i.e. energy-use intensity per million US dollars of MVA.

Sources: Kaufman et al. (2003) and World Bank (2004) for EG; UNIDO (2004) for CIP; Lall and Albaladejo (2002) for TI; IEA (2005) and UNIDO (2005) for EUI; and Archibugi and Coco (2004) for TC.

pollutant intensities, which were documented in Chapter 2. This relationship constitutes one part of the overall eight-country assessment in Chapter 12.

Environmental policy

Environmental policy with regard to industry aims primarily to reduce pollutant discharge into the environment. It could, but seldom does, explicitly require more efficient use of production inputs such as energy and water. It draws on a variety of policy instruments, described in some detail in the country chapters, to achieve its objectives.

Environmental policy works its way through the institutional network in several ways to influence plant-level behaviour. Its influence is primarily transmitted via governmental regulatory agencies to the extent that it empowers them to implement a command-and-control regulatory programme and to use supplemental environmental management instruments. Effective implementation normally results in plants making investments in PATs and to a lesser extent in CTs. The influence of environmental policy is also felt through civil society. In many countries it legitimizes NGOs and local communities to protest against the failure of plants to comply with environmental standards. It also encourages business associations to represent the interests of their members in negotiations about environmental regulation, to inform their members of regulatory requirements and in some cases to assist their members in complying with environmental standards.

Unfortunately there was no ready-made measure of the effectiveness of environmental policies available, as there were for most economic and technology policies.[4] Consequently an index of environmental governance (EG) was constructed by combining (a) a general measure of governmental effectiveness and (b) the pollutant intensity of countries (organic matter discharge per million US dollars of MVA). Kaufmann et al. (2003) calculated several governance indicators for 1996–2002. Their composite indicators for government effectiveness combine 'into a single grouping responses on the quality of public service provision, the quality of bureaucracy, the competence of civil servants, the independence of the civil service from political pressure and the credibility of the government's commitment to policies' (p. 3). The World Bank (2004) estimates of BOD discharge for the period 1980–2001 are described in Chapter 2 of this study. Countries were scored on a composite EG index for about 1990 and about 2002. The index for about 1990 combines government effectiveness in 1996 and BOD pollutant loadings per million US dollars of MVA in 1990, and for about 2002 it combines government effectiveness in 2002 and BOD pollutant loadings per million US dollars in 2001.

Using these data, it was possible to calculate index values for 65 countries for about 1990 and 66 countries for about 2001 and then rank order them. Countries were arbitrarily assigned to one of three categories based on their scores (one-third of the countries being placed in each category), with the higher category considered to have the more effective industrial environmental management regime and the lower category the least effective.

The rank ordering and associated indices of the EG index for the eight countries covered in this study are listed in Table 3.1. There is no score for Viet Nam in 1990 because it was not possible to estimate a BOD load for that year, whereas there is one for 2001 because there were sufficient employment data then to estimate one following the World Bank methodology (Hettige et al., 1996). In 2001, five countries fell into the medium effectiveness category in the order given (Tunisia, Thailand, China, Brazil and India) and three into the low effectiveness category (Viet Nam, Zimbabwe and Kenya).

Economic policy: industrial policies

Industrial policies, those which affect the expansion of the capital stock and the efficiency with which it is used, increase the incentive for plants to adopt EST, primarily CTs. In many cases new capital stock is more resource efficient than the stock it replaces in that it uses less energy, water and raw material per unit of output. More efficient use of the capital stock (process optimization) often requires the use of CTs.

The industrial policies considered to have the most influence on EST adoption in this way are those supporting openness to foreign direct investment (FDI), export promotion, privatization and the creation of industrial estates. These policies work their way through the institutional network in different ways to influence plant-level behaviour. Increased openness to FDI affects factor markets, in particular the availability of technology, finance and skills, when foreign firms bring more advanced (usually cleaner) technologies and the skills needed to operate them into a country. Governmental incentives for export affect product markets by supporting domestic producers in exporting since this normally requires the producers to manufacture more competitive goods, using more advanced techniques and technologies than those normally used in production for the domestic market.[5] Privatization of state-owned enterprises affects factor markets by forcing firms to be more efficient in their use of production inputs, which often results in the use of CTs. Finally, the creation of industrial estates affects factor markets by lowering the costs of basic services, such as communication and transport, as well as those of environmental services for collective abatement of pollutants.

The impact of industrial policies in transforming and expanding the capital stock can be measured approximately by a country's relative position on the competitive industrial performance (CIP) index, which ranks countries on the basis of their ability to produce and export manufactured goods competitively. UNIDO (2004) combined manufacturing value added (MVA) per capita, manufactured exports per capita, industrialization intensity (simple average of the share of MVA in gross domestic product and the share of medium- and high-technology activities in MVA), and export quality (simple average of the share of manufactured exports in total exports and share of medium- and high-technology products in manufactured exports) to create the revised CIP, calculated for three points in time (1980, 1990 and 2000) for 93 countries.

CIP index values and the associated rank ordering for the 93 countries in 1990 and 2000, the approximate time period used for most analysis in this study, can be found in UNIDO (2004). Lall and Albaladejo (2002) assigned the 93 countries to five categories based on 'natural breaks' in their scores: high, medium high, medium low, low and very low.

The rank ordering and indices of the CIP index for the eight countries covered in this study are listed in Table 3.1. A CIP score for Viet Nam, which was not included in the CIP index, was estimated for 2000 for this study, but could not be estimated for 1990 because of insufficient data.[6] In 2000, four of the countries fell into the medium high category in the order given (Thailand, China, Brazil and India), two into the medium low category (Tunisia and Zimbabwe), and two into the low category (Viet Nam and Kenya).

Economic policy: trade policies

Trade-related import policies, the lowering or raising of tariffs and non-tariff restrictions (quotas) work their way through the institutional network via factor and product markets. Low tariffs and few quantitative restrictions on 'intermediate inputs' affect factor markets by making imported cleaner chemicals and technologies less costly. Low tariffs and few quantitative restrictions on 'finished goods' affect product markets by putting cost pressure on domestic manufacturers to compete with imported goods, which gives them an incentive to use CTs to lower production costs.

The effectiveness of changes in import restriction policies can be measured by changes in the technology import (TI) index. It combines two forms of technology imports – capital goods imports and technology licensing payments overseas. Capital goods include all non-FDI-related capital transfers that fall within the current account; technology licensing (or royalties) includes payments 'for the authorized use of intangible, non-produced, non-financial assets and proprietary rights (such as patents, copyrights, trademarks, franchises and industrial processes) and for the use, through licensing agreements, of produced originals of pro-totypes (such as films and manuscripts)' (World Bank, 2004: 301). Adopting the methodology of Lall and Albaladejo (2002), both forms of technology are calculated on a per capita basis, indexed and then averaged to form the composite TI index. The time period, about 1990, includes data from 87 countries throughout the time period 1990–97 in order to capture as many countries as possible, given the limited avail-ability of data; for the comparison year, 2001, the TI index includes 91 countries.

The index values and associated rank ordering for 87 countries in about 1990 and for 91 countries in 2001 can be found in Lall and Albaladejo (2002). They assigned the countries to four categories, high, medium high, medium low and low, with a relatively large number of countries having a very low use of foreign technology.

The rank ordering and associated indices of the TI index for the eight countries covered in this study are listed in Table 3.1. In 2001 no country fell into the high TI category, two fell into the medium high category in the order given (Thailand and Tunisia), two fell into the medium low category (Brazil and China), and four fell into the low category (Viet Nam, Zimbabwe, Kenya and India).

In the case of trade policy, two common measures of policy outcome as well as the effectiveness measure, TI, are used in each country chapter. The outcome measures are the simple mean tariff on imported manufactured products (TMP)[7] and the trade restrictiveness index (TRI).[8]

Economic policy: resource pricing policies

In general, higher resource prices, those that reflect full production cost and, in a limited number of cases, pollution damage, are incentives for adopting EST, particularly CTs. Higher resource prices typically motivate plant managers to reduce total expenditure on resource input by using CTs that lower water and energy use per unit of output. The price effect depends on the share of resource costs in total production and the extent to which costs can be passed on to consumers.

Resource pricing policies work their way through factor markets to influence plant-level behaviour. Most often resource pricing policies inter-fere with free market prices by subsidizing the costs of production inputs, primarily for energy and water. In some cases, the policies are ones of neglect to the extent that they fail to set any price, which happens in the case of groundwater. Below-market prices for these production inputs encour-age their excessive use by plants.

No global assessment could be drawn on to estimate the effectiveness of resource pricing policies, as was done for other policies. As an alternative and very approximate measure, an energy-use intensity (EUI) index for the manufacturing sector in several countries was calculated for use in this study. The EUI index is the amount of energy used, measured in tons of oil equivalents (toe), in the manufacturing sector per million dollars (constant 1995) of MVA (IEA, 2005 and UNIDO, 2005).

Using these data, it was possible to calculate scores for 93 countries in 1990 and 2002 and then rank order them. Countries were arbitrarily assigned to one of three categories, high, medium and low, with approximately one-third of the countries in each category. Countries in the high category have lower energy-use intensity and those in the low category have high energy-intensity use.

The rank ordering and associated energy-intensity scores of the EUI index for the eight countries are listed in Table 3.1. In 2002 no country fell into the category of low energy-use intensity, three fell into the medium energy-use intensity category in the order given (Tunisia, Thailand and Brazil), and five into the high energy-use intensity category (China, Zimbabwe, Viet Nam, India and Kenya).

Technology policy
Technology policies have the potential to increase the adoption of EST, particularly CTs, by directing the technological infrastructure to support plant-level adoption of more productive technologies and to train workers to operate these technologies.

Technology policies work their way through the institutional network to influence plant-level behaviour in two ways. One pathway empowers inter-mediary agencies, mostly manufacturing or technical extension services, to enhance plant-level capabilities to adopt or utilize newer technologies and to use their existing technology more efficiently. The other pathway affects factor markets by supporting training programmes that improve the skills of the labour force.

One measure of the effectiveness of technology policy is the technologi-cal capabilities (TC) index of Archibugi and Coco (2004).[9] The three main components of their TC index are the creation of technology, the extent of the technological infrastructure and the development of human skills. Quantitative measures of these three components are patents, scientific articles, internet penetration, telephone penetration, electricity consump-tion, tertiary science and engineering enrolment, mean years of schooling and literacy rate.

TC index values and associated rank ordering for 162 countries in approxi-mately 1990 and approximately 2000 can be found in Archibugi and Coco (2004). They assign the countries to one of four categories: technology leaders, potential leaders, latecomers and marginalized, based on significant gaps among the country groupings.

The rank ordering and associated indices of the TC index for the eight countries investigated are listed in Table 3.1. In 2000, seven countries fell into the latecomers category in the order given (Thailand, Brazil, China, Tunisia, Zimbabwe, Viet Nam and India), and one (Kenya) into the marginalized group.

Perceived Factors: Perceptions of Plant Managers and Key Informants of Drivers for EST Adoption

In the second mode of investigation, plant managers and key informants were asked to identify the main drivers for the adoption of EST and to rate their importance. The purpose of this largely qualitative approach was to capture the range and heterogeneity of the perceptions of EST adoption factors of these two groups in different countries and sub-sectors. The richness of the perception data is, unfortunately, largely missing from the statistical analysis of factors observed by the survey teams, which is introduced in the next section of this chapter. This mode of investigation, however, does not capture the full range of factors internal to a plant that influence EST decisions; nor does it shed light on the relative importance of internal and external factors.

The drivers listed in the survey questionnaire were derived from the literature reviewed above. They constitute the incentive structure created by the policy regimes as perceived by plant managers and key informants and transmitted by the three pathways referred to earlier, namely, government, markets and civil society. They are listed in Table 3.2; their descriptions and hypotheses about their influence on the adoption of EST are presented in Chapter 12.

Table 3.2   Perceived drivers for the adoption of EST

Government	Markets	Civil society
Current environmental regulation	Environmental reputation	Peer pressure
Financial incentives	High costs of production inputs	Public pressure
Future environmental regulation	Product specifications in foreign markets	
	Requirements imposed by owners and investors	
	Supply chain demands	

Observed Factors: Analysis of Factors Observed by the Survey Teams

The third mode of investigation consisted of observations by the survey teams of the underlying factors, both plant-level characteristics and contextual factors external to plants, that affected the adoption of EST by the 98 plants in the eight countries, and the transformation of the data thus collected into the dependent and independent variables used in the statistical analysis. The advantage of using a statistical approach, in this case an ordered-choice model, is that it identifies factors that influence the adoption of EST regardless of what plant managers consciously identified as important factors.

The literature reviewed above was the basis for identifying the independent variables used in the statistical analysis. The variables were grouped into four categories: the three contextual pathways, government, markets and civil society, via which policy incentives influence plant-level behaviour, and, fourthly, plant-specific factors which reflect in their totality the capacity of plants to respond to the policy incentives to adopt EST as transmitted by the different institutions. (Many, but not all, of these variables are similar to the perceived factors of the previous section.) The contextual and plant-specific factors that could be quantified are listed in Table 3.3. and are briefly described below. Additional information about the observed factors hypotheses about their influence on the adoption of EST are presented in Chapter 12.

This list of contextual and plant-specific factors is not complete when compared to the number of factors identified in the heuristic model. The most striking absence is of market forces. While their importance is recognized and discussed in the literature, it was not possible to take all of them

Table 3.3   Observed factors determining EST adoption

Contextual/external to plant			Internal
Government	Markets	Civil society	Plant-specific
International donor assistance	Export to OECD markets	Business associations	Environmental commitment
Regulatory implementation strategy	Foreign involvement	Community groups and NGOs	Ownership Profitability
Technical assistance	Water and energy price perceptions		Size
			Technological capabilities

into account. In some cases the limitation was due to the limited number of countries and the absence of national data on EST utilization, while in others it was because of the non-availability of data, such as access to finance; in yet other cases it was due to the absence of a known way to quantify the factors, such as availability of skilled labour.

SUMMARY

The heuristic model used to direct this research into the determinants of EST adoption in developing countries was formulated from a review of the more general literature on technology diffusion and technological capabilities and, especially, from a review of the more specific literature on the adoption of EST in developing countries, in particular, the literature related to the World Bank's 'new model' of pollution control. The literature on EST adoption in developing countries documents the fact that plants in developing countries are complying with environmental standards more than many had thought. It found that improved environmental performance is influenced not only by environmental regulation but also by a combination of environmental regulation, market forces and community pressures.

The heuristic model is built around the understanding that a plant's incentive structure to adopt EST is created by three policy regimes, environmental, economic, and technology, and is transmitted to plant managers via the three pathways of governments, markets and civil society. In turn, plant-level characteristics determine the extent to which plants can respond to these incentives. This research investigated the effectiveness of policy regimes in creating incentives, the perceptions of 98 plant managers and 91 key informants of the influence of the three pathways in bringing about EST adoption, and the observed factors that are thought to have influenced EST adoption at the 98 plants. While the relative importance of several observed factors was taken into account in this research, it was not possible to quantify and take all of them into account, in particular, market forces.

NOTES

1. In this connection, Kemp (1997) observes that technologies whose environmental gains are considered in adoption decisions, that is, EST, require a specific model to study their diffusion. In general terms, most new technologies are more efficient in their resource use and are less pollution intensive compared with older versions. The distinction between new production/process technology and CT is therefore not sharp. Furthermore, many factors that affect EST adoption are identical to those that determine adoption of

'normal' technologies. While diffusion models for 'normal' technologies can thus provide insights into EST diffusion patterns, it is nevertheless desirable to examine the diffusion of EST in a specific model. Such an EST diffusion model should explicitly consider environmental costs and benefits in adoption decisions.

2. National innovation systems are defined 'as the elements and relationships which interact in the production, diffusion and use of new and economically useful knowledge . . . and are either located within or rooted inside the borders of a nation state' (Lundvall, 1992: 12).

3. This study and others on the topic of openness to trade are summarized in World Bank (2000).

4. The World Bank (2006) prepares annual quantitative assessments of country policies and institutional capacities including those for environmental governance. Although it has prepared ratings for environmental governance for 134 developing and new industrialized countries, these ratings are only publicly available for the 76 International Development Association countries for the year 2005. Because ratings were only available for only four of the eight countries included in this book, it was necessary to devise a rating scheme that covered all eight countries and the time period of concern (1990 to 2002).

5. van Dijk and Szirmai (2006) document how Indonesian industrial policy aimed at export promotion encouraged the installation of advanced production technology in the pulp and paper sub-sector. In particular the government offered support in the form of subsidies and grants to promote the diffusion of embodied technology.

6. The four components of the 2000 CIP index for Viet Nam were calculated as follows: (a) MVA and total population in 2000 were taken from the WDI (2004) to calculate the component 'MVA per capita', yielding an indexed score of 0.0072; (b) manufactured exports were taken from WITS (World Bank, 2005) and population from WDI (2004) to calculate the component 'manufactured exports per capita', yielding an indexed score of 0.0062; (c) the share of MVA in GDP was calculated from WDI (2004) and averaged with the share of medium- and high-tech MVA (UNIDO, 2005) in total MVA (WDI, 2004) for the component 'industrialization intensity', yielding an indexed score of 0.3695; (d) the share of manufactured exports in total exports was calculated from WITS (World Bank, 2005) and averaged with the share of medium- and high-tech exports in total manufactured exports for the component 'export quality', yielding an indexed score of 0.3625. Following UNIDO methodology, the four components were averaged, yielding a composite CIP value of 0.186. In the full CIP ranking this placed Viet Nam in position 67 in 2000.

7. The TMP is 'the un-weighted average of effectively applied rates or most favoured nations rates for all products subject to tariffs calculated for all traded goods' (World Bank, 2004). The time period '2002' includes tariff data for 52 countries ranging from 2001 to 2003, depending upon data availability; the time period '1994' includes tariff data for 47 countries ranging from 1993 to 1996 (World Bank, 2004).

8. The TRI provides a cumulative measure of import barriers by combining restrictions due to both tariff and non-tariff measures (Allen, 2005). The index ranks 66 countries on a scale from 1 to 10, with 10 being the most restrictive. Countries included in this study were ranked first according to their TRI score and then secondarily sorted based on their tariff rate.

9. Another measure of the effectiveness of technology policy similar to the technological capability index is the technology effort (TE) index, which only approximately reflects the intensity of technological activity in a country. The composite index is derived from two measures: R&D financed by productive enterprises, and enrolment in tertiary education (Lall and Albaladejo, 2002). Their index was not used because it reflects only one point in time and has data for only five of the eight countries included in this study.

REFERENCES

Aden, J. and M. Rock (1999), 'Initiating environmental behavior in manufacturing plants in Indonesia', *Journal of Environment and Development*, **6** (4), 357–75.

Aden, J., K. Ahn and M. Rock (1999), 'What is driving the pollution abatement expenditure behavior of manufacturing plants in Korea?', *World Development*, **27** (7), 1203–14.

Adeoti, J. (2002), *Technology and the Environment in Sub-Saharan Africa, Emerging Trends in the Nigerian Manufacturing Industry*, Burlington, US: Ashgate Publishing.

Allen, M. (2005), 'Review of the IMF's Trade Restrictiveness Index (Background Paper to the Review of Fund Work on Trade)', Policy Development and Review Department, International Monetary Fund (available on: http://www.imf.org).

Archibugi, D. and A. Coco (2004), 'A new indicator of technological capabilities for developed and developing countries (ArCo)', *World Development*, **32** (4), 629–54.

Blackman, A. (1999), 'The Economics of Technology Diffusion: Implications for Climate Policy in Developing Countries', Discussion Paper 99-42, Washington, DC: Resources for the Future.

Blackman, A. and G. Bannister (1998), 'Community pressure and clean technology in the informal sector: An econometric analysis of the adoption of propane by traditional Mexican brick makers', *Journal of Environmental Economics and Management*, **35** (1), 1–21.

Blackman, A. and A. Kildegaard (2003), 'Clean Technology Change in Developing Country Industrial Clusters: Mexican Leather Tanning', Discussion Paper 03-12, Washington, DC: Resources for the Future.

Dasgupta, S., H. Hettige and D. Wheeler (2000), 'What improves environmental compliance? Evidence from Mexican industry', *Journal of Environmental Economics and Management*, **39** (1), 39–66.

Freeman, C. (1987), *Technology Policy and Economic Performance: Lessons from Japan*, London: Pinter.

Hettige, H., M. Huq, S. Pargal and D. Wheeler (1996), 'Determinants of pollution abatement in developing countries: evidence from South and Southeast Asia', *World Development*, **24** (12), 1891–904.

IEA (2005), 'Online Data Services', IEA Energy Information Centre Paris: International Energy Agency (available on: www.iea.org).

Kaufmann, D., A. Kraay and M. Mastruzzi (2003), 'Government Matters III: Governance Indicators for 1996 to 2002', WPS 3106, Washington, DC: The World Bank.

Kee, H., A. Nicita and M. Olarreaga (2005), 'Estimating Trade Restrictiveness Indices', Washington, DC: The World Bank.

Kemp, R. (1997), *Environmental Policy and Technical Change: A Comparison of the Technological Impact of Policy Instruments*, Cheltenham, UK and Northampton, MA, US: Edward Elgar Publishing.

Lall, S. and M. Albaladejo (2002), 'Indicators of the Relative Importance of IPRs in Developing Countries', Working Paper 85, Oxford: QEH Working Paper Series (available on: http://www.qeh.ox.ac.uk/pdf/qehwp/qehwps85.pdf).

Lall, S. and W. Latsch (1999), 'The technological capability approach', in S. Lall (ed.), *The Technological Response to Import Liberalization in Sub Saharan Africa*, London: Macmillan.

Lall, S. and C. Pietrobelli (2002), *Failing to Compete: Technology Development and Technology Systems in Africa*, Cheltenham, UK and Northampton, MA, US: Edward Elgar Publishing.

Lundvall, B. (ed.) (1992), *National Innovations Sytems: Towards A Theory of Innovation and Interactive Learning*, London: Pinter.

Lundvall, B., D. Johnson, E. Sloth Anderson and B. Dalum (2002), 'National systems of production, innovation and competence building', *Research Policy*, **31** (2), 213–31.

Montalvo, C. (2002), *Environmental Policy and Technological Innovation: Why do firms adopt or reject new technologies?*, Cheltenham, UK and Northampton, MA, US: Edward Elgar Publishing.

Montalvo, C. and R. Kemp (2004), 'ESTO Project Report: Industrial Cleaner Technology Diffusion', TNO, Delft, The Netherlands, unpublished manuscript.

Reppelin-Hill, V. (1999), 'Trade and environment: an empirical analysis of the technology effect in the steel industry', *Journal of Environmental Economics and Management*, **38** (3), 283–301.

Romijn, H. (2001), 'Technology support for small-scale industry in developing countries: a review of concepts and project practices', *Oxford Development Studies*, **29** (1), 57–76.

Ruttan, V. (2002), 'Sources of technical change: induced innovation, evolutionary theory, and path dependence', in A. Gruebler, N. Nakicenovic and W.D. Nordhaus (eds), *Technological Change and the Environment*, Washington, DC: Resources for the Future, pp. 9–39.

Seroa da Motta, R. (2006), 'Analyzing the environmental performance of the Brazilian industrial sector', *Ecological Economics*, **57** (2), 269–81.

UNIDO (2002), 'Industrial Development Report 2002/2003: Competing through Innovation and Learning', Vienna: UNIDO.

UNIDO (2004), 'Industrialization, Environment and the Millennium Development Goals in Sub-Saharan Africa', Industrial Development Report 2004, Vienna: UNIDO.

UNIDO (2005), *International Yearbook of Industrial Statistics 2005*, Cheltenham, UK and Northampton, MA, US: Edward Elgar Publishing.

van den Bergh, J.C.J.M. (2003), 'Bounded rationality and environmental policy', *International Society for Ecological Economics*, Amsterdam: Free University.

van Dijk, M. and A. Szirmai (2006), 'Industrial policy and technology diffusion: evidence from paper making machinery in Indonesia', *World Development*, **34** (12), 2137–52.

Wang, H. and D. Wheeler (2000), 'Endogenous Enforcement and Effectiveness of China's Pollution Levy System', Policy Research Working Paper 2336, Washington, DC: The World Bank (available on: http://www.worldbank.org).

Wheeler, D. and P. Martin (1991), 'Prices, policies and the international diffusion of clean technology', in P. Low (ed.), *International Trade and the Environment*, World Bank Discussion Paper 159, Washington, DC: World Bank, pp. 197–224.

World Bank (2000), *Greening Industry: New Roles for Communities, Markets and Governments*, Oxford, UK: Oxford University Press.

World Bank (2004), 'World Bank Development Indicators (WDI) 2004', CD-ROM version, Washington, DC: The World Bank.

World Bank (2005), 'World Integrated Trade Solution (WITS)' (available on: http://wits.worldbank.org).

World Bank (2006), *Country Policy and Institutional Assessment*, Washington, DC: The World Bank.

4. Brazil

INTRODUCTION

A survey team from the Centro Nacional de Technologias Limpas of Brazil investigated the specific factors influencing the adoption of environmentally sound technology (EST) in Brazil's pulp and paper sub-sector. The team used semi-structured questionnaires provided by UNIDO to interview plant managers at seven of the 255 plants in this sub-sector, and key informants in four business associations, two technology centres, three chemical and equipment suppliers, four environmental non-governmental organizations (NGOs), and five environmental regulatory agencies. The team also collected background data on the country and the pulp and paper sub-sector.

This chapter describes the economic and environmental context in Brazil for EST adoption; relevant environmental, economic and technology policies; the pulp and paper sub-sector and the plants investigated; and key informants and international donors.

THE ECONOMIC AND ENVIRONMENTAL CONTEXT FOR EST ADOPTION

The following selected economic and environmental performance indicators define the context in which manufacturing plants made their technology adoption decisions and, in particular, their decisions to adopt EST in the late 1990s/early 2000s.

Economic Performance Indicators

Brazil's economic growth staggered several times during the 1990s due to persistent macroeconomic weaknesses at the national level and to international economic turbulence, including, for example, the Argentinean crisis. Despite these factors, gross domestic product (GDP) growth was sustained and continuous, although understandably modest at times, with an annual average growth rate of 2.7 per cent between 1990 and 2002. Between 1990 and 2002, GDP increased by 34 per cent and GDP per capita by 14 per cent

Table 4.1   Economic indicators for Brazil

Economic indicator	Year	Value	Percentage change
GDP (constant 1995 US$) (billion)	1990	603.5	34.0
	2002	809.9	
GDP per capita (constant 1995 US$)	1990	4079.0	14.0
	2002	4642.0	
Population (million)	1990	148.0	18.0
	2002	174.5	
GNI per capita at PPP (current international $)	1990	5120.0	46.0
	2002	7450.0	
MVA (constant 1995 US$) (billion)	1990	135.2	13.0
	2002	152.5	
MVA (percentage of GDP)	1990	27.4*	–14.2
	2002	13.2	
CPI (1995=100)	1990	0.0024	
	2002	166.1	
Interest rate (commercial lending rate)	1997	78.2	–15.3
	2002	62.9	
Exchange rate (BRR/US$)	1997	1.1	170.0
	2002	2.9	

Note: * Average of MVA shares for 1989 and 1991.

Source: World Bank (2004).

while the population increased by 18 per cent (Table 4.1). Gross national income (GNI) per capita at purchasing power parity (PPP) – a more accurate indicator of well-being – increased even more, by 46 per cent. Based on the latter, Brazil is classified by the World Bank as a lower-middle-income country.

The country's manufacturing value added (MVA) increased slightly, by 13 per cent, but the MVA share of GDP declined from 27.4 per cent in 1990 to 13.2 per cent in 2002, although its manufacturing sector was the second largest in Latin America. Despite being more export oriented, its performance abroad remained weak, with exports representing only 10 per cent of the country's GDP.

At the beginning of the 1990s inflation, as measured by the consumer price index (CPI), was very high, reaching 30 per cent per month in 1993. With the 'Real Plan' of 1994, Brazil emphasized the need to control inflation by adopting a fixed exchange rate and creating a quasi-independent Central Bank. The fixed exchange rate resulted in positive changes in investments and industrial output, but overvaluation of the real had a negative effect on exports and the government gradually abandoned it. Whereas in 1996 the real/dollar ratio was roughly 1:1, in 1999, following the adoption of a flexible exchange rate regime, the ratio reached 1.9:1 and finally in mid-2002 it climbed to 2.9:1. As a result Brazilian products became gradually more competitive in international markets and in 2001 the country announced a trade surplus of US$2.6 billion, something unique in its recent history.

Environmental Performance Indicators

The Brazilian economic miracle of the 1970s resulted in a significant expansion in the manufacturing industry, especially in the steel, pulp and paper, metallurgy and automotive manufacturing sectors. The enhanced manufacturing capacity generated excessive pollution, which contributed to environmental degradation. Since then many initiatives have been introduced to reduce pollution, encouraged not only by the central government and federal authorities but also by NGOs and the media.

Selected environmental indicators, namely, energy use, carbon dioxide (CO_2) emissions, organic matter effluent measured as biochemical oxygen demand (BOD) and water use, as well as the intensity of use of each of these, which provide an insight into the state of industrial environmental performance in the country, are presented in Table 4.2. Total energy use in the manufacturing sector, measured in tons of oil equivalents (toe), grew by 44 per cent between 1990 and 2002. Energy-use intensity also increased by 28 per cent. Associated CO_2 emissions increased by 62 per cent during the period, and CO_2-emission intensity increased more than energy-use intensity, by 44 per cent. However, total BOD effluent decreased by 19 per cent and BOD-effluent intensity by 28 per cent. While industrial water use increased by 7 per cent, water-use intensity decreased by 2 per cent from 1990 to 2000, the latest year for which data were available.

As of 1995 the distribution of BOD effluent among manufacturing subsectors was as follows: food and beverages, 44.4 per cent; primary metals, 17.7 per cent; pulp and paper, 12.9 per cent; textiles, 10 per cent; chemicals, 9.2 per cent; and others, 5.8 per cent. The BOD loadings of the pulp and paper sub-sector were the third highest among the sub-sectors (World Bank, 2004).

The number of ISO 14001 certificates increased from 63 in 1997 to 900 in 2002. Although Brazil ranked second among the eight countries included in this study in terms of the number of certificates issued, it lagged behind both China and India in terms of the number of certificates per million

Table 4.2   Environmental indicators for Brazil

Source code	Environmental indicator	Year	Value	Percentage change
1	Energy use in the manufacturing sector (million toe)	1990 2002	45.9 66.1	44.0
1&2	Energy-use intensity (toe per million US$ of MVA)	1990 2002	340.0 430.0	28.0
1	CO_2 emissions from the manufacturing sector (million tons)	1990 2002	58.0 94.0	62.0
1&2	CO_2-emission intensity (tons per million US$ of MVA)	1990 2002	420.0 610.0	44.0
2	BOD effluent from the manufacturing sector (thousand tons)	1990 2000	260.0 210.0	−19.0
2	BOD-effluent intensity (tons per million US$ of MVA)	1990 2000	1.9 1.4	−28.0
3	Water use in the manufacturing sector (billion m³)	1990 2000	9.9 10.7	7.0
3	Water-use intensity (thousand m³ per million US$ of MVA)	1990 2000	73.5 71.8	−2.0
4	Per cent of MVA produced by the most pollutant-intensive sub-sectors	1990 2002	37.5 35.0	−2.5
5	Number of ISO 14001 certificates	1997 2002	63.0 900.0	1330.0

Note: Data shown for 2000 on BOD for Brazil are from the year 1995, which is the latest year available.

Sources: 1. IEA (2005); 2. World Bank (2004); 3. FAO (2005); 4. UNIDO (2005); 5. ISO (2003).

US dollars of MVA. Brazil had 5.9 compared to 6.1 in China and 7.4 in India.

Implications for EST Adoption

During the period investigated by this study, the overall economic and environmental conditions in Brazil seemed conducive to the adoption of EST by the country's manufacturing sector. The government of this advanced developing country had compelled its manufacturing sector to make considerable investments in EST before 1990, as evidenced by its relatively low BOD-effluent intensity (1.9 tons per million US dollars of MVA) in 1990. However, from 1990 to 2002 the manufacturing sector, though large, grew only slowly, with a 1.6 per cent average annual growth rate in MVA and, in parallel, experienced an even smaller annual average growth rate in new investment, some of which would have been in EST.[1] A contributory factor in discouraging such investment would clearly have been the very high rate of inflation (the CPI increased over 10 000 per cent) and very high interest rates (78 per cent in 1997 and 63 per cent in 2002). The 13 per cent increase in MVA between 1990 and 2002 was accompanied by an increase in energy use of 44 per cent and energy-use intensity of 28 per cent, partially due to the structural change in the economy. However, BOD effluent decreased by 19 per cent and BOD-effluent intensity by 28 per cent, reflecting a small decline in the share of more polluting sub-sectors in MVA and a continuing but lower rate of EST adoption than in the 1980s, due to the tight monetary policy.[2]

ENVIRONMENTAL POLICY

Brazil had an efficient, democratic system for environmental management as well as one of the most advanced environmental legislative regimes in the world. It achieved significant institutional advances in environmental policy design and implementation following the Stockholm Conference on the Environment in 1972. Nevertheless, implementation and enforcement of these were far from ideal.

The institutional framework for environmental management was created between 1973, when the Special Secretariat for the Environment was established, and 1989, when the Brazilian Environmental Institute was established. From 1988 the Ministry of Environment (MMA) was the focal point for environmental activities at the federal level of government. MMA and associated organizations received between 0.3 and 0.5 per cent of the federal budget for their activities during the 1990s (Young and Roncisvalle, 2001).

As of 2002 there were key environmental organizations at three levels of government, federal, state and municipal. At the federal level, MMA administered the National Environmental Fund and allocated resources for implementation of the National Environmental Policy. The Institute of the Environment and Natural Renewable Resources, which reported to MMA, was responsible for monitoring and enforcement, as well as for providing technical assistance to state environmental protection agencies. The National Council of the Environment, an inter-ministerial organization, supported MMA by setting environmental standards. Each state had an environmental secretary and a regulatory body that issued licences to polluting activities. In addition, many municipalities had a citizen-led environmental council to address local issues. Finally, the Public Attorney

General was an important participant, with jurisdiction over environmental matters and responsive to public complaints.

State authorities could set environmental standards that were more stringent than the baseline standards prescribed by the federal government, but they did not prescribe the technology needed to comply with the standards. Hence firms had some degree of flexibility in selecting the technological configuration to meet the standards. In a few cases state authorities imposed technical requirements, such as the adoption of chlorine-free bleaching technologies on the pulp and paper sub-sector, but that was the limit of their imposition. Overall, emphasis on PATs was gradually replaced by initiatives that encouraged the adoption of CTs.

These organizations drew on a wide range of policy instruments for industrial environmental management. They are classified into four categories, command and control regulation, economic and fiscal incentives, voluntary programmes and transparency and disclosure.

First, as in many other countries, the environmental authorities relied mainly on the command-and-control regulatory approach of standard setting, permit issuance, compliance monitoring and enforcement. The effluent discharge standards set by Brazilian authorities for the pulp and paper sub-sector were very stringent and comparable to those in North America and the more demanding European countries. Since permitting was on a case-by-case basis, it sometimes resulted in negotiated compliance procedures that promoted the use of CTs or encouraged a more efficient use of water. Penalties were imposed on those firms that did not comply with the standards. The policy had, however, some degree of flexibility, with the first enforcement measure being only a warning to non-compliers.

Second, the government used some economic instruments, such as charges, taxes and fines, to improve environmental performance and encourage compliance with existing standards. Incentives included lower interest rates on loans for PATs and CTs from the National Bank for Economic and Social Development and subsidies for research and development (Shaman, 1996).

Third, several voluntary programmes with industry participating were under way. One was the cleaner production programme, started in 1995 with the establishment of the joint UNIDO–UNEP Centro Nacional de Tecnologias Limpas (CNTL) in Porto Alegre. This particular programme is described later in this chapter. The second is the ISO 14000 (environmental management system) certification programme, started in 1996. The impact of this programme was limited, with the participation of only 900 certificates as of 2002. However, most firms in the pulp and paper sub-sector were certified because of their export orientation. The third was environmental labelling both for final products and forestry practices. Although the labelling scheme has yet to be used for paper products, European schemes affect the pulp and paper industry because its products had to comply with European requirements. Wood and forestry certifications were a reality in Brazil, and the dominant certification procedures were those of the Forest Stewardship Council and the Brazilian Association of Standards.

Fourth, transparency and disclosure programmes were only recently emerging to address the need to report the industrial performance of firms to the public. Accordingly some firms were beginning to disclose environmental and social information through their sustainability and social balance reports.

Global Comparison

Overall, Brazil's environmental policies were progressively improving towards the end of the period of this study. They relied on all levels of government for their management and involved a variety of regulatory measures, which appear to have resulted in extensive investments in PATs to achieve compliance with environmental standards. Thus it is not surprising that Brazil's ranking improved modestly on the EG index, described in Chapter 3, from forty-second among 66 countries in 1990 to thirty-ninth in 2001. Similarly its ranking among developing countries improved from eighteenth among 39 developing countries in 1990 to fifteenth among 40 developing countries in 2001. However, it ranked only fourth among the eight countries included in this study, one place behind China, the other major pulp and paper producing country.

ECONOMIC POLICY REGIMES

Overviews of Brazil's three economic policy regimes, industrial, trade and resource pricing, the economic policies that most directly influence technological modernization in the manufacturing sector and thereby increase the likelihood of the adoption of EST (see Chapter 3), are presented in this section.

Industrial Policy

In 1990 the Brazilian government introduced the New Industrial Policy, which initiated a shift from a growth-focused to a competitiveness-oriented industrial policy. It redirected budget incentives and subsidies to finance investments and exports. This shift was seen as necessary because the rate of growth of the manufacturing sector had lagged behind that of GDP throughout the 1980s and both the labour force and labour productivity in the sector decreased during the second half of the 1980s (UNIDO, 1992). The Multi-Annual Plan 1996–99 and the Governmental Agenda 2000–2001 continued the emphasis on competitiveness, declaring that the central objective of development policies was to insert the Brazilian economy into the world economy in a competitive manner (Melo, 2001).

As a result of this shift there were major changes in three policy instruments that had the potential to stimulate the modernization of technology: foreign direct investment (FDI), export promotion and privatization.

FDI

The Brazilian government's reductions during the 1990s of restrictions on FDI allowed the manufacturing sector to invest in more advanced technologies. The particular instrument, called 'Investe Brasil' and put in place in 1995, eliminated the limitations on the inflow of foreign investment and provided equal treatment for national and foreign capital, except for sub-sectors that were considered strategic. In these sub-sectors, such as air transportation, health care, mineral exploration, shipping and telecommunications, FDI inflows were either banned or required majority ownership by a national entity (WTO, 2000).

As a result, by 2002 Brazil had become the second largest beneficiary of FDI among emerging economies (UNCTAD, 2004). Between 1990 and 2002, FDI inflows increased from $1.07 billion to $16.4 billion, an increase of over 1500 per cent and, as a percentage of GDP, from 0.2 per cent in 1990 to around 3.4 per cent in 2002 (World Bank, 2005).[3]

Export promotion

Export promotion, often leading to the use of the more advanced and cleaner technologies needed to produce more competitive goods, was introduced to solve the general anti-export bias in the Brazilian trade regime. Since the export promotion instruments of the 1970s and 1980s were largely viewed as unsuccessful, the focus in the 1990s moved to the more competitive sub-sectors (OECD, 2001).

The changes that were introduced can be classified into three broad categories – fiscal incentives, financial incentives, and export promotion assistance. The fiscal incentives included reduction of or exemption from import duties on machinery, equipment, and accessories through 'Special Export Programmes'. In 1992 such fiscal incentives amounted to almost US$300 million under 503 contracts. However, in the following years both the number of contracts and the value of the fiscal incentives continued to decrease until they were terminated in 2003. Although all exports were subject to a 30 per cent tax, which could be reduced to zero or increased up to 150 per cent, exemptions were more often granted on the basis of export destination (WTO, 2000).

Financial incentives in Brazil were provided through the 'Export Financing Programme' (PROEX) established in 1991. PROEX gave export credits to exporters directly or through interest rate equalization payments, depending on the maturity and terms of the loans. Having increased expenditure from US$121 million in 1994 to US$629 in 2000, PROEX provided financing for close to 15 per cent of all exports in 2000. In addition, the Export Guarantee Fund provided export insurance for political as well as commercial risk for periods exceeding two years (WTO, 2000).

The Export Promotion Agency began to provide export assistance in 1997 with the aim of increasing the participation of SMEs in national exports by targeting segments of low technological intensity, modernizing production processes, increasing product values, and providing the necessary training on how to access new foreign markets. In addition, firms operating in certain export processing zones could obtain duty, tax and foreign exchange exemptions, but were required to export 100 per cent of their product. Few firms in these zones, however, took advantage of this as most found it more financially attractive to sell in domestic markets (WTO, 2000).

Despite many weaknesses, the manufacturing sector remained the largest contributor to the country's exports, these doubling from US$16.3 billion in 1990 to US$32.6 billion in 2002, and its share of total merchandize exports increasing from 52 per cent in 1990 to 54 per cent in 2002 (World Bank, 2004).

Privatization
The Brazilian Privatization Programme, initiated in 1990, was aimed at improving fiscal balances and reducing the public sector. Between 1996 and 2000 it sold 24 out of 120 state-owned enterprises for US$74 billion, the remaining enterprises being in the areas of electricity, petrochemicals, transportation, and health (WTO, 2000). Carried out with the aim of making these enterprises operate more efficiently with less wasteful production, this policy had the potential to encourage technological modernization.

Global comparison
Overall, the change in industrial policy along with better monetary policies for inflation control and exchange rate management created a more competitive environment that slowed the decline in the manufacturing sector. The New Industrial Policy is considered relatively effective because Brazil maintained a reasonably high ranking between 1990 and 2000 on the CIP

index, described in Chapter 3. It ranked thirty-first among 94 countries as of 2000, falling from twenty-seventh in 1990 and twenty-fourth in 1980. While it experienced declines in MVA per capita and MVA share in GDP during the 1990s, it increased its manufactured exports per capita and its share of medium- and high-technology goods in manufactured exports, managing in spite of some slippage to remain in the group of countries considered to have medium high industrial performance. It ranked tenth among 68 developing countries in 2000, a slight drop from eighth place in 1990, and third among the eight countries included in this study.

Trade Policy

In early 1991 the government announced a series of tariff reductions to be phased in between 1991 and 1994. These were among the most far-reaching and significant reductions in Brazilian trade protection in several decades. Earlier reductions were often largely superficial, only reducing rates that were prohibitive to rates of a high level that still barred many imports. The reforms in 1991 went much further and in many sectors rates were reduced to about a third of their level in the early 1980s. Equally importantly, the reforms reduced the wide variability or dispersion of tariff rates that were once characteristic of Brazilian trade policies (Castelar et al., 1999).

The Common External Tariff of the Southern Common Market (MERCOSUR) came into force in 1995 and largely determined the subsequent structure and level of Brazilian tariffs in spite of the many sector-specific exceptions. Following the establishment of MERCOSUR, the tariff ceiling was set at 20 per cent but was collectively increased to 23 per cent between 1997 and 2000 (WTO, 2000).

The use of import licences was reduced and automated during the 1990s, though the licensing procedure still remained for goods that were similarly produced domestically. As of 2000, the fees for such licences had been eliminated and an estimated 70 per cent of the licences were issued automatically (WTO, 2000). Brazil was also a frequent user of anti-dumping measures, having initiated investigations 72 times between 1996 and 1999, though India with an MVA approximately half that of Brazil did so 250 times from 1995 (WTO, 2000 and 2002).

More specifically, a number of tariff concessions were introduced in the 1990s that reduced the cost of imported capital goods and production inputs. The major concessions were duty and tax reductions for capital goods not produced locally, a drawback scheme to reimburse tariffs paid on inputs for the production of exports, and exemptions from the industrial production tax. These tariff concessions were allotted for the purchase of intermediate goods from abroad, such as industrial machinery and electronic equipment. As a result, the share of investment using domestic versus imported machinery and equipment shifted from 85 per cent domestic and 15 per cent foreign in 1991 to 65 per cent domestic and 35 per cent foreign by 1999 (OECD, 2001).

The cumulative reduction of import restrictions on manufactured goods caused by numerous trade-related agreements is most clearly, but only partially, reflected in the change in the TMP. Overall, Brazil's TMP decreased significantly from 44.0 per cent in 1989 to 15.0 per cent in 2001, which would have lowered the barrier to import more advanced and therefore cleaner technology. Its ranking improved from forty-fourth to thirty-eighth among 53 countries between about 1990 and 2002 and it had the second lowest TMP in 2002 among the eight countries included in this study (World Bank, 2004).

Indeed, the import regime was only modestly restrictive, as indicated by Brazil's ranking on the more comprehensive TRI. Brazil received a medium high score (5 out of 10) as of 2004 based on all its restrictions. It ranked forty-second out of 66 countries and had the least restrictive ranking among the eight countries included in this study, indicating that the combined impact of all import barriers was not a serious limitation to technology import, which would have included EST.

Partially due to this modestly restrictive trade regime, the import of manufactured products increased by almost 190 per cent from US$13.1 billion in 1990 to US$37.5 billion in 2002. Similarly the import of capital goods, one sub-category of manufactured goods, increased by more than 210 per cent from US$6.2 billion in 1990 to US$19.3 billion in 2002. As a result, the share of capital goods as a percentage of imported manufactured goods increased from 47 per cent to 52 per cent between 1990 and 2002 (World Bank, 2005).

The pulp and paper sub-sector

The pulp and paper sub-sector, of special interest in this study, was relatively unshielded by tariffs (World Bank, 2005). The simple average tariff on pulp and paper machinery declined significantly from 34.6 per cent in 1990 to 13.0 per cent in 2002. In spite of this decline, the annual value of imported machinery for the sub-sector increased from only US$82.7 million to US$88.7 million. The tariff concessions on machinery and chemicals specifically for use in this sub-sector were not a strong incentive for accelerating the import of capital goods because the strength of these domestic equipment manufacturing sub-sectors had been built up during the 1970s. In the pulp and paper sub-sector, over 90 per cent of the required equipment was produced with technology licensed from abroad or by multinationals with factories in Brazil. The main constraint on investment, however, was the high domestic taxation and tariffs on the machinery, which varied between 43 and 53 per cent (CNTL, 2002). Most of the chemicals used were produced on site or by a domestic manufacturer. Only a few, such as antraquinone, talc, titanium dioxide, powerful brighteners for paper and dyes, were imported from abroad.

The tariff level on pulp import actually increased from 4.7 per cent to 5.5 per cent between 1990 and 2002. However, this had a negligible effect on pulp imports, which increased by 200 per cent over the same period.

Brazil's tariff level on paper products decreased from 25.5 per cent to 14.6 per cent between 1990 and 2002, the lowest among the pulp and paper-producing countries included in this study. Paper imports increased by 64 per cent between 1990 and 2002, although they unexpectedly decreased significantly (by 42 per cent) between 2000 and 2002 despite the lack of tariff protection, evidence of the strength of the Brazilian paper industry.

Global comparison

In summary, Brazilian trade liberalization policies reduced tariffs significantly during the 1990s, creating positive incentives for the import and adoption of more advanced and, therefore, CTs. However, because Brazil had very well-developed domestic machinery and chemical production industries, it relied relatively less on technology imports than countries that lack such domestic capabilities. It is therefore not surprising that, despite its unrestrictive import regime, it made only moderately low use of foreign technology based on the TI index. In 2001 Brazil ranked fifty-fifth among all 91 countries, twenty-third among 55 developing countries and third among the eight countries included in this study.

Resource Pricing Policy

As with all the countries included in this study, it was not possible to obtain information to provide a comprehensive overview of resource pricing policies, including the use of subsidies, for energy and water, nor to calculate an average change in resource prices over the period 1990 to 2002. This section therefore offers only limited information on resource pricing policies, prices *per se* and changes in energy and water use by the manufacturing sector. Higher resource prices, as described in Chapter 3, are often incentives for adopting EST, particularly CTs.

The government kept electricity prices low as part of its import substitution policy and its attempt to control inflation by restraining increases in public sector prices, which induced a considerable substitution of electricity for other sources of energy in the manufacturing sector. In the early

1990s it implemented a series of measures to reduce its intervention in the market, thus allowing a more realistic pricing of electricity.

Between 1990 and 2002 the consumption of energy (defined as energy derived from oil, coal, natural gas, nuclear power, renewable sources and electricity) by the manufacturing sector increased by 44 per cent, as shown earlier in Table 4.2. This sector accounted for 41 per cent of total energy consumption in both 1990 and 2002 (IEA, 2005).

The pulp and paper sub-sector used fossil fuels to meet energy demands for steam and electricity until the 1980s, when it realized the potential of using larger biomass boilers fired by bark and firewood. The great majority of pulp and paper mills then changed to burning biomass to meet their energy needs.

Energy consumption by this sub-sector increased by 83 per cent during the same period, from 3.6 million toe to 6.6 million toe. Energy-use intensity increased, or conversely energy-use efficiency decreased, by 11 per cent during the same period, from 810 to 900 toe per million US dollars of MVA. The sub-sector accounted for 8 per cent of energy consumption by industry in 1990 and 10 per cent in 2002 (IEA, 2005).

Regarding water management, there was no pricing for water used by pulp and paper mills as of 2002. This, however, has the potential to change in light of the experiment started in the Paraiba do Sul River basin in 2001. A double pricing system introduced a charge on both the volume of water extracted and the effluent discharged into the river. From the experience in the Paraiba do Sul, it was estimated that pricing water would add around US$1.2 to US$4.2 per ton of finished product. As the final price paid for water depends on both quantity and quality, its pricing can be assumed to have stimulated measures to use less water and to operate effluent treatment plant (ETPs) more effectively.

Water use per ton of manufactured pulp was reduced by half between 1975 and 2000, primarily to reduce the volume and thus the cost of effluent treatment. As of 2002 the most modern pulp and integrated paper mills ran with 25 to 60 cubic metres of water per ton of finished product, whereas in the early 1990s the same mills were using around 60 to 100 cubic metres. However, total water use by the sub-sector was about the same as it had been in the past because production of pulp more than doubled and that of paper almost doubled over the same period (CNTL, 2002).

Global comparison

There is no global assessment that can be drawn on to compare the relative effectiveness of Brazil's resource pricing policies, nor were studies found on the effect of pricing on resource use. As an alternative, an EUI score for the manufacturing sector was calculated for use in this study. Brazil's energy-use intensity increased during the 1990s, from 339 toe per million US dollars of MVA in 1990 to 434 in 2002. As a result, its position on the EUI rankings fell from thirty-seventh among 93 countries in 1990 to forty-seventh in 2002. Among developing countries its rank remained almost the same, dropping from seventeenth among 53 countries in 1990 to twenty-second in 2002. Among the eight countries included in this study, it ranked second in 1990 and third in 2002.

TECHNOLOGY POLICY

Brazil's technology policy and programmes and associated institutional arrangements, aimed at increasing productivity in the manufacturing sector, often with the concomitant of increased adoption of EST, are described in this section, in particular those relating to the pulp and paper sub-sector.

The New Industrial Policy of 1990 called for fundamental changes not only in industrial policy but also in technology policy. It introduced programmes for the diffusion of more advanced technology, the setting of performance standards and the development of technological capabilities. A new quality and productivity programme was intended to counteract the estimated loss of 40 per cent of industrial output through quality deficiencies and to provide a key input for enhanced industrial competitiveness. A new technological capability programme was set up to increase expenditure on science and technology with an emphasis on technology-related applications and more private sector participation.

In 1995 the government issued a policy document entitled 'Industrial, Technological and External Trade Policy' which supported firms in their transition from the defensive strategies used at the beginning of trade liberalization to more forward-looking strategies based on increased productivity and technological innovation. The Brazilian Multi-Annual Plan of 1996–99 reinforced the support for productive modernization (Melo, 2001).

At the federal level the central organization for science and technology was the Ministry of Science and Technology (MCT), established in 1985. It advised the government on the broad allocation of funding and activities to other agencies and administered a development programme for science and technology (MDIC, 2001).

During the 1990s national systems of innovation for various sub-sectors, including pulp and paper, began to emerge in response to the need to improve productivity and competitiveness. The participants in the pulp and paper network included pulp and paper firms, individual consultants and consulting firms, analytical laboratories, technical institutes, universities, environmental regulators, and equipment and chemical suppliers. They discussed environmental issues at fora, seminars, courses, congresses and exhibitions. The most important of these was the annual environmental seminar organized by the Brazilian Technical Association for Pulp and Paper, which usually took place at one of the leading mills in the country. The network also included involvement with the Technical Association of the Pulp and Paper Industry in the United States and the Pulp and Paper Association of Canada.

Global Comparison

In summary, Brazil responded aggressively to the need for modernization of its manufacturing sector in the 1990s. It put in place several new policy initiatives and supported an impressive technological infrastructure, involving both the private and public sectors. In the light of this response, it is surprising that Brazil was placed among the group of latecomers in the TC index described in Chapter 3.[4] In 2000 it ranked seventy-second among 162 countries, a small improvement over its rank of seventy-seventh in 1990, twenty-ninth among 114 developing countries and second among the eight countries included in this study.

PULP AND PAPER SUB-SECTOR

Economic Overview

Brazilian pulp for paper production increased by 69 per cent and paper and paperboard production by 52 per cent in the 13-year period 1990–2002, with 7.4 million tons of pulp and 7.4 million tons of paper and paperboard in 2002 (Table 4.3). This represented more than 8 per cent of global pulp production and over 2 per cent of global paper and paperboard production, making the country the world's seventh largest pulp producer and eleventh largest paper and paperboard producer (FAO, 2004). In spite of the large volume of domestic production, the per capita consumption remained comparatively low, rising from 26 kg per capita in 1990 to approximately 39 kg in 2000 (compared to 34 kg in South America and 54 kg in the world as a whole in that year (WRI, 2005).

As for paper-related trade, Brazil's paper and paperboard exports dropped by 46 per cent between 1990 and 2002, moving it from the world's fifteenth to twenty-ninth largest exporter; among countries included in this study only China ranked higher in both years. Pulp for paper exports, on the other hand, surged by almost 150 per cent, making Brazil the fourth

Table 4.3   Pulp for paper and paper and paperboard production, import and export

Year	Production	Import	Export	Import	Export
	Pulp for paper (thousand tons)			Pulp for paper (US$ million)	
1990	4364	48	1035	35	599
1995	5909	185	1958	153	1041
2002	7390	422	2579	209	1138
	Paper and paperboard (thousand tons)			Paper and paperboard (US$ million)	
1990	4844	234	840	152	502
1995	5856	932	1223	988	1025
2002	7354	509	452	396	311

Source: FAO (2004).

largest pulp exporter in the world, behind Canada, the United States and Sweden. Its two largest export markets were the United States and Argentina. Whereas the sub-sector accounted for 4.4 per cent of total Brazilian exports in 1997, by 2000 this figure had reached 6.9 per cent (World Bank, 2005).

Brazil had also become a significant importer of pulp for paper production (moving from fortieth to sixteenth on the global rankings), and was the thirty-first largest paper and paperboard importer in the world. An estimated 7 per cent of paper and paperboard demand was supplied by imports in 2002, more than doubling since 1990. Among the countries included in this study, only China and India imported more paper and paperboard. Brazil was the closest among the three countries to becoming a net exporter of these products, with a net export deficit of only 50 000 tons (China, by contrast, had a net export deficit of around 6 000 000 tons). Finally, Brazil was the only net exporter of pulp for paper among these countries.

Overall, the pulp and paper sub-sector (ISIC 341) made a significant contribution to Brazil's manufacturing sector in the 1990s. The value added of this sub-sector increased from US$4.4 billion in 1990 to US$7.3 billion in 2002, a 65 per cent increase, while total Brazilian MVA increased from US$135.2 billion in 1990 to US$152.5 in 2002, only a 13 per cent increase. Its percentage share of total MVA increased from 3 per cent in 1990 to 4.8 per cent in 2002 (UNIDO, 2005). In 2002, according to information provided by the industry association BRACELPA (2004), the sub-sector employed about 95900 workers, accounting for 1.8 per cent of total employment in manufacturing. According to UNIDO industrial statistics, it employed about 138 300 workers, or 2.6 per cent of total 'formal' employment in manufacturing (UNIDO, 2005).

Sub-sector Profile

As of 2002, the pulp and paper industry was dominated by six large groups, most of which had their own forests and pulp mills and, in some cases, paper mills. Overall, there were 220 firms with approximately 255 mills located in 16 states and 180 towns throughout the country.

The financial performance of the majority of domestic firms allowed them to expand and modernize their plants. The gross operating margin was around 50 per cent of the net pulp price. However, the return on investment was much lower, around 15 per cent, because of other unrelated costs, such as depreciation and taxes. Consequently the low return together with the macroeconomic risk offset the otherwise excellent gross operating margin.

The firms were also hindered by the size of their pulp and paper mills in comparison with other global players. The largest pulp mill in Brazil, Aracruz, was significantly smaller than those owned by the the the sector giants, namely, Georgia Pacific, International Paper, UPM Kymene, Norske Skog, Mead, and Domtar. For this reason the Brazilian mills were unable to take advantage of the economies of scale available to global players. Nevertheless the mills continued to be competitive because on average they had the lowest production costs worldwide, partially due to a favourable exchange rate, but mainly to low wood, energy and chemical costs.

The mills surveyed for this study were all located in the southern region, in the states of Parana, Rio Grande do Sul and Santa Catarina. This region produced the bulk of Brazilian pulp, around 30 per cent or 2.2 million tons, and was also the country leader for some pulp products in 2002. For example, it produced 89 per cent of fibred chemical pulp and 91 per cent of high-yield pulp (BRACELPA, 2004). Pulp production here was mainly for local markets, with only one firm, Klabin Riocell, exporting 20 per cent of its production. This limited export of pulp production stood in stark contrast to other regions, where the percentage exported was much higher. Finally, the region produced around 40 per cent of total Brazilian paper and paperboard production, with only a few firms producing for export purposes.

Out of 255 mills, seven were selected to be investigated in this study, based on variations in pulping processes, size, location and raw material input. The selected mills corresponded to the criteria as follows: three used kraft pulping and the others used different processes; five were large-scale and two were small-scale; three were located in the state of Parana, three in the state of Rio Grande do Sul and one in the state of Santa Catarina; six used mixes of hard (eucalyptus) and soft (pine) wood for making pulp, and one used purchased pulp for paper-making (Table 4.4).

Other characteristics worth noting are: six of the mills were privately owned by domestic parties and one was foreign owned; they sold mainly to the domestic market, with only four of them exporting more than 20 per cent of their output; and four mills were both ISO 9001/9002 and ISO 14001 certified.

Process Technology and CT Characterization

The most common manufacturing process found in the pulp and paper sub-sector was the kraft process, which was used by three of the mills investigated (Table 4.4). This is a very efficient process, both in terms of chemical recovery (over 95 per cent) and energy, as most of the dissolved wood used in production is converted into black liquid and burnt in a boiler. The main environmental problems with this technology are substantial discharges of various water pollutants and the release of noxious odour.

The seven pulp and paper mills used all kinds of equipment, with little variation compared to the mills surveyed in other countries included in this study. The survey team assigned the mills to one of two categories based on the predominant technological vintage of the pulp production equipment: five used standard-modern technology and two used best available technology (BAT) (Table 4.4).

They also classified the mills into three groups based on the highest order of complexity of the CTs used by the mill (low, medium and high). Of those investigated, not all used the most advanced CTs, but most were implementing, or had already implemented, many CT options. One mill used CTs of a higher order of complexity, four used CTs of a medium order of complexity and two used CTs of a lower order of complexity. In addition, four of the mills had implemented environmental management systems (Table 4.4).

CT options were used in all stages of the production process. Some of those used in specific process areas and the number of mills using them are identified in Table 4.5, which confirms the extensive use of CTs in the seven mills. Among the different process areas, CT use was most extensive in fibre handling and papermaking. Costly investments were made in the bleaching process in those mills that bleached pulps (both kraft and sulphite) in order to reduce or eliminate the discharge of chlorinated organics.

The potential of CTs to reduce water and chemical use and pollutant discharge into the aquatic environment has been documented in several demonstrations undertaken by the CNTL. The results achieved at one of the mills and investigated in this study are shown in Box 4.1.

Table 4.4 Profile of the seven mills investigated

Mill	Process/product	Scale, thousand TPY	Location: region	Sales orientation (in 2000)	Technology vintage	Ownership	EST score	Regulatory compliance	Donor assist.	EMS
B1	Wood, kraft pulp, 10% pulp to paper	Large	Guaiba/urban	23% D, 77% E	BAT	100% private – domestic	PAT + HCT	Yes now, but has been penalized in the past	No	Yes
B2	Wood, sulphite, 15% pulp to paper	Small	Cambara/rural	100% D	Standard–modern	100% private–domestic	PAT + MTC	Yes now, but was penalized in 1991	No	No
B3	Wood, kraft pulp only	Large	Parana/rural	100% D	Standard–modern	100% private–domestic	PAT + LTC	Yes now, but has been penalized in the past	No	No
B4	Wood, thermo-mechanical pulp, coated paper	Large	Parana/rural	68% D, 32% E	BAT	100% private–domestic	PAT + MTC	Yes	No	Yes

B5	Wood, kraft pulp, linerboard	Large	Otacilio Costa mill/ rural	20% D, 80% E	Standard– modern	100% private– domestic	PAT + MTC	Yes	No	Yes
B6	Wood, groundwood pulp, newsprint	Large	Parana/ rural	94% D, 6% E	Standard– modern	99.92% private– foreign	PAT + LTC	Yes	No	Yes
B7	Recovered paper and market pulp, packing bags and printing	Small	Guaiba/ rural	80% D, 20% E	Standard– modern	100% private– domestic	PAT + MTC	Yes now, but has been penalized in the past	No	No

Abbreviations: domestic (D); export (E); best available technology (BAT); pollution abatement technology (PAT); higher order technological complexity (HTC); medium order technological complexity (MTC); lower order technological complexity (LTC).

Source: CNTL (2002).

Table 4.5   CTs used in the seven mills

Process area	Option	Number of mills using practical equipment
Fibre handling	Biomass fuel	2
	Biomass composting	4
	Low-energy conveyors	6
	Adoption of sawdust	1
Pulping	Cooking modifications	2
	Antraquinone use	2
Bleaching	Oxygen delignification	2
	ECF bleaching	2
	Acid pre-treatment	1
Recovery of black liquor	Low odour or odourless boiler	1
	Burning gases in lime kiln or boiler	1
	Efficient multi-effect evaporators	2
	Condensate stripping column	1
	Burning vent gases in captive burner	1
	Reuse of the liquor to lignosulphonates	1
	Biomass power boiler	1
Chemical plant	Effluent-free chemical manufacturing	1
	Membrane cells to caustic soda making	1
Papermaking	Closed water system	7
	Automation/process control	7
	Recovery of fibres (save-all)	7
	Adoption of recovery fibre/waste paper	1
	Broke management	7

Source: CNTL (2002).

Implementation of CT options resulted in measurable reductions at little or no cost to the mill.

While the adoption of some CTs, particularly those reducing the discharge of chlorinated organics, can be attributed to increasingly stringent environmental norms, the adoption of most can be primarily attributed to the quality management programmes implemented by the mills. In the late 1980s and early 1990s the mills responded to governmental initiatives, mentioned earlier in the industrial and technology policy sections, supporting total quality management and related management tools. Efforts to increase productivity at the same time entailed the modernization of equipment to reduce wastes and residues through the recovery of fibre

---

BOX 4.1   CLEANER PRODUCTION CASE STUDY: BRAZIL

The mill is the sole producer of fluff paper in Cambara do Sul. In the early 1990s it was cited by the State of Rio Grande do Sul for violations of environmental norms. It invested US$900 000 in improving its activated sludge wastewater treatment plant and adopting several CT options. As of 2000 it functioned in full compliance with environmental standards and reduced its water use by 90 per cent.

Source: CNTL (2002).

---

losses and wastewater and to minimize energy and steam consumption. Later, mills with good-quality management programmes and excellent housekeeping were able to convert easily to the CP approach to environmental management.

PAT Characterization

All integrated pulp and paper mills and most non-integrated pulp mills in Brazil used relatively sophisticated effluent treatment technologies, while most non-integrated paper mills used relatively simple effluent treatment technologies. The exact configuration used by the integrated mills varied according to their location, but the majority were aerated lagoons (ABTCP, 2002).

All the mills investigated used PATs, for the most part primary and secondary ETPs. Five mills used secondary ETPs, three being aerated lagoons and two being activated sludge, and one used a tertiary ETP. The one non-integrated paper mill used only a physical chemical ETP because that was sufficient to meet environmental standards.

Environmental Performance

In spite of an impressive array of environmental legislation and institutions, the federal government did not set up a uniform and continuous pollutant monitoring system, relying instead on state environmental protection agencies, which used different monitoring protocols. Consequently the only estimate of pollutant release from the Brazilian pulp and paper sub-sector is the one prepared by the World Bank based on sub-sector data on effluent discharge per employee from 13 national environmental protection agencies (including São Paulo State) and sub-sector employment data from UNIDO (Hettige et al., 2000). The sub-sector was said to be responsible for approximately 13 per cent of organic water pollutant discharge, making it the third largest source after the food and beverages (44 per cent) and the primary metals (18 per cent) sub-sectors.

The seven mills included in this study reported that they were operating in full compliance with environmental standards in 2002. In earlier years the government had penalized four mills for failing to do so.

KEY INFORMANTS AND INTERNATIONAL DONORS

Four groups, in addition to government environmental regulatory agencies and technology centres, are in a position to influence the extent to which plants adopt EST: NGOs, business associations, international donors of technical assistance, and chemical and equipment suppliers. Some information on the first three is presented in this section; there was insufficient information to characterize the firms that supplied chemicals and equipment to Brazil's pulp and paper sub-sector.

NGOs

At the time of this study there were hundreds of NGOs throughout Brazil addressing environmental and socio-economic issues. They appear to have played a role in making the manufacturing sector more environmentally responsible in spite of what they perceived to be inadequate dialogue with the private sector. They also appear to have been satisfied with the stringency of environmental standards, but critical of the government for failing to be proactive rather than reactive and for not providing environmental information to the public.

The survey team interviewed four environmental NGOs that were active in the southern region, the location of the mills surveyed for this study. These four are briefly characterized as follows:

- Amigos do Meio Ambiente (Friends of the Environment) is a small NGO, founded in 1990, and an active critic of the largest pulp and paper mill in the region;
- Associacao Gaucha de Protecao ao Ambiente Natural (Gaucha Association for the Protection of the Natural Environment), founded in 1971, was the leader of the major campaign against pulp and paper mills in the state of Rio Grande do Sul in the 1990s;
- Fundacao Gaia (Gaia Foundation), founded in 1990, is a subsidiary of a European-based foundation promoting biodiversity, ecological justice and 'earth democracy';

- Nucleo Amigos da Terra (Friends of the Earth), founded in 1964 and renamed in 1998, is a well-known NGO in the southern region. It has led major campaigns against pulp and paper mills.

Business Associations

The survey team interviewed four business associations that were also active in the southern region. These four are briefly characterized as follows:

- The Brazilian Association of Pulp and Paper Manufacturers (BRACELPA) is the national association of the pulp and paper industry. It was founded in 1950 and is located in São Paulo. It lobbies the government in the interest of the sub-sector, collects statistics and publishes reports, and has an environmental committee that reviews equipment performance, environmental norms, and mill compliance.
- The Brazilian Pulp and Paper Technical Association is the technical association of pulp and paper manufacturers. Founded in 1967 and located in São Paulo, its main role is to share technology information with its members. It has an environment committee that reviews the performance of equipment, environmental norms and compliance monitoring procedures.
- The Parana Association of Pulp and Paper Manufacturers (SINPA-CEL), founded in 1969, is the state association of pulp and paper manufacturers and is linked to the Parana Industrial Federation and BRACELPA. It provides political and technical services, including testing, to its members.
- The Rio Grande do Sul Association of Pulp, Paper and Cork Manufacturers, founded in 1994, is the state association of pulp and paper manufactures and is linked to the Rio Grande do Sul Industrial Federation and to BRACELPA. Its objective is to assist its members in technical, political and environmental issues and in labour negotiations.

International Donors

Starting in the 1970s, the World Bank supported water pollution control projects in Brazil. In the 1980s the Bank funded its first Brazilian project on industrial pollution control in São Paulo and, in 1990, it initiated a project to address industrial pollution control in other states. The Inter-American Development Bank also supported capacity building for industrial environmental management in state environmental protection agencies and made loans for industrial pollution control.

The Government of Rio Grande do Sul financed the establishment of a UNIDO/UNEP National Cleaner Production Centre, Centro Nacional de Tecnologias Limpas Brazil (CNTL), in Porto Alegre in 1995. Later, minimal complementary support was provided by UNIDO. Its activities included plant-level demonstrations, training programmes/workshops and the dissemination of information on CP.

None of the mills included in this investigation, unlike some of those in the other countries included in this study, received international donor assistance to invest in PATs and CTs.

SUMMARY

Brazil's aggregate economic performance indicators suggest a relatively poor performance both for the economy as a whole and for the manufacturing sector, whereas its aggregate environmental performance indicators show a more mixed performance. While GDP increased by a relatively modest 34 per cent between 1990 and 2002, the percentage increase in MVA was even smaller, 13 per cent. As a result, the share of MVA in GDP decreased from 27.4 to 13.2 per cent. GNI per capita, however, increased by 46 per cent during the same period. Energy use in the manufacturing sector increased by 44 per cent, a larger percentage increase than that of MVA, and energy-use intensity increased by 28 per cent. BOD effluent, however, decreased by 19 per cent and BOD-effluent intensity decreased even more, by 28 per cent, an improvement primarily due to a strong regulatory effort on the part of the government and to community pressure.

Brazil's environmental policy was among some of the most advanced in the world, as of 2002, and environmental considerations were slowly being introduced in the economic development planning processes. Brazil used all levels of government for industrial environmental management and applied a variety of policy instruments, which appear to have resulted in extensive investments in PATs to achieve compliance with environmental standards.

The collective impact in the 1990s of three economic policy regimes, industrial, trade and resource pricing, on achieving the technological modernization that could be expected to have incorporated the use of EST was positive but probably limited. The new industrial policy measures introduced in the 1990s contributed to slowing down the decline in MVA and competitiveness, as measured by Brazil's rank on the CIP index in 1990 and 2000. They pushed the manufacturing sector more forcibly into the world economy, particularly in terms of the export of medium- and high-tech manufactured goods. Achieving these positive changes certainly demanded modernization of the capital stock, which would have contributed positively but to an unknown extent to greater adoption of EST. The decline in tariff and non-tariff barriers in the 1990s would have increased the incentive to import more advanced and, therefore, cleaner technologies, especially so by the pulp and paper sub-sector, but in practice such imports were limited because of a well-developed domestic industrial machinery sub-sector. The limited changes in resource pricing policies were not an incentive to improve resource-use efficiency; in fact, energy-use intensity in the manufacturing sector, including the pulp and paper sub-sector, increased during the 1990s, if the data are to be believed.

Brazil's technology policy and programmes responded aggressively to the need for modernization of its manufacturing sector in the 1990s. The government introduced programmes for the diffusion of more advanced technology, the setting of performance standards and the development of technological capabilities. National systems of innovation for various sub-sectors, including pulp and paper, emerged in response to the need to improve productivity and competitiveness. However, even closer cooperation among different institutions and the provision of technical support for industry could have further accelerated adoption of advanced technology, moving the manufacturing sector closer to the best practice in industrialized countries.

The pulp and paper sub-sector increased pulp for paper production from 4.4 to 7.4 million tons (a 70 per cent increase) and paper and paperboard production from 4.8 to 7.4 million tons (a 69 per cent increase) between 1990 and 2002. As of 2002, there were 225 pulp and paper mills in the sub-sector. The survey team investigated seven of these mills, of which three used the kraft process to pulp eucalyptus and pinewood and other four different processes. Not surprisingly, five of the mills used reasonably modern technology and two used BAT. In addition, one mill used CTs of a higher order of complexity; four used CTs of a medium order of complexity and two used CTs of a lower order of complexity. All the mills had installed PATs equivalent to secondary treatment. Finally, in 2002, all the mills were reported to be operating in full compliance with environmental standards.

Other institutional actors, NGOs, business associations and international donors played a significant role in encouraging the adoption of EST. Notably NGOs played an important role in exerting pressure on the pulp and paper sub-sector to comply with environmental standards – a role that was explicitly supported by Brazilian environmental legislation. Business associations were effective in representing the sub-sector and, importantly, providing advice on technology and environmental compliance to their members. International donors, primarily the World Bank and the Inter-American Development Bank, supported capacity building for environmental management and provided loans for pollution control projects.

Overall, with closer cooperation between different institutions, efficient and realistic resource pricing policies and effective policy implementation, including support for business, Brazil was, by 2002, moving closer to 'best practice' in EST, sustainable industrial development and effective environmental protection.

NOTES

1. This presumption is based on the economy-wide average annual growth rate in gross fixed capital formation of 0.6 per cent between 1990 and 2002 (World Bank, 2004).
2. A study conducted for the São Paulo State Government (the State of São Paulo represents nearly 60 per cent of the Brazilian industrial GDP), analysing economic activity in the years 1996 and 2001, has shown that investments had fallen by 40 per cent in pollution control equipment and 30 per cent in production processes, suggesting that only a smaller share of São Paolo's industrial sector was able to invest in EST. Another useful indicator of pollution abatement efforts undertaken by Brazilian firms is the surveys carried on by the Brazilian Institute of Geography and Statistics between 1997 and 2002, which included questions about the pollution abatement expenditures. The picture resulting from the surveys is that firms were spending less on pollution abatement. The output share for those firms that undertook abatement expenditures declined from 23 per cent in 1997 to 16 per cent in 2002. The high interest rate certainly played a major role in the declining propensity of firms to invest in pollution abatement, but it remained also true that many other factors influenced this behaviour (Seroa da Motta, 2006).
3. The FDI for 1990 has been taken as the three-year average of 1989–91 and for 2002 as the three-year average of 2001–3, in order to even out fluctuations in FDI flows.
4. Brazil was classified among the group of countries with moderate technology effort by Lall and Albaladejo (2002); these are equivalent to the group of countries called potential leaders by Archibugi and Coco (2004). The latter would appear to be more appropriate for Brazil than being classified among the latecomers.

REFERENCES

ABTCP (2002), 'Associacäo Brasileira Técnica de Celulose e Pape', internal report, Säo Paulo, Brazil.
Archibugi, D. and A. Coco (2004), 'A new indicator of technological capabilities for developed and developing countries (ArCo)', *World Development*, **32** (4), 629–54.
BRACELPA (2004), Associacao Brasileirade Celulose e Papel, BRACELPA, São Paulo: Brazil (available on: http://www.bracelpa.org.br).

Castelar Pinheiro, A., F. Giambiagi and J. Gostkorzewicz (1999), 'O Desempenho Macroeconômico do Brasil nos Anos 90', in F. Giambiagi and M.M. Moreira (eds), *Rio de Janeiro: A Economia Brasileira nos Anos 90*, Brasilia, Brazil: Brazilian Development Bank (BNDES) (available on: http://www.bndes.gov. br/conhecimento/livro/eco90_01.pdf).

Centro Nacional de Tecnologias Limpas Brazil (CNTL) (2002), 'Assessing the Uptake of EST by the Pulp & Paper Industry in the South of Brazil', Report prepared for UNIDO.

FAO (2004), 'FAOSTAT – Forestry Statistics', Rome: Food and Agriculture Organization of the United Nations (available on: http://www.fao.org).

FAO (2005), 'AQUASTAT: FAOSTAT', Rome: Food and Agriculture Organization of the United Nations (available on: http://www.fao.org).

Hettige, H., M. Mani and D. Wheeler (2000), 'Industrial pollution in economic development: the environmental Kuznets curve revisited', *Journal of Development Economics*, **62** (2), 445–76.

IEA (2005), 'Online Data Services', IEA Energy Information Centre, Paris: International Energy Agency (available on: www.iea.org).

ISO (2003), 'The ISO Survey of ISO 9000 and ISO 14001 Certificates', Geneva: International Organization for Standardization (available on: http://www.iso.org).

Lall, S. and M. Albaladejo (2002), 'Indicators of the Relative Importance of IPRs in Developing Countries', Working Paper 85, Oxford: QEH Working Paper Series (available on: http://www.qeh.ox.ac.uk/pdf/qehwp/qehwps85.pdf).

MDIC (2001), 'O Futuro da Industria Brasilia, Ciência, Tecnologia e Inovação: Desafio Para a Sociedade Brasileir', Brasilia, Brazil, Ministerio Do Desenvolvimento, Ministério da Indústria, do Comércio e do Turismo. Industria E Comercio (Ministry of Development, Industry and Foreign Trade) (available on: www.mdic.gov.br).

Melo, A. (2001), 'Industrial Policy in Latin America and the Caribbean at the Turn of the Century', Working Paper #459, Washington, DC: Inter-American Development Bank.

OECD (2001), 'OECD Economic Surveys: Brazil', Paris: Organization for Economic Cooperation and Development .

Seroa da Motta, R. (2006), 'Analyzing the environmental performance of the Brazilian industrial sector', *Ecological Economics*, **57** (2), 269–81.

Shaman, D. (1996), 'Brazil's Pollution Regulatory Structure and Background', Report 16635-PR, New Ideas in Pollution Regulation Background Paper, Washington, DC: The World Bank (available on: http://www.worldbank.org).

UNCTAD (2004), 'Development and Globalization: Fact and Figures', Geneva: United Nations Conference on Trade and Development.

UNIDO (1992), 'Brazil's Industrial Policy: an Assessment in the Light of the International Experience', Vienna: UNIDO.

UNIDO (2005), *International Yearbook of Industrial Statistics 2005*, Cheltenham UK and Northampton, MA, US: Edward Elgar Publishing.

World Bank (2004), 'World Bank Development Indicators (WDI) 2004', CD-ROM version. Washington, DC: The World Bank.

World Bank (2005), 'World Integrated Trade Solution (WITS)' (available on: http://wits.worldbank.org).

WTO (2000), 'Trade Policy Review Brazil 2000', Geneva: World Trade Organization.

WTO (2002), 'Trade Policy Review India 2002', Geneva: World Trade Organization.

WRI (2005), 'EarthTrends', Energy and Resources, Washington, DC: World Resources Institute (available on: http://earthtrends.wri.org).

Young, C.E. and C.A. Roncisvalle (2001), 'Expenditure, Investment, and Financing for Sustainable Development in Brazil', Brazilia, Brazil: United Nations Development Programme.

5.   China

INTRODUCTION

A survey team from the China National Cleaner Production Centre and the Chinese Research Academy of Environmental Sciences investigated the specific factors influencing the adoption of environmentally sound technology (EST) in China's pulp and paper sub-sector. The team used semi-structured questionnaires provided by UNIDO to interview plant managers at 11 out of 4600 plants in this sub-sector and key informants in one business association, three technology centres, two chemical and equipment suppliers, two environmental NGOs and six environmental regulatory agencies. The team also collected background data on the country and the pulp and paper sub-sector.

This chapter describes the economic and environmental context in China for EST adoption; relevant environmental, economic and technology policies; the pulp and paper sub-sector and the plants investigated; and key informants and international donors.

THE ECONOMIC AND ENVIRONMENTAL CONTEXT FOR EST ADOPTION

The following selected economic and environmental performance indicators define the context in which manufacturing plants made their technology adoption decisions and, in particular, their decisions to adopt EST in the late 1990s/early 2000s.

Economic Performance Indicators

During the 1990s China experienced a consistent and rapid growth, averaging 10.1 per cent gross domestic product (GDP) growth per year, with an increase of about 12 per cent on an annual basis during the Eighth Five Year Plan (1991–95) and of 8.3 per cent during the Ninth Five Year Plan (1996–2000). Between 1990 and 2002 GDP increased by 204 per cent and GDP per capita by 170 per cent while the population increased by 11 per cent (Table 5.1). Gross national income (GNI) at purchasing power

Table 5.1   Economic indicators for China

Economic indicator	Year	Value	Percentage change
GDP (constant 1995 US$) (billion)	1990	397.6	204.0
	2002	1208.9	
GDP per capita (constant 1995 US$)	1990	350.0	170.0
	2002	944.0	
Population (million)	1990	1155.0	11.0
	2002	1280.0	
GNI per capita at PPP (current international $)	1990	1310.0	245.0
	2002	4520.0	
MVA (constant 1995 US$) (billion)	1990	116.4	293.0
	2002	457.2	
MVA (percentage of GDP)	1990	32.9	2.5
	2002	35.4	
CPI (1995 = 100)	1990	55.6	96.0
	2002	108.8	
Interest rate (commercial lending rate)	1990	9.4	−44.0
	2002	5.3	
Exchange rate (Y/US$)	1990	4.8	73.0
	2002	8.3	

Source: World Bank (2004).

parity (PPP) – a more accurate indicator of well-being – increased by 245 per cent. Based on the latter, China is classified by the World Bank as a low–middle-income country.

The country's manufacturing value added (MVA) increased by almost 300 per cent during the same period, significantly more than the percentage increase in GDP, with the MVA share of GDP increasing from 32.9 per cent to 35.4 per cent between 1990 and 2002, and light industry, such as textiles and shoes, growing faster than heavy industry (EIU, 2004).

As a result of adopting strict measures for the issuance of currency and limiting credit, the government effectively controlled the rate of inflation during the same period. Whereas prices almost doubled between 1990 and 1995, as measured by changes in the consumer price index (CPI), they increased by only 9 per cent during the period 1990 to 2002.

Furthermore, the monetary policy achieved its aim of lowering interest rates, reducing them from 9.4 per cent in 1990 to 5.3 per cent in 2002.

Following the institution of economic reforms and the opening of the national economy to global markets, the international competitiveness of Chinese industries improved steadily, particularly for high-value-added, technical or capital-intensive industries such as the automotive sub-sector. However, the structure of industrial competitiveness did not change fundamentally and most of China's competitive strength continued to lie in labour-intensive sub-sectors with low value added, such as textiles and garments.

Environmental Performance Indicators

During the period of this study China had serious water and even more serious air pollution problems. Although the former remained serious, improvements were made in a number of river basins and the quality of water in major rivers did not appreciably deteriorate in the 1990s. Furthermore, industrial pollution control efforts, primarily large-scale water pollution control campaigns that targeted the most polluted rivers and lakes, reduced wastewater discharges. The share of industrial wastewater subject to treatment increased from approximately 60 per cent in 1990 to more than 80 per cent in 2000, but a comparable increase in compliance with environmental standards was not detected (World Bank, 2001).

The more serious air pollution problems were caused by the use of coal for household heating and cooking as well as for power generation and other industrial activities. Chinese coal contains high amounts of ash and sulphur, and boilers used old combustion technologies, producing significant emissions, particularly in urban areas. The government reported in the mid-1990s that acid rain affected 29 per cent of the country's land area. The damage caused by excessive pollution (both air and water) to human health and the environment was estimated in the mid-1990s to cost around 8 per cent of GDP (World Bank, 1997b).

Selected environmental indicators, namely, energy use, carbon dioxide (CO_2) emissions and organic matter effluent, measured as biochemical oxygen demand (BOD), and water use, as well as the intensity of use of each of these, which provide an insight into the state of industrial environmental performance in China, are presented in Table 5.2. Total energy use by the manufacturing sector, measured in tons of oil equivalent (toe), grew by 18 per cent between 1990 and 2002, much lower than MVA growth. Consequently energy-use intensity by this sector declined by 70 per cent. Associated CO_2 emissions decreased by 2.3 per cent during the same period, whereas CO_2-emission intensity decreased by 75 per cent. Total BOD effluent decreased by 13 per cent and BOD-effluent intensity decreased significantly, by 78 per cent. Finally, while China's industrial water use increased by 224 per cent, water-use intensity decreased by a slight 1.5 per cent between 1990 and 2000. This is a much more marked improvement than in India where, during the same period, water-use intensity increased by 31 per cent.

Table 5.2   Environmental indicators for China

Source code	Environmental indicator	Year	Value	Percentage change
1	Energy use in manufacturing sector (million toe)	1990	261.0	18.0
		2002	307.0	
1 & 2	Energy-use intensity (toe per million US$ of MVA)	1990	2240.0	−70.0
		2002	670.0	
1	CO_2 emissions (million tons)	1990	940.0	−2.0
		2002	920.0	
1 & 2	CO_2-emission intensity (tons per million US$ of MVA)	1990	8100.0	−75.0
		2002	2010.0	
2	BOD effluent from the manufacturing sector (thousand tons)	1990	2320.0	−13.0
		2000	2010.0	
2	BOD-effluent intensity (tons per millionUS$ of MVA)	1990	20.0	−75.0
		2000	4.8	
3	Water use in the manufacturing sector (billion m³)	1990	50.0	224.0
		2000	162.0	
2 & 3	Water-use intensity (thousand m³ per million US$ of MVA)	1990	429.0	−1.5
		2000	423.0	
4	Per cent of MVA produced by the most pollutant-intensive sub-sectors	1990	30.3	0.2
		2002	30.5	
5	Number of ISO 14001 certificates	1997	22.0	12 700.0
		2002	2803.0	

Sources: 1. IEA (2005); 2. World Bank (2004); 3. FAO (2005); 4. UNIDO (2005); 5. ISO (2003).

As of 2001, the distribution of BOD effluent among manufacturing sub-sectors was as follows: food and beverages, 28 per cent; primary metals, 21 per cent; chemicals, 15 per cent; textiles, 15 per cent; pulp and paper, 11 per cent; and others, 10 per cent (World Bank, 2004). While the pulp and paper sub-sector is a major source of BOD loadings, it is definitely not the largest.

Finally, the number of ISO 14001 certificates increased from 22 to 2803 between 1997 and 2002, a significantly large change compared to the other countries included in this study. There were 6.1 certificates per million US dollars of MVA in 2002, about the same as in Brazil (5.9) and India (7.4).

Implications for EST Adoption

During the period investigated by this study, the overall economic and environmental conditions in China seemed highly conducive to the adoption of EST by the country's manufacturing sector. The government of this accelerating developing country had not compelled its manufacturing sector to make significant investments in EST before 1990, as evidenced by its very high BOD-effluent intensity (20 tons per million US dollars of MVA) in 1990. From 1990 to 2002 the already large manufacturing sector grew rapidly, with an 11.9 per cent average annual growth rate in MVA. In parallel there was an even larger annual average growth rate of 13.2 per cent in new investment, some of which would have been in EST (Isaksson, 2006); this growth would have been encouraged to a significant degree by the moderate rate of inflation (the CPI increased by 156 per cent) and low and declining interest rates (9.4 per cent to 5.3 per cent) over this period. In spite of the 293 per cent increase in annual MVA between 1990 and 2002, energy use increased by only 18 per cent and energy-use intensity decreased by 70 per cent, the result of considerable industrial restructuring and a size-able investment in new technology. More surprisingly, BOD effluent decreased by 13 per cent and BOD intensity by an amazing 75 per cent due to a combination of several factors, including industrial restructuring, plant closures and investments in EST.

ENVIRONMENTAL POLICY

China's recent efforts in industrial environmental management started with the Law on Environmental Protection (LEP), which was tentatively promulgated in 1979 and finally promulgated in 1989 (Ma and Ortolano, 2000). This was followed by numerous other laws. The more recent legislation affecting industry was the cleaner production promotion and environmental impact assessment laws, both promulgated in 2002.

In addition to the legislative measures, the government put forward general strategies for protecting the environment. Of particular relevance for industrial environmental management is China's Agenda 21 of 1994, Chapter 12, which called for changing the industrial structure and its geographical distribution, developing CTs and green products and improving industrial management (Anon, 1994).

The government also set up the National Environmental Protection Agency (NEPA) in 1984 as part of the Ministry of Urban and Rural Construction and Environmental Protection (MURCEP). Its name was changed to the State Environmental Protection Agency (SEPA) when it was upgraded to ministerial status in 1998. It is responsible for implementing the environmental policies issued by the National People's Congress.

As of 2002, there were 31 provincial Environmental Protection Bureau (EPBs) and 1400 city-level EPBs. While the city-level EPBs reported to the provincial EPBs, which in turn reported to SEPA, the budgetary resources for the city-level EPBs were provided by the local governments, and a good share of their operating funds were obtained from retained pollution levies on industry. As a result, EPBs were reluctant to enforce compliance with environmental standards because doing so would reduce their main source of revenue (World Bank, 2001).

These organizations drew on a wide range of policy instruments for industrial environmental management. They are classified into four categories, command and control regulation, economic and fiscal incentives, voluntary programmes and transparency and disclosure.

First, as in many other countries, the environmental authorities relied mainly on the command-and-control regulatory approach of standard setting, permit issuance, compliance monitoring and enforcement. Initially the approach was based on concentration-based national standards, 29 for the most common water pollutants and 13 for the most common air pollutants. The permits issued to factories required them to comply with the standards within specified time limits. The environmental impact assessments requirements and the 'three synchronous policy', which required EPBs to review the design of pollution control equipment, supervise the construction of treatment plants and monitor operation of the newly constructed plants, were integral parts of this approach. The primary limitation to this approach was that these laws and regulations were not adequately enforced for a variety of reasons (Ma and Ortolano, 2000).

Regarding the pulp and paper sub-sector, SEPA issued wastewater concentration-based standards in 1992. These were made more stringent in 1999 and contained both concentration-based and, for the first time, load-based discharge criteria. In addition SEPA and the State Light Industry Agency published a guideline on straw pulp and paper industry wastewater prevention and treatment technology. It advised mills using agro-residues as raw material about improvements that could be made in process technologies to reduce pollutant discharge.

Second, these organizations used economic instruments, such as charges, taxes and fines, to improve compliance with environmental standards. The most widely used economic instrument was a pollution levy system that imposed a fee on pollutant concentrations that exceeded the standards. This fee varied depending on the difference between actual concentrations and the standards. EPBs also levied tariffs on wastewater treatment and solid waste disposal and, in some cases, applied environmental taxes on all pollutant discharges, even those within the pollutant concentration limits. The primary limitations with this approach were that the levy was applied only to the pollutant on which the assessed penalty was the highest, and the applicable rate of the levy system was too low. The result was that these measures had very minor effects on enterprise performance. In spite of the limitations, though, Wang and Wheeler (2000) found that plants had reduced their pollutant discharge in response to the levy. In addition to the levy, another important economic instrument for industrial pollutant reduction was the conditionality of loans from commercial banks and other social organizations. For example, the Agricultural Bank of China required a firm to be in compliance with national environmental standards as one condition for receiving a loan.

Third, several voluntary programmes with industry participating were under way. One was a cleaner production programme, started in 1993 with a World Bank and UNEP-funded large-scale cleaner demonstration project. Further funding was provided by UNIDO and UNEP to the China National Cleaner Production Centre in 1995 and for several bilaterally funded projects with provincial EPBs. The impact of this programme has been limited because the total number of industrial units that conducted CP audits since 1993 is still below 1000 (Han and Ma, 2002: 41). The second was an ISO 14000 (environmental management system) certification programme started in 1997. The impact of this programme has also been limited, with approximately 2800 certificates as of 2002 (Table 5.2). The third was an environmental labelling programme started in 1994. By early 2004 approximately 10 000 products from 800 enterprises had received such labels.

Fourth, transparency and disclosure programmes, in spite of their potential, were not yet comparable to those in developed and other developing countries. There was, however, a formal procedure for citizen complaints within EPBs, and there were ongoing experiments using information disclosure in two cities, Hohhot and Zhenjiang, along the lines of the 'program for pollution control, evaluation and rating' in Indonesia, which required public disclosure of pollutant releases (Wang et al., 2002).

In addition to the above policy instruments, the government in 1996 ordered the closure of many small town and village enterprise (TVE) production units, approximately 72 000 in 15 sub-sectors, due to severe pollution of the Huai River. As a result, more than 4000 small pulp and paper mills with an annual capacity of less than 5000 tons per year were closed between 1996 and 1997. These mills had no effluent treatment plants (ETPs) and produced mainly poor-quality packing grades of paper from agro-residuals. Besides, the operation of numerous printing and writing paper-producing machines was stopped (OECD, 2001). In Shandong Province alone, which had the largest number of mills and production volume using agro-residue pulp in the country and where seven out of the 11 mills surveyed for this study were located, more than 1000 mills were shut down in 1996. The Province then proceeded first to close many mills whose capacity was less than 25 000 tons per year and then to close all mills whose capacity was below 30 000 tons per year (Ma and Ortolano, 2000).

Global Comparison

In short, China had put in place a well-designed command-and-control regulatory system and was making use of several supplemental policy instruments, primarily a pollution levy during the period of this study. Improvements were certainly still necessary, such as increasing the pollution levy fee and strengthening the city-level EPBs, because compliance with environmental regulations remained low (OECD, 2001). This said, though, China's achievements in industrial environmental management were impressive, especially in light of the 293 per cent increase in industrial output between 1990 and 2002. The total volume of wastewater discharged decreased and the total discharge of major pollutants barely increased (World Bank, 2001). The reduction was reflected in the tremendous improvement in China's ranking on the EG index described in Chapter 3, from fifty-seventh among 65 countries in 1990 to thirty-sixth among 66 in 2001. Among developing countries its position improved from thirty-first among 39 in 1990 to twelfth among 40 in 2001. In that year it ranked third among countries included in this study and ahead of the other two large pulp and paper producing countries, Brazil and India.

ECONOMIC POLICY REGIMES

Overviews of China's three economic policy regimes, industrial, trade and resource pricing, the economic policies that most directly influence techno-logical modernization in the manufacturing sector and thereby increase the likelihood of the adoption of EST (see Chapter 3), are presented in this section.

Industrial Policy

Industrial development in China is a policy priority embedded in the central planning system, which has a tradition of placing emphasis on the development of industry. With the reforms and liberalization start-ing in 1978, and specifically for industry in 1984, China implemen-ted an extensive programme of economic measures that substituted a market-oriented economy within the context of macroeconomic control by the government for the previous rigidly planned economy. This was the so-called social-capitalist model. The main reforms were oriented towards the establishment of a modern corporate structure and pro-perty ownership in large and medium-sized state-owned enterprises (SOEs).

Three broad classes of reforms characterized these changes in industrial development policy:

- gradual improvements in firm-level autonomy in the selection of input and output mixes (manager responsibility system);
- more permissive product distribution that allowed a greater share of final output to be sold in the open market (dual-track pricing system); and
- emergence of a private manufacturing sector (guaranteed economic rights) (Xu, 2000).

These major shifts in industrial development policy included changes in three policy instruments: foreign direct investment (FDI), export promotion and privatization, all with the potential for stimulating the modernization of technology.

FDI

By the end of the 1990s China had eliminated almost all previous restrictions on private and foreign investments in the manufacturing sector and in the insurance and banking sectors. In general, China had now become the most favoured destination among emerging markets for FDI because of its rapid GDP growth, its healthy economic outlook and the opportunities offered by such a large market (EIU, 2005a).

This was a recent development. Although during the 1980s and the early 1990s, because of generous tax incentives and a seemingly infinite supply of cheap labour, the inflow of FDI into China had soared, accounting for as much as 17.3 per cent of all investment in 1994, by the late 1990s the attraction of these benefits had started to fade. Investors began to realize that chaotic rules and poor infrastructure made it difficult to realize profits. Subsequently, however, China's entry into the World Trade Organization (WTO), with the potential of this membership for strengthening a rule-based trading system, as well as opening up previously restricted areas of the economy to FDI, began to revive the interest of foreign investors (EIU, 2005b).

Preferential income tax policies were introduced in the late 1990s as an added inducement for foreign-invested firms. An income tax rate of 15 per cent was introduced in high-tech industrial development zones and 24 per cent for firms located in coastal areas and provincial capital cities, with a complete exemption from income tax during the first two years after registering profits and a 50 per cent reduction during the following three years (EIU, 2005a).

With the elimination of restrictions and these added incentives, China succeeded in securing an increase of over 1300 per cent in FDI between 1990 and

2002, from US$3.7 billion to US$49.0 billion.[1] As a share of GDP, it increased from 1 per cent to 3.9 per cent during this period (World Bank, 2004).

The successful increase in FDI during the 1990s resulted in both the import of embodied technology in plant and equipment and the improvement of managerial skills through licensing, joint ventures and wholly owned foreign subsidiaries.[2] However, the assimilation of imported technology remained low; for every yuan (Y) spent by industry on technology import, only Y0.09 was spent on its assimilation (IDRC, 1997). Assimilation was difficult because the national innovation system lacked the resources, dynamism and flexibility to respond fully to the changing needs of industry. Moreover, some 30 per cent of FDI invested in China in 1995 went into pollutant-intensive sub-sectors, with 13 per cent of this going into highly pollutant-intensive sub-sectors (Xian et al., 1999).

Export promotion
In the 1980s China reformed its export system in two significant ways. First it shifted its reliance on a few foreign trading corporations to a phenomenally large number of corporations that were allowed to trade internationally. Second, it did away with a many of controls on foreign exchange, thus allowing exporters to retain a portion of their foreign exchange receipts, and it continued to maintain a realistic exchange rate policy.

These changes led to increased competition between foreign trading corporations and better prices for export suppliers (World Bank, 1997a). As a result, Chinese manufactured exports increased by more than 600 per cent, from US$44.6 billion in 1990 to US$293.4 billion in 2002. Of greater relevance, the share of manufactured exports in total merchandise exports increased from 72 per cent in 1990 to 90 per cent in 2002 (World Bank, 2004). A large part of this increase can be linked to the rapid growth of foreign-invested firms, whose share of trade increased from less than 2 per cent in 1984 to an impressive 57 per cent in 2004. Particularly favoured were the eastern provinces of the country, where over 60 per cent of all industrial output was produced (EIU, 2005a).

Privatization
Changes in the governance and management of SOEs and town and village enterprises (TVEs), aimed at making them operate as if they were privately owned enterprises concerned with maximizing efficiency, had the potential to bring a greater modernization of technology. The initial Chinese reforms focused on decentralization, i.e., from central to local control. Cross-regional competition then forced local governments to privatize both SOEs and TVEs. In fact the privatization of TVEs was even faster than that of SOEs (Li and Zhang, 2004).

Data on change in the number of SOEs in China are unclear. Best estimates reveal that, in total, the number decreased from 262 000 in 1997 to 150 000 in 2003, when they controlled some US$2.4 trillion in assets (Mako and Zhang, 2004; EIU, 2005b). Of the 196 200 industrial enterprises with an annual sales income of more than US$600 000 registered in 2003, 34 280 were officially part or fully owned by the state (as state-owned and state-holding enterprises). The government probably also had a stake in many, if not all, of the 22 500 firms defined as 'collective' and the 9300 firms categorized as 'cooperative', not to mention the high number of non-industrial enterprises (EIU, 2005b).

There was also economic progress in the restructured SOEs. The SOE sector is reported to have made total profits of Y241 billion (US$29 billion) in 2000, up by more than 140 per cent year on year. Of the 6600 large and medium-sized SOEs that were running at a loss in 1997, 70 per cent had, by the end of 2000, started registering profits following restructuring or mergers (EIU, 2005b).

Global comparison

To conclude, industrial policies significantly altered the inefficient and energy- and resource-intensive heavy industry structure and inward economic orientation in China. The country showed consistent gains in all components of the CIP index described in Chapter 3. Its rank increased from twenty-sixth place among 94 countries in 1990 to twenty-fourth as of 2000, and it was among the countries considered as having medium high industrial performance during the 1990s. Among 68 developing countries, it ranked sixth in 2000. Although it had ranked lowest among the other two large developing countries included in this study (Brazil and India) in 1980, it ranked higher than these two in 2000, leading them in the share of MVA in GDP and making impressive gains in the share of medium- and high-technology goods in manufactured exports. Finally, it ranked second, one place below Thailand, among the eight countries included in this study.

Trade Policy

According to Zhang (1999), trade reforms in China went through four phases. Throughout the first series of reforms during the 1988–93 period, the operational efficiency of foreign trade corporations (FTCs) was targeted. In addition to the introduction in 1988 of a foreign trade contract responsibility system enabling FTCs to become financially independent, fiscal subsidies for exports were eliminated in 1991, and an export tax rebate system for all exported goods was introduced as the main tool for the export promotion policy. In 1993, when a move was made to enter the General Agreement on

Tariffs and Trade (GATT), the export and import quota and licence system reforms made the system more transparent. Furthermore, relaxation of tradable commodity control progressed very rapidly, allowing trade to be carried out more and more by decentralized FTCs and producers.

Throughout the second series of reforms between 1994 and 1998, China introduced additional fiscal and financial reforms, which significantly affected the foreign exchange regime. Exporters and importers were allowed to buy and sell foreign exchange freely from the Bank of China, and the yuan was made convertible on the current account. China also implemented a preferential policy for importing technologies with high technology content, and other preferential policies were introduced to facilitate industries identified as 'pillar' industries.

China achieved smooth accession to the World Trade Organization (WTO) in 2001. This entailed the removal of trade and investment barriers, thereby improving market access to foreign capital and imported technologies. The number of commodity categories subject to import licensing dropped from 26 in 2001 to 12 in 2002, including pulp and paper products. As of 2004, the only products subject to import quota licences were specific machinery and electronic products, and the only products subject to import tariff quota administration were grain, cotton, vegetable oil, sugar, wool, wool tops and chemical fertilizers (WTO, 2004).

The cumulative reduction of import restrictions on manufactured goods as a result of numerous trade-related agreements is clearly, but only partially, reflected in the change in the TMP. Overall China's TMP decreased significantly from 40.6 per cent in 1992 to 15.0 per cent in 2001, which would have lowered the barrier to import more advanced and therefore cleaner technologies. Its ranking improved modestly from forty-second out of 48 countries in about 1990 to fortieth out of 53 countries in about 2002, and in 2002 it had the fourth lowest TMP in 2002 among the eight countries included in this study (World Bank, 2004).

In fact the import regime was only modestly restrictive, as indicated by China's ranking on the more comprehensive TRI. China received a medium high score (5 out of 10) as of 2004 based on all its restrictions. It ranked forty-eighth among 66 countries, which indicates that the combined impact of all import barriers was only modestly restrictive, and it had the second lowest score among the eight countries included in this study.

In spite of the modestly restrictive trade regime, the import of manufactured products surged from US$43 billion in 1992 to US$245 billion in 2002, an increase of approximately 470 per cent. Similarly the import of capital goods, one sub-category of manufactured goods, increased from US$22 billion in 1990 to US$135 billion in 2002, an increase of approximately 520 per cent. As a result, the share of capital goods imports as a percentage of imported manufactured goods increased from 51 per cent to 55 per cent over this time period (World Bank, 2005).

The pulp and paper sub-sector

Changes in the tariff levels for the pulp and paper sub-sector were broadly in line with those for the overall manufacturing sector in 2002, which meant that the sub-sector was largely unshielded by tariffs. The tariff levels on machinery and pulp and paper products had fallen to relatively low levels by 2002 (World Bank, 2005). More specifically, the tariff level on pulp and paper machinery decreased from 22.7 to 12.1 per cent between 1992 and 2002, broadly in line with other paper-producing countries. This reduction was an additional incentive for large-scale pulp and paper mills to buy technology from foreign sources; the value of imported machinery was more than three times higher in 2002 than in 1992. China ranked first among the four pulp and paper-producing countries included in this study in terms of the percentage change in machinery import over this period.

The almost negligible tariff level on pulp had no impact on its import; it increased by 600 per cent over the same period. China had no alternative but to import pulp if it wanted to satisfy the domestic demand for paper and paper products.

Finally, China reduced the tariff level on paper imports from 36.3 per cent in 1992 to 17.5 per cent in 2001. This reduction of over 50 per cent from 1992 was greater than that applied by any other pulp and paper-producing country included in this study; the new tariff level was relatively low compared to India's 34 per cent level. This reduction contributed to some extent to the steady increase of almost 190 per cent in the value of paper imports over the same time period.

Global comparison

In summary, Chinese trade liberalization policies reduced tariffs significantly during the 1990s, creating positive incentives for the import of more advanced and therefore cleaner technology. Somewhat surprisingly, however, China ranked very low on the TI index. In 2001 it was sixty-sixth among 91 countries, a modest increase from sixty-eighth among 87 countries in 1990. Its rank among developing countries increased more significantly, from forty-fifth to thirty-third among 61 countries during this period. Finally, it ranked fourth in 2001 among the eight countries included in this study.

Resource Pricing Policy

As with all countries included in this study, it was not possible to obtain information to provide a comprehensive overview of resource pricing policies, including the use of subsidies, for energy and water, nor to calculate the average change in resource prices over the period 1990 to 2002. This section therefore offers only limited information on resource pricing policies, prices *per se* and changes in energy and water utilization by China's manufacturing sector. Higher resource prices, as described in Chapter 3, are often incentives for adopting EST, particularly CTs.

Reforms that affected electricity prices included two important components: power-generating stations were separated from power distribution networks, and they were allowed to sell their electricity to the power network, enabling the latter to have electricity at the lowest possible rates. Although the reforms were aimed at establishing a market mechanism to determine electricity prices, the State Power Corporation still controlled 90 per cent of the electricity supply as of 2002 (EIU, 2005b). In spite of this, the electricity rate, which averaged around US$0.02 per kwh at the beginning of the 1990s, was increased to US$0.06 in Beijing in 2000, and even higher in other provinces (CNCPC/CRAES, 2002).

Between 1990 and 2002, consumption of energy (defined as energy derived from oil, coal, natural gas, nuclear power, renewable sources and electricity) by the manufacturing sector increased by 18 per cent, as shown above in Table 5.2. This sector accounted for 38 per cent of national energy consumption in 2002, a decline from 54 per cent in 1990 (IEA, 2005).

Energy consumption by the pulp and paper sub-sector increased by 7 per cent during the same period, from 9.8 million to 10.5 million toe. Energy-use intensity, however, decreased by 73 per cent during the same period, from 3890 to 1050 toe per million US dollars of MVA. The sub-sector accounted for 4 per cent of energy consumption by industry in 1990 and 3 per cent in 2002 (IEA, 2005).

The setting of rates for water management was the responsibility of cities, which led to a distorted system that often caused water shortages, most frequently in the north (EIU, 2005b). Cities seldom imposed extraction fees for self-supplied groundwater or, if they did, the fees were nominal. The charges for water delivered from municipalities to enterprises varied considerably but were said to be below current household charges and far below the average incremental cost of new supply in virtually all cities. As a result, industrial water use per unit of output was five to ten times that of the OECD countries. The reuse rate of industrial water was 30 to 40 per cent, while in OECD countries it reached 75 to 85 per cent (OECD, 2001).

The water consumption of integrated pulp and paper mills in China averaged 300 tons per ton of output compared with 35 to 50 tons in the developed countries, while that of non-integrated paper mills averaged 100 tons compared with 10 to 20 tons in developed countries (CNCPC/CRAES, 2002).

The widespread inefficiency in water use is not surprising because water's contribution to industrial productivity was significantly undervalued. According to Wang and Lall (1999), the marginal value of water used by industry ranged between less than US$0.01 per cubic metre for the power sector to US$3.30 for transport equipment, with an average for the whole industry of US$0.30, said to be a low estimate. They state that the price of water in China was in the range of US$0.06 to US$0.15 per cubic metre in 2002, which means that the price was significantly below its use value.

Even though a more inclusive reform of national water prices was deleted from the Tenth Five Year Plan, reform efforts were observed in some regions and in large cities, such as Beijing and Shanghai. Wastewater treatment fees were introduced and the price of water consumed increased from US$0.08 per cubic metre to some US$0.45 for domestic use and US$0.35 for industrial and commercial use.

Global comparison

There is no global assessment that can be drawn on to measure the relative effectiveness of China's resource pricing policy, nor were studies found on the effect of pricing on resource use. As an alternative, an EUI score for the manufacturing sector was calculated for use in this study. China's energy-use intensity decreased considerably between 1990 and 2002, with a change from 2240 toe per million US dollars of MVA in 1990 to 670 toe in 2002. As a result, its position on the EUI ranking advanced from eighty-seventh in 1990 among 93 countries to sixty-sixth in 2002. Among 65 developing countries it progressed from sixtieth position in 1990 to thirty-ninth in 2002. Among the eight countries included in this study it improved from last (most intensive) in 1990 to fourth in 2002.

TECHNOLOGY POLICY

During the early 1990s the government organized and coordinated technology import activities and paid the full cost associated with such importation. Further, the government's involvement ensured some degree of cooperation and communication between technology development institutes and industrial enterprises, and usually encouraged the adoption of EST. However, following economic liberalization it substantially reduced its financial support, introducing new modalities of technological cooperation that required firms to follow market signals when making their technology choices and to participate in partnerships and joint ventures.

The main institutions that influenced Chinese technology policies and the development and diffusion of technologies, including EST, in the 1990s were:

- the Ministry of Science and Technology, which assumed responsibility for funding the development and demonstration of technologies;
- the State Development Planning Commission, which took the lead in importing and commercializing technology;
- the State Economic and Trade Commission (SETC), which played the leading role in diffusing energy-efficient technologies as well as EST;
- the State Administration of Quality, Technical Supervision and Quarantine, which formulated, implemented and oversaw the formulation of technological and safety standards, including those for environmental protection equipment.

China spent between 0.5 and 0.7 per cent of its GDP on research during the 1990s, which was mostly carried out by research institutes and universities. These public sector institutions accounted for approximately 55 per cent of R&D expenditure, or perhaps more, given that industry accounted for only 23 per cent; the remainder, classified as 'other', most likely came from governmental sources. In general, industrial needs for advanced technology were met, by and large, by technology imports from developed countries (Yao, 2003).

Overall, governmental programmes were numerous and mainly focused on the development and adoption of more advanced technologies. These included the setting up of engineering and productivity centres to transfer to engineering the know-how developed by research institutes. From 1991 the government funded the establishment of 84 engineering technology research centres and established 79 additional centres with World Bank support (Rakesh, 2000).

The government also started two new programmes for technology upgrading during the 1990s. One was the 'criterion and methods for the verification of high and new technology enterprises in national high and new technology industrial development zones'. The programme, which started in 1991, was modified in 1996 by the extension of tax reductions and exemptions to enterprises located outside the development zones.

The other was a comprehensive 'national technology innovation programme' launched by the SETC in 1996. Its main activities included pilot technological innovation projects in SMEs; the establishment of in-plant technology centres (294 in 2000); networking between universities, research institutes and industries to commercialize and diffuse R&D results (for example, with personnel exchanges); and the establishment of manufacturing sub-sector institutions for technological innovation. Between 1996 and 2000 SETC implemented more than 2400 key technological innovation projects with a total investment of Y54.5 billion (CNCPC/CRAES, 2002).

In addition, the government supported the development of a sub-sector for manufacturing pollution control equipment, which it initiated in 1990. SETC accelerated the pace of this programme in 1996. However, this led to conflicts of interest between different government departments. As a result, government policy and programmes failed to create an enabling business environment for the take-off of the sub-sector. A new approach was adopted in 1998, with SETC assuming responsibility for industrial policy and SEPA retaining only a participatory role in policy work related to the sub-sector manufacturing pollution control equipment.

Universities were the main education and training institutions for industrial environmental management in the 1990s. Each province had a light industry university, with most having a department concerned with pulp and paper-making. Moreover, due to weak R&D capacity within industrial enterprises, the publicly funded R&D institutes in universities played a crucial role in technological innovation and, in some cases, followed up with commercialization of the innovations.

With regard to the pulp and paper sub-sector, there were, as of 2002, ten research institutes, including the China National Pulp and Paper Research Institute; ten engineering and consultant institutes, including the Light Industry Beijing Design Institute; and more than ten universities that specialized in pulp and paper science and technology, including the South China University of Technology. The latter set up a key national laboratory for pulp and paper engineering. In addition there were 17 testing centres under national or provincial supervision actively working in quality control for raw material and products for the paper industry.

Communication between the technology infrastructure, the universities and the pulp and paper mills improved during the 1990s because universities and research institutes were in contact with international universities and researchers. Moreover, mills were willing to pay for technologies and information in order to improve their performance. Most mills needed to import foreign technologies because indigenous technologies had proven unsatisfactory, and turned to the technology infrastructure and universities for advice on such choices (Shi, 1996).

Global comparison

In summary, Chinese science and technology policy and infrastructure changed with the shift towards a market-oriented economy. New technology programmes offered opportunities for the increased use of more efficient production processes. According to Yao (2003), however, there was still too much emphasis on advanced technologies for heavy industry rather than on appropriate technologies for the labour-intensive industries, and government-funded institutes dominated domestic R&D. Furthermore, the lack of cooperative synergy between institutions as well as poor plant management limited the potential for technological transformation.

Not surprisingly, China ranked reasonably low on the TC index but improved its ranking between 1990 and 2000. It ranked eighty-fifth out of 162 countries in 2000, a considerable improvement on its ninety-seventh ranking in 1990, but between Brazil at seventy-second and Tunisia at ninety-second, placing it in the latecomers group. It ranked fiftieth among 115 developing countries in 1990, fortieth among 114 in 2000 and third among the eight countries included in this study in 2000, up one place from 1990.

PULP AND PAPER SUB-SECTOR

Economic Overview

By 2002 China had become a large global producer of both pulp for paper and paper and paperboard, ranking third and second respectively in the world. Between 1990 and 2002 its production of pulp for paper increased by 38 per cent and paper and paperboard production by 118 per cent, with 18.4 million tons of pulp and 37.9 million tons of paper and paperboard in 2002 (Table 5.3). This represented more than 10 per cent of global pulp production and over 12 per cent of global paper and paperboard production. Likewise, it had become the world's second largest paper-consuming country, after the United States, even though per capita consumption was still low compared to developed countries.

With regard to trade, China exported 2.6 million tons of paper and paperboard in 2002, making it the seventh largest global exporter (up from twelfth in 1990). Its largest export markets were Hong Kong SAR of China and the United States. However, it was only the twenty-ninth largest exporter of pulp and, indeed, was a massive net importer of pulp for paper by 5.7 million tons, ranking second only behind the United States as a global pulp importer. The trend was generally the same for paper and paperboard imports, where it was again a net importer of around 6 million tons and again second only to the United States. The story is clear: despite China's booming production, domestic demand had outpaced production, thus requiring huge imports of both pulp and paper.

Overall the pulp and paper sub-sector made a significant contribution to China's manufacturing sector in the 1990s. Its value added increased from

Table 5.3 Pulp for paper and paper and paperboard production, import and export

Year	Production	Import	Export	Import	Export
	Pulp for paper (thousand tons)			Pulp for paper (US$ million)	
1990	13 300	800	100	500	60
1995	24 600	1600	100	1100	40
2002	18 400	5800	50	2400	30
	Paper and paperboard (thousand tons)			Paper and paperboard (US$ million)	
1990	17 400	3100	1400	2300	800
1995	28 500	5500	2600	4400	1700
2002	37 900	10 400	4000	6000	2600

Source: FAO (2004).

US$2.5 billion in 1990 to US$10.0 billion in 2002, a fourfold increase, while total Chinese MVA increased from US$116.4 in 1990 to US$457.2 in 2002, a similar fourfold increase. Its percentage share of total MVA was around 2.2 per cent in both 1990 and 2002, about half of the percentage share in Brazil. In 2002 the sub-sector employed some 1.15 million workers, constituting approximately 2.5 per cent of employment in the manufacturing sector (UNIDO, 2005).

Sub-sector Profile

There were 12 000 mills nationwide in 1990 with 1.2 million employees, but by 2002 the number of mills had fallen sharply to around 4600, although the number of employees decreased only slightly to 1.15 million (UNIDO, 2005). Mills with a capacity below 5000 tons per year accounted for 83 per cent of national production at the beginning of the 1990s, but with their closure their minimal contribution to production ceased. By 2000, 44 mills had reached a capacity of 100 000 tons per year or more, whereas in 1995 only 15 mills had had that capacity. The capacity of the country's largest mill registered remarkable increases: 240 000 tons in 1995, 700 000 tons in 2000, and 1.3 million tons in 2003.

The ownership structure of the sector changed significantly during the 1990s. By 1999, SOEs accounted for only 30 per cent of the total number of mills, joint ventures for 28 per cent, and the remaining 42 per cent were privately or collectively owned.

The survey for this study focused on mills using non-wood (agricultural residues) rather than wood as the raw material input because the former are more pollutant intensive per unit of production. Most mills were located in Shandong Province. Nevertheless, other mills using wood and waste paper were also included in the survey to cover the whole range of raw materials used by Chinese mills. In fact wood pulp accounted for 12.5 per cent of the total pulp used for making paper and paperboard in 1995, and this increased to 19.1 per cent in 2000. On the other hand, wastepaper pulp increased from 37.2 per cent to 40.9 per cent between 1995 and 2000. During the same period, use of non-wood pulp dropped from 50.3 per cent to 40 per cent.

Of 4600 mills in operation in 2001–2, 11 were selected to be investigated in this survey, based on variations in the pulping process, size, location and raw material input. The selected mills corresponded to the criteria as follows: eight used principally chemical soda pulping, two used principally kraft pulping and one used principally sulphite pulping; seven were large-scale and four were small-scale; they were located in four different provinces (seven in Shandong, two in Guangxi, one in Xinjang, and one in Jilin); and one used wood as fibre raw material and ten used primarily agro-residues (and also some waste paper) (Table 5.4).

Other characteristics of the mills worth noting are: six were SOEs, three combined public/private ownership and two were completely privately owned; all sold mainly to the national market, reflecting the overall orientation of the Chinese pulp and paper sub-sector; all were accredited with ISO 9002 certification; and one had, and two were in the process of obtaining, ISO 14001 certification.

Each mill had a designated environment or technology department. However, it was mainly concerned with quality control and new technology implementation and adaptation. As described earlier, there was a lack of R&D capacities in pulp and paper mills, leaving research institutes with the responsibility of producing technical design blueprints and comprehensive construction specifications.

Process Technology and CT Characterization

The process of paper production became more user-oriented during the 1990s, moving from quantity to quality objectives. Low-level products were phased out gradually and products of middle and high levels increased some 30 to 40 per cent between 1995 and 2000. To produce higher-quality products, mills were forced to upgrade their production technologies and use higher-quality raw materials.

Table 5.4 Profile of the 11 mills investigated

Mill	Process and product type	Scale (thousand tons/year)	Location: province/rural or urban area/ industrial zone	Sales orientation (in 2000)	Technology vintage	Ownership	EST score	Regulatory compliance	Donor assist.	EMS
C1	AR pulp, CS, double pastern paper	Large (230)	Shouguang, Shandong Province/ urban	78% D, 22% E	BAT	42% private foreign, 31% government, 27% staff	PAT + HTC	Yes	Yes	Yes
C2	AR pulp, CS, enamelled paper	Large (127)	Gaotang, Shandong Province/rural	95% D, 5% E	BAT	49% private domestic, 51% government	PAT + MTC	Yes	No	No
C3	AR pulp, CS, offset paper	Large (120)	Bingzhou, Shangdong Province/ urban	100% D	Standard– modern	26% private domestic, 74% government	PAT + MTC	No (has been penalized)	Yes	No
C4	AR pulp, sulphate, white board	Large (380)	Yanzhou, Shandong Province/ urban	98% D, 2% E	BAT	82% private domestic, 18% private foreign	PAT + MTC	Yes	No	No
C5	AR pulp, CS, enamelled paper	Small (80)	Laiwu, Shandong Province/ rural	100% D	Standard– modern	100% government	PAT + MTC	Yes	No	No

Table 5.4 (continued)

Mill	Process and product type	Scale (thousand tons/year)	Location: province/rural or urban area/industrial zone	Sales orientation (in 2000)	Technology vintage	Ownership	EST score	Regulatory compliance	Donor assist.	EMS
C6	AR pulp, CS, PW paper	Small (60)	Huantai, Shandong Province/rural	100% D	Standard–modern	100% government	PAT + MTC	Yes	No	No
C7	AR pulp, kraft, machine-made paper	Large (200)	Guangrao County, Shandong Province/rural	–	BAT	100% private domestic	PAT + MTC	Yes	No	No
C8	AR pulp, CS, mechanically made paper	Large (100)	Guigang, Guangxi Province/urban, in the Ecology Industry Park	100% D	BAT	100% government	PAT + MTC	Yes	No	Yes (end 2002)
C9	AR pulp, CS, mechanically made paper	Small (40)	Guigang, Guangxi Province/urban, in the Ecology Industry Park	100% D	BAT	100% government	PAT + HTC	Yes	No	Yes (end 2002)

C10	AR pulp, CS, PW paper	Small (32)	Xiniang Province/rural, in an Ecology Industry Park	100% D	Standard–modern	100% government	PAT + MTC	Yes	No	No
C11	Wood, kraft pulp, Newsprint Sanitary	Large (220)	Shixian Tumen Jilin Province/ rural	100% D	Standard–modern	100% government	PAT + LTC	No (has been penalized)	No	No

Abbreviations: domestic (D); export (E); agro-residuals (AR); chemical soda (CS); printing and writing (PW); best available technology (BAT); pollution abatement technology (PAT); higher order technological complexity (HTC); medium order technological complexity (MTC); lower order technological complexity (LTC).

Source: CNCPC/CRAES (2002).

During the 1990s the technology infrastructure (research centres and universities) assisted many mills in making improvements in a number of ESTs, including: (a) alkali recovery systems in small soda straw pulp mills; (b) more comprehensive utilization of cooking waste liquor in small chemical straw pulp mills; (c) the development of ammonium sulphite pulp mills; (d) anaerobic digestion of semi-chemical pulp and of high-yield straw pulp waste liquor; (e) chlorine free bleaching and (f) improved PAT configurations.

As of 2001 the vast majority of Chinese mills used one of two processes: the kraft pulping process, commonly used by wood-based mills, or the soda pulping process, more frequently used by agro-residue-based mills. Most used a mix of pulping processes, the chemical soda process being the principal pulping process at eight mills in the survey, the kraft process at two, and sulphite at one mill (Table 5.4).

The survey team found a wide range of production equipment being used in the 11 mills they investigated. They assigned the mills to one of two categories based on the predominant technological vintage of the pulp production equipment – six mills primarily used best available technology (BAT) and the other five used standard–modern technology (Table 5.4).

They also classified the mills into three groups based on the highest order of complexity of the CTs used in each mill (low, medium and high). Of those investigated, not all used the most advanced CTs, but most were implementing, or had already implemented, some CT options. According to the survey findings, two mills used CTs of a higher order of complexity, eight used CTs of a medium order of complexity and one used CTs of a lower order of complexity (Table 5.4).

CT options were used at all stages of the production process. Some of those used in various process areas and the number of mills using them are identified in Table 5.5. Among the different process areas, most applications were for recovery of black liquor and paper-making. Improvements in other process areas were rare.

The potential of CTs to reduce water and chemical use and pollutant discharge into the aquatic environment was demonstrated by the United Nations Environment Programme (UNEP) in the 1990s for the Asia-Pacific pulp and paper industry. The UNEP project involved 50 pulp and paper mills in the region, of which 15 were in China. Implementation of about 250 CT options at nine mills significantly reduced pollutant loads, using mainly non- and low-cost options for a total investment of around US$600 000. Total savings were calculated at US$4.6 million (Swenningsen, 2001). More details about CT implementation at one mill that participated in the demonstration project are presented in Box 5.1.

Table 5.5   CTs used in the 11 mills

Process area	Option	Number of mills using practice/ equipment
Pulping	Return black liquor to digester	1
	Three-stage pre-impregnation of non-wood fibre	1
Washing	Installation of air water separator to increase vacuum in belt washer	1
	Installation of horizontal (belt) washer	1
Bleaching	ECF bleaching	2
Recovery black liquor/power boilers	Recycle alkali (recovery black liquor)	6
	Rebuilt power boiler	3
Paper-making	Closure water system	3
	Fibre recovery (save all)	2

Source: CNCPC/CRAES (2002).

BOX 5.1   CLEANER PRODUCTION CASE STUDY: CHINA

SEPA, with support from UNEP, undertook a CP assessment in the late 1990s in an agro-based mill that had the capacity to produce 18 500 tons of semi-chemical pulp and whose main products were various types of high-strength corrugated papers. The CP assessment identified 58 CT options, of which 12 were feasible (8 no/low-cost, 2 medium-cost and 6 high-cost options). Implementation of seven of the no/low-cost options generated approximately US$150 000 of savings per year, primarily from increased pulping efficiency and reduced coal consumption. Discharge of chemical oxygen demand decreased by 920 tons and suspended solids decreased by 230 tons per year. Implementation at a later date of some of the medium- and high-cost options yielded additional financial benefits and further reduced the discharge of chemical oxygen demand.

Source: SEPA (1999).

PAT Characterization

All the mills investigated had built some type of ETP and most were well maintained because of the legal requirements. The mills were concerned mainly with reducing water pollutant discharge, but paid less attention to the management of air emissions and solid waste disposal Ten of the 11 mills used secondary ETPs and one mill pretreated its waste before discharging into a municipal ETP.

It must be mentioned that the use of PATs in the 11 mills cannot be attributed to donor assistance programmes. None of them had benefited from international donor funds and only two mills had benefited from technical advice on CTs from the UNEP project described above.

Environmental Performance

Overall, based on national data, the environmental performance of the industrial sector in China showed considerable improvement in wastewater management. The total volume of wastewater discharged decreased from 27.9 billion cubic metres in 1989 to 20.2 billion cubic metres in 2001. During the same time period the discharge of chemical oxygen demand (COD) load from SOEs declined from 7.4 million tons in 1989 to 6.1 million tons in 2001 (World Bank, 2001).

After the chemical and iron and steel sub-sectors, the pulp and paper sub-sector was the third largest polluter measured in terms of BOD loadings, accounting for 12 per cent of total BOD loadings by the manufacturing sector (World Bank, 2004). It was also the largest Chinese polluter measured in terms of COD load (46 per cent), followed by the food (22 per cent) and chemical (8 per cent) sub-sectors (World Bank, 2001).[3] In addition the sub-sector was highly pollutant intensive. While it generated 46 per cent of industrial COD load, it produced only 1.8 per cent of gross industrial value added (World Bank, 2001).

According to the World Bank (2001), the proportion of the total wastewater discharged by the industrial sector (SOEs only) decreased in the 1990s, but the actual volume of wastewater discharged that complied with environmental standards declined. In fact treatment rates in the four sub-sectors (one being pulp and paper), which were the major sources of water pollution, were all significantly lower than the all-industry averages for 1997 and 1998. Less than 40 per cent of the wastewater discharged by the pulp and paper sub-sector met environmental standards (World Bank, 2001). However, among the investigated mills, only two out of 11 were reported to be out of compliance with environmental standards and to have been penalized.

KEY INFORMANTS AND INTERNATIONAL DONORS

Four groups, in addition to government environmental regulatory agencies and technology centres, were in a position to influence the extent to which plants adopt EST: NGOs, business associations, international donors of technical asssistance, and chemical and equipment suppliers. Some information on the first three is presented in this section; there was insufficient information to chartacterize the firms that supplied chemicals and equipment to China's pulp and paper sub-sector during the period of this study.

NGOs

The number of NGOs in China increased steadily before and during this period, and they gained strength in the 1990s under the more tolerant guidelines issued by the Chinese authorities. However, legal and financial red tape hindered their full development (Edele, 2004). Changes in the legal framework were still necessary to ease their social acceptability and fund-raising capacity (US Embassy, 2003).

The survey team interviewed representatives of two NGOs concerned with industrial pollution: one located in Beijing and the other in Shangdong Province, where seven out of the 11 mills interviewed were located. The Beijing NGO was the Student Association on Environment and Development at Peking University, founded in 1991; it promotes the use of economic measures to ensure compliance with environmental norms. The Shangdong NGO was the Women's Union of Dongying City, established in 1953; it has worked over the years for better compliance with environmental norms.

Business Associations

The survey team interviewed the main association in the pulp and paper sub-sector, the China Paper Industry Association, which was established in 1992. Its environmental committee works on the transfer and adoption of EST. In the mid-1990s it focused on wastewater treatment technology from wheat-grass pulp and also conducted several studies and investigations, as well as the preparation and organization of the first forum on wastewater treatment technology for the pulp and paper sub-sector and the forum on the alkaline recovery technology. In addition, the Association publishes a quarterly journal, *Paper Environmental Protection*.

International Donors

From the early 1990s the concept of CP was systematically put into practice in China through multilateral and bilateral technical cooperation projects. The World Bank and UNEP initiated the first CP project in 1993. Building on its success, UNIDO and UNEP funded the establishment of a

National Cleaner Production Centre in 1995. Fifteen bilateral or multilateral collaborative CP projects were implemented in two-thirds of the provinces in China. None the less, progress on CP implementation was only partial because the international collaborative programmes were insufficiently adapted to the Chinese context. In addition, government initiatives were not always well suited to industrial needs, and multilateral cooperation initiatives had limited spillover effects.

A major complement to CP promotion in China was the Network for Industrial Environmental Management undertaken by the United Nations Environment Programme between 1994 and 2000. It supported improvements in environmental management in the pulp and paper sub-sector in the Asia-Pacific region, including 50 CP assessments in pulp and paper mills. In China the counterpart for the project, SEPA, carried out CP assessments in 15 mills, including two mills investigated for this study (Swenningsen, 2001).

Finally, the Asian Development Bank provided technical assistance in 1995 to set up the Centre for Environmentally Sound Technology Transfer. Its mission is to assist China's industry, particularly SMEs, in pursuing higher economic competitiveness and environmental performance by adopting EST, particularly CTs.

Overall, the level of donor assistance for industrial environmental management was still comparatively low in the 1990s due to the limited national technical capacity to carry out CP assessments, disseminate information and advise on sub-sector-specific CT needs. Moreover, additional donor assistance was needed to enhance the effectiveness of the Chinese policy framework, the underlying driver for the adoption of EST.

SUMMARY

China's aggregate economic and environmental performance indicators reveal an outstanding performance as compared to other East Asian countries and economies in transition. While GDP increased by 204 per cent between 1990 and 2002, MVA increased even more, by 293 per cent. As a result the share of MVA in GDP increased from 32.9 to 35.4 per cent. GNI per capita, at PPP, moreover, increased by 245 per cent over the same period. Energy use in the manufacturing sector increased only slightly, about 18 per cent, during the 1990s, whereas energy-use intensity decreased by 70 per cent, mainly attributable to the extensive closure of SOEs and TVEs. BOD effluent increased by less than 13 per cent in spite of the more than 290 per cent increase in MVA. This was because of plant closures and the strong enforcement of environmental norms required to reduce extensive water pollution damage. Consequently BOD-effluent intensity decreased by 75 per cent between 1990 and 2000.

China's environmental policy regime consisted of a command-and-control regulatory system and several supplemental policy instruments, primarily a pollution levy, all of which were enhanced in the 1990s. Clearly improvements were still needed, such as increasing the pollution levy fee and strengthening the city-level EPBs. This said, China's achievements in terms of industrial environmental management were impressive in the light of the almost 300 per cent increase in industrial output in the 1990s. The total volume of wastewater discharged decreased and the total discharge of major pollutants barely increased (World Bank, 2001).

Changes in the three economic policy regimes, industrial, trade and resource pricing, created numerous and generally positive opportunities for the adoption of more advanced technologies, especially when compared to the other countries included in this study. The changes in the three industrial policy instruments, FDI, export promotion and privatization, increased the incentives to use more advanced production technologies. Changes in trade-related import measures were positive but mixed. The large reductions in import restrictions on production equipment lowered the cost of more advanced foreign technology, whereas the limited reduction in import restrictions on paper products muted any significant pressure on domestic producers of these products. Finally, while a significant decrease in energy-use intensity occurred, resource pricing changed little and was insufficient to promote a wider adoption of EST.

The country's technology policy and infrastructure changed with the shift towards a market-oriented economy. New technology programmes offered opportunities for the increased use of more efficient production processes. However, insufficient training facilities, excessive hierarchies and structural problems continued to plague the Chinese science and technology infrastructure. Furthermore, the lack of synergy between institutions as well as poor plant management continued to limit the potential for technological transformation.

While China has advanced more than many other countries in integrating industrial, environmental and technology policies, there are still many impending problems to be solved before sustainable industrial development can be pursued with more efficiency. There is too little cooperation between technology and environmental policymaking, though the new law on CP is a positive step forward as it offers new incentives for innovative CTs and would also strengthen the institutional network created through multilateral and bilateral support programmes during the 1990s.

The pulp and paper sub-sector increased pulp for paper production from 13.3 to 18.4 million tons (a 38 per cent increase) and paper and paperboard production from 17.4 to 37.9 million tons (a 117 per cent increase) between 1990 and 2002. As of 2002, there were approximately 4600 pulp and paper mills in this sub-sector, the vast majority of which were still small in spite of the closure of all mills with an annual capacity of below 5000 tons during the second half of the 1990s. The survey team investigated 11 of the 4600 mills, focusing on those using non-wood for pulp because of their pollutant intensity. Six of these mills used BAT and the other five used mainly standard–modern technology. Two used CTs of a higher order of complexity, eight used CTs of a medium order of complexity and one used CTs of a lower order of complexity. All of the mills had installed PATs equivalent to secondary treatment. Finally, most of the mills were reported to be in compliance with environmental standards.

The influence of other institutional actors, NGOs, business associations and international donors, on EST adoption was limited during the 1990s. Despite growing awareness of environmental problems, the role of NGOs and business associations remained insignificant owing to financial limitations and the absence of strong connections with the government. Donor assistance achieved some plant-specific results, but not enough attention was paid to improving the environmental regulatory system to the extent needed to accelerate the adoption of EST.

To conclude, although the pulp and paper sub-sector benefited from the general growth environment, it was confronted with serious problems because of the large number of small plants, and was, for the most part, constrained by old technology that resulted in high production costs and low-quality products, and a low ratio of wood pulp in raw material input. In spite of this, the sub-sector made substantial investments in EST that resulted in an improved economic and environmental performance.

NOTES

1. The FDI for 1990 has been taken as the three-year average of 1989–91 and for 2002 as the three-year average of 2001–3, in order to even out fluctuations in FDI flows.
2. A report by OECD (2001) describes a number of instances of FDI bringing more advanced technologies into China that were less pollutant, energy and resource intensive, as well as a number of instances of FDI bringing in less advanced, often second-hand, technologies that were more pollutant, energy and resource intensive.
3. The BOD percentage is based on World Bank engineering calculations and the COD percentage is based on at-source data collected by SEPA.

REFERENCES

Anon (1994), *China's Agenda 21*, Beijing, China: China's Environmental Science Press.

CNCPC/CRAES (2002), 'Research Report: Assessing the Adoption of EST in China', Beijing, China: China National Cleaner Production Centre (CNCPC) and the Chinese Research Academy for Environmental Sciences (CRAES). Report prepared for UNIDO.

Edele, A. (2004), 'Non-Governmental Organizations in China', Paper prepared for Casin-Programmme on NGOs and Civil Society, Geneva, Switzerland: Centre for Applied Studies in International Negotiations (available on: http://www. casin.ch/pdf/ngosinchina).

EIU (2004), 'China: Country Profile', London: Economic Intelligence Unit.

EIU (2005a), 'FDI Policy Outlook', London: Economist Intelligence Unit.

EIU (2005b), 'Country Report: China', London: Economist Intelligence Unit.

FAO (2004), 'FAOSTAT – Forestry Statistics', Rome: Food and Agriculture Organization of the United Nations (available on: http://www.fao.org).

FAO (2005), 'AQUASTAT: FAO STAT', Rome: Food and Agriculture Organization of the United Nations (available on: http://www.fao.org).

Han, S. and C. Ma (2002), 'China's Policies to Promote the Development and Diffusion of Environmentally Sound Technology', in *UNIDO Final Report: Evaluation and Adjustment of China's Sustainable Industrial Planning Policy*, Vienna: UNIDO.

IDRC (1997), 'A Decade of Reform: Science and Technology Policy in China', Ottawa, Canada: International Development Research Centre (IDRC) and the State Science and Technology Commission (available on: http://www.idrc.ca).

IEA (2005), 'Online Data Services', IEA Energy Information Centre, Paris: International Energy Agency (available on: http://www.iea.org).

Isaksson, A. (2006), 'World Productivity Database: Construction and Measurement Methods', unpublished working paper, Vienna: UNIDO.

ISO (2003), 'The ISO Survey of ISO 9000 and ISO 14001 Certificates', Geneva: International Organization for Standardization (available on: http://www. iso.org).

Li, S. and W. Zhang (2004), 'Cross-regional Competition and Privatization in China' (available on: http://www.gsm.pku.edu.cn/wuan1/EnglishPapers/PRIVA. rtf).

Ma, X. and L. Ortolano (2000), *Environmental Regulation in China: Institutions, Enforcement and Compliance*, Lanham, MD, Boulder, CO, New York and Oxford: Rowman and Littlefield.

Mako, W.P. and C. Zhang (2004), 'State Equity Ownership and Management in China: Issues and Lessons from International Experience', Paris: Organization for Economic Cooperation and Development (available on: http://www.oecd.org/ dataoecd/35/23/31226002.pdf).

OECD (2001), 'Environmental Priorities for China's Sustainable Development', CCNM/China (2001) 25, Paris: Organization for Economic Cooperation and Development (available on: http://www.oecd.org).

Rakesh, M. (2000), 'Enhancing Competitiveness through Industrial Restructuring: Options for Asia-Pacific Countries and the WTO', paper prepared for the Asia-Pacific Regional Forum on Industrial Development, Shanghai. Vienna: UNIDO.

SEPA and State Light Industry Bureau (1999), 'Review on CP Demonstration in Pulp and Paper Mills of China', Beijing, China: State Environmental Protection Bureau.

Shi, H. (1996), 'Current Status and Future Prospect of Networking Systems in China', paper prepared for Experts' Meeting for APEC Environmental Technology Exchange, 14 November (available on: http://www.estinfo.net.cn).

Swenningsen, N. (2001), 'Network for Industrial Environmental Management – a New Approach to old Challenges in the Asia-Pacific Pulp and Paper Industry', *Paperex Magazine* (Swedish Pulp & Paper Industry Association).

UNEP (2004), 'Environmental Information in China', Beijing, China: United Nations Environment Programme (available on: http://www.zhb.gov.cn).

UNIDO (2005), *International Yearbook of Industrial Statistics 2005*, Cheltenham, UK and Northampton, MA, US: Edward Elgar Publishing.

US Embassy in China (2003), 'Chinese NGOs – Carving a Niche Within Constraints', Beijing, China: US Beijing Embassy, Beijing (available on: http://www.usembassy-china.org.cn).

Wang, H. and S. Lall (1999), 'Valuing Water for Chinese Industries: a Marginal Productivity Assessment', Policy Research Working Paper 2236, Washington, DC: The World Bank.

Wang, H. and D. Wheeler (2000), 'Endogenous Enforcement and Effectiveness of China's Pollution Levy System', Policy Research Working Paper 2336, Washington, DC: The World Bank.

Wang, H., J. Bi, D. Wheeler, J. Wang, D. Cao, G. Lu and Y. Wang (2002), 'Environmental Performance Rating and Disclosure: China's Green-Watch Program', Policy Research Working Paper 2889, Washington, DC: The World Bank.

World Bank (2001), China's environment in the new century: clear water, blue skies', in *China 2020: Development Challenges in the New Century*, Washington, DC: The World Bank.

World Bank (2004), 'World Bank Development Indicators (WDI) 2004', CD-ROM version, Washington, DC: The World Bank.

World Bank (2005), 'World Integrated Trade Solution (WITS)' (available on: http://wits.worldbank.org).

WTO (2004), 'Committee on Import Licensing: replies to questionnaire on import licensing procedures', G/LIC/N/3/CHN/3, 30 September, Geneva: World Trade Organization.

Xian, G.M., C. Zhang, Y. Zhang, S. Ge and J. Zhan (1999), 'The Interface Between Foreign Direct Investment and the Environment: the Case of China', Report as part of UNCTAD/DICM Project Cross Border Environmental Management in Transnational Corporations, Geneva: United Nations Trade and Development Commission (available on: http://www.unctad-10.org/pdfs/preux_fdipaper3.en.pdf).

Xu, J. (2000), 'China's Paper Industry: Growth and Environmental Policy during Economic Reform', Singapore: Economy and Environment Program for South East Asia (EEPSEA).

Yao, Y. (2003), 'In search of a balance: technological development in China', in S. Lall and S. Urata (eds), *Competitiveness, FDI and Technological Activity in East Asia*, Cheltenham, UK and Northampton, MA, US: Edward Elgar Publishing.

Zhang, X. (1999), *China's Trade Patterns and International Comparative Advantage*, London: Macmillan.

6. India

INTRODUCTION

A survey team from the Centre for Technology Studies of India investigated the specific factors influencing the adoption of environmentally sound technology (EST) in India's pulp and paper sub-sector. The team used semi-structured questionnaires provided by UNIDO to interview plant managers at 14 out of the 450 plants in this sub-sector and key informants in one business association, one technology centre, five suppliers of chemicals and equipment, one environmental NGO and two environmental regulatory agencies. The team also collected background data on the country and the pulp and paper sub-sector.

This chapter describes the economic and environmental context in India for EST adoption; relevant environmental, economic and technology policies; the pulp and paper sub-sector and the plants investigated; and key informants and international donors.

THE ECONOMIC AND ENVIRONMENTAL CONTEXT FOR EST ADOPTION

The following selected economic and environmental performance indicators define the context in which manufacturing plants made their technology adoption decisions and, in particular, their decisions to adopt EST during the late 1990s/early 2000s.

Economic Performance Indicators

Following the financial crisis in 1991, India embarked on a process of accelerating economic growth by reversing its import substitution policies and reducing state interference in economic activities. As a result the average annual growth in gross domestic product (GDP) in the 1990s was 5.9 per cent in spite of the poor performance of the agricultural sector. Between 1990 and 2002 GDP increased by 88 per cent and GDP per capita by 52 per cent, while the population increased by 26 per cent (Table 6.1). However, net growth would have been higher if the agriculture sector – with a 23 per cent share of GDP in 2002 and employing about two-thirds of the Indian work-force – had not experienced negative growth (−5.2 per cent) in 2002. Gross national income (GNI) per capita at purchasing power parity (PPP) – a more accurate indicator of well-being – increased by 95 per cent. Based on the latter, India is classified by the World Bank as a low-income country.

The country's manufacturing value added (MVA) increased by 97 per cent, somewhat greater than the percentage increase in GDP. None the less, the MVA share of GDP decreased by 1.5 per cent. It was the country's service sector that outperformed all other sectors, with an average growth rate of 7.9 per cent, thereby increasing its share to 50.7 per cent. It should be noted that there was a high degree of variation in terms of economic performance among Indian states. Gujarat and Maharashtra, for example, achieved rates of growth comparable to the East Asian tigers in the 1990s, while growth in Bihar and Orissa was very poor.

India's fiscal deficit in the 1990s (over 5 per cent of GDP) was a severe impediment to economic growth (ADB, 2005). The deficits of the country's state governments made the picture look significantly worse. Furthermore, problems such as high real interest rates and a high inflation

Table 6.1   Economic performance indicators for India

Economic indicator	Year	Value	Percentage change
GDP (constant 1995 US$) (billion)	1990	275.6	88
	2002	517.3	
GDP per capita (constant 1995 US$)	1990	324.0	52
	2002	493.0	
Population (million)	1990	834.7	26
	2002	1048.6	
GNI per capita at PPP (current international $)	1990	1360.0	95
	2002	2650.0	
MVA (constant 1995 US$) (billion)	1990	41.4	97
	2002	81.5	
MVA (percentage of GDP)	1990	17.1	−1.5
	2002	15.6	
CPI (1995=100)	1990	60.8	156
	2002	155.8	
Interest rate (commercial lending rate)	1990	17.0	−30
	2002	11.9	
Exchange rate (INR/US$)	1990	17.5	178
	2002	48.61	

Source: World Bank (2004).

rate (over 10 per cent on average throughout the 1990s) as measured by the consumer price index (CPI) could not be solved because of mutually constraining fiscal and monetary policies.

Environmental Performance Indicators

The accelerated industrialization process generated an excessive amount of pollutant discharge, which severely affected the environment. The share of MVA of the most polluting industrial sub-sectors, such as chemicals, iron and steel and pulp and paper, increased from 31.1 per cent in 1990 to 33.6 per cent in 2001 (Table 6.2). Small-scale industries (SSIs), the Indian designation for small and medium enterprises (SMEs), continued to be a major source of pollution because of their failure to comply with environmental standards.

Selected environmental indicators, namely, energy use, carbon dioxide (CO_2) emissions, organic matter effluent measured as biochemical oxygen

Table 6.2   Environmental performance indicators for India

Source code	Environmental indicator	Year	Value	Percentage change
1	Energy use in the manufacturing sector (million toe)	1990 2002	75.5 104.5	38
1 & 2	Energy-use intensity (toe per million US$ of MVA)	1990 2002	1830.0 1280.0	−30
1	CO_2 emissions from the manufacturing sector (tons)	1990 2002	170.0 240.0	40
1 & 2	CO_2-emission intensity (tons per million US$ of MVA)	1990 2002	4060.0 2890.0	−29
2	BOD effluent from the manufacturing sector (thousand tons)	1990 2000	470.0 510.0	10
2	BOD-effluent intensity (tons per million US$ of MVA)	1990 2000	11.3 6.7	−40
3	Water use in the manufacturing sector (billion m³)	1990 2000	15.0 35.2	135
2 & 3	Water-use intensity (thousand m³ per million US$ of MVA)	1990 2000	360.0 480.0	31
4	Per cent of MVA produced by the most pollutant-intensive sub-sectors	1990 2001	31.1 33.6	2.5
5	Number of ISO 14001 certificates	1997 2002	28.0 605.0	2060

Sources: 1. IEA (2005); 2. World Bank (2004); 3. FAO (2005); 4. UNIDO (2005); 5. ISO (2003).

demand (BOD) and water use, as well as the intensity of use of each of these, which provide an insight into the state of industrial environmental performance, are presented in Table 6.2. Energy use by the manufacturing sector, measured in tons of oil equivalent (toe), increased by 38 per cent between 1990 and 2002, less than the increase in MVA. Thus energy-use intensity decreased by 30 per cent. Associated CO_2 emissions increased less than energy use, by only 40 per cent, whereas CO_2-emission intensity decreased by 29 per cent. BOD effluent increased by 10 per cent, significantly less than the percentage increase in MVA, while the BOD-effluent intensity decreased by more than 40 per cent. Finally, water use by industry increased by 135 per cent, while water-use intensity increased by 31 per cent. Water-use intensity was less than that for China in 1990 but greater than in 2000.

In 2000 the distribution of BOD effluent among manufacturing sub-sectors was as follows: food and beverages, 52 per cent; primary metals, 14 per cent; textiles, 13 per cent; chemicals, 9 per cent; pulp and paper, 7 per cent; and others, 5 per cent (World Bank, 2004). Although the BOD loadings from the pulp and paper sub-sector were small compared to other resource-intensive sectors, they were certainly not trivial.

In 2002 there were 605 ISO 14001 certificates, far below the 2803 certificates in China and 900 in Brazil. However, the number of ISO 14001 certificates per billion US dollars of MVA exceeded the two other large paper-producing countries included in this study. India had a ratio of 7.4 certificates per billion US dollars of MVA in 2002 compared to a ratio of 6.1 and 5.9 in China and Brazil respectively. Indeed, among countries included in this study only Thailand has more certificates, with 10.8 per billion US dollars of MVA.

Implications for EST Adoption

During the period of this study the overall economic and environmental conditions in India seemed particularly conducive to the adoption of EST by the country's manufacturing sector. The government of this accelerating developing country had not compelled its manufacturing sector to make substantial investments in EST before 1990, as evidenced by the high BOD-effluent intensity (11.3 tons of BOD per million US dollars of MVA) in 1990. From 1990 to 2002, the relatively modest manufacturing sector grew rapidly, with a 5.9 per cent average annual growth rate in MVA and, in parallel, an even larger percentage annual average growth rate of 14.2 per cent in new investment, some of which would have been in EST (Isaksson, 2006). The limited rate of inflation (the CPI increased by 156 per cent) and moderate interest rates (17.0 per cent to 11.9) over the period seems not to have discouraged new investment in capital stock. However, the 97 per cent increase in annual MVA between 1990 and 2002 resulted in an increase in energy use of 92 per cent and only a slight decrease in energy-use intensity of 3 per cent. In spite of the large annual increase in MVA, BOD effluent increased by only 10 per cent and BOD-effluent intensity decreased by 40 per cent, which suggests that there was increased regulatory and community pressure on manufacturing plants to accelerate their adoption of EST during this period.

ENVIRONMENTAL POLICY

Overall, India has made significant improvements in its environmental legislation (Kathuria and Haripriya, 2000). Some of the more important legislative acts affecting industrial environmental management are the Water Pollution Act of 1974 (amended in 1988 and 2003), the Water Cess Act of 1977 (amended in 2003) and the Air Act of 1981 (amended in 1987).

In addition to legislative measures, the government developed specific policies and strategies to protect the environment. In particular it promulgated the National Conservation Strategy and the Policy Statement on Environment and Development in 1992 and in the same year the Ministry of Environment and Forests (MOEF) published a Policy Statement for Abatement of Pollution.

The MOEF is one of the main administrative bodies of India's environmental institutional framework along with the Planning Commission and the Ministry of Science and Technology. It is the prime policy-making body, originally created as a department in 1980 and expanded into a ministry in 1985. It is entrusted with planning, promotion, operation and coordination functions as well as with regulatory powers. It oversees the national environmental information system, established in 1982, which grew to 81 partner nodes by 2005 (ENVIS, 2005). It has also built up seven centres of excellence to promote research and training, the most prominent of these being the National Environmental Engineering Research Institute, which, among other functions, designs and tests PATs.

Directly under the MOEF's control is the Central Pollution Control Board (CPBC) and indirectly under its supervision are the State Pollution Control Boards (SPCBs). The CPBC is responsible for coordinating the activities of SPCBs, providing them with technical assistance, carrying out investigations, setting up laboratories, training personnel and conducting public awareness campaigns. However, it has limited powers to force SPCBs to adopt certain standards and its role is therefore mainly advisory.

Various environmental policy instruments were used by the CPBC and SPCBs at the time of this study. These are classified into four categories: command-and-control regulations, economic and fiscal incentives, voluntary programmes with industry participation, and transparency and disclosure programmes.

First, as in many other countries, the environmental authorities relied mainly on the command-and-control regulatory approach of standard setting, permit issuance, compliance monitoring and enforcement. Until the early 1990s industrial discharge standards were based on the concentration of pollutants in waste streams. Due to the very low water-use charges, industry simply diluted effluents, causing a tremendous waste of water in an ineffective mode of compliance. In order to counter this, the Water Pollution Act was amended in 1998 to include mandatory load-based and process standards.

SPCBs were primarily responsible for plant-level monitoring and inspection, as well as the enforcement of environmental standards. They also issued a 'No Objection Certificate' for plant expansion and the construction of new plants. Consent was given only when an SPCB was convinced that the equipment required to control pollution had been installed and the plant was operating in full compliance with environmental standards. Consent was not always essential, and many plants, particularly those belonging to highly polluting categories, continued to operate without consent. For instance, according to a survey of the 24 paper and pulp mills, five did not receive any 'consent' and a further five mills only received 'deemed consent' (Agarwal, 1999).

SPCBs had the authority to fine non-compliers and issue administrative orders to close down non-compliant factories and disconnect their water and electricity supply. However, the degree of compliance depended on both appropriate monitoring and enforcement of the law by SPCBs, and their enforcement was often criticized for being too lax (Kathuria and Haripriya, 2000), with a high degree of variation in enforcement among different states (Pargal et al., 1997).

As a further part of its regulatory programme, the government introduced environmental impact assessments in 1994. These subsequently became mandatory for 29 different activities, including new industrial projects. The extent to which industrial projects had to be reviewed depended on the size of the investment and the sub-sector.

The second category, economic incentives, included customs waivers and soft loans used by SPCBs to encourage the installation of PATs. Companies who installed PATs were entitled to special depreciation and tax benefits. However, the contribution to pollutant reduction was small, as the tax benefits were linked to the installation of PATs rather than to their operation. Companies therefore installed equipment but did not use it (Kathuria and Haripriya, 2000). Consequently, in August 2003 India's Supreme Court established the 'polluter pays' principle to emphasize that prevention of pollution and waste management was a national priority. There were also some user and administrative charges, such as the water cess on water intake, introduced largely to augment the financial resources of the SPCBs. Twenty-five per cent of the collected cess could be rebated if it was used to build an effluent treatment plant (ETP). However, the effect of these incentives was marginal since the user fees, in particular the water cess, were too low in spite of fivefold to sixfold increases during the 1990s.

Third, several voluntary programmes with industry participation were under way. One was a nationwide cleaner production programme, started in 1995 by the India National Cleaner Production Centre (NCPC), whose operations are described later in this chapter. Both the World Bank, as part of its pollution control loans to India, and bilateral donors also funded cleaner production efforts. A second programme was an ISO 14000 certification programme, with the Quality Council of India administering the national accreditation board for certification bodies. The third was an eco-labelling scheme, known as 'Eco-mark', launched in 1991 for the easy identification of environmentally friendly products. Any product that was made, used or disposed of in a way that significantly reduced the harm it would otherwise cause the environment could be considered as an environmentally friendly product (MOEF, 2005).

Transparency and disclosure programmes, the fourth category, were not widely used. There was still no programme on public disclosure along the lines of the programme in Indonesia. There were, however, environmental performance awards given by trade associations and the more prestigious industrial associations such as the Confederation of Indian Industries.

Global Comparison

Overall, during the period of this study India had solid environmental legislation and an impressive legal regime. In its efforts to reduce industrial pollution it relied mainly on regulatory measures, which empowered government agencies to set and enforce environmental standards. However, the impact of these efforts was low, mainly due to the quality of public services and the limited enforcement of environmental standards. Thus it is not surprising that India ranked relatively low on the EG index. It was forty-third out of 66 countries in 2001, although this position was a considerable improvement on its fifty-eighth rank in 1990. Among all developing countries its position improved from thirty-third in 1990 to eighteenth of 40 countries in 2001. In that year it ranked fifth among the eight countries included in this study.

ECONOMIC POLICY REGIMES

Overviews of India's three economic policy regimes, industrial, trade and resource pricing, the economic policies that most directly influence techno-logical modernization in the manufacturing sector and thereby increase the likelihood of the adoption of EST (see Chapter 3), are presented in this section.

Industrial Policy

India, to a much greater extent than many countries included in this study, pursued several policies and strategies supporting its industrial sector in the 1990s. After a severe balance-of-payments crisis in 1990 it embarked upon a series of reforms. The beginning of the period witnessed the promulga-tion of the wide-ranging 'New Industrial Policy' in 1991, which emphasized deregulation, efficiency and international competitiveness. The core prob-lem with the Indian economy was the largesse of the state. During the early 1990s the state accounted for half of all investment and for 70 per cent of organized employment (EIU, 1996).

Traditionally, licensing had been a major instrument of India's industrial policy, and it used this to guide development along certain strategic and industrial lines. Since 1991 the relaxation of industrial licensing require-ments significantly reduced the number of industrial sectors needing licences. Only industries reserved for the public sector (defence, railways, atomic energy), those subject to location restrictions and those producing manufactures in the SSI sector, continued to need licences.

This major shift in industrial policy included changes in three policy instruments, foreign direct investment (FDI), export promotion and priva-tization, all with the potential for stimulating the modernization of tech-nology.

FDI

In the 1980s India sought foreign investment only in areas deemed to be of national importance. One of the first reforms of the 1990s was the intro-duction of an FDI regime that permitted FDI in almost every sector of the economy, including the pulp and paper sub-sector. In addition, the gov-ernment introduced a series of incentives to attract investments, in partic-ular FDI and technology.

The Foreign Exchange Regulation Act underwent significant amendments to eliminate restrictive provisions on the operations of companies with over 40 per cent foreign equity (Ahluwalia et al., 1996). All companies with foreign equity were treated in the same manner and could borrow and accept public deposits. FDI liberalization was even pursued, in a limited way, for the SSI sector, which had previously been completely shielded from FDI competition. However, India failed to attract as much FDI in export-oriented industries as other developing countries. The reasons for this included the anti-export bias of trade policies, labour rigidity, certain reservations for small-scale industries and weaknesses in the infrastructure (WTO, 2002).

Between 1990 and 2002, FDI increased almost 2100 per cent, from US$187 million to over US$3.9 billion, while the net external borrowing remained constant, at between US$7 and $9 billion. As a share of GDP, FDI remained relatively small, with an increase from 0.1 to 0.7 per cent between 1990 and 2002 (World Bank, 2005).[1] Incomplete economic reforms and the lack of second-generation reforms, as well as a loss of confidence in emerging markets, hampered FDI inflows. To a great extent internal borrowing, facilitated by a decline in commercial lending rates of almost 30 per cent, compensated for the shortage of FDI (ADB, 2005).

Export promotion
Three primary methods of export promotion were implemented in India in the 1990s to combat the anti-export bias found in industrial strategies that typically focused on selling goods to the huge domestic market: fiscal incentives, financial incentives and export promotion assistance.

As a fiscal incentive the government put into effect several export subsidy schemes. It introduced a duty drawback and advanced licensing programme that granted tariff exemption for imported input needed for products that were to be exported. The Export–Import Policy of April 1996 further streamlined this process by improving the advance licensing procedure and introducing the 'green channel' facility for strategic categories of exporters. By 2000, approximately 71 per cent of the exports qualified for a level of tariff exemption or repayment (WTO, 2002).

As a financial incentive, Indian banks were required to allocate 12 per cent of total lending for exports. Moreover, export credit had to be offered either in local or foreign currency, whichever was more beneficial to the industry; rates for export credits were likewise required to be 1.5 per cent lower than the prime lending rate, with a ceiling of 12 per cent per annum. The Export Credit Guarantee Corporation of India Limited offered insurance to exporters against political and commercial risks (WTO, 2002).

Export promotion assistance was provided through the India Brand Equity Fund, which gave marketing development assistance to promote

Indian exports. The Fund also offered medium-term loans to encourage Indian brands that had attained certain quality and performance requirements. The Department of Commerce also funded a marketing development assistance scheme to help exporters explore overseas markets and to provide them with market intelligence (WTO, 2002).

Unfortunately there was little evidence that the use of these various instruments to encourage export had a significant impact on export growth. Indeed, many of the export measures simply eliminated disincentives, as opposed to positively prodding export growth. For example, though exports from export processing zones increased by over 100 per cent between 1998 and 2001, their share of total exports increased only marginally, from 3.7 per cent in 1998 to 4.2 per cent in 2001 (WTO, 2002).

As a result of the export promotion measures, the export of manufactured goods increased from US$12.7 billion to US$36.9 billion between 1990 and 2002. While significant, this was a modest increase of 190 per cent compared to other countries in Asia. China's export of manufactured goods, for example, increased by more than 600 per cent over the same period. During this period, too, the share of manufactured exports in total merchandise exports rose from 71 per cent to 75 per cent, also less impressive when compared to China's rise from a 72 per cent to a 90 per cent share (World Bank, 2004).

Privatization

A combination of performance reviews and privatization that aimed to make state-owned enterprises (SOEs) operate more efficiently had the potential to encourage the modernization of technology. The Sick Industrial Companies Act (1985) necessitated referral of poorly performing SOEs to the Board of Industrial and Financial Reconstruction, which analysed firm-level reforms and recommended restructuring or partial privatisation into joint ventures (Ahluwalia et al., 1996). In March 1999 the government announced that 74 per cent of its non-strategic industries (excluding defence, atomic energy and railways) could be disinvested; a Ministry of Disinvestment was subsequently created to speed the process (WTO, 2002).

Nevertheless the process was slow, with only 42 enterprises undergoing disinvestment between 1991 and 2000. There were important reasons for this, mainly the way the process was carried out and political resistance from certain Indian states. Consequently SOEs, while still playing an important part in the economy, continued to be a financial burden for the government. Of the 240 nationally registered SOEs in 2000, 44 per cent recorded losses; and of the state-registered SOEs, 58 per cent recorded losses. In total, government support for SOEs required 3.9 per cent of GDP in 2002, a steady increase in absolute terms since 1997 (WTO, 2002).

Industrial policy also targeted the pulp and paper sub-sector throughout the 1990s. Removal of price and distribution controls on the sub-sector encouraged new investments and increased capacity. As a result, the pulp and paper sub-sector started registering positive returns on paper products. In 1992 the government took further steps by offering a tax rebate to small units, abolishing the customs duty on the import of paper-grade pulp and wood chips, eliminating statutory controls over the production, pricing and distribution of white printing paper, and increasing the allocation of coal for the sub-sector.

Global comparison
In summary, changes in India's industrial policies appear to have contributed to the increase in industrial output in the 1990s, including that of the pulp and paper sub-sector. Although policy reforms liberalized FDI, encouraged export and privatized some enterprises, these changes were limited compared to changes in other more advanced developing countries. Thus it is not surprising that India's rank on the CIP index actually declined between 1980 and 2000. It ranked fortieth among 93 countries as of 2000, falling from thirty-sixth in 1990 and thirty-eighth in 1980. In 2000 it ranked nearly last among the countries considered as having medium high industrial performance. Among developing countries it fell from thirteenth out of sixty-eight in 1990 to fifteenth in 2000. Compared to China, India showed only modest gains in most components in the CIP index and an actual decline in its share of medium- and high-technology goods in manufactured exports. Finally it ranked fourth among the eight countries included in this study.

Trade Policy

Until the reforms of the early 1990s India had maintained an import regime characterized by extensive quantitative restrictions and high tariffs. It had banned the import of consumer goods and had subjected raw materials, intermediate goods and capital to a restrictive licensing regime, using considerations of 'essentiality' and 'indigenous availability' as the criteria. Such quantitative restrictions were mostly eliminated in the 1980s by placing most intermediate and some capital goods on the 'Open General Licence' list for ready import. This, however, was offset by increased tariffs. In the 1990s the import regime still remained 'complex, discretionary, and inhibiting' (Ahluwalia et al., 1996).

In 1991 a marked transformation in this regime began to take place. Quantitative restrictions were eliminated for most goods, other than final consumer goods, and replaced by a single negative list, thus eliminating discretionary decisions and bureaucratic delays. As a result, manufactured goods on the negative list comprised 51 per cent of total manufacturing value added by 1995, compared to 90 per cent before the reforms (Ahluwalia et al., 1996). The 'Export–Import Policy', introduced in 1996, removed additional items from the negative list and liberalized restrictions on consumer goods, including pulp and paper. Although licensing restrictions were generally declining, there appears to have been an increase in other import barriers, namely anti-dumping measures. India was one of the major users of anti-dumping regulations, with some 250 cases initiated since 1995 (WTO, 2002). Likewise the import of certain goods was only allowed through specific ports.

During this period India actively pursued tariff reduction through its participation in multilateral agreements. It was a founding member of the WTO and offered most favoured nation (MFN) status to all its trading partners. It embarked upon numerous regional trade agreements, including the South Asian Association for Regional Cooperation in 1993 with Bangladesh, Bhutan, the Maldives, Nepal, Pakistan and Sri Lanka. This agreement granted preferential treatment to signatory countries, but its ultimate objective was the creation of a free trade zone (WTO, 2002). Free Trade Area Agreements were signed with Thailand and Sri Lanka and negotiations continued with Singapore.

The cumulative reduction of import restrictions on manufactured goods of these numerous trade-related agreements is clearly but only partially reflected in the change in the TMP. Overall India's TMP was reduced enormously from a highly restrictive 80 per cent in 1991 to 31 per cent in 2001, which would have lowered the barrier to import more advanced and therefore cleaner technology. Its TMP ranking, however, only improved from forty-seventh to fifty-third between 1990 and about 2002, showing that its tariff reform had progressed much more slowly than in other countries. It ranked last; that is, it had the highest TMP among the countries included in this study.

Its import regime, in fact, remained highly restrictive, as indicated by its ranking on the more comprehensive TRI. It received a high score (7 out of 10) as of 2004, based on all its restrictions, ranking sixty-first among 66 countries, which indicates that the combined impact of all the import barriers was still highly restrictive. Among the eight countries included in this study it had the sixth most restrictive score.

Despite the restrictive trade regime, the import of manufactured products increased from US$12.8 billion in 1990 to US$30.9 billion in 2002, a modest increase of 140 per cent. Similarly the import of capital goods, one sub-category of manufactured goods, increased from US$4.3 billion in 1990 to US$11.5 billion in 2002, an increase of 170 per cent. As a result the import of capital goods as a percentage of manufactured goods increased from 33 per cent to 37 per cent between 1990 and 2002 (World Bank, 2005).

The pulp and paper sub-sector

Change in import restrictions for the pulp and paper sub-sector and the levels of these restrictions were broadly in line with those for the overall manufacturing sector in 2002, which meant that the sub-sector was largely shielded by tariffs (World Bank, 2005). The tariff levels on machinery, pulp and paper products had decreased by 2000 but not to low levels. More specifically, the tariff level on pulp and paper machinery decreased from 42.8 to 25.0 per cent between 1990 and 2002 but remained twice as high as that of China. However, this reduction, along with relaxations in quantitative restrictions, increased the incentive to import machinery, the value of these imports more than doubling between 1990 and 2002. A substantial portion of the imported machinery was second-hand equipment that had become available at throwaway prices when pulp and paper mills in Europe and North American upgraded their equipment.

The tariff level on imported pulp decreased from 40 to 5 per cent between 1990 and 2001 but still remained high compared to China and Viet Nam, each with a 1 per cent tariff level, and was comparable with Brazil (5.5 per cent). Despite the lower rate, the value of imported pulp increased only slightly between 1990 and 2001 because of the limited need for chemical pulp to improve the quality of pulp produced in India.

The simple average tariff on paper and paper products decreased from 97.6 per cent to 34.1 per cent between 1990 and 2001. However, the tariff level escalated from 1997, going from 28.2 per cent to 34.1 per cent. This was especially high when compared to that of the other paper-producing countries in 2001: Viet Nam (20 per cent), China (17 per cent) and Brazil (14 per cent). In spite of this high tariff level, however, the import of paper and paper products increased by 78 per cent.

Global comparison

In summary, though Indian trade liberalization policies reduced import restrictions during the 1990s, the end result was that the trade regime remained relatively restrictive. The reality was that tariff levels for the manufacturing sector in general and for the pulp and paper sub-sector in particular remained absolutely high compared to other countries and thus probably discouraged the import of technology; liberalization in the area of quantitative restrictions was simply replaced by increased tariffs. Overall, it is not surprising to find that India ranked very low on the TI index. In fact its rank dropped from seventy-fifth among 87 countries in 1990 to eighty-fourth among 91 countries in 2001. Among developing countries its rank improved slightly from fifty-second to forty-eighth among 61 countries, but it ranked last for both years among the eight countries included in this study.

Resource Pricing Policy

As with all countries included in this study, it was not possible to obtain sufficient information to provide a comprehensive overview of resource pricing policies, including the use of subsidies for energy and water, nor was it possible to compute the average change in resource prices between 1990 and 2002. This section therefore contains only limited information on resource pricing policies, prices *per se* and changes in energy and water utilization by the manufacturing sector. Higher resource prices, as described in Chapter 3, are often incentives for adopting EST, particularly CTs.

India's power sector was in need of urgent reform, according to the WTO (WTO, 2002). All power generation, transmission and distribution facilities were under the control of state electricity boards. Electricity tariffs differed from state to state and even within a state, depending on the user category. As a result there was no uniformity in electricity rates. According to the national planning commission, no state electricity board was recovering the full cost of power supplied and thus all were operating at a loss (WTO, 2002).

Between 1990 and 2002 energy consumption (defined as energy coming from oil, coal, natural gas, nuclear power, renewable sources and electricity) by the manufacturing sector increased by 38 per cent, as shown earlier in Table 6.2. The manufacturing sector accounted for 27 per cent of national energy consumption in 2002, a decline from 46 per cent in 1990 (IEA, 2005).

Energy consumption by the pulp and paper sub-sector decreased by 8 per cent during the same period, from 1417 kilotons of oil equivalent (ktoe) in 1990 to 1306 ktoe in 2002. The sub-sector accounted for 1.2 per cent of energy consumption by industry in 2002, whereas it had been 2 per cent in 1990. Energy-use intensity also decreased by 41 per cent during the same period, from 1740 to 1030 toe per million US dollars of MVA. The steep increase in the cost of energy was the main driver for this reduced intensity (IEA, 2005).

Regarding water management, there was a nationally mandated charge on water use. The main objective of this charge was to encourage a more rational use of water and to further increase the income of the SPCBs. The charges varied from US$1–2 per kilolitre of water depending on the degree of toxicity and biodegradability of the water consumed (Water Cess Act of 1977, Schedule II). Water charges varied from state to state and sub-sector to sub-sector, and reflected whether the water source was ground or tap water. The state-determined water charges appear to have been very low, which suggests that the pricing system would have had only a limited effect on water use.

The limited effect of charges for water use is confirmed by a study that compared resource use by the Indian pulp and paper industry in the late 1990s to world standards (Agarwal, 1999). For instance, where the world average water use was 55 cubic metres water per ton of paper, some Indian mills used more than 400 cubic metres. Moreover, the average water consumption had remained constant at 250–300 cubic metres per ton of paper since 1990, even with the introduction of water charges.

Global comparison
There is no global assessment that one can draw on to compare the relative effectiveness of resource pricing in India, nor could any study be found that compares current prices for these resources to the actual cost of their production. As an alternative, an EUI score for the manufacturing sector was calculated for use in this study. India's energy-use intensity declined only slightly during the 1990s, changing from 1315 toe per million US dollars of MVA in 1990 to 1268 in 2002. In a global comparison this absolute improvement seems even more modest, as India's ranking on the EUI dropped from eighty-third in 1990 to eighty-fourth in 2002, among 93 countries. Among sixty-five developing countries, India ranked fifty-sixth in 1990 and fifty-seventh in 2002. Among the eight countries included in this study, it ranked seventh, only more intensive than Kenya.

TECHNOLOGY POLICY

During the early 1990s Indian policy was aimed at promoting indigenous technologies. This had a dual purpose. First, it facilitated the control of technology entering the country via joint ventures and other licensing collaboration arrangements, and, second, it fostered local R&D activities. Although successful, such policies hindered the expansion of FDI and the introduction of foreign technologies into India, thus contributing to the technological stagnation of industry during the early 1990s. Indeed, only companies using sophisticated technologies were allowed to have large foreign equity. Furthermore, much of the research carried out by the public sector did not focus on the needs of industry. The industrial sector, for its part, did not want to risk using local unproven technologies and preferred to import expensive foreign technologies.

In the mid-1990s there was the beginning of a policy reversal that reduced the price of technology imports. Restrictions were eased on the use of imported technologies, large foreign equity shares were permitted, controls on technology payments were removed, and royalty taxes and technical fees reduced.

The Ministry of Science and Technology, established in 1985, guided the implementation of the evolving science and technology policy in India, working through the following institutional network:

- Central government and science and technology departments
- State governments and science and technology departments
- Private industry R&D
- Independent research institutes.

The government took several steps to strengthen the technological capabilities of this network. In 2001 it spent 0.78 per cent of GDP on R&D (Dahlman and Utz, 2005). It required public research institutions to generate at least 30 per cent of their budgets from consultancy services to the private sector. It provided financial support for technological absorption and development through a new technology development fund. In addition, through a Patent Information Centre created in 1997, it promoted innovation, fostered patent awareness, provided information and facilitated the filing of patent applications.

This institutional network included research centres for the pulp and paper sub-sector. The foremost of these were the Central Pulp and Paper Institute, part of the Federal Ministry of Industry, the Institute of Paper Technology and the Cellulose and Paper Division of the Forest Research Institute. However, these institutes transferred little technology to industry, giving industrialists the impression that the research carried out by the centres did not correspond to their needs.

Global comparison

In summary, India has a long history of implementing science and technology policies and supporting R&D, both in terms of the large number of organizations involved in R&D and its measurable financial contribution. Considerable encouragement is given to enterprise R&D. None the less, governmental influences are still contradictory in some cases and are not sufficiently focused on industrial needs for technological modernization. Because of these contradictions, India ranked modestly on the TC index, coming one hundred and eleventh among 162 countries on the TC index in 2000, a slight improvement on its position of one hundred and sixteenth in 1990. Its 2000 rank, sixty-third among 114 developing countries, which placed it in the group of countries classified as latecomers. Among the eight countries included in this study it ranked seventh.

PULP AND PAPER SUB-SECTOR

Economic Overview

Pulp for paper production in India increased by about 70 per cent and paper and paperboard production by 88 per cent during the period 1990 to 2002, with 2.9 million tons of pulp and 4.1 million tons of paper and paperboard, as shown in Table 6.3. This large increase in output occurred in spite of many traditional hindrances. All through the period Indian mills suffered from high production costs, low productivity, excessive resource consumption (especially with regard to fibre deficits), low output quality, obsolete technologies and under-utilization of installed capacity.

On a global scale, India ranked tenth in aggregate pulp production and seventeenth in aggregate paper and paperboard production in 2002; among the paper-producing countries included in this study it ranked third in both categories, trailing behind China and Brazil.

In spite of the increased domestic output, the growing domestic demand could only be met through a combination of local production and imports, which was permitted by the trade liberalization policies introduced in 1992. Not surprisingly, Indian paper and paperboard producers were not export oriented in such a situation. In 1990 the export share of the national

Table 6.3   Pulp for paper and paper and paperboard production, import and export

Year	Production	Import	Export	Import	Export
	Pulp for paper (thousand tons)			Pulp for paper (US$ million)	
1990	1750	76.5	–	37.6	–
1995	1870	174.2	4.8	109.0	3.9
2002	2950	240.9	25.5	104.7	14.8
	Paper and paperboard (thousand tons)			Paper and paperboard (US$ million)	
1990	2185	124.1	8.7	160.2	8.7
1995	3025	216.8	10.7	164.7	8.2
2002	4104	636.5	55.6	372.1	46.7

Source: FAO (2004).

production of paper and paperboard was less than 0.1 per cent and had increased only slightly by 2002. Similarly, the sub-sector accounted for less than 0.1 per cent of India's manufactured exports in 1990, increasing only to slightly more than 0.1 per cent in 2002 (World Bank, 2005).

As for trade in this sub-sector, India ranked forty-fifth in 1990 as a paper and paperboard exporter and dropped to forty-eighth position in 2002. Pulp for paper exports increased form zero in 1990 to 25 500 tons in 2002, in both cases behind China and Brazil. Its four largest export markets were the United States, Sri Lanka, Bangladesh and Nigeria. It remained a net importer of pulp for paper (by about 215 000 tons), ranking twenty-third globally, and of paper and paperboard (by about 600 000 tons), ranking twenty-fifth globally. The significant increase in imported paper and paper products pointed to the failure of the sub-sector to keep up with booming demand.

Overall, the pulp and paper sub-sector made only a modest contribution to India's economy during the 1990s. The value added of this sub-sector increased from US$0.9 billion to US$1.6 billion, an increase of almost 80 per cent, while total Indian MVA increased from US$41.4 billion to US$76.6 billion, a slightly larger increase of 85 per cent. As a result, its percentage share of MVA remained approximately the same, 2.1 per cent, during the 1990s. Finally, its percentage share of total employment was 1.5 per cent in both 1990 and 2001, with approximately 130 000 employees in both 1990 and 2000 (UNIDO, 2005).

Sub-sector Profile

The Indian pulp and paper sub-sector consisted, at the time of this study, primarily of approximately 450 registered mills with a total installed capacity of about 4.3 million tons per annum. Aside from the registered mills there were around 2000 small, non-registered mills with a production capacity of one ton per day (USAID, 2001). Among the 450 registered mills there were 37 large-sized mills with an installed capacity of 33 000 tons per year or above. These mills were primarily forest-based, with bamboo accounting for between 60 and 65 per cent of the raw material input and hard wood for the remaining 35 to 40 per cent. There were 120 medium-sized paper mills with an installed capacity of between 10 000 and 33 000 tons per year. Typically their raw material input was 80 per cent agricultural residues, 15 per cent waste paper and 5 per cent purchased pulp. Finally there were 288 small mills, defined as having an installed capacity of less than 10 000 tons per annum (Pöyry, 2002).

Of approximately 450 registered mills, 14 were selected for this study based on criteria that called for variations in the pulping process, size, location and raw material input. The selected mills corresponded to the criteria as follows: eight used the chemical soda process, two used the hydro-pulping process and four used the kraft sulphate process; four were large, nine medium-sized and one small; they were located in six different states (Maharashtra, Orissa, Punjab, Tamil Nadu, Uttaranchal and Uttar Pradesh); and four used primarily wood, eight used primarily agro-residues and two used recycled paper (Table 6.4).

Other characteristics of the mills worth noting are: all were under private domestic ownership; all produced only for the domestic market; six were ISO 9001/9002 certified and one was ISO 14001 certified; and four had integrated R&D departments, engaged mainly in quality control and in the installation and adaptation of new technology.

Process Technology and CT Characterization

As of 2000, the average age of plants and machinery in the pulp and paper sub-sector exceeded 20 years. Only a few mills had modern technologies, such as continuous digesters and high-speed paper machines. Consequently the energy and raw material efficiency at most mills was in general low.

As of 2000, the majority of Indian pulp and paper mills used one of three processes, mainly determined by the availability of raw material and capacity. Large mills as well as wood-based mills used the sulphate process, and medium-sized agro-based mills and recycled fibre-based mills used the soda process and hydro-pulping process respectively. Chemical soda was the dominant pulping process used by more than half of the mills included in the survey; the remainder used either hydro-pulping or kraft sulphate (Table 6.4).

The 14 mills used all kinds of equipment, ranging from very old to modern automated equipment in some of the newer plants. The survey team assigned the mills to one of two categories based on the technological vintage of the pulp production equipment: 11 used mainly standard–modern equipment and three used best available technology (BAT) (Table 6.4).

The extent of CT adoption in the sub-sector was low. Obsolete, inefficient and highly polluting technologies for bleaching, such as batch digesters and elemental chlorine, were still used. Only a few mills used fluidized bed boilers or lime kilns, which gave lower production costs and generated fewer pollutants. Most large mills, however, had installed modern and efficient chemical recovery units.

The extent of CT adoption in the 14 mills, in line with overall adoption in the sub-sector, was relatively limited. According to the survey findings, eight of the mills used CTs of only a low order of complexity, three used CTs of a medium order of complexity, and the remaining three did not use any. Only two mills had an environmental management system (Table 6.4).

Table 6.4 Profile of the 14 mills investigated

Mill	Process/Product	Scale ('000 tons/year)	Location (state)	Sale orientation (2000)	Technology vintage	Ownership	EST score	Regulatory compliance	Donor assist.	EMS
I1	Chemical soda, PW paper	Large (153)	Lal Kuan, Uttar Pradesh	99% D, 1% E	BAT	100% private domestic	PAT + MTC	Partial	World Bank	Yes
I2	Hydro-pulping, kraft paper	Medium (68)	Meerut, Uttar Pradesh	100% D	Standard–modern	100% private domestic	PAT	No	No	No
I3	Sulphate, kraft pulp, PW paper	Large (150)	Rayagada, Orissa	96% D, 4% E	BAT	100% private domestic	PAT + MTC	Yes	No	Yes
I4	Hydro-pulping, kraft paper	Medium (30)	Khatima, Uttaranchal	99% D, 1% E	BAT	100% private domestic	PAT + LTC	Yes	No	No
I5	Chemical soda, PW paper	Small (17)	Bijnor, Uttar Pradesh	100% D	Standard–modern	100% private domestic	PAT	No	No	No
I6	Chemical soda, corrugated board	Medium (41)	Aurangabad, Maharashtra	100% D	Standard–modern	100% private domestic	PAT + LTC	No	No	No
I7	Chemical soda, speciality paper	Medium (36)	Pune, Maharashtra	99% D, 1% E	Standard–modern	100% private domestic	PAT + LTC	No	No	No

I8	Chemical soda, PW paper	Medium (40) Punjab	100% D	Standard– modern	100% private domestic	PAT	No	No	No
I9	Sulphate, PW paper	Large (115) Erode, Tamil Nadu	86% D, 14% E	Standard– modern	100% private domestic	PAT + LTC	Partial	No	No
I10	Chemical soda, PW paper	Medium (20) Rampur, Uttar Pradesh	99% D, 1% E	Standard– modern	100% private domestic	PAT + LTC	Partial	No	No
I11	Sulphate, PW paper	Medium (66) Ropar, Punjab	100% D	Standard– modern	100% private domestic	PAT + LTC	Yes	Loan from USAID	No
I12	Chemical soda, PW paper	Medium (64) Saharanpur, Uttar Pradesh	100% D	Standard– modern	100% private domestic	PAT + LTC	Yes	No	No
I13	Sulphate, newsprint, PW paper	Large (230) Karur, Tamil Nadu	87% D, 13% E	Standard– modern	100% private domestic	PAT + LTC	Partial	No	No
I14	Chemical soda, PW paper	Medium (34) Barnala, Punjab	100% D	Standard– modern	100% private domestic	PAT + MTC	No	No	No

Abbreviations: printing and writing (PW); domestic (D); export (E); best available technology (BAT); pollution abatement technologies (PATs); higher order technological complexity (HTC); medium order technological complexity (MTC); lower order technological complexity (LTC).

Source: CTS (2002).

133

Table 6.5   CTs used in the 14 mills

Process area	Option	Number of mills using practice/ equipment
Handling fibre raw material	Washing fibre raw material	1
	Screw press for reducing pith moisture	1
Pulping	Digester laggings	1
Bleaching	Oxygen delignification	2
	Addition of washers in bleaching plant	1
Black liquor recovery in power boilers	Efficient multi-effect evaporators	4
	Installation of black liquor chemical recovery	3
	Installation of co-generation plant	4
	Fluidized bed power boiler	1
Paper-making	Installation of hoods in paper machine	1
	Closure of water system	1
	Recovery of fibre (save all)	2
	Improvement of press section paper machine	1

Source: CTS (2002).

CT options were used in all stages of the production process. Some of the CTs used in the various processes and the number of mills using them is identified in Table 6.5. Black liquor recovery in power boilers was the only technological configuration used, and their use was limited to a few mills. Only one or two mills used best practices in other unit processes.

Overall, the potential of CTs to improve the financial performance and reduce the generation of pollutants was high, as illustrated by the case study presented in Box 6.1. In this particular example the mill reduced the capital outlay needed for pollution control equipment and cut back significantly on the generation of pollutants.

In spite of this potential, the adoption of CTs was limited for several reasons. First, many mills were set up during the 1970s by the government in an attempt to expand production capacity rapidly and were encouraged to import old and inefficient plant machinery from developed countries. Since then the equipment had further deteriorated. Second, financially viable technology for chemical recovery in small mills was still not available. Third, inadequate financial resources had prevented them from investing in new technology. Due to the cyclical nature of the industry, banks and financial institutions were reluctant to lend money for technological upgrading. Fourth, the uncertainty caused by trade liberalization, which had allowed increased paper imports, made small mills particularly hesitant

---

BOX 6.1   CLEANER PRODUCTION CASE STUDY: INDIA

The National Productive Council of India and UNIDO undertook a CP assessment in the mid 1990s at an agro-based pulp and paper mill with a production capacity of 30 tons per day. As a result, the mill implemented 28 preventive measures, achieving savings of around US$400 000 at a cost of US$140 000. The achievements were as follows:

- Reduced capital investment cost for PAT by 25 per cent and its maintaining costs by 35 per cent;
- Reduced residual discharge by 20–40 per cent;
- Reduced secondary pollution;
- Increased output by 22 per cent due to quality improvements and new products.

Source: UNIDO (1995).

---

to invest. In fact, about 150 small mills were closed or standing idle in 2000 due to a combination of high production cost and the availability of cheaper imported products.

PAT Characterization

In general, large and most medium-sized Indian mills have constructed ETPs. However, their capacity was often insufficient to treat the volume of effluent, and in most instances they were not used regularly but only at the time of inspections by the SPCBs. Eleven used anaerobic lagoons and two used activated sludge; one mill used only primary treatment.

All 14 mills used some form of PAT because of legal requirements. Most of their attention was focused on effluent treatment, while applications for air pollution control and solid waste management were more limited.

In the case of India, international technical cooperation programmes had a limited role in encouraging the adoption of PATs in the pulp and paper sub-sector. Only two of the 14 mills surveyed benefited from subsidies or loans from international donors.

Environmental Performance

The MOEF classified the pulp and paper sub-sector as a significant source of water pollutants. Pollutant discharge from SSIs was significantly more serious than the problems caused by large wood-based mills because the SSIs used outdated technology and did not have resources to install PATs.

A 30-tons-per-day small, agro-based paper mill was estimated to be almost three times as polluting as an integrated paper mill of 200 tons per day (Schumacher and Sathaye, 1999).

In spite of the MOEF support for a national Environmental Information System, there were no consistently collected data on pollutant release from pulp and paper mills. The only estimate of pollutant loadings from the sub-sector is the one prepared by the World Bank (World Bank, 2004). The sub-sector was estimated to be responsible for one-fifth of BOD loadings, which seems high considering that it accounted for only 2 per cent of MVA in 2001.

Overall, only four of the 14 mills interviewed operated in full compliance with Indian environmental standards, as shown in Table 6.4. A further four mills partially complied, while the remainder did not comply at all.

KEY INFORMANTS AND INTERNATIONAL DONORS

Four groups, in addition to national enviromental regulatory agencies and technology centres, can influence the extent to which plants adopt EST: NGOs, business associations, international donors of technical asssistance, and chemical and equipment suppliers. Some information about the first three is presented in this section; there is insufficient information to characterize those firms that supplied chemicals and equipment to India's pulp and paper sub-sector.

NGOs

Many international and national NGOs were engaged in environmental protection efforts in India during the time of this study. They had some success at the village level in forcing industry to reduce pollutant discharge. Some SPCBs responded to public requests for more rigorous enforcement of environmental regulations. However, NGOs do not appear to have had sufficient influence to modify Indian environmental policy or to correct the general lack of law enforcement.

The only substantial information on the role of NGOs in reducing industrial pollution comes from a World Bank survey in 1997. The survey asked 250 plant personnel whether pollution control authorities were affected by local community pressure: 51 plants indicated that they had undertaken abatement in response to NGO pressure and 102 said they had done so in response to complaints from neighbouring communities (World Bank, 1997).

The survey team interviewed one NGO, the Centre for Science and Environment, founded in 1980. The Centre aims to increase public awareness on environment and development issues and is concerned about environmental threats such as ecological poverty, extensive land degradation and rapidly increasing pollution. It has an equipped pollution-monitoring laboratory that documents pesticide residues, conducts water quality analyses and monitors ambient air quality in cities and communities across India. It publishes a state-of-environment report and rates enterprises on the basis of their environmental behaviour.

Business Associations

The survey team interviewed one of the two national pulp and paper industry associations, the India Agro and Recycled Paper Mills Association (IARPMA). The other association, the India Paper Manufacturers' Association, which represented large, wood-based mills, was not interviewed.

The IARPMA represents mills using agro-based products as raw materials and had around 110 members in 2002. It liaises with the government and assists in the diffusion of information on new technology and government policy. It also publishes a trade journal, organises international exhibitions (Paperex) and maintains a directory of members. Furthermore, it provides training courses on waste minimization, CTs and energy conservation.

Overall, the business community was not directly involved in the law-making process. Even if business representatives were requested to make suggestions, they were not formally represented in the decision-making bodies.

International Donors

Official development assistance in the environment sector totalled US$9.9 billion or about US$1.9 billion per year between 1995 and 2000 (World Bank, 2002). Of this total, about 17 per cent was directed to industry and energy projects. Within this category, about 41 per cent (US$670 million) went for industrial pollution control, 31 per cent for co-generation and renewable energy projects (US$519 million) and 28 per cent (US$473) for emissions reductions and energy efficiency. The major donor during this period was the World Bank, which provided 39 per cent of total environmental overseas development assistance (ODA). The Japanese Bank for International Cooperation followed, with a 16 per cent share.

Starting in 1991, the Government of India, with technical and financial assistance provided by the World Bank, the Governments of Denmark, Norway, Japan and other parties, launched a comprehensive effort to address the root causes of industrial pollution in the country. The World Bank supported this effort with two projects, one operational from 1990 to 1996 and the other operational from 1996 to 2002. Both projects consisted of three components: (a) an institutional component designed to strengthen the CPCB and SPCBs of selected states; (b) an investment component via the Industrial Development Bank of India and the Industrial Credit and Investment Corporation of India (ICICI) to provide financial support for industry to comply with regulations, both for plant-specific ETPs and common effluent treatment plants (CETPs) for clusters of SSIs; and (c) a technical assistance component to prepare various technical reports, support an industrial extension service for promoting waste minimization (CP) and assist development financial institutions in preparing feasibility and pre-investment studies (World Bank, 1991 and 1994).

UNIDO/UNEP established a National Cleaner Production Centre (NCPC) in 1995 with the aim of spreading the CP concept, in particular to SSIs. The NCPC was located at the National Productivity Council of India and its activities included: plant-level demonstrations, training programmes/workshops and the dissemination of CP information. Together with the state governments, NCPC and UNIDO established regional cleaner production centres in Karnataka and Gujarat. These centres served as independent sub-centres of NCPC and undertook four specific activities: in-plant assessments, training, information dissemination and policy advice.

None of the mills in the survey received technical assistance from NCPC or other donor-funded CP programmes, and only two received international funds for implementing EST projects.

SUMMARY

India's manufacturing sector performed reasonably well between 1990 and about 2002, as indicated by aggregate economic and environmental performance indicators. While GDP increased by 88 per cent between 1990 and 2002, MVA increased by more, 97 per cent. However, the share of MVA in GDP in current prices decreased from 17.1 to 15.6 per cent. GNI per capita, at PPP, moreover, increased by 95 per cent over the same period. Energy use by this sector surged during the 1990s with an increase of 38 per cent, and energy-use intensity decreased by 30 per cent. Between 1990 and 2000 total BOD effluent, however, increased by only 10 per cent in spite of an increase in MVA of almost 100 per cent, and BOD-effluent intensity decreased by 40 per cent.

Overall, India has developed an impressive environmental policy since the 1970s, relying mainly on regulatory measures in its efforts to reduce industrial pollution. These empowered government agencies to set and enforce environmental standards. However, the impact of its regulatory efforts was low, mainly due to the quality of public services and limited enforcement of environmental standards.

Changes in three economic policies, industrial, trade and resource pricing, had mixed effects on industrial output and technology upgrading. Industrial policies could be expected to have promoted the expansion of industrial output by lifting restrictions and offering incentives to domestic and foreign investors, but probably did not do so to the fullest extent possible. Liberalization of trade-related import restrictions, though significant, was limited compared to other countries. None the less, the import of pulp and paper products increased slightly and, more surprisingly, the import of pulp and paper machinery boomed. Finally, the modest changes in resource pricing do not appear to have provided a stimulus for technology upgrading; indeed, energy-use intensity decreased only modestly and energy-use intensity remained high compared to many other countries.

India has a long history of using technology policy to support R&D, both in terms of a large number of organizations and a measurable financial contribution. Considerable encouragement was given specifically for enterprise R&D. None the less, governmental influences were still contradictory in some cases and were not sufficiently focused on industrial needs for technological modernization.

Government policies had mixed results in the pulp and paper industry. While output increased by almost 70 per cent in the 1990s, this was not sufficient to meet the demands of the country. Trade liberalization, which allowed for a significant increase in imports to meet demand, flooded the domestic market with better-quality paper at lower prices. As a result, around 150 small mills were standing idle by 2000. Most Indian mills continued to use obsolete and inefficient equipment because of the limited technological support given to the sub-sector and the reluctance of financial institutions to provide financial support. Consequently the mills were wasting large amounts of energy, water and raw material, which generated unnecessary pollutant loads. Most SPCBs lacked the resources and political support to carry out tasks efficiently, and to provide the industry with sufficient advice and information on how to solve environmental problems.

India's pulp and paper sub-sector increased pulp for paper production from 1.7 to 2.9 million tons (a 70 per cent increase) and paper and paperboard production from 2.2 to 4.1 million tons (a 88 per cent increase) between 1990 and 2002. As of 2002 there were approximately 450 registered pulp and paper mills in the sub-sector. Approximately 60 per cent of these mills were SSIs. The survey team investigated 14 of the 450 mills with a focus on those using non-wood for pulp because of their pollutant intensity. Eleven of these mills used mainly standard–modern production equipment and three used BAT. Eight of the mills used CTs of a low order of complexity, three used CTs of a medium order of complexity and three used no CTs. All of the mills had installed PAT equivalent to secondary treatment. However, only four of the mills were reported to be in compliance with environmental standards.

The influence of other institutional actors, NGOs, business associations and international donors on EST adoption was limited during the 1990s. NGOs had some influence but only at the state and local levels of government. Business associations were not involved in shaping the national environmental policy agenda and in providing advice on more advanced production technologies. The amount of donor assistance directed towards reducing industrial pollution was small in comparison to the scale of industrial pollution, with the largest efforts being made by the World Bank to upgrade the capacity of SPCBs in several states.

In conclusion, as of 2002, the government needed to improve the effectiveness of its economic, environmental and technology policy regimes if they were to benefit the pulp and paper sub-sector. Additional policies *per se* were not necessary, but rather standards and delivery of environmental and technological advice to plants needed to be enforced to enable them to compete in an increasingly competitive global economy and meet their environmental obligations.

NOTE

1. The FDI for 1990 has been taken as the three-year average of 1989–91 and for 2002 as the three-year average of 2001–3, in order to even out fluctuations in FDI flows.

REFERENCES

ADB (2005), 'Key Indicators – Labor Markets in Asia: Promoting Full, Productive and Decent Employment', Manila: Asian Development Bank.
Agarwal, Anil (1999), 'The five leaf award: the green rating project', *Down To Earth*, **8**(5), 5–10.
Ahluwalia, I., R. Mohan and O. Goswami (1996), 'Policy Reform in India', Development Centre, Paris: Organization for Economic Cooperation and Development (OECD).

CTS (2002), 'Adoption of EST: A Study of India's Paper and Pulp Industry', Gorgon, India: Centre for Technology Studies (CTS). Report prepared for UNIDO.

Dahlman, C. and A. Utz (2005), 'India and the Knowledge Economy: Leveraging Strengths and Opportunities', Overview, Finance and Private Sector Development Unit of the World Bank's South Asia Region and The World Bank Institute, Washington, DC: The World Bank (available on: http://www.worldbank.org).

EIU (1996), 'Country Report: India', London: Economist Intelligence Unit.

EIU (2004), 'Country Report: India', London: Economist Intelligence Unit.

ENVIS (2005), 'Environmental Information System of India' (available on: http://www.envis.nic.in).

FAO (2004), 'FAOSTAT – Forestry Statistics', Rome: Food and Agriculture Organization of the United Nations (available on: http://www.fao.org).

FAO (2005), 'AQUASTAT: FAO STAT', Rome: Food and Agriculture Organization of the United Nations (available on: http://www.fao.org).

Government of India (1991), 'Notification' [GSR 93(E) February 21, 1991], New Delhi, India: Government of India.

Government of India (2002), 'Annual Report (2001–02) on the Working of State Electricity Boards and Electricity Departments', Annexure 4.28: 137, New Delhi, India: Planning Commission (Power & Energy Division) (available on: http://planningcommission.nic.in).

IEA (2005), 'Online Data Services', IEA Energy Information Centre, Paris: International Energy Agency (available on: http://www.iea.org).

Isaksson, A. (2006), 'World Productivity Database: Construction and Measurement Methods', unpublished working paper, Vienna: UNIDO.

ISO (2003), 'The ISO Survey of ISO 9000 and ISO 14001 Certificates', Geneva: International Organization for Standardization (available on: http://www.iso.org).

Kathuria, V. and G.S. Haripriya (2000), 'Industrial pollution control: choosing the right option', Bombay: *Economic Political Weekly*.

MOEF (2001), 'Indian Environment Institutional Framework', New Delhi, India: Ministry of Environment and Forests.

MOEF (2005), 'Eco-mark scheme of India', New Delhi, India: Ministry of Environment and Forests (http://www.envfor.nic.in/cpcb/ecomark).

Pargal, S., M. Mani and M. Huq (1997), 'Regulatory Inspections, Informal Pressure and Water Pollution – A Survey of Industrial Plants in India', Policy Research Department, Washington, DC: The World Bank (available on:http://www.worldbank.org).

Pöyry, Jaakko (2002), 'Global Competitiveness of the Indian Paper Industry', Vantaa, Finland: Jaakko Pöyry Consulting.

Schumacher, K. and J. Sathaye (1999), 'India's Pulp and Paper Industry: Productivity and Energy Efficiency', Berkeley, US: Lawrence Berkeley National Laboratory (available on: http://ies.lbl.gov/iespubs/41843.pdf).

UNIDO (1995), 'DESIRE – Demonstration in Small Industries for Reducing Waste Project, From Waste to Profits – Experiences', Vienna: UNIDO.

UNIDO (2005), *International Yearbook of Industrial Statistics 2004*, Cheltenham, UK and Northampton, MA, US: Edward Elgar Publishing.

USAID (2001), 'Report on Pulp and Paper Industry: Survey of Industrial Environment', Washington, DC: United States Agency for International Development (available on: http://www.cleantechindia.com/neweic/bhup.htm).

World Bank (1991), 'Staff Appraisal Report India: Industrial Pollution Control Project, May 7, 1991', Washington, DC: The World Bank.

World Bank (1994), 'Staff Appraisal Report India: Industrial Pollution Prevention Project, June 9, 1994', Washington, DC: The World Bank.

World Bank (1997), 'Pulp and Paper Mills Share in Total Industrial Pollution', Washington, DC: The World Bank.

World Bank (2002), 'Compendium of Donor Assisted Projects in the Environment Sector in India', Compiled by the Confederation of Indian Industry, Washington, DC: The World Bank (available on: http://www.worldbank.org).

World Bank (2004), 'World Bank Development Indicators (WDI) 2004', CD-ROM version, Washington, DC: The World Bank.

World Bank (2005), 'World Integrated Trade Solution (WITS)', Washington, DC: The World Bank (available on: http://wits.worldbank.org).

WTO (2002), 'Trade Policy Review India 2002', Geneva: World Trade Organization.

7. Kenya

INTRODUCTION

A survey team from the Kenya National Cleaner Production Centre investigated the specific factors influencing the adoption of environmentally sound technology (EST) in Kenya's leather processing sub-sector. The team used semi-structured questionnaires provided by UNIDO to interview plant managers at nine out of 12 tanneries and key informants in five business associations, one technology centre, two chemical suppliers, one environmental NGO and three environmental regulatory agencies. The team also collected background data on the country and the leather processing sub-sector.

This chapter describes the economic and environmental context in Kenya for EST adoption; relevant environmental, economic and technology policies; the leather processing sub-sector and the plants investigated; and key informants and international donors.

THE ECONOMIC AND ENVIRONMENTAL CONTEXT FOR EST ADOPTION

The following selected economic and environmental performance indicators define the context in which manufacturing plants made their technology adoption decisions and, in particular, their decisions to adopt EST during the late 1990s/early 2000s.

Economic Performance Indicators

Agriculture dominated Kenya's economy during the period of this study, though its industrial, commercial and tourism base was much more developed than that of many other sub-Saharan countries, one exception being Zimbabwe, the other African country examined in this study, whose manufacturing sector was more developed than Kenya's. Over the post-independence era (1964–2000) Kenya had transited from a high-growth path in the 1960s (6.6 per cent average annual growth from 1964 to 1972) to an ever-declining path in subsequent decades, the average annual growth rate of gross domestic product (GDP) during the 1990s being a disappointing 1.2 per cent.

Between 1990 and 2002 GDP increased by 21 per cent but GDP per capita decreased by 10 per cent as the population increased by 34 per cent (Table 7.1). Gross national income (GNI) per capita in purchasing power parity (PPP) – a more accurate measure of well-being than GDP per capita – increased by 15 per cent. Based on the latter, Kenya is classified by the World Bank as a low-income country.

The manufacturing sector performed modestly during the 1990s, with an increase of 23 per cent in manufacturing value added (MVA), its share of GDP increasing from 11.8 per cent in 1990 to 13.0 per cent in 2002. Within the manufacturing sector the most economically important sub-sectors were food processing, textiles, petroleum and chemical products, metals and machinery. Although the leather processing sub-sector represented a small fraction of MVA, it was singled out by policy-makers as a priority in Kenya's export-oriented industrialization drive, largely because of its export potential and its linkage with agriculture.

Table 7.1   Economic performance indicators for Kenya

Economic indicator	Year	Value	Percentage change
GDP (constant 1995 US$) (billion)	1990	8.4	21.0
	2002	10.1	
GDP per capita (constant 1995 US$)	1990	358.0	−10.0
	2002	322.0	
Population (million)	1990	23.3	34.0
	2002	31.3	
GNI per capita at PPP (current international $)	1990	880.0	15.0
	2002	1010.0	
MVA (constant 1995 US$) (billion)	1990	0.7	23.0
	2002	0.8	
MVA (percentage of GDP)	1990	11.8	1.2
	2002	13.0	
CPI (1995=100)	1990	34.3	374.0
	2002	162.2	
Interest rate (commercial lending rate)	1990	18.8	−2.0
	2002	18.5	
Exchange rate (KESh/US$)	1990	22.9	244.0
	2002	78.7	

Source: World Bank (2004).

The manufacturing sector registered an average annual growth rate of 2.1 per cent during this period, a very discouraging performance in light of the government's ambition to turn it into an engine of growth and achieve the status of a newly industrialized country by 2020. Poor performance of the sector can be attributed in part to structural factors, such as the poor state of the country's infrastructure, particularly the dilapidated state of the road network, which increased freight costs and extended delivery times (EIU, 2003).

Macroeconomic policies were not particularly conducive to investment and foreign technology adoption over the period 1990–2002. Interest rates remained high (over 18 per cent), reflecting high rates of inflation, with the consumer price index (CPI) increasing by 374 per cent over the period, corresponding to an annual average price increase of 12.9 per cent. Furthermore the value of the Kenyan shilling (KES) declined by 244 per cent against the US dollar over this period, largely as a result of the government's removal of most foreign exchange controls in 1993 and its decision to allow the shilling to float freely. However, the government's decision to liberalize the foreign exchange regime effectively alleviated one of the widely perceived constraints to industrial development in the country, namely the chronic lack of foreign exchange (UNIDO, 1996).

An unfriendly donor and international environment during the 1990s encouraged the government to run a burgeoning deficit, funded by domestic borrowing. This strategy not only put pressure on interest rates but also significantly reduced the flow of funds to the productive sectors, with undesirable consequences for productivity. Combined with political stagnation and the ever-present spectre of corruption, Kenya's economic growth was compromised (Kimuyu, 2005).

Environmental Performance Indicators

For the most part environmental problems attributed to industry were not widespread throughout the country during the period of this study. They were found primarily in the large urban centres of Nairobi, Mombassa and Kimusu, and mainly regarded as being caused by food processing activities such as, *inter alia*, grain milling, beer production, and sugarcane crushing.

Selected environmental indicators, namely energy use, carbon dioxide (CO_2) emissions, organic matter effluent measured as biochemical oxygen demand (BOD), and water use, as well as the intensity of use of each of these, which provide an insight into the state of industrial environmental performance in Kenya, are presented in Table 7.2. Energy use in the manufacturing sector, measured in tons of oil equivalent (toe), increased by 17 per cent from 1990 to 2002, significantly less than the 23 per cent change in

Table 7.2   Environmental performance indicators for Kenya

Source code	Environmental indicator	Year	Value	Percentage change
1	Energy use in the manufacturing sector (million toe)	1990 2002	1.07 1.25	17.0
1 & 2	Energy-use intensity (toe per million US$ of MVA)	1990 2002	1610.0 1520.0	−5.0
1	CO_2 emission (million tons)	1990 2002	1.42 1.52	7.0
1 & 2	CO_2-emission intensity (tons per million US$ of MVA)	1990 2002	2130.0 1850.0	−13.0
2	BOD effluent from the manufacturing sector (thousand tons)	1990 2000	14.1 17.5	24.0
2	BOD-effluent intensity (tons per million US$ of MVA)	1990 2000	21.0 21.5	2.0
3	Water use in the manufacturing sector (billion m³)	1990 2000	0.08 0.1	25.0
2 & 3	Water-use intensity (thousand m³ per million US$ of MVA)	1990 2000	120.0 124.0	3.0
4	Per cent of MVA produced by the most pollutant-intensive sub-sectors	1990 2002	13.1 12.3	−0.8
5	Number of ISO 14001 certificates	2000 2002	2.0 1.0	−50.0

Sources: 1. IEA (2005); 2. World Bank (2004); 3. FAO (2005); 4. UNIDO (2005); 5. ISO (2003).

MVA. Consequently energy-use intensity of MVA decreased by 5 per cent. Associated CO_2 emissions increased by 7 per cent, whereas CO_2 intensity decreased by 13 per cent. BOD effluent increased by 24 per cent, approximately the same as the increase in MVA. As a result there was a slight increase of 2 per cent in BOD-effluent intensity in the manufacturing sector. Finally, water use by industry increased by 25 per cent from 1990 to 2000, while water-use intensity increased by only 3 per cent.

In 2000 the distribution of BOD effluent among manufacturing sub-sectors was as follows: food and beverages, 66.7 per cent; pulp and paper, 12.2 per cent; textiles, 8.8 per cent; chemicals, 6.1 per cent; primary metals, 4.1 per cent; wood, 1.9 per cent; stone and ceramics, 0.1 per cent; and others, 0.1 per cent. The leather processing sub-sector's BOD effluent was small compared to other sub-sectors, so small indeed that it is included in the aggregated 'other' category (World Bank, 2004).

The number of ISO 14001 certificates relative to MVA was low in Kenya, with two certified companies in 2000 and just one in 2002. It had a ratio of 1.2 certificates per billion US dollars of MVA compared to Zimbabwe with a ratio of 5.5 and Thailand with a ratio of 10.7.

Implications for EST Adoption

During the period investigated by this study the overall economic and environmental conditions in Kenya did not seem particularly conducive to the adoption of EST by the country's manufacturing sector. The government of this lesser developed country had not compelled the manufacturing sector to invest in EST before 1990, as evidenced by the very high BOD-effluent intensity (21.5 tons of BOD per million US dollars of MVA) in 1990. From 1990 to 2002 the manufacturing sector grew modestly, with a 1.8 per cent average annual growth rate in MVA and, in parallel, a somewhat higher average annual growth rate of 3.1 per cent in new investment, some of which would have been in EST. The high rate of inflation (the CPI increased by 374 per cent) and the modest interest rate (18.8 per cent in 1990 and 18.5 in 2002) over the period, along with political and economic uncertainties, discouraged long-term investment. The 23 per cent increase in annual MVA between 1990 and 2002 was accompanied by only a modest increase in energy use of 17 per cent and a slight decline in energy-use intensity of 5 per cent, some of which could be attributed to investment in new technology. On the other hand, the increase of 24 per cent in BOD effluent and 2 per cent in BOD-effluent intensity suggest only a minimal adoption of EST.

ENVIRONMENTAL POLICY

Environmental policy in Kenya has been strongly influenced by mainstream international trends, in particular by the outcomes of the UN Conference on the Human Environment (1972) and the UN Conference on Environment and Development (1992). Over the years the country has developed its institutional capacity through legislation and administrative measures that include the National Environmental Action Plan of 1994 and the Environmental Management and Coordination Act (EMCA) of 1999.

Until 1999 many different laws, such as those for factories, land tenure and use, water and agriculture, addressed environmental issues. What was lacking was an appropriate institution for the overall management of cross-cutting environmental issues such as policy formulation, planning, and institutional coordination and conflict resolution (Frijns and Van Vliet, 1999). The EMCA was enacted in 1999 to address this weakness. The Act created a number of bodies for the effective implementation of its provisions, with the National Environment Management Authority (NEMA) as the key institution for coordinating all matters relating to the management of the environment. It was followed by the Water Act of 2002, which provided the institutional and legal framework for implementing the national water policy.

The government set up the National Environmental Secretariat in 1971 to administer environmental legislation, and provincial and district environment offices in 1988 to decentralize the administration of environmental laws. The NEMA under the Ministry of Environment and Natural Resources replaced the National Environmental Secretariat in 2000. It was given responsibility for the implementation of all policies relating to environmental affairs and for exercising supervision and coordination on all matters relating to the environment; it had several bodies reporting to it:

- the National Environment Council, responsible for policy formulation on the management of the environment;
- provincial and district environment committees, responsible for the proper management of the environment within their respective provinces and districts;
- the Public Complaints Committee, responsible for independent investigations of complaints against the NEMA as well as complaints/allegations relating to environmental damage and degradation;
- the National Environment Trust Fund, responsible for facilitating research on matters relating to but not limited to environmental management, capacity building and environmental awards.

The NEMA and the provincial and district committees drew on several environmental policy instruments in the 1990s for industrial environmental management, classified into four categories. These are command and control regulation, economic and fiscal incentives, voluntary programmes and transparency and disclosure.

First, the command-and-control regulatory approach was introduced in the 1970s and strengthened by the EMCA in 1999. The current generic water discharge standards, set as part of this approach, covered all industrial sub-sectors but were only concentration-based rather than a combination of concentration-based and load-based standards. They specified sewer discharge requirements under the generalized effluent standards from the Ministry of Water as well as under municipal by-laws and the export processing zone regulations. At 20 mg/l BOD for direct discharge into watercourses, Kenya's standards were very stringent. In comparison, the BOD standard for most countries at that time was in the range of 20 to 100 mg/l (in India it was 30 mg/l but in Zimbabwe it was 1000 mg/l). For discharge into sewers the concentration limit was 500 mg/l, an average figure for most developing countries. In addition, there were standards for the discharge of suspended solids into both watercourses and sewers, but unfortunately none for chemical oxygen demand. These discharge standards were, however, poorly enforced, and fines imposed on violators were too low to be a deterrent.

Environmental impact assessments and audits were also part of the command-and-control regulatory approach. The EMCA required proponents of new industrial projects to undertake an assessment and to make annual environmental audit reports to the NEMA. Existing enterprises were also required to undertake yearly environmental audits.

Second, Kenya only recently introduced a wide array of economic instruments with passage of the EMCA. These included:

- waiver of customs and excise taxes on imported capital goods which prevented or substantially reduced environmental degradation caused by industry;
- tax rebates to industries or other establishments that invested in plants, equipment and machinery for pollution control, recycling wastes, water harvesting and conservation, and for using new and renewable energy resources as substitutes for hydrocarbons;
- tax disincentives to deter environmental behaviour that led to depletion of environmental resources or that caused pollution;
- user fees to ensure that those using environmental resources should pay proper value for the utilization of such resources.

Third, two voluntary programmes with industry participation were under way. One was the cleaner production programme run by the Kenya National Cleaner Production Centre (KNCPC), described later in this chapter. The other was the ISO 14000 certification programme that was actively promoted by the Kenya Bureau of Standards. There was no national eco-labelling programme.

Fourth, the government had yet to promote transparency and disclosure programmes, such as a pollutant release inventory or corporate reporting. However, several industry associations, including both the Kenya National Chamber of Commerce and Industry and the Kenya Association of Manufacturers, acknowledged outstanding annual environmental performance by their members.

Global Comparison

In summary, it appears that at the time of this study Kenya lagged behind most countries when it came to sound environmental policies and implementation. Mismanagement coupled with the lack of adequate legislation from its independence until the late 1990s contributed to the deficiency in the implementation of established environmental standards. In addition, Kenya's priorities of dealing with poverty reduction and economic growth seem to have further contributed to these deficiencies, which are reflected in the EG index. It is not surprising that Kenya ranked sixty-second out of 65 countries in 1990 and sixty-fourth out of 66 in 2001. Among developing countries, it fell slightly, from thirty-sixth out of 39 in 1990 to thirty-eighth out of 40 in 2001. Amongst the eight countries included in this study, it ranked last in 1990 and 2001.

ECONOMIC POLICY REGIMES

Overviews of Kenya's three economic policy regimes, industrial, trade and resource pricing, the economic policies that most directly influence technological modernization in the manufacturing sector and thereby increase the likelihood of the adoption of EST (see Chapter 3), are presented in this section.

Industrial Policy

Inspired by the 'Asian tiger' model of the Republic of Korea, Taiwan Province of China, Hong Kong and Singapore, Kenyan economic policy endeavoured to follow strict macroeconomic management; establish an outward orientation which would not overvalue the shilling and would allow ready access to foreign exchange; establish trade policies which would foster an export bias; and stimulate private foreign investment. In addition, it aimed to develop the country's human resources through education and training and to rely especially on the private sector to further industrial expansion. The government's intentions were set forth in a number of key policy documents, principally 'Sessional Paper No. 1 of 1986 on Economic Management for Renewable Growth', 'Sessional Paper No. 1 of 1994 on Recovery and Sustainable Development to the Year 2010' and 'Sessional Paper No. 1 of 1996 on Industrial Transformation to the Year 2020' (Government of Kenya, 1986, 1994 and 1996). Taken together, they set out national policies and strategies that were meant to lay the foundation for the structural transformation required for Kenya to join the league of newly industrialized countries by 2020.

Two phases were identified in the industrial transformation strategy. The first, spanning the period 1997–2006, was to emphasize processing industries in which Kenya had operational and technological capabilities. During this phase, Kenya set out to expand and modernize existing firms and attract new investments in light manufacturing and resource-based activities. In this regard, manufacturing sub-sectors with many SMEs that utilized and added value to local raw materials and required relatively modest capital investment were identified. The leather sector was selected as one of the priority sub-sectors (WTO, 2000).

Despite good policy intentions, the main problems faced by Kenyan manufacturing enterprises over the period were not remedied. Key among these were: accessing affordable credit in a country where manufacturing activities were particularly costly; a chronic lack of foreign exchange; an insufficient demand for its products; power shortages and poor infrastructure in general; lack of good governance and security; an underdeveloped legal framework; poor export promotion; and environmental degradation. None the less, the reform process initiated in 1996 resulted in some improvements for the manufacturing sector.

The major shift in industrial development policy involved changes in three policy instruments: foreign direct investment (FDI), export promotion and export processing zones, all with the potential for stimulating the modernization of technology.

FDI

Increasing the flow of FDI to alleviate the lack of investment funds and modernize the economy through technological transfers (managerial skills and embodied technology) was an important element of Kenya's economic reform policy in the 1990s. The government actively pursued FDI, and all sectors of the economy were open to FDI as long as there were no adverse effects on the environment and national security. Most of the earlier regulations on foreign-controlled firms were dismantled and there were generally no restrictions on foreign ownership of firms engaged in commerce and industry. UNCTAD (2005) concluded that Kenya's investment framework was generally an appropriate one, at least on paper.

None the less, despite its strategic position in the region and the quality of the country's workforce, FDI passed Kenya by. Between 1990 and 2002 the country experienced an increase in FDI inflows, from US$46 million to US$53.4 million, an increase of 16 per cent but, as a share of GDP, FDI decreased from 0.6 to around 0.3 per cent (World Bank, 2004).[1] Kenya's failure to attract FDI in manufacturing can be partly attributed to the government's neglect of infrastructure and its failure to ensure that backbone services, utilities, telecommunications and transport, were provided on a competitive basis. FDI in the leather and leather products subsector was minimal and most of it was in the leather products segment (UNIDO, 2003).

Export promotion

To improve its outward orientation, Kenya set up institutions such as the Export Promotion Council (EPC) in 1992 and the Export Processing Zones Authority (EPZA) in 1990 (described in more detail below). The EPC is the leading institution in the field of export promotion. It participates in trade fairs and exhibitions, sponsors contacted promotion programmes and sales missions, and undertakes market surveys. Unfortunately the export promotion and marketing efforts undertaken by the EPC and the EPZA during the period of this study had only a limited effect on expanding export-oriented activities. Between 1990 and 2002 the export of manufactured products increased from US$0.3 billion to only US$0.33 billion, an increase of less than 14 per cent, and at the same time the manufacturing sector's share of merchandise exports decreased from 30 to 24 per cent (World Bank, 2004). The export performance of the leather and leather products sector was poor. Local producers did not have the capacity to produce competitive leather products and therefore would not have benefited from promotion efforts by the EPC. The EPC failed to address the supply-side constraints that faced local producers of leather and leather products.

Export processing zones

The EPZA established designated export processing zones in Nairobi (two, both privately owned), Mombassa and Athi River (publicly owned) (Gerrishon et al., 2004). The law under which the zones were established required developers to install common effluent treatment plants (CEPTs) before a licence to operate was granted. They therefore had the potential to encourage the sharing of CT knowledge and the increased adoption of EST, in particular PATs. At the time of this study there were no tanneries in these zones. Textile manufacturers, who assembled garments for the US market under the African Growth and Opportunity Act, occupied the majority of the facilities (EPZA, 2003).

Global comparison

The limited effect of Kenya's industrial policies during the period under study was reflected in the deterioration in the performance of the manufacturing sector as measured on the CIP index. Kenya had ranked sixty-sixth among 93 countries on the CIP index in both 1980 and 1990 and fell to seventy-ninth in 2000, placing it in all three years among the countries with a low industrial performance. Among developing countries, it dropped from forty-first to fifty-fourth out of 68 countries between 1990 and 2000, and in 2000 ranked last among the eight countries included in this study.

Trade Policy

Before the introduction of structural adjustment policies in the early 1980s Kenya's import regime was highly restrictive, with high tariffs and a cumbersome and discretionary licensing mechanism (Wignaraja and Ikiara, 1999). Import liberalization started modestly in the mid-1980s when import bans were replaced by tariffs and two broad categories of imports were established, unrestricted licensing items and quota-restricted items. A few years later tariffs were reduced and more items became unrestricted. Under donor pressure for more rapid and substantial economic reform, the Kenyan authorities accelerated economic liberalization between 1992 and 1995, and import tariffs were significantly reduced. As a result of becoming a member of the World Trade Organization (WTO) in 1995 the country took further measures, which included a progressive dismantling of quantitative restrictions, a rationalization of the tariff structure, and a lowering of the average tariff rate. Import duties in Kenya, as of 2002, ranged from 0 to 35 per cent (EAC, 2004).

The cumulative reduction of import restrictions on manufactured goods is most clearly, but only partially, reflected in the change in the TMP. The TMP in Kenya stood at 19.6 per cent in 2001, down from 31.9 per cent in 1994. Kenya's TMP was thus slightly less than that of Zimbabwe, the other country in this study where the leather processing sub-sector is examined, which was 20.9 per cent, but Zimbabwe made a significantly larger reduction during the 1990s. Kenya ranked forty-eighth among 53 countries in 2002, relatively high for a developing country; in 1990 it had ranked fortieth out of 48 countries. Among developing countries it fell from twenty-ninth out of 37 in 1990 to thirty-sixth out of 41 in 2002. It had the fifth highest TMP among the eight countries included in this study in 2002, down three places from second in 1990.

Indeed, the restrictiveness of the import regime lay between modest and reasonable, as indicated by Kenya's ranking on the more comprehensive TRI. Kenya received a medium high score (6 out of 10) on the TRI as of 2004, based on all its restrictions. It ranked fifty-ninth among 66 countries, which indicates that the combined impact of all tariff barriers was a partial limitation to technology import, and it had the fourth lowest score among the eight countries included in this study.

The relatively small increase of approximately 50 per cent in the import of manufactured goods from US$1.4 billion in 1990 to US$2.1 billion in 2002 was partially attributable to the generally restrictive tariff and non-tariff regime. Similarly the import of capital goods, one sub-category of manufactured goods, only increased from US$0.9 billion to US$1.0 billion during the same period. As a result, the share of capital goods as a percentage of imported manufactured goods decreased from 60 to 46 per cent (World Bank, 2005).

Leather processing sub-sector

Tariffs in the leather processing sub-sector changed considerably over the period of this study (World Bank, 2005). There were no non-tariff barriers for the sub-sector other than the WTO-mandated ones relating to the import and export of animals and animal products. The steep decline in tariffs on equipment and chemicals used in the leather industry however did not stimulate additional imports because of the difficult economic situation of the leather sub-sector. In fact the import of hide preparation equipment declined from approximately US$1.1 million in 1990 to US$0.008 million in 2002, and the import of chemicals for dyeing declined from roughly US$2.6 million in 1990 to US$0.7 million in 2002. The drop in tariffs for finished leather is seen as the main reason behind the precarious situation of tanneries. Indeed, as discussed later, leather processing in the country declined significantly as a result of a fall in domestic demand for locally produced finished leather.

In summary, the process of import liberalization was slow in Kenya. Donor pressure and WTO membership eventually resulted in a dedicated move towards greater trade liberalization. In comparison with other developing countries, and using the TMP and TRI as a guide, Kenya's import regime can be seen as still rather restricted at the end of this period. Nevertheless, greater import competition has certainly made an impact on the country's manufacturing sector. As Wignaraja and Ikiara (1999) note, the effects for certain sub-sectors were devastating and the technological responses of firms were generally inadequate. This is underscored by the import of industrial machinery and equipment, which declined in value by 30 per cent. Leather processing, in fact the leather goods sector in general, was seriously hit. Import data for chemicals and equipment illustrate that the technological response was lacklustre. It is thus not surprising that Kenya ranked low on the TI index. It ranked sixty-fourth among 87 countries in 1990 and even lower in 2001, seventy-fourth among 91 countries, which placed it among the group of countries with low technology import. In 1990 it ranked forty-first among 64 developing countries and in 2001 it was thirty-ninth out of 55. Finally, it ranked sixth among the eight countries included in this study in 1990 and declined further to seventh place in 2001.

Resource Pricing Policy

As with all countries reviewed in this study, it was not possible to obtain sufficient information to provide a comprehensive overview of resource pricing policies for energy or water, including the use of subsidies, nor to calculate the average change in resource prices over the period 1990 to 2002. This section therefore provides only limited information on resource pricing policies, prices *per se* and resource use in response to price changes. Higher resource prices, as described in Chapter 3, are often incentives for adopting EST, particularly CTs.

The average cost of electricity rose steeply during the 1990s due to an increase in overheads as a result of the liberalization of the power sector and the splitting of power generation and distribution into two separate companies. Purchases of power from independent power producers and increases in fuel costs contributed further to the escalation of the cost of electricity. Costing for electricity use was on a cost recovery basis as the full direct costs of production and distribution were usually passed on to the consumers. For example, when the exchange rate and/or price of fuel went beyond their level at the time a tariff was established, the full cost of the increase was passed on to consumers. If, however, these costs decreased, then consumers were given full rebates on their bills. None the less, there was no indication that power companies were required to meet the indirect environmental costs relating to their activities and it is therefore unlikely that these costs were included in the prices that consumers paid.

From 1990 energy consumption (defined as energy derived from oil, coal, natural gas, nuclear power, renewable sources and electricity) by the manufacturing sector increased by 17 per cent, as shown in Table 7.2, significantly less than the 23 per cent increase in MVA. As a result energy-use intensity decreased by 5 per cent, from 1610 toe per million US dollars to 1520 toe. The manufacturing sector accounted for 11 per cent of the energy consumption in both 1990 and 2002 (IEA, 2005).

Energy consumption by the leather sub-sector was estimated to have decreased by 38 per cent from 5.2 ktoe in 1990 to 3.2 ktoe in 2002.[2] Energy-use intensity declined much less, by only 5 per cent, from 1610 toe per million US dollars of MVA in 1990 to 1520 toe in 2002 because the decline in value added was much greater than the decline in energy consumption. The leather sector accounted for 0.5 per cent of total energy consumption by industry in 1990 and 0.25 per cent in 2002.

Regarding water management, the pricing of water was greatly influenced by the fact that the water services were publicly managed until 2002 when the applicable law was revised to require local authorities to allow water companies to manage the provision of water to consumers. To the extent that public resources underwrote the production and distribution of water, there was no inbuilt pressure to recover the full cost from the consumer. A 1990 report found that the local authorities did not have pricing systems that would promote efficient use of water (Price Waterhouse Associates, 1990). It was then recommended that (a) minimum charges should be fixed at a level that covered the fixed costs of providing water and sewerage service to consumers and (b) each council should undertake regular reviews of tariffs, including costs analysis of current and future performance.

The government accepted these recommendations and required the local authorities to implement them from 1993. Consequently the guidelines issued in 1993 by the Water and Sanitation Operations Unit of the Ministry of Local Government provided that 'the charges by councils should ensure that the pricing of the utility and services reflect the real cost of operations, maintenance and the long term replacement of the capital investment'. The water rates, which the councils were charging thereafter, were expected to reflect these costs. None the less, although the necessary legal basis existed for proper pricing for water services between 1993 and 2002, the extent to which the councils' water rates reflected the real cost of production and distribution could not be determined.

The most common pricing policy for water consumption in Kenya was graduated billing whereby larger consumers of water paid more than smaller ones. In addition to paying for water supplied by the councils, firms using freshwater had to acquire a temporary permit for five to ten years, costing between 2800 and 40 000 KES. This policy was not conducive to a more rational use of water because the cost was not based on the amount of water used.

This situation was expected to change in 2003 with the New Water Act, which privatized water management and changed the permit system to levy fees based on the amount of water used. This was indeed a significant shift from previous policies where water was a free resource; moreover, pricing water would reduce waste, vital in Kenya since it had the highest water deficit in East Africa (Otieno, 2003).

Over the period of this study, water use in the manufacturing sector increased slightly more than the increase in MVA, as did water-use intensity (Table 7.2). All of the business associations interviewed were of the opinion that the increasing cost of water, as well as of energy, had an impact on operational practices and improvements in technology in the tanning sub-sector, largely in terms of energy conservation and the recycling of water.

Global comparison

There was no global assessment that could be drawn upon to compare the relative effectiveness of Kenya's resource pricing; nor could a country study be found, other than that of 1990, that compared current prices for these resources to the actual cost of their production. As an alternative, an EUI index for the manufacturing sector was calculated for use in this study. In the case of Kenya, energy-use intensity increased slightly during the 1990s, from 1610 toe per million US dollars of MVA in 1990 to 1520 toe in 2002. Still its global ranking dropped from seventy-ninth out of 93 countries in 1990 to eighty-sixth in 2002. Among 65 developing countries it declined from fifty-second in 1990 to fifty-ninth in 2002. Among the eight countries included in this study, it dropped from sixth in 1990 to last in 2002.

TECHNOLOGY POLICY

The National Council for Science and Technology was charged with the task of developing technology policies and approving research activities. It served as the catalyst for the creation of a conducive national policy environment for the acquisition, adoption and/or adaptation and transfer of technology into the country. However, since its role was largely facilitative, the impact of the Council in technological development was minimal.

The Kenyan Industrial Research and Development Institute and the Kenyan Bureau of Standards were the two major organizations that constituted Kenya's technological support infrastructure for the manufacturing sector. Both organizations were governmental bodies under the Ministry of Trade and Industry. The Institute offered technology advisory services and hosted a quality control laboratory; it also addressed the needs of industry for improved technologies and technically trained employees. It was concerned with the development of better linkages between the public and private sectors and the way they marketed their services. It was, however, underfunded for most of the period under review and consequently was not able to offer its services at levels that would have enabled many local manufacturers to upgrade their technologies. The Bureau formulated national standards and technological regulations. It was in charge of performing inspections and certification on quality standards to ensure that individual products met minimum requirements, and issued the 'Diamond Mark of Quality' seal, which was a legal requirement for products made in the country. It also inspected imported goods to ensure they met ISO quality standards.

The Kenya Industrial Property Office was founded in 1989 in Nairobi. It was a governmental department in the Ministry of Research, Technical Training and Technology. It was charged with the task of studying applications for industrial property rights as well as technology transfer agreements, patents and trademarks, and sought to promote technology innovation in the country.

Another organization concerned with technological improvement in Kenya was the Engineering Development Services Centre, which was established as a joint initiative by the government of Kenya and UNIDO. It offered services for the design, manufacture and repair of industrial tools, equipment and components.

Universities carried out R&D activities focused on adopting and adapting foreign technologies for local use, particularly for SMEs and micro-enterprises. Recent encouragement had been given to research on the use of natural resources so as both to make better use of these resources and alleviate the shortage of foreign exchange for the import of raw materials.

Due to the lack of sufficient resources to support the technological infrastructure described above, Kenya relied to a great extent on imported technology, especially for the manufacturing sector. As a result of financial difficulties in many sectors, most of the technology and equipment was acquired second-hand and adapted to the needs of the specific plant where it was to be operated. There were, however, some engineering centres, based mainly in Nairobi, such as the Numerical Machines Complex, that had the capacity to manufacture and repair some technological equipment.

The leather processing sub-sector relied entirely on process technologies developed in Europe. The survey team found that, as of 2002, there were no local technology developers associated with the sub-sector and that the links between local developers and tanneries were indeed very weak. There were, though, freelance manufacturers of good-quality drums, and some companies used these locally made drums. The links between local developers and tanneries were in need of enhancement, as well as more support for such developers in terms of training and engineering facilities. Overseas sourcing for technology was often very expensive for local tanneries, hence the tendency to source second-hand reconditioned machines and equipment, costing less and typically arranged by external stakeholders. For instance, the Sagana Tannery was helped by UNIDO in the purchase of machinery from an old tannery in the Netherlands.

Global Comparison

In summary, the scientific and technological infrastructure appeared, as of the time of the survey, to be incomplete and inefficient. The country had a record of limited policy implementation for the previous decades that had resulted in setbacks and distortions. Although policies were formulated, the government's limitations in putting them into practice were a major obstacle to the proper development of technological capabilities. However, in the previous few years some organizations had started to become more capable providers of services.

Given the overall economic situation and the weakness of the technological infrastructure in the 1990s, it is not surprising that Kenya ranked relatively low on the TC index. It was one hundred and fourteenth out of 162 countries in 1990 and declined slightly to one hundred and sixteenth in 2000. Similarly, among developing countries it moved from sixty-seventh out of 115 countries in 1990 to sixty-eighth out of 114 in 2000, which placed it in both years in the group of marginalized countries. Among the countries included in this study, it dropped from sixth in 1990 to eighth in 2000.

LEATHER PROCESSING SUB-SECTOR

Economic Overview

The production of raw hides and skins in Kenya was approximately the same from 1990 to 2000, 31 000 tons (Table 7.3). The production of semi-finished and finished leather decreased significantly between 1990 and 2000, declining by 38 per cent over the period. The country's production of raw hides and skins accounted for 0.5 per cent of global production in 2000, and its semi-finished and finished leather accounted for 0.8 per cent, making it the thirty-first largest producer of raw hides and skins among 158 countries and the thirty-sixth largest producer of semi-finished and finished leather among 116 countries (FAO, 2004).

The performance of the leather sector gradually deteriorated from 1995, a phenomenon observed in the entire production chain, from the production of raw materials and the processing of leather to shortcomings in footwear and other leather products and poor marketing. Between 1995 and 1999 the sector exhibited an extremely low utilization capacity, estimated at 20 per cent of its potential, with only 12 active tanneries. This situation contrasts with the previous 1990–95 period when 16 tanneries were operating at 80 per cent of their capacity (Ministry of Trade and Industry, 2001).

Table 7.3   Production, import and export of raw hides and skins and semi-finished and finished leather

Year	Raw hides and skins (thousand tons)[1]			Raw hides and skins (US$ million)[2]	
	Production	Import	Export	Import	Export
1990	31.1	0.2	0.9	7.4	0.9
1995	30.8	0.3	1.2	0.6	6.1
2000	31.0	0.3	9.8	0.01	6.5

Year	Semi-finished and finished leather from bovine, sheep and goats (ft^2 million)[1]			Semi-finished and finished leather from bovine, sheep and goats (US$ million)[2]	
	Production	Import	Export	Import	Export
1990	100.3	0	82.5	0.002	20.6
1995	74.8	0	24.5	0.007	18.4
2000	61.7	0	22.0	0.09	6.37

Sources: 1. FAO (2004); 2. World Bank (2005).

The main reason for this steep decline was the fall in the demand for finished leather in the local market caused by the liberalization of the economy. Liberalization led to an increase in import of second-hand footwear and other leather products, as well as the export of raw hides and skins. Whereas 95 per cent of the hides and skins produced between 1990 and 1995 were processed as value added product, only 15 per cent of production was processed in the following period, and 85 per cent was exported in raw form. This was mainly due to lower duties on the exported hides and skins, but domestic problems in acquiring tanning chemicals and other technologies also contributed to the decline in production of finished leather for export.

The export statistics reflect the declining trend in leather processing. On the one hand, the export of hides and skins was only 900 tons with a value of US$0.9 million in 1990 but increased to 9800 tons with a value of US$6.5 million in 2000. On the other hand, the export of finished and semi-finished leather declined from 82.5 million square feet with a value of US$20.6 million in 1990 to 22 million square feet with a value of slightly under US$6.4 million in 2000. As of 2000, Kenya was the seventy-first largest exporter of finished leather in terms of value in US dollars. Its two largest export markets were Italy and the Netherlands (World Bank, 2005).

Overall, the leather processing sub-sector (ISIC 3231) did not make a significant contribution to Kenyan MVA in the 1990s. Its share of MVA in 1990 was 0.47 per cent and even less in 2000, 0.26 per cent. The value added of the sub-sector actually declined from US$3.2 million in 1990 to US$2.1 million in 2002. In 2000 the sub-sector employed about 1700 workers, about 0.8 per cent of the workforce in manufacturing (UNIDO, 2005).

Sub-sector Profile

The leather processing sub-sector in Kenya consisted, as of 2002, of 19 small- to large-scale tanneries, ranging from semi- to fully mechanized, some of them using modern technologies, and with a total capital investment of about US$50 million. However, it is important to keep in mind that out of 19 tanneries only 16 were operational from 1990 to 1995 and then only 12 from 1995 to 1999, nine of which were investigated for this study.

The tanneries were set up between 1940 and 1991 and were still operating in 2002 with the second-hand equipment purchased from Italy, Holland and Spain. The average employment per tannery, across all the tanneries, was 70 employees, mostly local staff except for one tannery, which had an international expert working there for more than 30 years.

Most tanneries had installed at least wet-blue (i.e. semi-finishing) leather processing technology. In addition, six tanneries had installed crust leather and finished-stage leather technology. Indeed, of all hides produced in Kenya, 60 per cent was processed to the wet-blue stage while crust and finished leather accounted for 25 and 15 per cent respectively. In the case of skins, 90 per cent were processed to wet-blue, 6 per cent to crust and only 4 per cent to finished leather.

Of the 12 tanneries, nine were selected for this study based on criteria that called for variations in production process, size, location and raw material input. The selected tanneries corresponded to the criteria as follows: five had only wet-blue processing technology and the other four had, in addition, finishing technology; six were large-scale and three were small-scale operations; and one produced only finished leather, five produced hides and skins and semi-finished leather, and three produced finished leather, semi-finished leather and hides and skins (Table 7.4).

Other characteristics of the mills worth noting are: all were under private domestic ownership; all produced only for the domestic market; six were ISO 9001/9002 certified and one was ISO 14001 certified; and four had integrated R&D departments, engaged mainly in quality control and in the installation and adaptation of new technology.

Process Technology and CT Characterization

The survey team reported that the tanneries used a wide range of production equipment, in many cases second-hand equipment, coming mainly from

Table 7.4 Profile of the nine tanneries investigated

Tannery	Process and product type	Scale	Location	Sales orientation (in 2000)	Technology vintage	Ownership	EST score	Regulatory compliance	Donor assist.	EMS
K1	Hides and skins, SF	Large	Kitale	50% D, 50% E	Standard –modern	100% private domestic	PAT	Yes	No	No
K2	Hides and skins, SF	Large	Sagana	10% D, 90% E	Standard –modern	100% private domestic	PAT + MTC	Yes	Yes	No
K3	Sheep and goat hides and skins, SF	Large	Nakuru	60% D, 40% E	Standard –modern	100% private domestic	PAT + LTC	No (has been penalized)	Yes	No
K4	Hides and skins, SF, F kips and linings	Small	Embu	50% D, 50% E	Standard –modern	100% private domestic	PAT + MTC	Yes	Yes	No
K5	Hides and skins, SF and F	Large	Thika	15% D, 85% E	Standard –modern	100% private domestic	PAT + MTC	Yes	Yes	Own EMS
K6	F (upper/ sole), leather shoes	Large	Limuru	80% D, 20% E	BAT	100% private foreign	PAT + HTC	Yes	Yes	Own EMS
K7	Hides and skins, SF, F	Large	Thika	15% D, 85% E	Standard –modern	100% private domestic	PAT + HTC	Yes	Yes	No

| K8 | Hides and skins, SF, kips | Small | Nairobi | 50% D, 50% E | Standard –modern | 100% private domestic | PAT + HTC | Yes | No | No |
| K9 | Hides and skins, SF, vegetable tanning; small leather | Small | Nairobi | 5% D, 95% E | Standard –modern | 100% private domestic | PAT | Yes | No | Own EMS |

Abbreviations: semi-finished (SF); finished (F); domestic (D); export (E); best available technology (BAT); pollution abatement technology (PAT); higher order technological complexity (HTC); medium order technological complexity (MTC); lower order technological complexity (LTC).

Source: KNCPC (2002).

Europe. Often the equipment had been upgraded with international aid and assistance. As part of the investigation the survey team was requested to assign the plants to one of four categories based on the overall technological vintage of their production processes. In the case of Kenya the team classified eight tanneries as using standard–modern technology and one tannery, a multinational, as using best available technology (BAT) (Table 7.4).

The survey team also classified the nine tanneries based on the highest level of complexity of CTs being used into four groups (none, low, medium and high). Three tanneries used CTs of a higher order of complexity, three used CTs of a medium order of complexity and one used CTs of a lower order of complexity. Two tanneries were reported to be using no CTs.

Some of the firms had implemented technically advanced CT measures (Table 7.5). Four had the capacity to import new machines and equipment and had implemented more CT options than the other five. They had also undertaken massive retrofitting of their processes, making them more efficient in raw material utilization. CT implementation at one tannery is described in Box 7.1.

PAT Characterization

All six of the tanneries that directly discharged into water bodies had effluent treatment plants (ETPs), the management of which differed from company to company, with some performing very well, whereas others per-

Table 7.5   CTs used in the nine tanneries

Process area	Option	Number of tanneries using practice/ equipment
Soaking	Green hide fleshing	9
Liming	Hair save un-hairing	2
Deliming, bating	Carbon dioxide deliming	2
Tanning	Recycling of chrome floats	1
	Tanning products and methods that improve exhaustion rate	4
	Wet-white production to reduce chrome	2
	Other material tanning (e.g. vegetable)	4
Wet finishing	Post-tanning products and methods to improve exhaustion rates	5
Finishing	Reduction in solvent based products	4

Source: KNCPC (2002).

BOX 7.1   CLEANER PRODUCTION CASE STUDY: KENYA

KNCPC undertook a CP audit at a tannery that processes hides and skins to semi-finished leather in 1999. The audit showed that the tannery was using excessive amounts of water and chemicals that were consequently discharged with no attempt to recycle or reuse them. The audit team identified 30 CT options that could be implemented in the liming and de-hairing stages of production. Following the audit, the tannery implemented ten options that reduced chemical and water consumption and saved US$40 000 per year.

Source: KNCPC (2002).

---

formed below average. These six tanneries used different secondary treatment technologies to comply with environmental norms, four used aerated lagoons and two used activated sludge. Two of these had well-managed ETPs, involving separate treatment of the chrome waste from the lime waste. The other three tanneries, which discharged into sewers, had the equivalent of an ETP because they pre-treated their wastewater, which was then discharged into CETPs operated by municipalities.

Environmental Performance

Pollutant releases from the six tanneries that directly discharged into watercourses were governed by NEMA discharge standards, and pollutant releases from the three tanneries discharging into sewers were governed by municipal by-laws. The NEMA does not collect or publish data on pollutant discharge by industry. The only available data on compliance with discharge standards by tanneries were those collected during the survey. Eight of the nine tanneries were reported to be in compliance with the discharge standards (Table 7.4). Interestingly enough, those discharging into sewerage systems were reported to be performing well. This can be attributed to pressure from the municipal authorities. In addition, most tanneries were keeping up-to-date environmental monitoring records.

KEY INFORMANTS AND INTERNATIONAL DONORS

Four groups, in addition to government environmental regulatory agencies and technology centres, are in a position to influence the extent to which plants adopt ESTs: NGOs, business associations, international donors of technical asssistance, and chemical and equipment suppliers. Some information about the first three is presented in this section; there is insufficient information to chartacterize the firms that supplied chemicals and equipment to Kenya's leather processing sub-sector.

NGOs

The level of environmental pressure being exerted on Kenyan industry from civil society at the time of this study was modest but increasing. This can be attributed to the newly enacted EMCA in 1999, which entitled every Kenyan to a clean and healthy environment and also empowered them to safeguard and enhance the quality of their environment. As the awareness of the provisions of the EMCA continued to grow, more and more civil society groups could be expected to put pressure on companies to comply with environmental norms.

Most pollution-related problems were brought to the fore by the media. When this happened with Kamiti Tanners, the relevant government authorities took measures that led to its closure. In Nakuru a civil society group initiated a pollutant release and transfer register as a way of pressuring local companies, including Nakuru Tanners, to adopt responsible environmental behaviour. As a result, an inventory of all the toxic industrial wastes was prepared and passed on to the community. On the basis of their increased knowledge of the dangers, the community pressured local companies to improve their environmental performance. The campaign was a success and eventually all industrial establishments in Nakuru were exercising more responsible environmental stewardship than their counterparts in other Kenyan cities.

The survey team interviewed one NGO, the World Wide Fund for Nature, which was established in Kenya in 1988 with support from the international World Wide Fund for Nature. The Fund works with municipal authorities concerned with occupational health and safety to bring about compliance with environmental laws. It has requested the government to set up environmental committees in various governmental departments.

Business Associations

The survey team interviewed four business associations representing the interests of industry on environmental matters:

- The Kenya National Chamber of Commerce and Industry, the paramount business association in Kenya, was founded in 1965 with the aim of dealing with trade issues, both restricting imports and expanding exports as appropriate, and supporting members' participation in local and international trade fairs.

- The Kenya Association of Manufacturers, an association exclusively for manufacturers, was founded in 1959. It lobbies the government to grant special tax and tariff concessions to manufacturers and provides technical advice and training courses for members.
- The Federation of Kenyan Employers, an ILO-sponsored organization founded in 1959, aims to develop good relationships between employers and employees as well as to improve workplace health and safety conditions. It provides management consultancy services, particularly on ISO 9000 and ISO 14000.
- The Kenyan Tanners' Association, founded in the early 1960s, represents the interests of leather tanners to the government. The association has remained largely dormant after the performance of the sub-sector was weakened by the massive importation of second-hand leather products.

International Donors

Kenya lost out on donor funding as a result of its poor record of tackling government corruption in the 1990s, unlike neighbouring countries, Tanzania and Uganda, both recipients of substantial bilateral and multilateral donor funding (EIU, 2003).

Environmental assistance to the Kenyan leather processing sub-sector at the time of this study essentially came from UNIDO. As part of its comprehensive regional leather programme in Eastern and Southern Africa (which also included Zimbabwe), UNIDO has provided pollution control assistance to a number of tanneries since 1988. The programme, which offered tanneries technical assistance in sourcing and installing hardware and a conducive financial mechanism (interest-free loans from a revolving fund) led to the establishment or upgrading of many effluent treatment facilities. In some cases PAT and CT options were combined to reduce waste to desirable levels, as was the case with Nakuru Tanners. For example, this tannery was assisted in acquiring and using a hair-separation unit to replace the antiquated hair-burn process in the liming operation.

The promotion of CTs gained momentum in the late 1990s, largely due to the encouraging results of prior CT trial projects. UNIDO developed a regional demonstration project for members of the Eastern and Southern Africa Leather Industry Association, aimed at facilitating the adoption of a number of CTs, such as high-exhaustion chrome tanning, low-sulphide de-hairing, compact retanning, carbon dioxide deliming and wet-white processing. In Kenya the project involved two tanneries, giving a series of workshops and seminars that ensured the exchange of experience and dissemination of information to a wider population.

In 2000 UNIDO secured donor funding for KNCPC, whose purpose was to introduce and promote the concept of CP in Kenya's industrial sector, with a particular focus on SMEs. With regard to the leather sector, the KNCPC, together with the Leather Development Centre, provided technical services (including environmental audits) and undertook training and awareness-raising activities.

SUMMARY

Kenya's aggregate economic performance indicators suggest an overall poor performance for the economy as a whole and for the manufacturing sector, whereas its aggregate environmental performance indicators show an encouraging trend. Both GDP and MVA growth were low between 1990 and 2002: GDP increased by only 21 per cent and MVA only slightly more, by 23 per cent. As a result, the share of MVA in GDP increased slightly, from 11.8 to 13.0 per cent. GNI per capita at PPP increased by only a modest 15 per cent. However, even with a 17 per cent increase in energy use, energy-use intensity decreased by 5 per cent between 1990 and 2002. Although BOD effluent increased by 24 per cent, the same as the percentage increase in MVA, BOD-effluent intensity increased by only 2 per cent.

Kenya lagged behind most countries in the 1990s when it came to sound environmental policy and implementation. Mismanagement coupled with the lack of adequate legislation from the time of the country's independence until the late 1990s contributed to the deficiency in the implementation of established environmental standards. Kenya's priorities of dealing with poverty reduction and economic growth further contributed to these deficiencies.

The combined impact of three economic policies, industrial, trade and resource pricing, on technological modernization and EST adoption in particular appears to have been very limited mainly due to the overall economic instability and the country's limited resource capacity. Clearly, industrial policies, particularly the three policy instruments described – FDI, export promotion and export processing zones – did not have a substantial effect on reversing the decline in the competitiveness of the economy or on technological investments in manufacturing processes. The effects of trade policy for certain sub-sectors were devastating and the technological responses of firms were generally inadequate. Finally, rapidly rising utility costs appear to have induced some conservation efforts, albeit mostly of a lower order of technological complexity. While the encouragingly limited increase of energy and water use was probably a reflection of this, the small decrease in energy-use intensity suggests the need for greater technological efforts at firm level.

Kenya's technology policy and infrastructure changed little with the shift towards a market-oriented economy, because of the weakness of the government's implementation efforts. Technology was mainly second-hand and obsolete, and required constant repairs. International donor institutions still played an important role in implementing technology policies. Nevertheless, implementation of the policies was not very effective and was undermined by factors such as corruption.

Kenya's leather processing sub-sector experienced serious hardships over the period of this study. As a result, the production levels of semi-finished and finished leather declined significantly from 100.3 to 61.7 million square feet, tanneries closed down and capacity utilization levels generally dropped. As of 2002 there were 12 operational tanneries in the sub-sector. The survey team investigated nine of these and found that most used standard–modern production technology but that there was considerable variation in the use of CTs. Three tanneries used CTs of a higher order of complexity, three used CTs of a medium order of complexity, one used CTs of a lower order of complexity and two tanneries were reported to use no CTs. All tanneries had invested in PATs, six operating their own ETPs and three pre-treating their wastewater before discharge into municipal sewers. Consequently eight of the nine tanneries were reported to be in compliance with the environmental standards.

Other institutional actors, NGOs, business associations and international donors, played a role in encouraging the adoption of EST, with international donors playing a more significant role than the other two parties. Among donors, UNIDO was active in supporting numerous efforts to improve industrial environmental performance with PAT demonstration projects at tanneries and with advice on CTs as part of its leather sub-sector and NCPC programmes. While environmental NGOs had only a modest effect on improving industrial environmental performance, community organizations in combination with media pressure had notable positive impacts. Business associations, however, were noticeably inactive in assisting their members in improving their environmental performance.

To conclude, the leather processing sub-sector encountered serious economic problems in the period 1990 to 2002. As a result, value added from the sub-sector declined by 34 per cent and its small contribution to MVA became even smaller, declining from 0.46 to 0.26 per cent. However, in spite of the economic difficulties, the environmental performance of the sub-sector improved in the period of the study.

NOTES

1. The FDI for 1990 has been taken as the three-year average of 1989–91 and for 2002 as the three-year average of 2001–3, in order to even out fluctuations in FDI flows.
2. The IEA does not provide exclusive energy consumption data for the leather sub-sector; it was therefore calculated according to the proportion of MVA of the textile and the leather sub-sectors, for which the IEA provides information as one sub-sector.

REFERENCES

EAC (2004), 'East African Community Common External Tariff', Arusha, Tanzania: East African Community.

EIU (2003), *Country Profile: Kenya*, London: Economist Intelligence Unit.

EPZA (2003), 'Export Processing Zones Authority Annual Report 2003', Export Zone Processing Authority (EPZA) (available on: http://www.epzakenya.com).

FAO (2004), 'World Statistical Compendium for Raw Hides and Skins, Leather and Leather Footwear, 1984–2002', Rome: Food and Agriculture Organization of the United Nations (available on: http://www.fao.org).

FAO (2005), 'AQUASTAT: FAO STAT', Rome: Food and Agriculture Organization of the United Nations (available on: http://www.fao.org).

Frijns, J. and J. Van Vliet (1999), 'Small-scale industry and cleaner production strategies', *World Development*, **27** (6), 967–83.

Gerrishon, I., J. Olewe-Nyunya and W. Odhiambo (2004), 'Kenya: formulation and implementation of strategic trade and industrial policies', in C. Soludo, O. Ogbu and H. Chang (eds), *The Politics of Trade and Industrial Policy in Africa – Forced Consensus?*, Trenton, NJ: Africa World Press.

Government of Kenya (1986), 'Sessional Paper No. 1 of 1986: Economic Management for Renewable Growth', Nairobi: Government Printer.

Government of Kenya (1994), 'Sessional Paper No. 1 of 1994: Economic Recovery and Sustainable Development to the Year 2010', Nairobi: Government Printer.

Government of Kenya (1996), 'Sessional Paper No. 1 of 1996: Industrial Transformation to the Year 2020', Nairobi: Government Printer.

IEA (2005), 'Online Data Services', IEA Energy Information Centre, Paris: International Energy Agency (available on: http://www.iea.org).

ISO (2003), 'The ISO Survey of ISO 9000 and ISO 14001 Certificates', Geneva: International Organization for Standardization (available on: http://www.iso.org).

KNCPC (2002), 'Assessing the Adoption of EST in Kenya's Leather Tanning Sector', Kenya National Cleaner Production Centre. Report prepared for UNIDO.

Kimuyu, P. (2005), 'Productivity Performance in Kenya: a Contribution to UNIDO's Productivity Performance Project'. Report prepared for UNIDO.

Ministry of Trade and Industry (2001), 'Status Report on the Leather and Leather Products Sub-sector, 2001', Nairobi: Government Printer.

Otieno, J. (2003), 'Tough rule on water harvesting', *Horizon Magazine*, **22**, May (available on: http://www.nationaudio.com).

PriceWaterhouse Associates (1990), 'Financial Management of Municipal Operated Water Supply, Sewerage and Sanitation Service Systems'. Report prepared for the Ministry of Local Government, Nairobi, Kenya.

UNCTAD (2005), 'Investment Policy Review Kenya', February, New York and Geneva: United Nations Conference on Trade and Development.

UNIDO (1996), 'Kenya: Paving the Road to NIC Status', Industrial Development Review Series, Vienna: UNIDO.

UNIDO (2003), 'Africa Foreign Investor Survey, 2003', Vienna: UNIDO.

UNIDO (2005), *International Yearbook of Industrial Statistics 2005*, Cheltenham, UK and Northampton, MA, US: Edward Elgar Publishing.

Wignaraja, G. and G. Ikiara (1999), 'Adjustment, technological capabilities, and enterprise dynamics in Kenya', in S. Lall (ed.), *The Technological Response to Import Liberalization in Sub-Saharan Africa*, London: Macmillan, pp. 57–111.

World Bank (2004), 'World Bank Development Indicators (WDI) 2004', CD-ROM version, Washington, DC: The World Bank.

World Bank (2005), 'World Integrated Trade Solution (WITS)' (available on: http://wits.worldbank.org).

WTO (2000), 'Trade Policy Review Kenya', Geneva: World Trade Organization.

8. Thailand

INTRODUCTION

A survey team from the Thailand Environment Institute (TEI) investigated the specific factors influencing the adoption of environmentally sound technology (EST) in Thailand's textile sub-sector. The team used semi-structured questionnaires provided by UNIDO to interview plant managers at 28 out of 412 plants engaged in dyeing and finishing operations and key informants in one business association, four technology centres, five chemical and equipment suppliers, one environmental NGO and two environmental regulatory agencies. The team also collected background data on the country and the textile sub-sector.

This chapter describes the economic and environmental context in Thailand for EST adoption; relevant environmental, economic and technology policies; the textile sub-sector and the plants investigated; and key informants and international donors.

THE ECONOMIC AND ENVIRONMENTAL CONTEXT FOR EST ADOPTION

The following selected economic and environmental performance indicators define the context in which manufacturing plants made their technology adoption decisions and, in particular, their decisions to adopt EST during the late 1990s/early 2000s.

Economic Performance Indicators

Based traditionally on agricultural exports, Thailand's economy had, over the 25 years up to 2002, been transformed into one of the most diverse economies in South East Asia. Its industrial structure had changed significantly and become primarily export oriented. However, gross domestic product (GDP) growth was not constant. Thailand experienced impressively high rates of real GDP growth between 1987 and 1995, when it grew by 9.1 per cent per year due to market-oriented structural reforms, such as a reduction in barriers to imports and exports and the liberalization of the investment regime, but a slowdown began in 1996 when GDP growth fell to 5.9 per cent and decreased further to a negative 1.4 per cent in 1997 and a negative 10.5 per cent in 1998. Overall the average growth rate was 4.6 per cent between 1990 and 2002.

Between 1990 and 2002 GDP increased by 67 per cent and GDP per capita by 50 per cent, while the population increased by 10 per cent (Table 8.1). At the same time gross national income (GNI) per capita at purchasing power parity (PPP) – a more accurate indicator of well-being than GDP per capita – increased by 93 per cent. Based on the latter, Thailand was classified by the World Bank as a low–middle-income country.

The growth of the manufacturing sector contributed to the very high economic performance from 1990 to 2002; the country's manufacturing value added (MVA) more than doubling in this period. As a result, the share of MVA in GDP increased from 27.2 per cent in 1990 to 33.9 per cent in 2002. The fastest growth was in higher-technology goods, such as computer accessories and motor vehicle parts (EIU, 2002).

The growing economy was supported by a monetary policy that encouraged borrowing by industry. Flexible interest rates were reduced on two

Table 8.1   Economic performance indicators for Thailand

Economic indicator	Year/s	Value	Percentage change
GDP (constant 1995 US$) (billion)	1990	111.0	67.0
	2002	184.8	
GDP per capita (constant 1995 US$)	1990	1997.0	50.0
	2002	3000.0	
Population (millions)	1990	55.8	10.0
	2002	61.6	
GNI per capita at PPP (current international $)	1990	3580.0	93.0
	2002	6890.0	
MVA (constant 1995 US$) (billion)	1990	28.3	119.0
	2002	62.2	
MVA (percentage of GDP)	1990	27.2	6.7
	2002	33.9	
CPI (1995 = 100)	1990	79.1	59.0
	2002	125.6	
Interest rate (commercial lending rate)	1990	14.0	−51.0
	2002	6.9	
Exchange rate (THB/US$)	1990	25.6	73.0
	2002	44.4	

Source: World Bank (2004).

occasions, falling from 14 per cent in 1990 to 6.9 per cent in 2002. However, the monetary stimulus significantly increased interest payment obligations.

Environmental Performance Indicators

During the recession in the second half of the 1990s the country concentrated on improving its economic performance rather than on environmental management. Despite this, some significant improvements were made in industrial environmental management. The only exception was the failure to deal with the increasing amount of hazardous waste generated primarily by the increased production of higher-technology goods (APO, 2002).

Selected environmental indicators, namely, energy use, carbon dioxide (CO_2) emissions, organic matter effluent measured as biochemical oxygen demand (BOD) and water use, as well as the intensity of use of each of these, which provide an insight into the state of industrial environmental performance in Thailand at the time, are presented in Table 8.2. Energy use in the manufacturing sector, measured in tons of oil equivalent (toe), more than doubled between 1990 and 2002, reflecting the significant growth of the manufacturing sector, and energy-use intensity increased by 15 per cent. Associated CO_2 emissions increased by a correspondingly large percentage (204 per cent) and CO_2-emission intensity increased by 39 per cent. Given the significant expansion in MVA, BOD loadings increased by a relatively small 22 per cent, resulting in a decrease of BOD intensity in the manufacturing sector by 41 per cent. Water use in the sector increased by approximately 50 per cent, but water-use intensity decreased by 26 per cent. Not surprisingly, water-use intensity of 37.3 cubic metres per US$ billion of MVA in 2000 was higher than that of Tunisia, the other textile-producing country reviewed in this study, which was 25.0 cubic metres per US$ billion of MVA.

The significant reduction in BOD-loading intensity can partially be attributed to a shift to less polluting manufacturing sub-sectors, the share of pollutant-intensive sub-sectors in MVA declining by 33 per cent during the 1990s. The reduction in BOD pollutant intensity must also be attributed to a change in EST adoption brought about primarily by the construction of common wastewater treatment plants at industrial estates and the development of an effective environmental regulatory programme.

In 1994 the distribution of BOD effluent among manufacturing subsectors was as follows: food and beverages, 42 per cent; textiles, 35 per cent; primary metals, 6 per cent; pulp and paper, 5 per cent; chemicals, 5 per cent; and other, 6 per cent (World Bank, 2004). The BOD effluent from the textile sub-sector was the second highest.

Table 8.2   Environmental performance indicators for Thailand

Source code	Environmental indicator	Year	Value	Percentage change
1	Energy use in the manufacturing sector (million toe)	1990 2002	8.6 21.8	153.0
1 & 2	Energy-use intensity (toe per million US$ of MVA)	1990 2002	304.0 351.0	15.0
1	CO_2 emissions from the manufacturing sector (million tons)	1990 2002	14.3 43.5	204.0
1 & 2	CO_2-emission intensity (tons per million US$ of MVA)	1990 2002	505.0 700.0	39.0
2	BOD effluent from the manufacturing sector (thousand tons)	1990 2000	96.2 117.4	22.0
2	BOD-effluent intensity (tons per million US$ of MVA)	1990 2000	3.4 2.0	−41.0
3	Water use in the manufacturing sector (billion m^3)	1990 2000	1.4 2.1	49.0
2 & 3	Water-use intensity (thousand m^3 per million US$ of MVA)	1990 2000	50.7 37.3	−26.0
4	Percentage of MVA produced by the most pollutant-intensive sub-sectors	1990 2000	30.4 20.3	−10.1
5	Number of ISO 14001 certificates	1997 2002	61.0 671.0	1000.0

Note: Data shown for 2000 on BOD for Thailand are for 1994, the latest year available from World Bank (2004).

Sources: 1. IEA (2005); 2. World Bank (2004); 3. FAO (2005); 4. UNIDO (2005); 5. ISO (2003).

Following the introduction of ISO 14001 in 1996, 671 certificates had been issued as of 2002, relatively high compared to other developing countries. Thailand had a ratio of 10.8 certificates per billion US dollars of MVA, while other countries at the same level of development had lower ratios; for example, Malaysia had 10.5 and Indonesia 3.8. Overall, Thailand ranked first among ASEAN countries and fourth among APEC countries in ISO certificates in 2000 (APO, 2002).

Implications for EST Adoption

During the period investigated by this study the overall economic and environmental conditions in Thailand seemed highly conducive to the adoption of EST by the country's manufacturing sector. The government of this advanced developing country had already compelled its manufacturing sector to invest in EST before 1990, as evidenced by its reasonably low BOD-effluent intensity (3.4 tons of BOD per million US dollars of MVA) in 1990. From 1990 to 2002 the manufacturing sector grew rapidly, with a 6.1 per cent average annual growth rate in MVA. At the same time there may be presumed to have been a decline in the average annual growth rate in investment as a result of the Asian financial crisis that started in 1997.[1] However, the low rate of inflation (the consumer price index (CPI) increased by 59 per cent) and the relatively low and declining interest rate (14 per cent to 6.9 per cent) over this period would have encouraged new investments, some of which would have been in EST. The 119 per cent increase in annual MVA between 1990 and 2002 resulted in a large increase in energy use of 153 per cent and a 15 per cent increase in energy-use intensity, attributable also, to some extent, to the limited investment in energy-efficient technology. However, BOD effluent increased by only a modest 22 per cent and BOD-effluent intensity by 41 per cent, largely explained by a shift in the industrial structure away from the more pollutant-intensive sub-sectors and, to a lesser extent, by the adoption of EST.

ENVIRONMENTAL POLICY

Thailand's recent environmental protection legislation on industrial pollution started with the Factory Act of 1969, amended in 1992, which put in place the basic regulatory framework for controlling air and water pollutants from industry. The Hazardous Waste Act of 1992 expanded the regulatory programme to include hazardous wastes. The National Environmental Quality Enhancement and Conservation Act of 1992 introduced the 'polluter-pays' principle (including emission charges), which created a more effective regulatory regime by instituting penalties for violations.

As well as legislative measures, the government also put forward plans and strategies for protecting the environment. One of the four principal objectives of the Seventh National Development Plan (1992–96) called for pursuing ecologically sound patterns of industrial development. Specifically, the Plan set targets for reducing hazardous wastes, called for meeting environmental quality targets for water pollution, and aimed at increasing the capacity for the treatment and disposal of industrial wastes. It was supplemented by two plans, the Environmental Quality Management Plan (1999–2006) and the Enhancement and Conservation of National Environmental Quality Management Plan (1997–2016). The former established the framework for coordination among the several institutions, and the latter promoted, *inter alia*, a paradigm shift to sustainable development, focusing on CTs. It emphasized the need to upgrade the country's capability in science and industrial technology through increasing efficiency in the adoption and adaptation of more advanced production technology. The Plan also advocated the creation of systems to disseminate information on production technologies (APO, 2002).

The National Environment Board (NEB) was, at the time of this study, the apex organization responsible for implementing environmental legislation in Thailand. It managed the Environment Fund and set ambient environmental standards. Two ministries – the Ministry of Science, Technology and the Environment (MOSTE) and the Ministry of Industry (MOI) – played major roles in industrial environmental management. MOSTE was responsible for carrying out environmental policy planning and implemented NEB's mandate. MOI was responsible for, *inter alia*, monitoring the pollutant reduction efforts of factories and assisting them in solving environmental problems.

These organizations drew on a wide range of environmental policy instruments for industrial environmental management, classified into four categories. These are command and control regulation, economic and fiscal incentives, voluntary programmes and transparency and disclosure.

First, these organizations relied primarily on those instruments associated with the traditional command-and-control approach to environmental management: standard setting, permit issuance, compliance monitoring and enforcement. The Pollution Control Department (PCD) in MOSTE, in consultation with other ministries, prescribed emission and effluent standards for controlling air and water pollutants and solid and hazardous wastes; the Department of Industrial Works in MOI set plant-specific discharge limits, issued annual discharge permits, monitored industrial discharge and carried out inspections of plants outside industrial estates; the Industrial Estate Authority of Thailand (IEAT – see below) operated common effluent treatment plants (CETPs) on industrial estates and required pre- treatment of effluent before it was released into a CETP; and the Office of Environmental Policy and Planning in MOI implemented the Environmental Impact Assessment System, including the review of reports.

The effluent standards issued by the PCD required that industrial effluent measured as BOD should not exceed 20 mg/l, except for some manufacturing sub-sectors, including textiles, which should not exceed 60 mg/l. Industrial effluent measured as COD should not exceed 120 mg/l, except for some manufacturing sub-sectors, again including textiles, where it should not exceed 400 mg/l (PCD, 2004).

Second, Thailand employed a number of economic instruments to reduce pollutant discharge. All industrial estates collected user charges based on the volume and concentration of pollutants in the effluent and for the disposal of solid and hazardous wastes. The Environmental Fund, created in 1992, provided grants to governmental agencies and low-interest loans to both public and private parties for building wastewater treatment plants. In addition, the Board of Investment used tax incentives to encourage high-technology (low-polluting) industries and offered special privileges, such as customs duty exemption for pollution control equipment.

Third, several voluntary programmes with industry participating were under way as of 2002. Perhaps the most extensive was the promotion of cleaner production (CP) as a way to stimulate the use of CTs, which involved several initiatives. The Department of Industrial Works promoted CTs in 12 industrial sub-sectors, including textile dyeing and finishing, and offered CT advice to plants as part of its overall mandate to provide technical assistance. The PCD published 'Pollution Management Policy and Planning' (1997), which set guidelines for establishing prevention systems and action plans, and called for the establishment of criteria and methods for solid waste reduction, promotion of CTs and increased investment in pollution prevention and control. This effort by the government to promote CP was complemented by several donor-funded technical cooperation programmes, described later in this chapter. A second voluntary programme was ISO 14001 certification, administered by the Thai Industrial Standards Institute, the national standards organization under MOI. Of the 670 establishments certified to ISO 14001, 22 were in the textile sub-sector. The third voluntary programme was the Green Label Project of Thailand, launched in October 1993 by the Thailand Business Council for Sustainable Development. This project defined specifications for textile products.

Fourth, transparency and disclosure programmes were not widely used in Thailand. There was not yet a programme on public disclosure along the lines of the programme in Indonesia. However, there were of course environmental performance awards, given by trade associations and the more prestigious industrial associations such as the Federation of Thai Industries.

Global Comparison

In summary, as of 2002 Thailand possessed comprehensive environmental legislation, developed since the 1970s and further expanded in the 1990s. The government relied mainly on command-and-control regulation, which empowered governmental agencies to set and enforce environmental standards and, to a lesser extent, on economic/fiscal incentives as well as on voluntary programmes. It did not make use of more innovative instruments such as transparency/disclosure. It also appears to have effectively inserted

environmental considerations into other policy arenas such as export promotion and industrial location.

Given the comprehensiveness of the industrial environmental management regime, it is not surprising that Thailand ranked reasonably high on
the EG index. It improved its rank from thirty-fourth among 66 countries
in 1990 to thirty-second in 2001, and in 2001 ranked sixteenth among 40
developing countries and second among the countries included in this
study, coming just behind Tunisia.

ECONOMIC POLICY REGIMES

Overviews of Thailand's three economic policy regimes, industrial, trade
and resource pricing, the economic policies that most directly influence
technological modernization in the manufacturing sector and thereby
increase the likelihood of the adoption of EST (see Chapter 3), are presented in this section.

Industrial Policy

From the mid-1960s Thailand experienced a remarkable expansion in industrial production, which accelerated after 1987/88. When the domestic market
reached the limit of its capacity to absorb manufactured goods in the 1970s,
industrial policy shifted to an export orientation with some vestiges of
import substitution. Increased capital investments were accompanied by the
spread of new technologies and increasing product diversification. From the
1980s there was significant industrial expansion in automotive assembly, textiles, electronic goods and electronics. The decline in economic growth in the
mid-1990s was due to financial mismanagement, financially unjustified
excessive credit, declining productivity and a dramatic shortage of skilled
workers (Kraas, 1998).

Thailand's national development plans, two of which were operative in
the 1990s, included an industrial development strategy. The Seventh
National Economic and Social Development Plan (1992–99) shifted the
sole emphasis on export promotion to a more balanced outward orientation by providing similar incentives to manufacturers for exports and the
domestic market (NESDB, 1992). The Plan aimed at sustaining high rates
of industrial output and manufacturing export, improving the efficiency of
industrial production and stimulating competitiveness. It also explicitly
addressed environmental issues, calling for enforcement of environmental
regulations and the use of EST. The Eighth National Economic and Social
Development Plan (1997–2001) was revised significantly in light of the

financial crisis in 1997 (NESDB, 1997). The resulting Economic Restructuring Programme (1998–2002) targeted the financial, social, agricultural and industrial sectors. Strategic objectives for the industrial sector included technology upgrading, increased productivity, worker training, promotion of CTs and a more even distribution of growth within the country.

These major shifts in industrial development policy included changes in four policy instruments: foreign direct investment (FDI), export promotion, capacity expansion restrictions and industrial estate development, all with the potential for stimulating the modernization of technology.

FDI

Thailand, along with its neighbour Malaysia, had always been open to FDI and became even more so with the Investment Promotion Act of 1993. As the government continued to maintain its openness to FDI following the financial crisis, FDI actually remained positive compared to other capital inflows. In 1990, FDI inflows stood at US$2.3 billion and decreased to US$0.8 billion in 2002, a negative change of almost 200 per cent. As a share of GDP, FDI decreased over the same time period from 2.9 to 0.7 per cent (World Bank, 2004).[2] The textile industry (textiles and clothing) accounted for 1.9 per cent of the total in 1995 and 0.7 per cent in 1999 (WTO, 1999).

Export promotion

Government efforts to support exports began in the 1980s along with several other reforms in industrial policy; these efforts included both tax and non-tax incentives. In 1993 the government set up the Export–Import Bank of Thailand, a major provider of export finance, insurance and guarantees. Its capacity for financing and guarantees expanded considerably following the 1997 financial crisis. Overall, Thai manufactured exports increased by 250 per cent, from US$14.6 billion in 1990 to US$51.0 billion in 2002, and the share of manufactured exports in total exports increased from 63 to 74 per cent in the same period (World Bank, 2004).

Capacity expansion restrictions

In 1986 the restrictions on capacity expansion at existing textile mills were abolished, and new textile mills, which had limited investment in more modern (cleaner) production technologies, were established. The import of textile machinery and equipment increased significantly, from US$296 million in 1988 to US$559 million in 1990 and remained at approximately the same level until the financial crisis of 1997. By 2001 it had declined significantly to US$392 million (World Bank, 2005).

Industrial estates
The Thai government set up the Industrial Estate Authority of Thailand (IEAT) in 1972, under the MOI, to support the systematic and orderly development of industry. As of 2002 there were 30 industrial estates located in 13 provinces; nine were fully owned by the IEAT and the other 21 were joint ventures between IEAT and the private sector. All estates operated CETPs and solid and hazardous waste disposal facilities, and provided opportunities for sharing CT knowledge.

Global comparison
Overall, the industrial policies of the 1990s improved the country's competitiveness and at the same time encouraged, explicitly in the case of five-year development plans and implicitly through several industrial policy instruments, the upgrading of technology. The success of Thailand's industrial development policies is reflected in its high and improved ranking on the CIP index. It ranked twenty-third among 93 countries on the CIP index in 2000, placing it among the countries showing medium high industrial performance. More impressive were its changes in ranking over the period from 1980 to 1990; it moved from forty-seventh in 1980 to thirty-second in 1990. Among 68 developing countries it ranked fifth, with only Taiwan Province of China, China, Republic of Korea and Malaysia ranking higher in 2000. It was first among the eight countries included in this study, where it had ranked below Brazil and China in both 1980 and 1990.

Trade Policy

Thailand's trade policies are set forth in the five-year development plans that had evolved over the years. Starting in the mid-1970s, the government switched from an emphasis on protecting industry (an import substitution regime) to encouraging exports, as mentioned in the previous sub-section. In response to rising unit production cost and infrastructure constraints, it moved in the early 1990s towards an outward orientation, which required equalizing incentives between producers for export and those for the domestic market. At the core of this new orientation was a further opening of the economy, which exposed industry to international market forces and which the government maintained and even attempted to expand, despite the financial turmoil following 1997.

Thailand's trade policy was pursued in the context of several bilateral, regional and multilateral trade agreements. It was one of the founding members of the World Trade Organization in 1994. It participated in several regional arrangements, principally the Association of South East Asian Nations (ASEAN), as one of the founding members in 1967, and the

Asia Pacific Economic Cooperation programme. Under the ASEAN Free Trade Agreement, initiated in 1993, it reduced tariffs in order to expand regional trade and to attract FDI. In 1998 an ASEAN extension, introduced to promote joint manufacturing activities and provide tariff preferences on inputs sourced in the region, was established. In addition Thailand participated in 34 bilateral trade agreements (WTO, 1999).

The pursuit of an outward orientation resulted in lowering and sometimes even eliminating tariffs or quantitative restrictions on the import of capital equipment and raw materials. Investments in projects that were primarily for export production or that were located in specified industrial zones were entitled to duty-free import of machinery and raw and essential materials, as were those for the development of rural areas even if production was for the domestic market. Moreover, relatively high duties on imported pigments and chemicals, essential for dyeing and finishing and not produced locally, decreased steadily in the latter half of the 1990s.

The cumulative reduction of import restrictions on manufactured goods caused by numerous trade-related agreements was most clearly but only partially reflected by the change in the TMP. Overall Thailand reduced its TMP from 39.0 per cent in 1989 to 14.6 per cent in 2001, which would surely have lowered the barrier to import more advanced and therefore CTs, and its ranking improved from forty-first among 48 countries in about 1990 to thirty-seven among 53 countries in about 2002. It had the lowest TMP among the eight countries included in this study (World Bank, 2004).

Indeed, the import regime was only modestly restrictive, as indicated by its ranking on the more comprehensive TRI. Thailand received a medium high score (5 out of 10) as of 2004, based on the cumulative effect of all restrictions; it ranked fifty-fifth among 66 countries and had the third lowest score among the eight countries included in this study.

To some extent the relatively unrestrictive tariff regime contributed to the increase in the import of manufactured products from US\$25.5 billion in 1990 to US\$48.0 billion in 2002, an increase of 88 per cent. Similarly the import of capital goods, one sub-category of manufactured goods, increased from US\$13.4 billion in 1990 to US\$28.1 billion in 2002, an increase of 109 per cent. As a result of this large increase, the share of capital goods as a percentage of imported manufactured goods increased from 53 to 58 per cent over this period (World Bank, 2005).

The textile sub-sector
In line with the overall reduction in tariff levels there were significant tariff reductions in the textile sub-sector. A very high tariff on textile fabric of 48.1 percent in 1990 was reduced to 18.1 per cent in 2001, a much lower rate

than the 33.1 per cent of Tunisia, the other textile-producing country included in this study (World Bank, 2005). The reduction was clearly an added incentive to import textile fabric for garment production and resulted in an increase in textile fabric from US$0.9 billon in 1990 to US$1.5 billion in 2001. Thailand also virtually did away with the tariff on imported textile washing and dyeing machinery, reducing it to 6 per cent by 2001, and it cut the tariff on imported colouring agents used in dyeing operations by approximately 55 per cent. It did not reduce the latter further because of its policy of promoting the domestic production of colouring agents used in dyeing operations. While a comparison between the import of textile washing and dyeing machinery in 1990 and 2001 shows a decrease in annual import, the data for these two years are misleading because the import of such machinery increased dramatically from US$34 million in 1988 to US$104 million in 1990 and averaged US$95 million per year before the financial crisis in 1997. Despite the reasonably high tariff on synthetic organic colouring agents, their import too increased significantly, by 100 per cent, between 1990 and 2001.

One exception to the increased import of dyestuffs was the restriction on the import of those that contained lead, chromium or cadmium, which came into effect in 2000. This measure reduced extreme chemical contamination problems by an estimated 95 per cent, according to the Association of Thai Textile, Bleaching, Dyeing Printing and Finishing Industries (TEI, 2002).

Global comparison

In summary, Thailand's commitment to trade liberalization resulted in a significant lowering of trade-related import restrictions on manufactured goods in the 1990s. Reducing these restrictions clearly contributed to the overall increase in the import of manufactured goods. The lowering of tariff restrictions in the textile sub-sector contributed to an increase in the import of textile fabric, textile machinery and dyeing agents. Partially in response to the reduced cost of imported items and the increased pressure to compete with imported finished goods, Thailand made moderately high use of foreign technology, as shown on the TI index. Thailand ranked thirty-eighth among all 91 countries covered by the TI index in 2001, twelfth among 55 developing countries, far behind Malaysia, whose ranking was five times greater than Thailand, and second among the eight countries included in this study.

Resource Pricing Policy

As with all countries included in this study, it was not possible to obtain sufficient information to provide a comprehensive overview of resource pricing policies, including the use of subsidies for energy and water; nor to calculate an average change in resource prices between 1990 and 2002. This section therefore consists of only limited information on energy and water resource pricing policies, prices *per se* and changes in energy and water use by the manufacturing sector. Higher resource prices, as described in Chapter 3, are often incentives for adopting EST, particularly CTs.

Regarding energy management, the government liberalized the energy market and encouraged competition by allowing foreign-owned plants to provide energy services in the 1990s. A transparent regulatory framework emerged for the petroleum, electricity and gas sectors in 2000, followed by privatization of state-owned enterprises (SOEs) (WTO, 1999). However, the distribution and usage of electricity continued under state monopoly.

As part of the 1999 economic stimulus package, the government reduced the price of electricity in 1999 in order to reduce production costs and stimulate the economy. Between 1995 and 2000 the price dropped from 1.71 baht/kWh to 1.59 baht/kWh, a fall of 7.1 per cent. However, these measures were temporary and in 2000 the electricity price rose considerably, reaching 1.78 baht/kWh, an increase of 11.6 per cent. The Electricity Generating Authority of Thailand (EGAT) claimed that the base tariff now covered the marginal cost of power generation, financial requirements and customer load patterns.

Between 1990 and 2002 the manufacturing sector's energy consumption (defined as energy derived from oil, coal, natural gas, nuclear power, renewable sources and electricity) increased by 153 per cent, as shown above in Table 9.2. The manufacturing sector accounted for 28 per cent of the total final energy consumption in 1990 and 39 per cent in 2002 (IEA, 2005).

Energy consumption by the textile sub-sector increased by 46 per cent during the same period, from 303 ktoe to 443 ktoe,[3] and energy-use intensity by 2 per cent, from 108 to 111 toe per million US dollars of MVA. The textile industry accounted for 3.4 per cent of energy consumption by industry in 1990, but only 2 per cent in 2002 (IEA, 2005).

Regarding water management, the government actively intervened in the pricing of groundwater and tap water in the 1990s. Before 1996, groundwater could be used free of charge, but between 1996 and 1999 a payment of 3.50 baht/m^3 had to be made for its use. In 2000 the rate was increased to 4.50 baht/m^3 and in 2001 it reached 6.50 baht/m^3, 86 per cent higher than that charged in 1999. In 2003 it was increased further to 8.50 baht/m^3, around 145 per cent more than that in 1999 (MOI, 2005).

As for tap water prices, the average rate of increase was 21 per cent between 1992 and 2000. For example, for consumption in the range of 31–50 m^3 the rate was increased by 36 per cent from 14 baht/m^3 in 1992 to 19 baht/m^3 in 2000. The lowest increase occurred in the range of 301–1000 m^3, a 9 per cent increase during that period, with the rate rising from 20 baht/m^3 to 21.75 baht/m^3 (MOI, 2005).

As a result of these price increases there was a change in the share of input costs as a percentage of total production cost for the textiles mills. In 1992 the highest cost share was for raw materials, which was 50 per cent of the total production cost. In 2002 this decreased to 35 per cent while the share of energy cost increased from 15 to 25 per cent. The share of water cost doubled between 1992 and 2002, rising from 1.5 to 3 per cent, and the share of pollution control cost increased from 2 to 5 per cent between 1992 and 2002 (THTI, 2002).

Global comparison

There is no global assessment that can be drawn on to compare the relative effectiveness of Thailand's resource pricing policies; nor were studies found on the effect of resource pricing on resource use. As an alternative, an EUI score for the manufacturing sector was calculated for use in this study. In the case of Thailand, energy-use intensity increased during the 1990s from 303 tons of oil equivalent (toe) per million US dollars of MVA in 1990 to 350 toe in 2002. As a result, Thailand's EUI ranking fell from thirty-second among 93 countries in 1990 to thirty-fifth in 2002. Among developing countries it moved up from fourteenth out of 65 countries in 1990 to thirteenth in 2002. None the less, compared with the eight countries included in this study, Thailand's energy-use intensity is low, second in 2002 (behind Tunisia) and first in 1990.

TECHNOLOGY POLICY

At the beginning of the 1990s there was a broad consensus in Thailand that the country lacked the scientific and technological capabilities needed to provide a major stimulus to its economic development. First, research and development (R&D) expenditures were low and were almost non-existent in the private sector. In 1987 total R&D expenditures accounted for only 0.22 per cent of GDP compared to 0.5 per cent for the Republic of Korea, a country at a comparable level of development, and 2 per cent in the late 1980s. More troubling was the fact that the private sector carried out only 3 per cent of total R&D compared to 35 per cent in 1987 and 80 per cent in late 1991 in the Republic of Korea. Second, while there were a number of governmental organizations dealing with science and technology, their effectiveness was limited for several reasons, including staffing problems, lack of institutional cooperation among various R&D institutions, limited industry-related applied research and a lack of client orientation in the dissemination of information and the provision of services (UNIDO, 1992).

The Seventh Five Year Plan (1992–96) (based on input from the National Research Council of Thailand) included a science and technology policy for the industrial sector. It called for the technological infrastructure to increase industrial productivity by increasing public and private R&D expenditures for industry and building up a sufficient pool of technically qualified manpower. Specific targets for the textile sub-sector included the efficient use of modern machinery, the improvement of production management, and the expanded production of chemicals for use in the sub-sector.

Specialized divisions in MOSTE and MOI were responsible for implementing science and technology for industry. The National Science and Technology Development Agency (NSTDA) was set up in MOSTE in 1991. It managed three centres of excellence (biotechnology, metals and material technology, and electronic and computer technology), operated three technical outreach programmes (industrial technical assistance; standards, testing and quality control; and company-directed technology development) and funded R&D activities in universities. The Department of Industrial Promotion was a specialized division within MOI for providing technical services, and within it was the Textile Industry Division, which was responsible for promoting the textile industry by providing technical training, consultancy services and quality testing services, as well as carrying out research and experiments in the textile field. It was also responsible for organizing training programmes and providing testing services on bleaching and dyeing.

There were also autonomous institutes that had been affiliated with MOI as a result of efforts to re-invigorate MOI in the mid-1990s, two of which were the Thai Textile Institute and the Thai Productivity Institute. The Thai Textile Institute, established in 1996 on the initiative of the various textile associations, aimed to improve the quality of textile manufacturing and to equip the textile industry with the ability to compete effectively in global markets. The government intended to gradually transfer the functions of the Textile Industry Division to it. The Thai Productivity Institute promoted general awareness and understanding of productivity and provided direct consultancy and training services in quality assurance and productivity to individual firms in all sub-sectors.

In addition to governmental organizations, private associations were also part of the technological infrastructure. The most prominent was the Federation of Thai Industries, which facilitated industrial development and represented industry in governmental committees and councils. The Federation's Industrial Environment Management Programme tries to overcome several difficulties in promoting CP, including the lack of environmental awareness and information, the lack of resources, mainly in the case of SMEs, and the lack of efficient management practices (TEI, 2002). Specific associations for the textile sub-sector were the Thai Textile Manufacturing Association and the National Federation of Thai Textile Industries, which included five associations dealing respectively with synthetic fibres, textile manufacturing, weaving, garment making and silk making.

In spite of new initiatives and organizational mandates, governmental research and technology institutes still appeared, as of 2002, to face several challenges in delivering technology-upgrading services to firms. First, there was limited awareness in the industrial sector of the need for such services in the institutes and universities. Second, there was duplication and a lack of specialization in the institutional infrastructure. Third, MOI played only a limited role in formulating technology policy and securing financial resources for technological development. Finally, MOI's goal of financially self-supporting sub-sectoral institutes which charged for their services was counter-productive to the aim of upgrading firms, particularly SMEs, which had limited financial resources for paying for advisory services (Arnold et al., 2000; UNIDO, 2002).

Global Comparison

In summary, the scientific and technological infrastructure appears to have been working below its capacity to deliver technology advisory services to firms and to supply technically trained manpower during the 1990s. Part of the problem was the low demand on the part of firms themselves for technological services, and even for financial services during the financial crisis. Thus major challenges for the technological infrastructure were to raise the awareness of firms of the necessity of technology upgrading and to provide specialized, cost-effective services that would be attractive to firms. Given the situation as of 2000, it is not surprising that Thailand ranked among the 'latecomers' on the TC index. It ranked sixty-eighth among 162 countries on the TC index in 2000, still a considerable improvement over its rank of eightieth in 1990, twenty-sixth among 114 developing countries, and first among the eight countries included in this study.

THE TEXTILE SUB-SECTOR

Economic Overview

The textile industry is the common collective designation for two manufacturing sub-sectors, textiles (ISIC 321) and wearing apparel (ISIC 322). Textile production in Thailand increased by 106 per cent and wearing

*Table 8.3   Textile and wearing apparel production and textile import
and export*

Year	Textiles and wearing apparel (thousand tons)[a]		Textiles (US$ million)[b]	
	Textiles	Wearing apparel	Import	Export
1990	1215	318	898.1	927.8
1995	2013	459	1534.4	1937.4
2002	2504	458	1534.6	1887.8

Sources: [a] Textile Industry Division (MOI, 2005); [b] World Bank (2005).

apparel production by 44 per cent between 1990 and 2002 (Table 8.3). Most of the increase occurred between 1990 and 1995, with textile production only increasing by 27 per cent between 1995 and 2002 and wearing apparel production declining by 1 per cent. However, while production of textiles stagnated between 1995 and 1999 because of the financial crisis, it accelerated between 2000 and 2002.

Although textile exports more than doubled between 1990 and 2002, the export value was much the same in 2002 as it had been in 1995, as a result of increased costs of production and competition from producers in other countries. It lost its market share in the United States and Europe to strong competition from lower-cost countries (China, India, Indonesia and Viet Nam). The textile sub-sector's share of manufactured export declined from 6 per cent in 1990 to 4 per cent in 2001. However, it essentially retained its position as a global exporter of textiles, ranking nineteenth out of 65 textile exporting countries in 1990 and twentieth out of 79 textile exporting countries in 2001. Its largest export markets were in the United States, Australia, the Lao Republic and Malaysia (World Bank, 2005).

It should be mentioned that Thailand's export of both textiles and wearing apparel during the 1990s was constrained, first by the Multi-Fibre Arrangement (MFA), which came into force in 1974, and then by the Agreement on Clothing and Textiles, which came into effect in 1995. Both agreements set quotas on the amount of textiles and garments that developing countries could export to developed countries (Kyvik-Nordas, 2004). All constraining agreements subsequently ended in 2005.

Overall, the textile sub-sector made a significant contribution to the economy in 2002, only slightly less than the wearing apparel sub-sector. Its value added increased by 43 per cent, from US$2.8 billion in 1990 to US$4.0 billion in 2002, while total Thai MVA increased by 119 per cent over the same period (UNIDO, 2005). Its percentage share of total MVA was 10 per cent in 1990 but only 6.4 per cent in 2002. In 2002 the sub-sector employed around 241 000 workers, approximately 4.7 per cent of the manufacturing workforce (MOI, 2005).

Sub-sector Profile

The textile industry is a sequential manufacturing operation (complete production cycle), comprising the following five major stages: (a) fibre production (natural or man-made); (b) spinning; (c) weaving and knitting; (d) dyeing/printing and finishing; and (e) garment production. Each stage is related to the others in that the product in one stage may be a raw material for the subsequent stage. The last stage of the process, garment production, is considered a separate sub-sector in terms of industrial statistics and in this chapter.

There were about 4500 textile industry operations in 2000, of which 90 per cent were SMEs. Of these, 1880 were engaged in textile production and 2670 in garment production. Most were located in Bangkok and its satellite provinces.

Although the wearing apparel manufacturing stage had the largest number of plants and was the main exporting stage, weaving and spinning plants were also competitive in the international markets. This was attributed to Thailand's low labour costs compared with some other developing countries. Mills in China and Viet Nam, however, were, as of 2000, adversely affecting the competitiveness of some textile firms in Thailand (MOI, 2005).

The dyeing/printing and finishing stage, the most pollutant-intensive stage of textile production, consists of one of two processing configurations. In one configuration this stage is part of an integrated mill, which combines several textile-processing operations in one place, while in the other it is the only stage at the mill. In the latter, commonly called a commission mill, production starts with fabric preparation, that is, desizing, scouring and bleaching, and continues through dyeing/printing and finishing. Of the 412 dyeing and finishing mills, 68 per cent were classified as small-scale, 24 per cent as medium-scale and 8 per cent as large-scale. In terms of employment figures, the Thai dyeing/printing and finishing segment employed 47 810 workers, accounting for 4.4 per cent of the total textile sub-sector employment in 2000.

Geographically, around 90 per cent of the dyeing/printing and finishing mills were located in the Bangkok Metropolitan Region, as of 2002. There were two main reasons for this: the need to be close to dyestuff suppliers as well as raw material suppliers like those for grey fabric, and the need for proximity to the next stage of the production process, the garment manufacturers in the region.

Of the 412 mills, 28 were selected for this study based on criteria that called for variations in their degree of integration, size and location. The selected mills corresponded to the criteria as follows: seven were integrated mills and 21 were commission mills; 13 were small-scale and 15 were large-scale; 17 were located in Samutprakam, the most industrialised province in Thailand, six in Nakornpatom province and the remaining five in Bangkok, Nonthaburi and Kanchanaburi provinces (Table 8.4).

Other characteristics of the mills are worth noting: all were under private domestic ownership; all produced only for the domestic market; six were ISO 9001/9002 certified and six were ISO 14001 certified; and four had integrated R&D departments, engaged mainly in quality control and in the installation and adaptation of new technology.

Process Technology and CT Characterization

The dyeing and finishing segment of the textile sub-sector, comprising mostly small plants, mainly used outdated (between 10 and 30 years old) and locally made equipment. The owners were generally not interested in modernizing their equipment. Most plants used batch-dyeing techniques. Colour fastness and quality control remained major problems because most small plants had neither an inspection system nor checking equipment. Because this stage of textile manufacturing required highly skilled technical workers, trained and qualified personnel were needed to produce the required quality products. Failure to meet quality demands in the 1990s led to an increased use of imported fabrics in the garment-making stage.

Compared to other stages in textile manufacturing, the dyeing and finishing stage is an equipment-intensive operation. Thus the 28 dyeing and finishing mills investigated used a wide array of production technology, depending on whether the operation was an integrated or a commission mill and on the volume of production. For the most part, medium- and large-scale integrated plants used suitable technology. The survey team assigned the mills to one of three technology categories based on the technological vintage of the dyeing equipment: three used best available technology (BAT), 22 used standard–modern and three used traditional technology (Table 8.4).

The survey team also classified the mills into three groups based on the highest order of complexity of the CTs used in each mill (low, medium and high). Given that most of the mills included in the survey had undertaken CP projects, it is not surprising that they used many CTs in their operations. According to the survey team, five mills used CTs of a higher order of complexity, 12 used CTs of a medium order of complexity, ten used CTs of a lower order of complexity and one used no CTs (Table 8.4).

Table 8.4 Profile of the 28 mills investigated

Mill	Process	Scale	Location: province	Sales orientation (in 2000)	Technology vintage	Ownership	EST Score	Regulatory compliance	Donor assist.	EMS
TH1	Bleaching, dyeing and finishing	Large	Samutprakarn	40% D, 60% E	Traditional	51% private domestic; 49% private foreign	PAT + HTC	Yes	n.a.	On-going
TH2	Weaving, bleaching, dyeing and finishing	Large	Samutprakarn	100% D	Standard–modern	100% private domestic	PAT + HTC	Yes	DANCED	No
TH3	Bleaching, dyeing and finishing	Small	Samutprakarn	100% D	Standard–modern	100% private domestic	PAT + HTC	Yes	No	No
TH4	Bleaching, dyeing and finishing	Small	Samutprakarn	50% D, 50% E	Traditional	100% private domestic	PAT + MTC	Yes	DANCED	No
TH5	Weaving, bleaching, dyeing and finishing	Large	Samutprakarn	56% D, 44% E	Standard–modern	100% private domestic	PAT + MTC	Yes	No	On-going
TH6	Bleaching, dyeing and finishing	Small	Samutprakarn	50% D, 50% E	Standard–modern	100% private domestic	PAT + MTC	Yes	n.a.	No
TH7	Weaving, bleaching,	Large	Bangkok	100% E	Standard–modern	100% private	PAT + MTC	Yes	n.a.	On-going

Table 8.4 (continued)

Mill	Process	Scale	Location: province	Sales orientation (in 2000)	Technology vintage	Ownership	EST Score	Regulatory compliance	Donor assist.	EMS
	dyeing and finishing					domestic				
TH8	Weaving, bleaching, dyeing and finishing	Large	Samutprakarn	92% D, 8% E	Standard–modern	100% private domestic	PAT + MTC	Yes	n.a.	Yes
TH9	Printing only	Small	Samutprakarn	95% D, 5% E	Traditional	100% private domestic	PAT + LTC	Yes	n.a.	No
TH10	Printing only	Small	Samutprakarn	100% D	Standard–modern	100% private domestic	PAT + LTC	Yes	n.a.	No
TH11	Weaving, bleaching, dyeing and finishing	Large	Samutprakarn	30% D, 70% E	Standard–modern	100% private domestic	PAT + MTC	Yes	Thai Govt	Yes
TH12	Bleaching, dyeing and finishing	Large	Samutprakarn	60% D, 40% E	Standard–modern	66% private domestic, 34% private foreign	PAT + LTC	No (has been penalized)	n.a.	No
TH13	Bleaching, dyeing and finishing	Large	Samutprakarn	90% D, 10% E	Standard–modern	100% private domestic	PAT + LTC	Yes	n.a.	No

ID	Process	Size	Location	D/E	Technology	Ownership	Incentive		Foreign funds	
TH14	Knitting, bleaching, dyeing and finishing	Small	Samutprakarn	100% D	Standard-modern	100% private domestic	PAT + HTC	Yes	Foreign funds	Yes
TH15	Bleaching, dyeing and finishing	Small	Samutprakarn	100% D	Traditional	100% private domestic	PAT + MTC	Yes	Loan	No
TH16	Weaving, bleaching, dyeing and finishing	Large	Nakonpathom	10% D, 90% E	Standard-modern	100% private domestic	PAT + LTC	Yes	n.a.	No
TH17	Dyeing and finishing	Small	Samutprakarn	95% D, 5% E	Standard-modern	100% private domestic	PAT + LTC	Yes	n.a.	No
TH18	Bleaching, dyeing and finishing	Large	Nakhonpratom	100% E	Standard-modern	100% private domestic	PAT + LTC	Yes	n.a.	Yes
TH19	Bleaching, dyeing and finishing	Large	Nakonpahtom	70% D, 30% E	Standard-modern	100% private domestic	PAT + HTC	Yes	JETRO	Yes
TH20	Bleaching, dyeing and finishing	Small	Nonthaburi	100% E	BAT	100% private domestic	PAT + LTC	Yes	JETRO	No
TH21	Bleaching, dyeing and finishing	Large	Nonthaburi	85% D, 15% E	Standard-modern	100% private domestic	PAT + LTC	Yes	Company and loan	No
TH22	Bleaching and dyeing	Small	Bangkok	100% D	Standard-modern	100% private domestic	PAT + LTC	Yes	Company	No

Table 8.4 (continued)

Mill	Process	Scale	Location: province	Sales orientation (in 2000)	Technology vintage	Ownership	EST Score	Regulatory compliance	Donor assist.	EMS
TH23	Printing, dyeing and finishing	Small	Bangkok	70% D, 30% E	Standard–modern	100% private domestic	PAT	Yes	Company	No
TH24	Knitting, bleaching and dyeing	Large	Samutsakorn	100% D	Standard–modern	100% private domestic	PAT + MTC	Yes	Company	On-going
TH25	Bleaching and dyeing	Large	Samutprakarn	100% D	Standard–modern	100% private domestic	PAT + MTC	Yes	n.a.	No
TH26	Weaving, bleaching and dyeing	Large	Bangkok	100% D	Standard–modern	100% private domestic	PAT + MTC	Yes	n.a.	No
TH27	Bleaching, dyeing and finishing	Large	Samutsakorn	100% D	BAT	100% private domestic	PAT + MTC	No (has been penalized)	n.a.	Yes
TH28	Bleaching, dyeing and finishing	Small	Samutprakarn	90% D, 10% E	BAT	100% private domestic	PAT + MTC	Yes	n.a.	No

Abbreviations: domestic (D); export (E); best available technology (BAT); pollution abatement technology (PAT); higher order technological complexity (HTC); medium order technological complexity (MTC); lower order technological complexity (LTC).

Source: TEI (2002).

CTs were used in all stages of the dyeing and finishing of textiles. The survey team did not document the type and extent of CT options used by the 28 mills. As an alternative they relied on an assessment undertaken by the Association of Thai Textile Bleaching, Dyeing, Printing and Finishing Industries for the Asian Productivity Organization to characterize the use of CTs applied in these operations. The findings of the assessment are presented in Table 8.5.

Table 8.5   CTs used in dyeing and finishing mills in Thailand

Practice	High use	Moderate use	Low use	No use
Built-in bath and reuse on dye machine	x			
Caustic and size recovery		x		
Chemical dosing system			x	
Continuous knit dyeing range		x		
Control, automation, and scheduling management system		x		
Counter-current washing	x			
Heat recovery system	x			
Humidity sensors and advanced controls for drying	x			
Incinerator dryers				x
Low bath-ratio dyeing systems	x			
Mechanical finishing		x		
Pad-batch dyeing machines for fibre-reactive dyes	x			
Quick-change pads on continuous ranges		x		
Low add-on finishing	x			
Water recovery systems	x			
Vacuum system for chemical recovery		x		
Computerized colour matching system	x			

Source: APO (2002).

An example of the use of CTs in one of the 28 mills surveyed is given in Box 8.1 The emphasis in the CP audit was energy conservation, given the rising cost of energy inputs into the production process.

PAT Characterization

Because industry has a great impact on water quality, PATs were legally required and environmental norms strictly enforced in Thailand. Con-

BOX 8.1   CLEANER PRODUCTION CASE STUDY: THAILAND

This producer of knitted fabric and dyed and finished fabric is located in Samutprakan. It invested US$37 000 in several energy conservation options including replacement and insulation of steam pipes, heat recovery and boiler efficiency. These options all contributed to fuel savings. The investment paid for itself in 15 months.

Source: TEI (2002).

sequently most medium- and large-scale mills had either built their own effluent treatment plants (ETPs) or discharged their effluent into CETPs operated by industrial estates. About 10 per cent of the mills, almost exclusively large-scale mills, treated their own effluent using an activated sludge system. Most small mills were either located in industrial estates with CETPs or discharged into sewers that were connected to a CETP operated by a municipality. All of the 28 mills included in the survey were located outside industrial estates and consequently had installed their own ETPs, mostly activated sludge. One mill used physical chemical treatment and then discharged its effluent into a CETP.

Environmental Performance

Textile effluent includes rinsing and cooling water, and concentrated waste process water, which consists of natural impurities extracted from the fibres and a mixture of process chemicals, such as inorganic salts, dyes and heavy metals. It is usually highly coloured and high in organic and chemical matter. Generally speaking, the more sophisticated textile dyeing and finishing mills were well designed and often operated at levels that met international standards. Smaller mills, however, had difficulty in providing adequate treatment and often discharged untreated wastewater into adjacent canals. In the provinces compliance with discharge standards showed signs of decline.

National at-source data on industrial effluent were not available. As stated earlier, the textile sub-sector was estimated to be the second largest source of BOD in the manufacturing sector, accounting for some 35 per cent of the total loadings from the manufacturing sector (World Bank, 2004). Based on a survey of 100 mills, around 83 per cent of the dyeing and finishing mills operated in compliance with the BOD standard of 60 mg/l (TEI, 2002).

All 28 mills surveyed had PAT that would have allowed them to comply with effluent limitations. Twenty-six were reported as being in compliance with effluent limitations, while the other two were in violation.

KEY INFORMANTS AND INTERNATIONAL DONORS

Four groups, in addition to government environmental regulatory agencies and technology centres, are able to influence the extent to which plants adopt EST: NGOs, business associations, international donors of technical assistance, and chemical and equipment suppliers. The following section presents some information on the first three; there is insufficient information to characterize the nature of firms that supplied chemicals and equipment to Thailand's textile sub-sector.

NGOs

Although Thailand has been a democratic country since 1932, public participation in government decision making assumed importance only after the Thai Constitution was drawn up in 1997. At that time environmental NGOs became a significant factor in environmental decision making.

The survey team interviewed the Samutprakan Environment Society, an NGO set up in 1997 with support from the Thailand Environmental Institute. The Society is active in Samutprakarn Province (outskirts of Bangkok), a highly industrial area with acute pollution and transportation problems. It monitors targets set for reducing pollutant discharge from industrial sources.

Business Associations

Business associations have been active and effective in Thailand since the 1980s. In terms of the textile industry, major associations are the Thai Textile Manufacturing Association and the National Federation of Thai Textile Industries, which, as of 2002, included five associations dealing respectively with synthetic fibres, textile manufacturing, weaving, garment making and silk making.

The survey team interviewed one business association, the Association of Thai Bleaching, Dyeing, Printing and Finishing Industries, established in 1991, and with 131 firms at the time of the survey. Its short-term objective is to contribute to the technology upgrading of its members. It trains mill personnel and supports the efforts of members to obtain ISO 9000 and ISO 14000 certification. Its long-term objective is to increase the value added of textile products.

International Donors

During the 1990s several international technological cooperation initiatives were undertaken to promote the application of CP in Thai industries, the main activities being training, outreach projects and demonstrations. Some of the major CP initiatives are described briefly below.

The United States Agency for International Development (USAID) funded the Industrial Environmental Management Programme of the Federation of Thai Industries in 1990–95. An awareness programme was initiated for several sub-sectors, including textile dyeing and finishing, pulp and paper, food processing and chemicals. The programme promoted technology transfer and increased cooperation between different institutions.

USAID also funded the ASEAN Environmental Improvement Programme (ASEAN–EIP) between 1992 and 1996. This programme operated in the six member nations of ASEAN at that time: Brunei, Indonesia, Malaysia, Philippines, Singapore and Thailand. The programme design was complex, with interlinking actions in several areas, including technology and management demonstration, policy development and regional rationalization, institution building, information networking, technology transfer and trade promotion.

The Carl Duisberg Gesellschaft (CDG) assisted SMEs in the textile, electroplating and food sub-sectors through a number of training, capacity-building and industrial audit activities. The project was implemented in cooperation with three educational institutions: the Asian Institute of Technology, Chulalongkorn University and Chiang Mai University.

The Danish Cooperation for Environment and Development (DANCED) funded the 'Promotion of CT in Thai Industry' project, implemented between 1996 and 1998 by TEI and the Federation of Thai Industries. The project aimed to strengthen CP auditing and CT advisory services. In addition, CP audits were carried out in the food, electroplating and textile industries.

The Asian Development Bank and the Japanese Overseas Economic Cooperation Fund were funding the construction of a large-scale CETP in Samutprakarn Province, where much of the textile industry is located. This four-year programme aimed to promote and develop CP and industrial energy efficiency among industries in the province. The essential features of the programme include the establishment of a resource centre, provision of advice to local industry and demonstrations of applied CT processes.

SUMMARY

Thailand's aggregate economic performance indicators show that it performed remarkably well in the 1990s despite the East Asian financial crisis of 1997, although its environmental performance indicators show mixed results. While GDP increased by 67 per cent between 1990 and 2002, MVA increased even more, by almost 120 per cent. As a result, the share of MVA in GDP increased from 26 to 34 per cent. GNI per capita at PPP increased by 150 per cent during the same period. Energy use in the manufacturing sector surged in the 1990s and energy conservation efforts were largely unsuccessful, with increases in energy-use and CO_2-emission intensities. However, BOD effluent increased by only a small percentage compared to the percentage change in MVA, which resulted in a dramatic decrease in BOD-effluent intensity of 41 per cent.

Thailand introduced a comprehensive environmental policy in the 1970s and further expanded it in the 1990s. The country relied mainly on command-and-control regulatory instruments that empowered governmental agencies to set and enforce environmental standards. The government also introduced incentives to encourage the adoption of EST and appears to have effectively taken into account the need for environmental management in establishing industrial estates.

The combined impact of major changes in the 1990s in three economic policies, industrial, trade and resource pricing, had a positive impact on technological modernization that would have included the use of more EST. Clearly the outward orientation of industrial policies, particularly the continued openness to FDI and export promotion, rapidly transformed the economy and brought about a degree of technological modernization in the manufacturing processes. The abolition of the restriction on capacity expansion enhanced the import of more modern production equipment, and the creation of industrial estates ensured proper treatment of the wastewater from the plants located in the estates. The reduction of trade-related import restrictions encouraged the adoption of more advanced technologies both by lowering the cost of imported capital equipment and material input and by increasing the need for domestic producers to respond to competitive pressures by upgrading their production technology. Finally, it appears that resource pricing increased the need for firms to introduce more resource-efficient technologies in order to reduce their use of energy and water. Despite the increase in energy-use intensity, as measured by the EUI index, Thailand continued to rank quite high in this regard among developing countries, especially among those included in this study.

Thailand's technological policy supported the development of an infrastructure to deliver technological advisory services to firms and to supply technically trained manpower during the 1990s, but these services appear to have been under-utilized. Part of the problem was the low demand on the part of the firms themselves for technological services and even financial services during the financial crisis. Thus major challenges for improving the technological infrastructure were to raise the awareness of firms of the necessity of technology upgrading in order to remain competitive and to provide specialized, cost-effective services that were attractive to firms.

Thailand's textile sub-sector, as distinct from the garment sub-sector, increased its production from 1215 to 2504 tons between 1990 and 2002, approximately doubling output. As of 2002, some 412 dyeing and finishing mills were involved in textile production, some of these being part of integrated mills and others non-integrated or commission mills. Approximately 70 per cent of the mills were small-scale operations using outdated production technology. The other 30 per cent were medium- and large-scale operations that used modern production technology. The survey team investigated 28 of the 412 mills. Three used mainly BAT, 22 used mainly standard–modern process technologies, and three used mainly traditional technologies. Five used CTs of a higher order of complexity, 12 used CTs of a medium order of complexity, 10 used CTs of a lower order of complexity and one used no CTs. Twenty-seven mills either operated their own ETP; one mill pre-treated its effluent and then discharged it into a municipal CETP. Finally, 26 of the 28 mills were reported to be in compliance with effluent standards in 2002.

The influence of other institutional actors – NGOs, business associations and international donors – on EST adoption varied among the actors during the 1990s. The informal regulation of NGO pressure was limited because they became active only in the late 1990s. However, business associations played a role in the formulation of environmental policy during this period and assisted their members in technology upgrading. Finally, international donors funded numerous programmes to promote better industrial environmental management with significant support for adoption of CTs in several manufacturing sub-sectors, including textile dyeing and finishing.

Overall, the Thai textile sub-sector performed well during the first half of the 1990s but less so between 1995 and 2002. Its output doubled between 1990 and 2002 amid significant international competition. Most of the mills operated in full compliance with environmental norms, even at the most polluting stage of textile production, namely dyeing and finishing. A range of government policies, those supportive of both increased output and of pollution control, contributed to the reasonable economic and environmental performance of the textile sub-sector.

NOTES

1. This presumption is based on the economy-wide average annual growth rate in gross fixed capital formation of −4.1 per cent between 1990 and 2002 (World Bank, 2004).
2. The FDI for 1990 has been taken as the three-year average of 1989–91 and for 2002 as the three-year average of 2001–3, in order to even out fluctuations in FDI flows.
3. The IEA does not provide exclusive energy consumption data for the textile sub-sector; it was therefore calculated according to the proportion of MVA of the textile and the leather sub-sectors, for which the IEA provides information as one sub-sector.

REFERENCES

Arnold, E., M. Bell, J. Bessant and P. Brimble (2000), 'Enhancing Policy and Institutional Support for Industrial Technology Development in Thailand – The Overall Policy Framework and The Development of the Industrial Innovation System', Bangkok, Thailand: National Science and Technology Development Board.

Asian Productivity Organization (2002), 'Thailand: Country Environmental Profile', Tokyo: Asian Productivity Organization (available on www.apo-tokyo.org/gp/e_publi/gpp/02).

EIU (2002), 'Country Profile – Thailand', London: Economist Intelligence Unit.

FAO (2005), 'AQUASTAT: FAO STAT' Rome: Food and Agriculture Organization of the United Nations (available on: http://www.fao.org).

IEA (2005), 'Online Data Services', IEA Energy Information Centre, Paris: International Energy Agency (available on: http://www.iea.org).

ISO (2003), 'The ISO Survey of ISO 9000 and ISO 14001 Certificates', Geneva: International Organization for Standardization (available on: http://www. iso.org).

Kraas, F. (1998), 'Industrial structure and spatial strategies for industrial competitiveness in Thailand', in Johanna Witte and Stefan Koeberle (eds), *Competitiveness and Sustainable Economic Recovery in Thailand*, volume II, Bangkok, Thailand: National Economic and Social Development Board and World Bank, pp 235–79.

Kyvik-Nordas, H. (2004), 'The Global Textile and Clothing Industry post the Agreement on Textile and Clothing', Discussion Paper No. 5, Geneva: World Trade Organization.

MOI (2005), 'Textile Economics Study and Research Group, Textile Industry Division, Department of Industrial Promotion', Personal Communication, Bangkok, Thailand: Ministry of Industry, Government of Thailand.

NESDB (1992), 'The Seventh National Economic and Social Development Plan (1992–1999)', Bangkok, Thailand: National Economic and Social Development Board, Government of Thailand.

NESDB (1997), 'The Eighth National Economic and Social Development Plan (1997–2001)', Bangkok, Thailand: National Economic and Social Development Board, Government of Thailand.

PCD (2004), 'Thai Environmental Regulations – Water Quality Standards', Bangkok, Thailand: Pollution Control Division, Ministry of Natural Resources and Environment, Government of Thailand (available on: http://www pcd.gov.th).

TEI (2002), 'Assessing the Adoption of EST in Thailand's Textile Sub-sector', Bangkok, Thailand: Thailand Environment Institute. Report prepared for UNIDO.

THTI (2002), 'The Association of Thai Textile Bleaching, Dyeing, Printing and Finishing Industry', Bangkok, Thailand: Thailand Textile Institute (available on: http://www.thaitextile.org/atdp).

UNIDO (1992), *Thailand: Coping with the Strains of Success*, Industrial Development Review Series, Oxford, UK and Cambridge, MA, US: Blackwell Publishers.

UNIDO (2002), 'Thailand's Manufacturing Competitiveness: Promoting Technology, Productivity and Linkages', Vienna: UNIDO.

UNIDO (2005), *International Yearbook of Industrial Statistics 2005*, Cheltenham, UK and Northampton, MA, US: Edward Elgar Publishing.

World Bank (2000), 'Thailand Environment Monitor', Washington, DC: The World Bank.

World Bank (2004), 'World Bank Development Indicators (WDI) 2004', CD-ROM version, Washington, DC: The World Bank.

World Bank (2005), 'World Integrated Trade Solution (WITS)', Washington, DC: The World Bank (available on: http://wits.worldbank.org).

WTO (1999), 'Trade Policy Review – Thailand 1999', Geneva: World Trade Organization.

9. Tunisia

INTRODUCTION

A survey team from the Centre International des Technologies de l'
Environnement de Tunis investigated the specific factors influencing the
adoption of environmentally sound technology (EST) in Tunisia's textile
sub-sector. The team used semi-structured questionnaires provided by
UNIDO to interview plant managers at ten out of 37 mills that had dyeing
and finishing operations and six key informants in one business association,
two technology centres, one chemical supplier, one environmental NGO
and one environmental regulatory agency. The team also collected background data on the country and the textile sub-sector.

This chapter describes the economic and environmental context in
Tunisia for EST adoption; relevant environmental, economic and technology policies; the textile sub-sector and the plants investigated; and key
informants and international donors.

THE ECONOMIC AND ENVIRONMENTAL CONTEXT
FOR EST ADOPTION

The following selected economic and environmental performance indicators define the context in which manufacturing plants made their technology adoption decisions and, in particular, their decisions to adopt EST
during the late 1990s/early 2000s.

Economic Performance Indicators

During the 1990s Tunisia's economic growth was reasonably high, though
not in all of these years. Gross domestic product (GDP) grew by 7.8 per
cent in 1992, but in 1993 a slowdown began when it fell to lower than 2.5
per cent and continued decreasing steadily until 1995. This was reversed in
1996, when it registered 7.1 per cent, but it fell again in 1997 to 5.4 per cent
and remained at an average of 5 per cent for the remainder of the decade
(World Bank, 2004). Between 1990 and 2002 GDP increased by 69 per cent
and GDP per capita by 41 per cent, while the population increased by

20 per cent (Table 9.1). Gross national income (GNI) per capita at purchasing power parity (PPP) – a more accurate indicator of well-being than GDP per capita – increased even more, by 81 per cent. Based on the latter, Tunisia is classified by the World Bank as a low–middle-income country.

The high growth was mainly due to the increase in the manufacturing sector. Manufacturing value added (MVA) increased by 85 per cent between 1990 and 2002, significantly more than the percentage increase in GDP. As a result, the share of MVA in GDP increased from 16.9 per cent in 1990 to 18.6 per cent in 2002. Within the manufacturing sector several sub-sectors, such as food processing and mechanical and electrical equipment, grew rapidly (EIU, 2003).

The growing economy was supported by a monetary policy that encouraged borrowing by industry. Whereas prices increased by 32 per cent between 1990 and 1995, as measured by changes in the consumer price index (CPI), they increased by only 23 per cent between 1996 and 2002. As a result of the declining rate of inflation the interest rate fell from 11.5 per cent in 1990 to 6.0 per cent in 2002 (EIU, 2004).

Table 9.1   Economic performance indictors for Tunisia

Economic indicator	Year	Value	Percentage change
GDP (constant 1995 US$) (billion)	1990	14.9	69.0
	2002	25.2	
GDP per capita (constant 1995 US$) (billion)	1990	1.8	41.0
	2002	2.6	
Population (million)	1990	8.2	20.0
	2002	9.8	
GNI per capita at PPP (current international $)	1990	3560.0	81.0
	2002	6440.0	
MVA (constant 1995 US$) (billion)	1990	2.6	85.0
	2002	4.8	
MVA (percentage of GDP)	1990	16.9	1.7
	2002	18.6	
CPI (1995=100)	1990	75.5	63.0
	2002	122.8	
Interest rate (commercial lending rate)	1990	11.5	−48.0
	2002	6.0	
Exchange rate (Tunisian Dinars/US$)	1991	0.93	53.0
	2002	1.42	

Source: World Bank (2004).

Environmental Performance Indicators

Rapid economic and urban growth was not matched by adequate environmental protection measures. As a result, Tunisia was facing several environmental problems in 2002, including water pollution and the depletion of freshwater resources, land degradation, air pollution, untreated sewage and uncontrolled waste disposal.

Selected environmental indicators, namely energy use, carbon dioxide (CO_2) emissions, organic matter effluent measured as biochemical oxygen demand (BOD), and water use, as well as the intensity of each of these, which provide an insight into the state of industrial environmental performance in Tunisia in the period from 1990 to 2002, are presented in Table 9.2. Energy use in the manufacturing sector, measured in tons of oil equivalent (toe), grew by 25 per cent, much less than the growth of MVA,

Table 9.2   Environmental performance indicators for Tunisia

Source code	Environmental indicator	Year	Value	Percentage change
1	Energy use in the manufacturing sector (million toe)	1990	1.3	25
		2002	1.6	
1 & 2	Energy-use intensity (toe per million US$ of MVA)	1990	500.0	−32
		2002	340.0	
1	CO_2 emissions from the manufacturing sector (million tons)	1990	3.3	23
		2002	4.0	
1 & 2	CO_2-emission intensity (tons per million US$ of MVA)	1990	1290.0	−34
		2002	850.0	
2	BOD effluent from the manufacturing sector (thousand tons)	1993	14.7	11
		2000	16.3	
2	BOD-effluent intensity (tons per million US$ of MVA)	1993	5.7	−39
		2000	3.5	
3	Water use in the manufacturing sector (million m³)	1990	86.0	28
		2000	110.0	
2 & 3	Water-use intensity (thousand m³ per billion US$ of MVA)	1990	33.4	−25
		2000	25.0	
4	Percentage of MVA produced by most pollutant-intensive sub-sectors	1990	43.0	−19
		2002	23.6	
5	Number of ISO 14001 certificates	1997	4.0	325
		2002	13.0	

Note: BOD data shown for 2000 for Tunisia are from the year 2001.

Sources: 1. IEA (2005); 2. World Bank (2004); 3. FAO (2005); 4. UNIDO (2005a); 5. ISO (2003).

and as a result energy-use intensity declined by 33 per cent. Likewise, associated CO_2 emissions increased by 23 per cent but CO_2-emission intensity decreased by 34 per cent. BOD loadings increased by 11 per cent but BOD-effluent intensity decreased by 39 per cent. Likewise, associated water use increased by 28 per cent but water-use intensity decreased by 25 per cent. Given the water scarcity in the country, water-use intensity of 25 cubic metres per billion US dollars of MVA in 2000 was lower than the 37.5 cubic metres intensity of Thailand, the other textile-producing country in this study.

Between 1990 and 2002 there was a shift away from the most pollutant-intensive sub-sectors as their percentage of MVA declined from 43.0 to 23.6 per cent. This partially explains the decreasing energy-use and BOD-effluent intensities of the manufacturing sector at this time. The reduction in BOD-effluent intensity is also attributed to a growing adoption of EST by this sector, with the increasing construction of wastewater treatment plants and the development of an adequate environmental regulatory programme.

In 2000 the distribution of BOD effluent among the manufacturing sub-sectors was as follows: food and beverages, 41 per cent; textiles, 34 per cent; pulp and paper, 8 per cent: primary metals, 6 per cent; chemicals 6 per cent: and others, 5 per cent (World Bank, 2004). The BOD effluent from the textile sub-sector was the second highest among the manufacturing sub-sectors.

While the number of ISO 14001 certificates increased from 4 to 13 between 1997 and 2002, the number of certificates per billion US dollars of MVA was relatively low. In terms of certificates per million US dollars of MVA, Tunisia had a ratio of 2.7 certificates, between Kenya with 1.2 certificates and Mexico with 4.9. Only Kenya and Zimbabwe among the nine countries included in this study had a lower number.

Implications for EST Adoption

During the period investigated for this study the overall economic and environmental conditions in Tunisia seemed reasonably conducive to the adoption of EST by the country's manufacturing sector. The government of this advanced developing country had compelled its manufacturing sector to make some investment in EST before 1990, as evidenced by its modest BOD-effluent intensity (5.7 tons per million US dollars of MVA) in that year. From 1990 to 2002 the manufacturing sector grew rapidly, with a 5.5 per cent average annual growth rate in MVA. In parallel there was an even larger annual average growth rate of 12.7 per cent in new investment, some of which would have been in EST; the relatively low rate of inflation

(CPI increased 63 per cent) and the relatively low and declining interest rate (11.5 per cent to 6.0 per cent) over the period would have contributed to this. The 85 per cent increase in annual MVA brought a surprisingly modest increase in energy use of 25 per cent, some of this attributable to the 39 per cent decrease in energy-use intensity caused, in part, by investments in new technology. BOD effluent increased by a modest 11 per cent and BOD-effluent intensity decreased by 39 per cent, largely explained by a shift in the industrial structure away from the more pollutant-intensive sub-sectors and, to a lesser extent, by the adoption of EST.

ENVIRONMENTAL POLICY

Tunisia's efforts to strengthen its environmental protection legislation began with its water regulations. From the mid-1960s its environmental strategy consisted of extending wastewater treatment to all urban areas, as well as implementing a policy calling for an increase in the percentage of treated effluent that was to be reused. This gradual approach culminated in the Water Pollution Law, promulgated in 1975. This law was later backed up by a 1989 decree that set water quality standards and regulated agricultural reuse of wastewater after adequate treatment. This law and its related decree paved the way for the adoption of laws on air pollution in 1995.

In addition to these legislative measures, the government adopted several strategies, starting with its commitment to sustainable development. To this end it established the National Commission for Sustainable Development in 1993 and in 1995 adopted the National Plan of Action for the Environment and for Sustainable Development for the 21st Century (Tunisian Agenda 21) (MEAT, 1996). As a consequence, sector-specific environmental considerations in Agenda 21 were incorporated in the Eighth Socio-Economic Development Plan (1992–96), and the entirety of Agenda 21 was directly incorporated into the Ninth Socio-Economic Development Plan (1997–2001). The result of this was that the budget allocation for activities related to environmental protection increased by 67 per cent in the Ninth Plan as compared to the Eighth Plan, which was meant to lead to an allocation of 1.6 per cent of GDP to these activities (MEAT, 1997).

In 1991 the Ministry of Environment and Land Use Planning was established to promote environmental legislation and to anticipate, reduce and remove environmental risks for human beings, flora, fauna and all natural resources. This particular ministry included the National Environment Protection Agency (ANPE), created in 1988, the National Renewable Energy Agency, the National Office of Sanitation and the Tunis International Centre for Environmental Technologies (CITET). ANPE was responsible for implementing the environmental policies issued by the Ministry of Environment and Land Use Planning.

ANPE drew on a wide array of policy instruments for industrial environmental management, classified into four categories. Those are command-and-control regulation, economic and fiscal incentives, voluntary programmes and transparency and disclosure.

First, ANPE relied primarily on the traditional command-and-control regulatory approach of setting standards, issuing permits, monitoring compliance and enforcing actions. Discharge standards were set for wastewater disposal for all industries; plants were penalized for not investing in pollution control measures, though the penalties were not rigorously enforced; and the preparation of environmental impact assessments was required for all new industrial enterprises and the expansion of existing enterprises.

The effluent standards, or Normes Tunisiennes (NT 106-603, 1989), issued by ANPE conformed to the World Health Organization guidelines. They required that industrial effluent measured as BOD should not exceed 30 mg/l and, measured as COD (chemical oxygen demand), should not exceed 90 mg/l, except for some manufacturing sub-sectors, including the textile sub-sector.

Second, the government employed a number of economic instruments to reduce pollutant discharge, including reduced taxes of about 50 per cent on operating revenue invested in PATs and a 20 per cent subsidy of the value of an environmental investment. Environmental funds, such as the Foundation for the Cleaning of Pollution, were available for financing investments in EST. This foundation provided a 20 per cent subsidy for investments in pollution control equipment and funded investments in PATs by 37 textile mills between 1994 and 2000. It provided soft loans and, within the framework of projects funded by banks, incentives were provided in the form of reimbursements of up to 5 per cent of the costs (CETTEX, 2005).

Third, two voluntary programmes involving the participation of industry were under way in Tunisia at this time. One, the Environmental Pollution Prevention Programme, launched by the United States Agency for International Development in 1993, encouraged the use of CTs. The newly established Tunisian Cleaner Production Centre, funded jointly by UNIDO and UNEP, continued its work in 1996. The second voluntary programme was the ISO 14000 certification programme, established in 1997. The impact of this programme was limited, with only 13 firms certified as of 2002. Like many developing countries, Tunisia continued to encounter difficulties in participating in international standardization; in particular, the lack of financial resources to train experts, the cost of translating standards into the national language in order to disseminate information, and the lack of private sector support for standardization. There was not, at this time, a voluntary programme for product labelling.

Finally, the country's transparency and disclosure programmes could not compare with those in many developed and some developing countries. There was not yet any national reporting on environmental compliance or the release of pollutants; nor was there public access to information on industrial compliance with environmental norms.

Global comparison

Overall, Tunisia's environmental protection strategy during the 1990s was twofold. First, it applied corrective action to reverse the environmental damage caused by years of growth and development during which the environment was neglected. Second, it encouraged preventive action by requiring environmental impact assessments for new industrial investments, promoting the use of CTs and supporting the integration of environmental factors into investment decisions. Thus it is not surprising that the effectiveness of Tunisia's environmental governance, as measured by the EG index, was high. Tunisia ranked twenty-fifth among 65 countries in 1990 and dropped only to twenty-seventh in 2001. In both years it ranked fifth out of 40 developing countries and first among the countries included in this study.

ECONOMIC POLICY REGIMES

Overviews of Tunisia's three economic policy regimes, industrial, trade and resource pricing, the economic policies that most directly influence technological modernization in the manufacturing sector and thereby increase the likelihood of the adoption of EST (see Chapter 3), are presented in this section.

Industrial Policy

A comprehensive reform process was initiated in Tunisia in the 1980s. Incorporated in the Seventh Socio-Economic Development Plan (1987–91) and extended in the Eighth Socio-Economic Development Plan (1992–96) and the Ninth Socio-Economic Development Plan (1997–2001), it was aimed at changing the country's development strategy from a socialist-style interventionist one based on import substitution to one based on free markets and an export orientation (MDC, 1987, 1992, 1997). The new policy orientation emerged from the liberalization of the economy towards a more market-oriented structure and the opening up of the domestic economy to the international economy.

This shift in industrial policy included changes in three policy instruments: foreign direct investment (FDI), export promotion and industrial zones, all with the potential for stimulating the modernization of technology.

FDI

The use of FDI as an instrument of industrial policy in Tunisia in the 1990s would have resulted in foreign firms bringing more advanced (and usually less resource-intensive) technologies into the country. With a small domestic market, close proximity to major markets and capital suppliers, and with largely complementary patterns of comparative advantage with its neighbouring countries, Tunisia was, in any case, always somewhat dependent on foreign trade and investment. Through the promulgation of the Investment Incentives Code in 1994 it succeeded in attracting more FDI (MIE, 2000). Between 1990 and 2002, FDI inflows increased dramatically from US$0.09 billion to US$0.59 billion, an increase of almost 650 per cent; as a share of GDP, FDI increased from 0.8 to 3.4 per cent (World Bank, 2004).[1] The European Union (EU), with more than 70 per cent of Tunisia's total trade in merchandise and services in 2002, was the major source of foreign investment in the country.

Export promotion

Government efforts to boost exports had begun in Tunisia in the 1970s. In 1973 the Tunisian Centre for Export Promotion was created under the supervision of the Ministry of Trade to investigate export opportunities in new markets, particularly in difficult new markets outside the EU. The Centre also assisted with information and technical advice and administered an export promotion fund – Fonds de promotion des exportations – set up in 1984. Additional responsibilities include financing market prospects, promoting companies abroad and participating in foreign fairs and salons. Another export promotion agency – Fonds d'Accès aux Marchés – was set up in 2000. In the second phase of the programme at the time of this study, Fonds d'Accès aux Marchés 2 provided exporting firms with technical and financial aid in order to develop marketing strategies. Overall, manufactured exports increased by approximately 130 per cent, from US$2.4 billion in 1990 to US$5.6 billion in 2002, and the share of manufactured exports in total exports increased from 69 per cent to 82 per cent over the same period (World Bank, 2004).

Industrial estates

The establishment of industrial zones and export processing zones in the 1990s, which were required by law to build and operate common waste-water treatment plants (CEPTs), encouraged the adoption of EST, in particular of PATs. Under the Ninth Socio-Economic Development Plan the government renovated the existing industrial estates and established 28 new ones, seven of which were located in Greater Tunis (MDC, 1997). Two export processing zones (Bizerta and Zarzis) were established offering additional incentives, primarily exemptions from most taxes and customs duties.

Global comparison

In summary, the industrial policies of the 1990s contributed considerably to improving the competitiveness of the country and at the same time encouraged the adoption of more advanced and therefore cleaner technology, especially in the case of the five-year development plans. As a result Tunisia's ranking in terms of the CIP index improved, both overall and in all of the individual components of the index. In 2000 it ranked forty-sixth among 93 countries, placing it among those with medium low industrial competitiveness, improving its ranking from forty-ninth in 1990 and fifty-fifth in 1980. Among 68 developing countries it ranked twentieth in 2000, a slight improvement from twenty-fourth in 1990. It ranked fifth among the eight countries included in this study.

Trade Policy

The broad outlines of Tunisia's trade policies were formulated in the five-year development plans that had evolved over the years. Since the 1970s Tunisian trade policy has rested on two pillars: (a) export promotion by means of incentives intended to attract foreign direct investment and (b) a well-protected and -regulated domestic market. During the 1990s Tunisia, aiming to reinforce the success of its export policy, modified its trade strategy by introducing structural adjustment and privatization programmes. This orientation, designed primarily to improve the competitiveness of the local industries, resulted in further liberalization of the economy and exposed industry to international market forces (WTO, 2005).

The main drivers leading to reductions in tariff and non-tariff measures were Tunisia's participation in the Uruguay Round Agreement between 1986 and 1994 and its joining the World Trade Organization in 1995. Its trade liberalization was pursued further through several bilateral and regional trade agreements. Tunisia enjoyed preferential trading relations with African, Middle East and Mediterranean countries, and had trade agreements with 41 developing and developed countries (EIU, 2003).

In 1995, Tunisia and the EU signed the Association Agreement, which replaced the Cooperation Agreement of 1976 and was aimed at establishing a free trade zone with the EU by the year 2008 (EU, 2004: 3). To smooth the process towards the establishment of this zone, the EU, in cooperation with the Ministry of Industry and Energy and the Industrial Promotion Agency, set up a technical assistance programme in 1998 for the development of the private sector, namely, the Euro-Tunisie-Entreprise Programme (ETE). The purpose of this programme was to modernize industry with the objective of improving the competitiveness of Tunisia's SMEs in local and foreign markets. For the period 1998–2003 the EU allocated EUR 20 million to fund several activities, such as enterprise diagnostics, the introduction of new equipment and management tools, quality improvement and the establishment of support structures for enterprises. In addition the ETE Programme focused on transferring research results to industry as well as strengthening public and private organizations that provided support to enterprises, such as l'Agence de Promotion de l'Industrie and other technical centres. The ETE Programme was designed for a period of five years and was completed in 2002. Another programme was set up in its place in 2003 for a period of five years and was also funded by the EU, in cooperation with the Ministry of Industry and Energy.

The failure to reduce import restrictions on manufactured goods caused by the numerous trade-related agreements was most clearly but only partially reflected by the change in the TMP. Overall, Tunisia increased its TMP from 28.3 per cent in 1994 to 28.7 per cent in 2002. While this small increase would not have been a disincentive to import manufactured (including capital) products in the 1990s, the overall level of TMP certainly would have been. Tunisia's TMP ranking dropped from thirty-ninth among 48 countries in about 1990 to fifty-second among 53 countries in about 2002. It ranked seventh among the eight countries included in this study (World Bank, 2004).

A more comprehensive measure of import restrictiveness, one that captures the impact of both tariff and non-tariff measures, is the TRI. Tunisia received a high score (8 out of 10) on the TRI as of 2004, based on the cumulative effect of all restrictions. It ranked sixty-fourth among 66 countries, which indicates that the combined impact of all tariff and non-tariff measures remained highly restrictive for the import of manufactured goods. It ranked seventh among the eight countries included in this study.

Partially as a result of Tunisia's highly restrictive import regime, the import of manufactured goods increased from only US$4.0 billion in

1990 to US$7.2 billion in 2002, an increase of 82 per cent. Similarly the import of capital goods, one sub-category of manufactured goods, increased from US$1.5 billion in 1990 to US$2.8 billion in 2002, an increase of 79 per cent. Thus in both years the share of imported capital goods as a percentage of imported manufactured goods remained approximately the same, 39 per cent in 1990 and 38 per cent in 2002 (World Bank, 2005).

The textile sub-sector
In line with the overall maintenance of a high tariff level in the 1990s, Tunisia maintained a relatively high tariff level on two of the categories of imports used in the manufacture of textiles. The tariff level on textile yarn and fabric imports decreased only from 36.1 per cent in 1990 to 33.1 per cent in 2002. The 2002 tariff level was nearly twice as high as Thailand's 18.2 per cent in 2001, the latest year for which data were reported by the World Bank (2005). However, in spite of the relatively high tariff level, the value of imported textile yarn and fabric increased by 80 per cent. The tariff level on the import of synthetic organic colour agents actually increased, from 21.3 to 23.0 per cent, between 1990 and 2002. The value of imported colour agents nevertheless increased by 40 per cent, though this was a relatively low increase compared to the 100 per cent increase in imported colour agents in Thailand. However, the tariff level on textile machinery was low in 1990 (17 per cent) compared to Thailand (30 per cent) and was done away with totally in 2002. This partially contributed to the higher value of imports of textile machinery in 2002 compared to 1990.

Global comparison
In summary, Tunisia's commitment to trade liberalization policies did not involve any significant lowering of trade-related import restrictions on manufactured goods in the 1990s. The relatively high restrictions were one cause of the restraint in the import of manufactured goods, including capital goods, between 1990 and 2002. However, the tariff levels for textile machinery declined and textile machinery imports increased and, in spite of the small increase in the tariff level on dyeing agents, imports of dyeing agents also increased, by more than 40 per cent. Even though Tunisia had a relatively restrictive import regime, it ranked relatively high on the TI index, coming forty-first among all 91 countries covered by the index in 2001, and declining from its thirty-seventh rank in 1990, which placed it among the group of countries with medium high technology import. In 2001 Tunisia ranked second among the eight countries included in this study.

Resource Pricing Policy

As with all the other countries reviewed in this study, it was not possible to obtain sufficient information to provide a comprehensive overview of resource pricing policies, including the use of subsidies for energy and water, nor was it possible to calculate the average change in resource prices between 1990 and 2002. This section therefore provides only limited information on resource pricing policies, prices *per se* and changes in energy and water use by the manufacturing sector. Higher resource prices, as seen in Chapter 3, are often incentives for adopting EST, particularly CTs.

The public sector continued to play a dominant role in energy management. The electricity sector was controlled by the Ministry of Industry and Energy and managed by the Société Tunisienne de l'Electricité et du Gaz, a public company founded in 1962 which produced, transported and distributed power as well as natural gas. It had the monopoly of these activities until 1996, when the power generation market was opened to the private sector. The private companies subsequently operating in the sector were mainly involved in production, exploration and distribution. However, the government continued to hold a monopoly over pricing, and between 1998 and 2003 it reduced the price of electricity from 0.062 to 0.047/EUR/kWh to stimulate the economy (CETTEX, 2005).

From 1990 the consumption of energy (defined as energy derived from oil, coal, natural gas, nuclear power, renewable sources and electricity) in the manufacturing sector increased by 25 per cent, as shown in Table 9.2. This sector accounted for 39 per cent of the national energy consumption in 1990 and 27 per cent in 2002 (IEA, 2005).

The textile sub-sector's energy consumption is estimated to have increased by 246 per cent during this period, from 15 ktoe to 36 ktoe[2] and its energy intensity by 4 per cent during the same period, from 138 to 148 toe per million US dollars of MVA. The sub-sector accounted for 1.1 per cent of energy consumption by industry in 1990 and 2.2 per cent in 2002 (IEA, 2005).

Policies on water management were strongly marked by the complicated institutional framework. The Ministry of Agriculture had primary charge of water resources, but several other departments played an administrative role in water-related policies, namely, the Secretary of State, the Department of Water Resources, the Department of Public Infrastructure Projects and the Department of Civil Engineering.

Before 1997 the price of tap water varied between 35 and 95 per cent of the established government price for water. In 1997 a decree on the pricing of water was promulgated that set the price at $.01 per cubic metre, a very nominal price. The price of tap water increased with the level of consumption, thus providing some incentive for water conservation (SONEDE, 2005).

Water supply facilities, either tap or well water, were usually available at the factory site. Since there were no regulations regarding the industrial use of well water, it was used free of charge so there was no economic incentive for its rational use, a crucial issue for an arid country with chronic water shortages.

According to the state water authority, the Tunisian National Water Supply and Exploitation Society, water consumption by all sectors increased by about 15 per cent from 1990 to 2000, whereas water consumption by the manufacturing sector increased by 28 per cent. The manufacturing sector consumed around 20 per cent of all processed water distributed by the Society in both 1990 and 2000. However water-use intensity decreased by approximately 20 per cent during this period (see Table 10.2).

Global comparison
There is no global assessment that can be used to compare the relative effectiveness of Tunisia's resource pricing; nor are there any studies available on the effect of pricing on resource-use efficiency on pricing. As an alternative, an EUI score for manufacturing sectors was calculated for use in this study. In the case of Tunisia, energy-use intensity decreased considerably during the 1990s, from 500 toe per million US dollars of MVA in 1990 to 340 toe in 2002. Tunisia improved its EUI ranking from fifty-second out of 93 countries in 1990 to thirty-third in 2000. It made the greatest reduction in energy-use intensity between 1990 and 2002 of all the eight countries included in this study, ranking first in 2002.

TECHNOLOGY POLICY

The formulation and implementation of scientific and technological policy has a relatively long history in Tunisia, a history that had seen the birth of the most developed and sophisticated scientific community in North Africa. The current technology policy evolved from the collective science and technology programmes of three universities, 18 national research institutes and one private R&D institute, as well as a growing number of international joint ventures.

The Ministry of Higher Education, Scientific Research and Technology, established in 1991, was responsible for boosting R&D and technology transfer in every sector of the economy. In 2001 it was merged with the State Secretariat of Scientific Research and Technology to improve the generally low technological level of enterprises and to stimulate technological innovation. The main tasks of the Secretariat were the strategic planning, coordination and evaluation of all Tunisian R&D funded from the state budget (CITET, 2002).

The annual budget dedicated to R&D activities grew during the 1990s, its share of GDP increasing from 0.5 per cent to 1 per cent (CITET, 2002). Funding provided by the State Secretariat of Scientific Research and Technology alone increased from US$1 million to US$10 million between 1992 and 2002. A major outcome of this increased funding was the passing of the country's first legislation dedicated to the organization of R&D in 2001. As a result, all industries, including the textile and clothing sub-sectors, were now benefiting from new laboratories, with research units established in 13 different organizations by 2002.

Overall, government programmes focused on the development and adoption of more advanced technologies by specific manufacturing sub-sectors. These included the strengthening of branch-level technical centres that provided enterprises with efficient, demand-driven services: the Technical Centre for Food Processing and Agro Industry, the Technical Chemical Centre, the Technical Centre for the Wood and Furniture Industry, the Technical Centre for Textiles and the Technical Centre for Packaging.

Two other organizations were key players in the development and diffusion of technology, including EST. One was the National Scientific and Technical Research Institute, which was developing industrial waste-water treatment and recycling methods with particular focus on textile industry effluent. The other was the Tunis International Centre for Environmental Technologies (CITET), which was playing a key role in mastering and adapting EST and transferring it to industry.

In order for Tunisia to prepare its industry for the trade agreement with the EU, the Tunisian government launched a National Programme for Industry Upgrading (PMN: Programme de Mise à Niveau) in 1996 (UNIDO, 2000). This programme was implemented by the Tunisian Ministry of Industry and Energy and targeted on 4000 key industrial enter-prises for public support over a ten-year period. It was a voluntary effort and included all aspects of the internal and external needs of enterprises. It supported diagnostic studies of vital business functions (management, accounting, marketing, technical and financial structure, etc.), which in turn formed the basis for formulating short- and medium-term action plans. However, no diagnostic studies on environmental matters were undertaken as part of the programme. Between 1996 and 2003 it involved approximately 1100 companies, of which 640 were from the textile sub-sector.

To further support technology transfer, the government established the

Fund for Promoting the Transfer of Technology under the new 1994 Investment Incentives Code. Between 1994 and 1997 the Fund provided support to approximately 660 companies. In 1999 it was replaced by the Fund for Industrial Restructuring, Quality and Competitiveness Improvement, which provided financial support to enterprises participating in the PMN. However, the results of technology transfer failed to meet expectations because many plants continued to act as mere passive receptors of technology (UNIDO/UNDP, 2001).

During the 1990s various reforms in the educational and vocational training system were undertaken, and these led to improvements in technical education, including the training of textile engineers in specialized institutions, the main institutions being the National Engineers School of Monastir and the Ksar–Hellal Institute of Superior Technological Studies. The capacity of these schools increased during the 1990s with the addition of complementary subjects to their curricula. For example, during the academic year 2001–2, the National Engineers' School of Monastir introduced a master's programme in mechanics and textile materials. The number of students sent abroad for further specialization also increased during the 1990s.

Global Comparison

In summary, Tunisia's science and technology policy and infrastructure changed during the 1990s with the shift towards a market-oriented economy. The government recognized the importance of technology upgrading services and training of its labour force. Investment funds were made available for technological modernization, both by the government and the EU. The PMN, complemented by branch-level technical centres, focused on improving the productivity of the manufacturing sector in order to enable it to compete in the global economy. In spite of these changes Tunisia ranked low on the TC index being placed ninety-second among 162 countries in 2000, a slight improvement on its rank of ninety-eighth in 1990, which put it among the group of countries with low technological activity. It was forty-fifth out of 114 developing countries. Its ranking was similar to that of most of the other countries included in this study, particularly China, which ranked eighty-fifth and Zimbabwe, which ranked ninety-sixth among the 162 countries; among the eight in this study it ranked fourth.

THE TEXTILE SUB-SECTOR

Economic Overview

The textile industry is the common, collective designation for two manufacturing sub-sectors, textiles (ISIC 321) and wearing apparel (ISIC 322). In the case of Tunisia there are no historical data on the production of textiles or wearing apparel for 1990, only for 1995 and 2002. Between these years the production of textiles increased by 40 per cent and of wearing apparel by 10 per cent (Table 9.3).

The export value of textiles more than doubled between 1990 and 2002, increasing from US$112 million to US$227 million, and in 2002 Tunisia was the twenty-first largest global exporter of textiles. Virtually all exports of textiles were directed to Europe (95 per cent), making Tunisia the fourth largest supplier to the EU after China, Hong Kong and Turkey. This strong European dependence explains why the textile industry was to become one of the most important beneficiaries of the free trade zone with the EU.

Overall, the textile sub-sector made a notable contribution to the Tunisian manufacturing sector in the 1990s. Its value added increased from US$107 million in 1990 to US$253 million in 2002, approximately 135 per cent, while total Tunisian MVA increased from US$2.6 billion to US$4.8 billion, approximately 85 per cent (UNIDO, 2005). Its percentage share of MVA was about 4 per cent in 1990 and 5 per cent in 2002. In 2002 the textile sub-sector employed about 52 000 workers, and the wearing apparel sub-sector employed 152 000 workers; combined they accounted for approximately one half of employment in the manufacturing sector (CETTEX, 2005).

Table 9.3   Textiles and wearing apparel production and textile import and export

Year	Textiles and wearing apparel production (thousand tons)[a]		Textiles (US$ million)[b]	
	Textiles	Wearing Apparel	Import	Export
1990	n.a.	n.a.	790.4	111.7
1995	55	122	1289.4	164.9
2002	75	134	1424.7	226.9

Sources: [a] CETTEX (2005); [b] World Bank (2005).

Sub-sector Profile

The textile industry is a sequential manufacturing operation (complete production cycle), comprising five major stages: (a) fibre production (natural or man-made); (b) spinning; (c) weaving and knitting; (d) dyeing/printing and finishing; and (e) wearing apparel production. Each stage is related in that the product from one stage may be a raw material for the subsequent stage. The last stage, garment production, is considered in this section as a separate sub-sector in terms of industrial statistics, and in this chapter.

There were about 2300 textile industry operations in 2002. The textile sub-sector consisted of approximately 355 industrial units employing more than ten persons each. The remainder, 1945 units, were engaged in wearing apparel production. Approximately 60 per cent of units in the textile sub-sector and 80 per cent of the wearing apparel units produced exclusively for export (API, 2003). Most of the firms in the textile industry were SMEs. In the wearing apparel sub-sector there was a predominance of large firms, some of them employing more than 500 workers (UNIDO, 2001). Textile and wearing apparel production was mainly concentrated in the Greater Tunis region, Sahil (Sousse and Monastir) and in the Sfax province in the south. The government offered tax incentives to encourage the establishment of mills in industrial zones that were far from the cities.

Of the 355 textile mills, 60 per cent were small-scale operations, likely to use outdated production technology, and the remainder were medium- and large-scale operations using modern production technology (CETTEX, 2005).

The dyeing/printing and finishing stage, the most pollutant-intensive stage of textile production, consists of one of two processing configurations. In one configuration this stage is part of an integrated mill, which combines several textile-processing operations in one place, while in the other configuration it is the only stage at the mill. In the latter, commonly called a commission mill, production starts with fabric preparation, that is, desizing, scouring and bleaching, and continues through dyeing/printing and finishing.

Of the 37 dyeing and finishing mills, ten were selected for this study based on criteria that called for variations in their degree of integration, size and location. The selected mills corresponded to the criteria as follows: seven were integrated mills and three were commission mills; four were large and six were small; and all were located mostly in the Greater Tunis region and in the cities of Ben Arous, Ariana and Monastir (Table 9.4).

The ten selected dyeing and finishing mills represented about 25 per cent of these in the sub-sector and about 40 per cent of production capacity. Their age ranged from seven to 28 years. Other characteristics of the mills worth noting are: nine were privately owned and one was government

Table 9.4 Profile of the ten mills investigated

Mill	Process	Scale	Location: region	Sales orientation (% in 2000)	Technology vintage	Ownership	EST score	Regulatory compliance	Donor assist.	EMS
T1	Dyeing and finishing	Small	Hammam Lif	100% E	Standard–modern	33% private domestic, 67% private foreign	PAT + LCT	Yes	None	No
T2	Dyeing and finishing	Large	Jebel Jeloud	50% D, 50% E	Standard–modern	100% private domestic	PAT + LCT/ Municipal ETP	Yes	UNIDO	No
T3	Dyeing and finishing	Small	Ksar Said	85% D, 15% E	Standard–modern	100% private domestic	PAT + LCT	Yes	USAID	No
T4	Dyeing and finishing	Large	Kasar Hellal	20% D, 80% E	BAT	100% government	PAT + MCT	Yes	UNIDO/ WCPS	No
T5	Dyeing and finishing	Small	Kasar Hellal	100% D	Standard–modern	100% private domestic	PAT + LTC	Yes	UNIDO	EMS
T6	Dyeing and finishing	Large	Menzel Temime	100% E	BAT	100% private domestic	PAT + MCT	Yes		No

					BAT		PAT + MCT		EC	No
T7	Dyeing and finishing	Large	Menzel Temime	100% E	BAT	100% private domestic	PAT + MCT	Yes	EC	No
T8	Dyeing and finishing	Small	Ben Arous	100% D	Standard–modern	100% private domestic	PAT + LTC Municipal ETP	Yes	UNIDO/WCPS	No
T9	Dyeing and finishing	Small	Charguia	70% D, 30% E	Standard–modern	100% private domestic	PAT + LTC	Nn (has been penalized)		No
T10	Dyeing and finishing	Small	Ben Arous	50% D, 50% E	Standard–modern	100% private domestic	PAT + LTC Industrial Estate ETP	Yes	UNIDO/WCPS	No

Abbreviations: domestic (D); export (E); best available technology (BAT); pollution abatement technology (PAT); higher order technological complexity (HTC); medium order technological complexity (MTC); lower order technological complexity (LTC); effluent treatment plant (ETP).

Source: CITET (2002).

owned; three exported all of their production, three exported 50 per cent or more and the other four exported less than 50 per cent; and 30 per cent were certified ISO 9001 but none were certified ISO 14001 and only one was in the process of certification. It should be noted that in the overall textile and wearing apparel sector only 22 companies were certified ISO 9001 at the time of this study (CETTEX, 2005).

Process Technology and CT Characterization

The long life of dyeing equipment and the high capital cost of installing new equipment discouraged its replacement. Hence around 55 per cent of the equipment used by the textile sub-sector had an average life span of ten years or more.

Mills in the textile sub-sector, as of 2000, used a mixture of different types of machines. Some still imported second-hand machines, but an increasing number used new automated ones that regulated water and injected chemicals automatically, thus optimizing resource inputs. The survey team assigned the mills to one of three technology categories, traditional, standard–modern and best available technology (BAT), based on the technological vintage of the dyeing equipment. Seven of the mills selected used standard–modern technology and three used BAT (Table 9.4). The absence of any traditional operations can be explained by the fact that nine of the ten mills were built after 1980. One was constructed in 1959 and it modernized its equipment in the early 1990s.

The survey team also classified the mills into three groups based on the highest order of complexity of the CTs used in each mill (low, medium and high). Given that most of those in the study were involved in CP projects, it is not surprising that they used some CTs in their operations. Seven used CTs of a lower order of technological complexity and three used CTs of a medium order of technological complexity. What is surprising is that none used CTs of a higher order of technological complexity. What is not surprising, though, is that (a) the three mills that operated their own wastewater treatment systems had adopted CTs of a medium order of complexity to reduce pollutant generation and (b) the three that discharged into municipal or industrial estate-managed wastewater treatment systems had adopted only CTs of a lower order of complexity.

CTs were used in all the stages of dyeing and finishing textiles. The survey team did not document specific types of CTs used or the frequency of their use. As an alternative they asked CETTEX to estimate their use based on their work with dyeing and finishing mills (Table 9.5).

The use of CTs to conserve water and minimize chemical use was common in textile operations, despite the limited number of engineers.

Table 9.5   CTs used in dyeing and finishing mills in Tunisia

Practice	High use	Moderate use	Low use
Build-in bath and reuse on dye machine			x
Caustic and size recovery			x
Chemical dosing system			x
Continuous knit dyeing range			x
Control, automation, and scheduling management system		x	
Counter-current washing		x	
Heat recovery system			x
Humidity sensors and advanced controls for drying		x	
Incinerator dryers			
Low bath-ratio dyeing systems		x	
Mechanical finishing		x	
Pad-batch dyeing machines for fibre-reactive dyes		x	
Quick-change pads on continuous ranges			x
Low add-on finishing		x	
Water recovery systems		x	
Vacuum system for chemical recovery			x
Computerized colour matching system		x	

Source: CETTEX (2005).

Of particular concern was the use of pumps and buffer tanks to reuse water, which resulted in a reduction of water consumption. Plant managers were aware of this possibility and many were already recycling water, while others were investigating the possibility of doing so. In addition, because of their high cost, chemicals were, on the whole, carefully prepared to prevent spilling and overdosing. An increasing number of mills used computer-assisted dyeing to determine the quantities and mixture of dyes.

The potential of CTs to reduce water, energy and chemical usage in the textile sub-sector is well documented in Tunisia. For example, a CP assessment at one mill resulted in the implementation of several CT options, which led to measurable reductions at a low cost (Box 9.1).

PAT Characterization

The use of PATs was required of all industrial establishments in Tunisia that discharged directly into water bodies and was subsidized to some

BOX 9.1   CLEANER PRODUCTION CASE STUDY: TUNISIA

The company is a commissioned dyer and finisher and employs some 20 persons. Its annual production is approximately 550 000 kg. The company treats woven and knitted fabrics of polyester, polyester/cellulosic blends and cotton together with small amounts of other fibres. Its implementation of CT options included water recycling and reduced water consumption (by 31 000 m³/year), reduced energy consumption (by 30 per cent, saving 165 000 m³/year of natural gas) and improved process optimization by minimizing chemical use and improving product quality. The use of CTs led to annual savings of US$98 000 for a total investment of US$94 000. Housekeeping measures accounted for more than 60 per cent of the savings, and water and energy conservation measures accounted for 37 per cent of the savings.

Source: UNIDO (2005b).

extent by the government, as described in the section on environmental policy. In addition, several initiatives were launched to promote their use in the context of the PMN. As of 2000, 50 per cent of all mills in the sub-sector had built effluent treatment plants (ETPs) and 40 per cent were in the process of doing so (CITET, 2002).

All ten mills included in the survey had installed appropriate pollution control equipment. Seven that discharged directly into watercourses had operational ETPs, the management of which differed from mill to mill. They used a version of secondary treatment described as extended aeration activated sludge. It has a longer detention time than normal for activated sludge treatment (24 rather than eight hours) in order to break down the chemicals in the effluent. The other three mills had the equivalent of an ETP, two of them pre-treating their wastewater before discharging into a common effluent treatment plant (CETP) operated by a municipality and one pre-treating it before discharging it into a CETP managed by an industrial estate.

Environmental Performance

The annual report of the Ministry of Agriculture, Environment and Hydraulic Resources (2003) did not include data on pollutant discharge from the manufacturing sector or its sub-sectors. The only estimate of the textile sub-sector's pollutant load and share of BOD effluent is the one made by the World Bank (2004). The Bank estimated that the textile sub-sector accounted for some 35 per cent of total organic water pollutants discharged by the manufacturing sector in 2000.

A survey conducted by the National Sewerage Company in 1996 identified approximately 3530 polluting plants, of which 250 were in the textile and leather sub-sectors. In 2002 the National Sewerage Company took approximately 1600 industrial wastewater samples and performed 22 000 analyses (levels of chloride, BOD, COD and various heavy metals). ANPE found that 1440 of these samples did not conform to national environmental standards (ONAS, 2002).

Of the seven mills that discharged directly into watercourses, six were reported to be in compliance with environmental standards, while all three that discharged into CETPs were reported to be in compliance. However, ANPE's inability to provide data about compliance on a regular basis raised questions about its ability to ensure continuous compliance with environmental standards.

Many dyeing and finishing mills phased out environmentally harmful chemicals during the 1990s as a result of pressure from buyers from abroad. For example, sodium hypochlorite in bleaching processes ceased to be used, and oxidizing sulphur dyes superseded sodium bi-chromate. Tunisian managers now tended to buy dyes from manufacturers belonging to the Ecological and Toxicological Association of Dyes and Organic Pigment Manufacturers, which ensured the usage of more environmentally friendly dyes.

KEY INFORMANTS AND INTERNATIONAL DONORS

Four groups, in addition to environmental regulatory government agencies and technology centres, are able to influence in different ways the extent to which plants adopt EST: NGOs, business associations, international donors of technical assistance, and chemical and equipment suppliers. The following section provides some information only on the first three because there is insufficient information to characterize companies that supplied chemicals and equipment to Tunisia's textile sub-sector.

NGOs

Around 90 different civil associations were actively involved in environment and sustainable development at the time of this study. These associations participated in national and regional meetings on planning and regulation for environmental management and sustainable development.

The survey team interviewed one NGO, the Tunisian Association for Protection of Nature and the Environment, which was established in 1971 and joined the Friends of the Earth International in 1995. It represents Northern African NGOs in the World Conservation Union.

Business Associations

The survey team interviewed the main association for the textile sub-sector, the National Textile Federation, which is part of the Tunisian Private Business Federation of Industry, Commerce and Crafts (UTICA). It was founded in 1969 and represents all the textile firms. It aims to harmonize their actions, defend their interests in social, economic, financial and fiscal areas, and promote the development of the sub-sector. It participates in the elaboration of Tunisia's national development plan and is also an umbrella organization for the 14 trade unions representing different branches of the textile sub-sector.

International Donors

In the 1990s international donors played a comparatively important role in accelerating the adoption of EST and promoting linkages between enterprises and governments and between plants and research institutes. Their main activities were to provide information, technical advice and financial services.

The Environmental Pollution Prevention Project, funded by the United States Agency for International Development, was the first systematic effort to introduce CP into Tunisia. During the implementation of the project (1993–97) it provided training to 200 participants, mainly consulting engineers and engineering students, raised awareness of CP among 250 industry representatives and conducted CP assessments in 11 plants, including two textile dyeing and finishing mills. The professionals who were trained under this project became the core of the UNIDO/UNEP Tunisian Cleaner Production Centre established at CITET in 1998. That same year the Norwegian World Cleaner Production Society initiated a CP capacity-building programme with CITET to train professionals to conduct CP assessments and disseminate CP principles. As a result of this support, 25 CP assessors were trained and CP assessments undertaken in ten plants, and on average the pollutant loadings from the participating plants were reduced by 25 per cent.

The EU was an important donor to Tunisia, particularly its support for meeting the 2008 deadline for the establishment of a free trade zone. Its training programmes provided information on improved materials and more efficient production processes.

Tunisia was the single largest partner of the German Technical Cooperation Agency in the environmental sector. Cooperation in this sector included solid waste management, pollution control, and adoption of new and renewable energies, economic use of water, climate protection and desertification control.

The Spanish-funded ENORME–CETIME Initiative (Initiative Enorme du Centre Technique des Industries Mécaniques et Electriques) helped industrial enterprises to implement environmental management systems (ISO 14001) and offered courses on the preparation of CP and of environmental impact assessments during the 1990s.

SUMMARY

Tunisia's aggregate economic and environmental indicators showed a promising performance compared to other North African countries. While GDP increased by 69 per cent between 1990 and 2002, MVA increased by 85 per cent. As a result, the share of MVA in GDP increased from 16.9 to 18.6 per cent. GNI per capita at PPP increased by 81 per cent during the same period. Energy use in the manufacturing sector increased by 25 per cent, a much smaller percentage increase than that of MVA, and energy-use intensity decreased by 33 per cent. Total BOD effluent, however, increased by 11 per cent while BOD-effluent intensity decreased by 39 per cent.

Tunisia's environmental policy for industrial environmental management improved progressively during the 1990s and environmental considerations were introduced into the economic development planning processes. Furthermore, the government offered some incentives for adopting PATs, and it seems to have effectively included environmental considerations in technology modernization programmes.

The impact of the three economic policies, industrial, trade and resource pricing, on the adoption of EST in the 1990s was significant. The government's industrial restructuring and reforms, including the three specific policy instruments – FDI, export promotion and industrial zones – rapidly transformed the economy and brought about a high degree of technological modernization. In the textile sub-sector, in particular, changes in trade policy in the form of tariff and non-tariff measures were not sufficient to stimulate domestic textile producers to use more advanced production techniques and technologies. Because of significant industrial restructuring and new investment, there was a decrease in industrial energy-use intensity. Similarly, water-use efficiency in the manufacturing sector improved, but this was probably not attributable to appropriate or complete pricing of water. These improvements were most likely an indirect result of the national drive for technological modernization to increase manufacturing productivity.

The country's technology policy and infrastructure changed during the 1990s with the shift towards a market-oriented economy. The government recognized the importance of technology upgrading services and of training its labour force. Investment funds were made available, both from the government and the EU, for technological modernization. The PMN, complemented by branch-level technical centres, focused on improving the productivity of the manufacturing sector to enable it to compete in the global economy.

The textile sub-sector increased its production from 55 to 75 thousand tons between 1995 and 2002. As of 2002 there were approximately 355 industrial units involved in textile production, some of which were part of integrated mills and others non-integrated or commission mills. Approximately 60 per cent of the mills were small-scale operations using outdated production technology and the remainder were medium- and large-scale operations using modern production technology. The survey team conducted interviews at ten dyeing and finishing mills that accounted for approximately 50 per cent of production capacity in dyeing and finishing. Seven mills used standard–modern production technology and three mills used BAT. Seven used CTs of lower order technological complexity and three used CTs of medium order technological complexity. The seven mills that discharged directly into watercourses had installed secondary PATs and the other three that discharged into municipal or industrial estate sewers pre-treated their wastewater before discharge. Because of the high level of investment in PATs, nine of the ten plants were reported to be in compliance with environmental standards in 2002, probably as a result of carrying out proper operation and maintenance activities.

The influence of other institutional actors, NGOs, business associations and international donors, on EST adoption was limited primarily to international donors during the 1990s. NGOs concerned with pollution issues appear to have been few, and business associations appear to have not yet taken a strong interest in improving the environmental performance of the industrial sector. In contrast, international donors funded several programmes to improve industrial environmental performance, which complemented donor programmes aimed at increasing industrial productivity.

To conclude, there was extensive adoption of EST in the textile sub-sector, yet, at the time of this study, the sub-sector still contributed significantly to pollution and to unsustainable water and energy use. The majority of the mills were constrained by old technology. However, the adoption of EST was on the rise, particularly by mills that had an international partner and/ or were export oriented. Additional competitive pressures as well as enforcement of environmental regulations would encourage mills to adopt additional EST.

NOTES

1. The FDI for 1990 has been taken as the three-year average of 1989–91 and for 2002 as the three-year average of 2001–3, in order to even out fluctuations in FDI flows.
2. The IEA does not provide exclusive energy consumption data for the textile sub-sector; it was therefore calculated according to the proportion of MVA of the textile and the leather sub-sectors, for which the IEA provides information as one sub-sector.

REFERENCES

API (2003), 'Textile and Clothing Industry. Sector Overview', Tunis: Agence de Promotion de l'Industrie (API) (Industry Promotion Agency) (available on: http://www.tunisianindustry.nat.tn/en/doc.asp?docid=620&mcat=3&mrub=24# Exportations).
CETTEX (2005), personal communication, Tunis: Centre Tunisien de Textile.
CITET (2002), 'Survey of the Uptake of Environmentally Sound Technologies in the Industrial Subsector Textiles in Tunisia', report prepared for UNIDO, Tunis, Tunisia: Centre International des Technologies de l'Environnement de Tunis (CITET) (Tunis International Centre for Environmental Technologies).
EIU (1996), 'Country Report: Tunisia', London: Economist Intelligence Unit.
EIU (2003), 'Country Profile: Tunisia', London: Economist Intelligence Unit.
EIU (2004), 'Country Report: Tunisia', London: Economist Intelligence Unit.
EU (2004), 'European Neighbourhood Policy. Country Report – Tunisia', COM(2004)373 final. Brussels: European Commission (available on: http://ec.europa.eu).
FAO (2005), 'AQUASTAT: FAOSTAT', Rome: Food and Agriculture Organization of the United Nations (available on: http://www.fao.org).
IEA (2005), 'Online Data Services', IEA Energy Information Centre, Paris: International Energy Agency (available on: http://www.iea.org).
ISO (2003), 'The ISO Survey of ISO 9000 and ISO 14001 Certificates', Geneva: International Organization for Standardization (available on: http://www.iso.org).
MDC (1987), '7th Socio-Economic Development Plan (1987–1991)', Tunis, Tunisia: Ministère du Développement Economique (Ministry of Economic Development).
MDC (1992), '8th Socio-Economic Development Plan (1992–1996)', Tunis, Tunisia: Ministère du Développement Economique (Ministry of Economic Development).
MDC (1997), '9th Socio-Economic Development Plan (1997–2001)', Tunis, Tunisia: Ministère du Développement Economique (Ministry of Economic Development).
MEAT (1996), 'National Plan of Action for the Environment and Sustainable Development for the 21st Century', Tunis: Ministère de l'Environnement et de l'Aménagement de Territoire (MEAT) (Ministry of Environment and Land Use Planning).

MEAT (1997), 'Report on the State of the Environment', Tunis, Tunisia: Ministère de l'Environnement et de l'Amenagement de Territoire (MEAT) (Ministry of Environment and Land Use Planning).

MIE (2000) 'Investment Incentives Code', Tunis, Tunisia: Ministère de l'Industrie, de l'Energie et des petites et moyennes entreprises (Ministry of Industry and Energy and Small and Medium-sized Enterprises).

Ministries of Agriculture, the Environment and Hydraulic Resources (2003), *State of the Environment*, Tunis: Government of Tunisia.

ONAS (2002), 'Annual Report 2002', Tunis: Office National de l'Assainissement (ONAS) (National Sewerage Company).

SONEDE (2005), 'Informations Utiles: Quel est le Tarif de l'Eau?', Tunis, Tunisia: Société Nationale d'Exploitation et de Distribution des Eaux (SONEDE) (National Society of Water Supply and Exploitation) (available on: http://www.sonede.com.tn).

UNIDO (2000), 'Programme Cadre pour la Mise à Niveau et l'Amélioration de la Compétitivité de l'Industrie en Tunisie', Vienna: UNIDO.

UNIDO (2005a), *International Yearbook of Industrial Statistics 2005*, Cheltenham, UK and Northampton, MA, US: Edward Elgar Publishing.

UNIDO (2005b), 'UNIDO Cleaner Production, Success Stories/ NCPC Database', Vienna: UNIDO (available on: http://www.unido.org).

UNIDO/UNDP (2001), 'Support to SMEs in the Arab Region, the Case of Tunisia', Vienna: UNIDO.

World Bank (2004), 'World Bank Development Indicators (WDI) 2004', CD-ROM version, Washington, DC: The World Bank.

World Bank (2005), 'World Integrated Trade Solution (WITS)', Washington, DC: The World Bank (available on: http://wits.worldbank.org).

WTO (2005), 'Trade Regime in Need of Further Liberalization, Trade Policy Review: Tunisia', Geneva: World Trade Organization.

10. Viet Nam

INTRODUCTION

A survey team from the Institute for Environmental Science and Technology, Hanoi University of Technology, investigated the specific factors influencing the adoption of environmentally sound technology (EST) in Viet Nam's pulp and paper sub-sector. The team used semi-structured questionnaires provided by UNIDO to interview plant managers at nine out of approximately 300 plants in the sub-sector, and key informants in one business association, one technology centre, one chemical supplier, one environmental NGO and one environmental regulatory agency. The team also collected background data on the country and the pulp and paper sub-sector.

This chapter describes the economic and environmental context in Viet Nam for EST adoption; relevant environmental, economic and technology policies; the pulp and paper sub-sector and the plants investigated; and key informants and international donors.

THE ECONOMIC AND ENVIRONMENTAL CONTEXT FOR EST ADOPTION

The following selected economic and environmental performance indicators define the context in which manufacturing plants made their technology adoption decisions and, in particular, their decisions to adopt EST during the late 1990s/early 2000s.

Economic Performance Indicators

Viet Nam's economic achievements were impressive during the 1990s, with an average annual gross domestic product (GDP) growth rate of 7.6 per cent. Between 1990 and 2002 GDP increased by137 per cent, and GDP per capita by 96 per cent, while the population increased by 21 per cent (Table 10.1). This was Viet Nam's 'economic boom', which raised the country to the ranks of the Asian tigers in terms of growth: its growth rate more than doubled during this period and was second only to that of China.

Table 10.1 Economic performance indicators for Viet Nam

Economic indicator	Year	Value	Percentage change
GDP (constant 1995 US$ billion)	1990	14.0	137.0
	2002	33.2	
GDP per capita (constant 1995 US$)	1990	211.0	96.0
	2002	413.0	
Population (million)	1990	66.2	21.0
	2002	80.4	
GNI per capita at PPP (current international $)	1990	920.0	150.0
	2002	2300.0	
MVA (constant 1995 US$ billion)	1990	1.9	246.0
	2002	6.6	
MVA (percentage of GDP)	1995	12.3	8.3
	2002	20.6	
CPI (1995=100)	1995	100.0	24.0
	2002	123.8	
Interest rate (commercial lending rate)	1990	32.0	−72.0
	2002	9.1	
Exchange rate (VND/US$)	1990	6482.0	136.0
	2002	15279.0	

Source: World Bank (2004).

Gross national income (GNI) per capita at purchasing power parity (PPP) – a more accurate indicator of well-being – increased by 150 per cent. Based on this, Viet Nam was classified by the World Bank as a low-income country.

Such growth in GDP can be attributed to the very high economic performance of the country's manufacturing sector. Manufacturing value added (MVA) increased by 246 per cent between 1990 and 2002, with the MVA share of GDP increasing from 12.3 per cent in 1990 to 20.6 per cent in 2002. Within the manufacturing sector several sub-sectors grew especially rapidly, such as food processing and beverages, 24.1 per cent, electricity and fuel, 19.1 per cent and textiles and garments and footwear, 12.3 per cent (EIU, 2004). In addition, Viet Nam developed high-tech industrial sub-sectors, such as automobiles, precision mechanics, and electronics and telecommunication. Foreign direct investment (FDI) contributions, capital inflow and technology transfer played a major role in accelerating the industrialization process.

The country was also successful in managing the rate of inflation after experiencing hyperinflation in the 1980s. The consumer price index (CPI), which had increased significantly in the late 1990s – by 24 per cent from

1995 to 2002 – increased by only 0.8 per cent in 2001 and 4.0 per cent in 2002.[1]

Environmental Performance Indicators

Viet Nam's rapid industrialization brought the expected negative impact on the environment, made worse by the absence of an effective environmental regulatory programme. However, technological modernization, which often included the use of cleaner technology, brought some promising results, though pollution remained severe in several locations near industrial centres and in highly populated areas, which often overlapped.

Selected environmental indicators, namely, energy use, CO_2 emissions, organic matter effluent, measured as biochemical oxygen demand (BOD), and water use, as well as the intensity of use of each of these, provide an insight into the state of Viet Nam's industrial environmental performance at this time. These are presented in Table 10.2. Energy use in the manufacturing sector, measured in tons of oil equivalent (toe), surged by 249 per cent between 1990 and 2002, approximately the same as the growth of MVA. Consequently energy-use intensity in the manufacturing sector remained approximately the same. Associated CO_2 emissions increased by 230 per cent between 1990 and 2000 and CO_2-emission intensity decreased by 2 per cent. Total BOD effluent could be estimated only for 2001, when it was 74 000 tons and BOD-effluent intensity was 12.8 tons per million US dollars; sufficient data were not available to estimate them for 1990.[2] Data on water use and water-use intensity were also not available, as for other countries included in this study.

In 2001 the distribution of BOD effluent among manufacturing sub-sectors was as follows: food and beverages, 58 per cent; pulp and paper, 25 per cent; industrial chemicals, 11 per cent; others, 6 per cent. The BOD loadings of the pulp and paper sub-sector were second highest among the manufacturing sub-sectors.

The number of ISO 14001 certificates increased from two to 33 during the period 1998–2002. The country still lagged far behind many others in this regard, but was ahead of three other countries in this study, Kenya, Zimbabwe and Tunisia. Taking a comparison in the Asian region, it had five certificates per billion US dollars of MVA in 2002 whereas China had 6.1 and India 7.4.

Implications for EST Adoption

During the period investigated for this study the overall economic and environmental conditions in Viet Nam seemed highly conducive to the adoption

Table 10.2　Environmental perfomance indicators for Viet Nam

Source code	Environmental indicators	Year	Value	Percentage change
1	Energy use in the manufacturing sector (million toe)	1990 2002	1.7 6.0	249
1&2	Energy-use intensity (toe per million US$ of MVA)	1990 2002	903.0 912.0	1
2	CO_2 emissions from the manufacturing sector (million tons)	1990 2002	5.5 18.1	230
2	CO_2-emission intensity (tons per million US$ of MVA)	1990 2002	2800.0 2750.0	−2
2	BOD effluent from the manufacturing sector (thousand tons)	1990 2001	n.a. 74.2	−
2	BOD-effluent intensity (tons per million US$ of MVA)	1990 2001	n.a. 12.6	−
3	Water use in the manufacturing sector (billion m³)	1990 2000	n.a. n.a.	−
2&3	Water-use intensity (thousand m³ per million US$ of MVA)	1990 2000	n.a. n.a.	−
4	Percentage of MVA produced by the most pollutant-intensive sub-sectors	1990 2001	n.a. 19.8	−
5	Number of ISO 14001 certificates	1998 2002	2.0 33.0	1650

Sources:　1. IEA (2005); 2. World Bank (2004); 3. FAO (2005); 4. UNIDO (2004); 5. ISO (2003).

of EST by the country's manufacturing sector. The government of this accelerating developing country was assumed to have made only a limited effort to compel its manufacturing sector, the source of extensive pollution problems, to invest in EST before 1990.[3] From 1990 to 2002, this sector grew rapidly, with an 11.2 per cent average annual growth rate in MVA. In parallel there was an even larger percentage average annual growth in investment, some of which would have been in EST.[4] The low rate of inflation (the CPI was only 24 per cent from 1995 to 2002 but is said to have been very high from 1990 to 1994) and the declining interest rate (from 32.1 per cent in 1990 to 9.1 per cent in 2002) would have facilitated this large growth in new investment. The 246 per cent increase in the annual MVA between 1990 and 2002 was accompanied by a 249 per cent increase in energy use and a 1 per cent increase in energy-use intensity, which suggests that only limited investment took place in energy-efficiency technology. There were no BOD effluent data for 1990, but it can reasonably be assumed that BOD-effluent intensity was higher in 1990 than in 2002. The relatively high BOD-effluent intensity in that year compared to other countries suggests that the adoption of EST was limited.

ENVIRONMENTAL POLICY

Viet Nam's efforts in environmental protection legislation began with the Law on Environmental Protection, promulgated in 1993. This law was a general legal document and provided only a basic framework. Its 55 articles broadly established the country's policies on environmental protection. The government then promulgated numerous decrees to implement it, the most significant of these being Government Decree No. 175/CP on Providing Guidance for the Implementation of the Law on Environmental Protection, which set out the responsibilities of the National Environmental Agency (APCEL, 1998a).

Besides the legislative measures, the government put forth general strategies for protecting the environment, starting with the National Conservation Strategy in 1998. In 1992 it adopted the National Plan for Environment and Sustainable Development for the period 1990 to 2000, and a second national plan in 1999. The latter advanced various action programmes on: (a) natural resource conservation and rehabilitation; (b) urban and industrial pollution control; and (c) an institutional framework for the enhancement of environmental planning, management and protection. Following this strategy, the government promulgated a number of industrial environment-related policies in the National Strategy for Environmental Protection 2001–2010 (2003) and the National Action Plan for Cleaner Production (2003).

Until the recent government reorganization, the Ministry of Science, Technology and Environment was the organization primarily responsible for environmental governance. In 2002 it was split into the Ministry of Natural Resources and Environment (MONRE) and the Ministry of Science and Technology (MOST); both ministries became operational in 2003. The Viet Nam Environment Protection Agency (VEPA) was assigned to MONRE, as were the provincial environmental management offices, the Departments of Natural Resources and Environment (DONREs). Other industrial environmental management units were established in the Ministries of Industry, of Agriculture and Rural Development, and of Fishery.

The resources committed to implementing environmental management were limited in the 1990s. While some 400 people worked at the central level in ministries and government agencies engaged in natural resource and environmental management and 13 450 at the provincial and local levels, only 1300 were engaged in environmental management. Public expenditure on environmental management was less than 1 per cent of the national budget in the 1990s. Official development assistance bridged the financial gap in part, providing US$1 billion between 1985 and 1999 (UNDP, 1999).

These organizations drew on a wide range of policy instruments for industrial environmental management classified into four categories. These are command-and-control regulation, economic and fiscal incentives, voluntary programmes and transparency and disclosure.

First, national and provincial organizations relied primarily on the traditional command-and-control regulatory approach, which consisted of standard setting, permits issuance and compliance monitoring and enforcement. Their objective was to achieve compliance with the 1995 concentration-based national standards for water and air pollutants.

These authorities directed their enforcement efforts to the more polluting facilities. In particular, provincial and city authorities (DONREs) listed 4300 polluting establishments that were considered to cause serious environmental pollution. Many of these were SOEs. During the late 1990s the authorities' enforcement effort was concentrated on 439 of the most polluting establishments (INEST, 2002), including 14 pulp and paper mills. Four of the nine mills whose managers were interviewed for this study were included in the list (INEST, 2002).

Environmental impact assessments were required for new development projects as of 1994 and also for existing factories, which was not the case in most countries. Unfortunately the Ministry of Planning and Investment and sectoral agencies did not systematically inform VEPA about new projects that required an environmental review, thus undermining the effectiveness of the process (VEPA, 2002).

Second, the government used some economic instruments, such as charges, taxes and fines, to improve environmental performance and encourage compliance with existing standards. Furthermore, environmental funds, such as the Viet Nam Environmental Protection Fund, were available for financing EST projects. Nevertheless, the economic incentives structure needed to be enhanced, and the management of environmental funds needed to be strengthened (UNIDO, 2005).

Given Viet Nam's context, it was vital to establish an effective financing mechanism for the adoption of EST by SMEs, including those in the pulp and paper sub-sector. Some measures had already been taken: subsequent to the regulation on water pollution in rivers and lakes, small paper mills with an annual capacity under 1000 tons per year were restructured immediately and those with a capacity between 1000 and 10 000 tons per year initiated a modernization process. However, there were no effective financial mechanisms or institutions to support these technical transformation activities or to facilitate the adoption of EST.

Finally, some voluntary programmes in which industry participated were under way. Among the several cleaner production projects, the Viet Nam Cleaner Production Centre (VNCPC) was the main initiative. This and other multilateral and bilateral programmes and projects are described later in this chapter. The Directorate for Standards and Quality put into operation the mechanism of partial financial support for enterprises to establish their quality and environmental management, following ISO 9000 and ISO 14 000.

Global Comparison

Overall, Viet Nam's environmental policies on industrial environmental management were making progress at the time of this study, but still lacked plant-level monitoring and enforcement. It is therefore not surprising that it ranked fifty-ninth among 66 countries in 2001 on the environmental governance (EG) index, coming thirty-third among 40 developing countries. It was sixth among the eight countries included in this study, just ahead of Zimbabwe and Kenya. A historical comparison is not possible because there are no BOD loadings data to calculate the EG index for 1990.

ECONOMIC POLICY REGIMES

Overviews of Viet Nam's three economic policy regimes, industrial, trade and resource pricing, the economic policies that most directly influence technological modernization in the manufacturing sector and thereby increase the likelihood of the adoption of EST (see Chapter 3), are presented in this section.

Industrial Policy

With the adoption of the renewed 'doi moi' (reforms) policies in 1986 and their effective introduction in 1989, the government of Viet Nam began its transition from a centrally planned to a market-oriented economy. The 'doi moi' policies tackled numerous issues to do with the economy, including fiscal and monetary policies, macroeconomic issues such as the trade regime, microeconomic problems such as SOEs, and private sector development. The overriding goal of industrial policy in the 1990s was to achieve the status of 'industrial nation' by 2020. The Socio-Economic Development Strategy to the Horizon 2010, adopted by the IX Party Congress in 2001, reinforced the 'doi moi' policies with its priorities on less restrictive policies in trade and finance, liberalization of private investment, efficiency improvements in SOEs and better governance.

These major shifts in industrial policy included changes in four policy instruments: FDI, export promotion, privatization and industrial estates, all with the potential for stimulating the modernization of technology.

FDI

With the promulgation of the Law on Foreign Investment in 1988, Viet Nam began a successful effort to attract FDI. Between 1988 and 2001, some 3050 foreign investment projects committed a total of approximately US$38 billion (Leproux and Douglas, 2004); between 1990 and 2002, FDI inflows increased from US$186 million to US$1.4 billion, an increase of almost 750 per cent. As a share of GDP, FDI increased over the same time period from 2.5 to 3.9 per cent (World Bank, 2005).[5]

Initially more than half of the registered FDI flowed into the construction and service sectors. As of 1995, less than half was in the manufacturing sector, but this share increased to over three-quarters by 2001 (Martin, 2002). In terms of ownership composition, most FDI was originally in the form of joint ventures with SOEs to supply the domestic market in services and heavy industry, but more recently this developed into many fully foreign-owned ventures in light manufacturing. The potential of FDI in manufacturing to encourage the use of superior technologies was, however, limited compared to other Asian countries, including China, because joint ventures with the domestic private sector were not encouraged. Private firms with competitive incentives to pursue the latest technological capabilities were excluded from this significant means for the adoption of new technology (Martin, 2002).

Export promotion

Government efforts to support exports began in the 1980s along with several other reforms in industrial policy. These efforts included allowing all legal entities to export most goods, with only a few exceptions, progressively reducing foreign exchange surrender requirements and putting in place a duty drawback system for materials used in producing exports (CIE, 1999a). Unfortunately bureaucratic discretion limited their effectiveness and some necessary actions were not taken. In spite of these limitations, Viet Nam's non-oil exports increased sixfold between 1991 and 2002, twice as much as any other East Asian country. More importantly, the share of manufactured goods accounted for 50 per cent of total merchandise exports in 2002 (World Bank, 2004), and within manufactured goods, labour-intensive goods dominated resource-based goods by 2000 (Martin, 2002).

Privatization
Changes were made in the governance and management of SOEs, starting in 1989 and aimed at making them operate as if they were privately owned firms concerned with efficient (including less wasteful) production. The government initiated reforms of SOEs in the mid-1980s but failed to deal adequately with their continuing financial difficulties, so in the 1990s it started a second wave of reforms that included improved management of SOEs, consolidation of enterprise activities and equitization (divestiture) (CIE, 1996). Overall, the reforms helped to reduce the number of SOEs from 12 000 in 1990 to approximately 4000 in 2005, although in terms of assets and outputs the state remained the largest industrial operator.

Industrial estates
The establishment of industrial estates and export processing zones in the 1990s, with the requirement that plants pre-treat and then discharge their effluent into a common effluent treatment plant (CETP), had the potential to encourage the sharing of CT knowledge and, in particular, the increased use of PATs. The first industrial estate following unification was established in 1992 in Ho Chi Minh City. By the end of 2000, 67 estates had been established, including three export processing zones and one hi-tech park. Despite legal requirements, approximately 20 per cent of the 800 plants that were required to either pre-treat their wastewater and/or discharge it into a CEPT did not do so. Moreover, many of the pre-treatment facilities and effluent treatment plants (ETPs) were not always operated to the extent necessary to comply with environmental standards (Thong and Ngoc, 2004).

Global comparison
In sum, as of 2002, the set of 'doi moi' policies was in the process of rapidly transforming the manufacturing sector, making it more competitive and export oriented, but much more needed to be done to complete the transition to a market-oriented economy. Viet Nam's industrial performance for 1990 and 2000 was not included by UNIDO in the CIP index but sufficient data were available to assess its performance for 2000. It ranked sixty-seventh among all 94 countries and forty-first among 68 developing countries in 2000, and seventh among the eight countries included in this study. Clearly this relatively low ranking among developing countries in 2000 was not reflective of its achievements between 1990 and 2000. Viet Nam in fact achieved outstanding growth in GDP (137 per cent), MVA (246 per cent) and manufactured exports (1000 per cent) between 1990 and 2002, the highest among the East Asian economies in transition (Martin, 2002).

Trade Policy

Trade policy reform was one of the cornerstones of the 'doi moi' strategy in Viet Nam at the time of this study. The previous trading system had been based on foreign trading corporations, which had a monopoly on import and export transactions. Within this system the planned quantity of goods was more important than the price, which was used only for accounting purposes. Furthermore, domestic prices were not aligned to world prices. Thus the first set of reforms was designed to align domestic to world prices by restructuring the trade regime of tariffs and quotas and progressively deleting quotas. Immense progress was made in order to achieve the goal of entering the World Trade Organization by 2006.

As part of the trade policy reform process Viet Nam signed many bilateral and multilateral trade agreements. As a member of the ASEAN Free Trade Area from 1995, it followed a strict agenda of liberalization by gradually reducing tariffs to between 0 and 5 per cent for approximately 6300 goods imported from other ASEAN countries subject to domestic content rules. The most significant bilateral trade agreement in terms of enhancing exports was the United States–Viet Nam Bilateral Trade Agreement formalized in 2001. Subsequently the European Union and Viet Nam signed agreements to reduce tariffs on agricultural, fishery and industrial products as part of a bilateral accord on Viet Nam's accession terms to the WTO.

The cumulative reduction of import restrictions on manufactured goods caused by numerous trade-related agreements was most clearly but only partially reflected in the change in the TMP. Overall, the TMP actually increased from a relatively low 13.9 per cent in 1994 to 15.0 per cent in 2001, which would have reduced the incentive to import more advanced (and therefore cleaner) technology. As a result, Viet Nam's ranking dropped from eighteenth among 48 countries in 1994 to thirty-ninth among 53 countries in 2001, though it still had the third lowest TMP in 2002 among the eight countries included in this study (World Bank, 2004).

Indeed, the import regime remained highly restrictive, based on the more comprehensive TRI. Viet Nam received a high score (9 out of 10, with 10 being the most restrictive) on the TRI as of 2004, based on all its restrictions. It ranked last among 66 countries, which indicates that the combined impact of all import barriers was highly restrictive, and it had the highest score among the eight countries included in this study.

In spite of this restrictive trade regime, the import of manufactured products increased by 61 per cent, from US$9.0 billion in 1997 to US$14.4 billion in 2002. Although the import of capital goods, one sub-category of manufactured goods, increased by 44 per cent, from US$3.3 billion in 1997 to US$4.7 billion in 2002, the actual share of capital goods as a percentage of imported manufactured goods decreased slightly from 37 to 33 per cent (World Bank, 2005).

The pulp and paper sub-sector

The pulp and paper sub-sector was not, as of 2002, subject to any significant tariff on the import of machinery or pulp as raw material. The tariff level on machinery was zero and on pulp as raw material was only 1 per cent, primarily because these tariffs were applied to imports needed by SOEs. The low and then zero tariff level on machinery had the expected result of boosting such imports from US$17.4 million to US$31.3 million between 1997 and 2002.

The tariff level for the import of paper and paper products was very different. Among the pulp and paper-producing countries included in this study, Viet Nam had imposed the third highest average tariff level on pulp and paper products, which increased from 17 per cent to 20.3 per cent between 1994 and 2002 (World Bank, 2005). None the less, Viet Nam's paper imports increased by over 120 per cent between 1997 and 2002, from US$149 to US$333 million.

As a result of the high tariff level on finished products, the pulp and paper sub-sector was still highly protected from international competition. In addition, the intermittent use of quotas and prohibitions on imports of competing products assured producers that their market was guaranteed, regardless of the price or quality of the paper. Sometimes quotas were set so high that importers built up large stocks, hoping that the quota would be reduced later. In some cases quotas were replaced with direct prohibitions on imports of paper. Such prohibitions were either manipulated or exempted on a regular basis, destabilizing the domestic paper market and causing swings from windfall losses to profits for traders and consumers alike.

Global comparison

In summary, under the impetus of the 'doi moi' policies from 1986, Viet Nam was slowly but steadily being integrated into world markets, with total trade exceeding GDP as of 2002. However, it still retained its protective policy on imports of types of consumer goods produced by SOEs, including those by the pulp and paper sub-sector. Despite negligible import restrictions on pulp and paper machinery, actual imports were only as high as countries with very high tariffs on machinery, such as India and China. This reflects the limited incentive for SOEs to import these technologies to improve their competitive position. Overall, Viet Nam, as expected, made low use of foreign technology, as seen in the TI index. In 2001 it ranked sixty-ninth among all 91 countries in the TI index and thirty-fifth among

55 developing countries, a slight increase from its rank in 1990. It ranked fifth among the eight countries included in this study.

Resource Pricing Policy

As was the case for all the countries included in this study, it was not possible to obtain information for a comprehensive overview of resource pricing policies, including the use of subsidies, for energy and water. Since it was also not possible to calculate an average change in resource prices between 1990 and 2002, this section provides only limited information on resource pricing policies, prices *per se* and changes in energy and water use by the manufacturing sector. Higher resource prices, as described in Chapter 3, are often incentives for adopting EST, particularly CTs.

Before the introduction of the 'doi moi' policies, the government fixed resource prices. However, as a result of these policies, market forces started influencing the prices in many different sectors. Whether directly or indirectly (through SOEs), the government still set the price of several commodities and resources, including charges for water and energy. The fact that the fixed price was usually lower than the market price continued to distort economic decision-making among Vietnamese firms.

In the case of electricity, the State Pricing Committee fixed the selling price. This price was much lower than actual cost and did not include environmental protection costs. However, it introduced a new electricity tariff in 1999, raising the average price by 3.6 per cent compared to 1998.

Between 1990 and 2002 the manufacturing sector's consumption of energy (defined as energy derived from oil, coal, natural gas, nuclear power, renewable sources and electricity) increased by 249 per cent, as shown above in Table 10.2. This sector accounted for 39 per cent of national energy consumption in 2002 (IEA, 2005).

Energy consumption by the pulp and paper sub-sector increased by 27 per cent during the same period, from 66.8 ktoe to 84.8 ktoe. However, energy-use intensity in this sub-sector increased by only 1 per cent, from 903 to 912 toe per million US dollars of MVA. The sub-sector accounted for 3.9 per cent of energy consumption by industry in 1990 but only 1.4 per cent in 2002 (IEA, 2005).

In water management, the organizational and financial framework was based on the de-collectivization policy implemented since the 1980s. The government tried to combine liberalization, which meant that production costs should be covered by fees, with protection of farmers, which meant that prices should be subsidized for poor farmers who were unable to pay all the costs. Beginning in the early 1990s, the decentralization policy to put water management under provincial control led to variations in water fees in different provinces.

As there were no charges for groundwater consumption in Viet Nam, exorbitant amounts of groundwater were extracted for industrial use, resulting in a dramatic decrease in groundwater levels in the main industrial centres of Ha Noi and Ho Chi Minh City. Moreover, owing to the absence of an appropriate mechanism for groundwater regulation, plants on industrial estates evaded payments on wastewater discharges and treatment charges, which were based on the volume of water obtained from municipal authorities. Government Decree Number 67/CP on environmental protection fees for wastewater, enacted only in 2003, was the first step in applying an economic instrument to improve water resource management.

Global comparison
There is no global assessment that can be used to compare the relative effectiveness of Viet Nam's resource pricing; nor were any studies found on the effect of pricing on resource use. As an alternative, an EUI score for the manufacturing sector was calculated for use in this study. In the case of Viet Nam, energy-use intensity increased slightly during the 1990s, from 903 toe per million US dollars of MVA in 1990 to 912 toe in 2002. This deterioration was even more dramatic when compared to other countries, with Viet Nam's ranking dropping considerably during this period, from sixty-eighth in 1990 to seventy-third in 2002 among 93 countries and from forty-first in 1990 to forty-sixth in 2002 among 65 developing countries. Among the eight countries included in this study, it ranked sixth in 2002, ahead of only India and Kenya.

TECHNOLOGY POLICY

As with other policies, the government's approach to science and technology started changing in 1987 when a decision was taken to eliminate the state monopoly on science and technology development and to assign priority to a technology-over-science policy, that is, improved adoption of the available scientific potential. The 'doi moi' policy did not alter the overall political direction of subsuming science under the economy's needs but rather supplemented political pressure on science with economic pressure (Meske and Thinh, 2000). These changes occurred in three phases as follows:

- a first phase (1988–91) resulted in reduced direct governmental influence;

- a second phase (1992–95) shifted basic research from national research centres to universities, and sub-sector-specific research from sub-sectoral institutes to newly founded enterprise corporations;
- a third phase (1996 onward) established and consolidated a new R&D system better adapted to market conditions in Viet Nam. This orientation of science and technology for industrialization and modernization was reinforced through the Law on Science and Technology, promulgated in 2000.

Measures of immediate relevance for enhancing productivity in the manufacturing sector included allowing R&D institutes to enter into direct contracts with industry, encouraging them to provide a full range of advisory services for industry, and requiring them to enter into cost sharing with industry for basic research.

As of 1998, the Vietnamese industrial R&D system consisted of 32 organizations: six R&D institutes were directly controlled by the MOI and 19 R&D institutes and seven R&D centres were managed by MOI corporations. The workforce of this industrial R&D system comprised approximately 3300 persons, including 157 scientists with PhDs and 1636 engineers. About one half of the workforce received their salaries from the state budget and the other half from contract earnings. The Research Institute of Pulp and Paper, one of the 21 affiliated R&D institutes, was affiliated with the Viet Nam Paper Corporation (Meske and Thinh, 2000).

The impact of the reoriented science and technology policy on the adoption of scientific knowledge in the 1990s is well summarized in an evaluation of the technological levels of firms (UNIDO, 2000), which indicated that many problems still existed. These included:

- a low level of backward linkages between those manufacturing intermediate and consumer goods, a lack of capabilities on the part of both researchers and plant managers to communicate, and a scarcity of SOE managers who saw the need for external support;
- a generalized shortage of skilled technicians and engineers and an excess of low- and semi-skilled workers currently employed;
- training institutions that did not produce the skills and aptitudes required by firms;
- constraints on obtaining technologies, including the lack of financing and reasonably priced credits, complex and time-consuming bureaucratic procedures, and an inadequate legal framework.

The legal and the policy frameworks for technology promotion contained too many explicit policies and, at times, conflicting priorities, due to the lack of coordination between the Ministry of Science and Technology, the Ministry of Industry and the Ministry of Planning and Investment.

Global comparison

In summary, the influence of changes in science and technology policy and associated institutional arrangements on the use of more advanced production technologies, many of which were CTs, was at best ambiguous. The change in policy, that is, the emphasis given to technology over science and modifications in institutional arrangements, was aimed at achieving a better alignment between the needs of firms and the services provided by newly designated R&D institutes for technology upgrading, but, based on interviews with manufacturers, the extent to which this was achieved is doubtful. According to them, the majority of the imported technologies were of average standard, outdated or completely obsolete; they caused environmental problems; their prices were often inflated; and state organizations were incapable of assessing their vintage or of identifying their potential negative environmental impact. The fundamental constraint lay not only in the declining capabilities of R&D institutes, but also in the inability of firms to absorb new capabilities and the limitations in their manufacturing technology (Meske and Thinh, 2000).

This overall critical assessment of the limited effectiveness of changes in Viet Nam's technology policies and associated infrastructure is consistent with the country's modest ranking on the TC index. It ranked one hundred and seventh among 162 countries in 2000, a marked improvement in its rank of 118 in 1990 but still in the group of countries with a low technology effort. It was forty-ninth among 114 developing countries in 2000 and sixth among the eight countries included in this study.

THE PULP AND PAPER SUB-SECTOR

Economic Overview

Reflecting the effectiveness of the 'doi moi' policies, Viet Nam's pulp for paper production increased by approximately 520 per cent, and paper and paperboard production by more than 500 per cent, between 1990 and 2002, giving 314 000 tons of pulp and 384 000 tons of paper and paperboard in 2002 (Table 10.3). This performance improved Viet Nam's global position as a paper and paperboard producer from fifty-eighth to forty-fifth during this period, and from forth-eighth to thirty-third as a pulp for paper producer, though, as expected, it ranked last among the pulp and paper countries included in this study. Its annual average growth rate of production

Table 10.3   Pulp for paper and paper and paperboard production, import and export

Year	Production	Imports	Exports	Imports	Exports
	Pulp for paper (tons thousand)			Pulp for paper (US$ million)	
1990	67	–	–	–	–
1995	133	35	0.8	26	0.3
2002	314	33	–	14	–
	Paper and paperboard (thousand tons)			Paper and paperboard (US$ million)	
1990	62	–	9.0	–	6.0
1995	125	67	3.0	59	1.0
2002	384	140	2.0	90	2.0

Source: FAO (2004).

between 1996 and 2000 was 3.6 per cent, with a growth rate of only 2.9 per cent on the part of SOEs.

The pulp and paper sub-sector managed to increase production because of its experience in large-scale pulp and paper production in a few mills, and also because it had a low-cost and relatively well-trained manpower. However, its growth was constrained by several factors, including inappropriate trade and commodity management policies, outdated production technology and limited financial resources.

In regard to trade, the export of paper and paperboard dropped by 83 per cent, eliminating the lead that Viet Nam had had over India as a global exporter in 1990 and placing it fifty-eighth globally in terms of exports in 2002. The import of pulp for paper, however, increased from zero in 1990 to over 33 000 tons in 2002 and placed it forty-ninth globally in terms of imports, as did paper and paperboard, which increased from zero in 1990 to 140 000 tons in 2002 and placed it sixty-third globally in terms of imports. This level of import reflected the inability of local producers to meet the ever-increasing local demand; in fact they met only around 25 per cent of the demand.

Overall, the pulp and paper sub-sector made a small contribution to Viet Nam's economy in the 1990s. The value added of the sub-sector (ISIC 210) increased from US$74 million in 1990 to US$93 million in 2000 (the latest year for which data are available), a 26 per cent increase, while total MVA increased from US$1.9 billion in 1990 to US$5.3 billion in 2000, a 180 per cent increase. The GDP share attributed to the pulp and paper industry decreased from 3.8 per cent in 1990 to 1.7 per cent in 2000; its percentage share of total MVA rose from 3.9 per cent in 1990 to 7.9 per cent in 2000. At the end of 2003 the sub-sector employed approximately 50 000 workers out of the 2.4 million employed in manufacturing (GSO, 2005).

Sub-sector Profile

There were some 300 pulp and paper production facilities (excluding a small number of village-level operations) in Viet Nam at the time of this study. These consisted of 27 pulp mills, 93 paper mills and a large number of small-scale paper converters and trimmers. There were only three large-scale mills (according to Viet Nam's standards) and two medium-scale mills. Together the five biggest mills produced around 75 per cent of the country's pulp for paper and 60 per cent of its paper and paperboard (VNCPC, 2004).

Approximately 80 per cent of the mills were SOEs, as of 2002, while the others were mainly township and village enterprises. There were also some private and joint stock firms, but the presence of joint ventures was limited. The Viet Nam Paper Corporation, a state holding company, controlled most paper production facilities. The three biggest mills were all member units of the Corporation. As of 2002 it was attempting to enlarge its production capacity by investing in new facilities, but financial resources were scarce and banks were not prone to risk-taking. Without state funding, implementation of these projects was impossible.

As pointed out above, pulp and paper production in Viet Nam showed sustained growth during this period. Sales performance, however, was erratic because of large swings in world prices and destabilizing changes in government policies towards the import of production inputs and the pricing of paper. Thus the financial performance of the sub-sector was difficult to gauge, although an assessment of the largest mill in 1996 showed that it had traded profitably in previous years (CIE, 1999b).

Of approximately 300 mills, nine were selected for this study, based on criteria that called for variations in their pulping process, size, location and raw material input (Table 10.4). The selected mills corresponded to these criteria as follows: four used chemical soda, three hydro-pulping, one kraft and one chemical mechanical pulping; two were large-scale, one medium-scale and six small-scale; they were located in six different provinces (Dong Nai, Ho Chi Minh City, Binh Duong, Khanh Hoa, Thai Nguyen, and Phu Tho); and as raw material input one used wood, three used a mix of wood and agro-residuals, three used only agro-residuals and two used recycled wastepaper.

Other characteristics of the mills worth noting were: all were under private domestic ownership; all produced only for the domestic market; six

Table 10.4 Profile of the nine mills investigated

Name of mill	Process and Product type	Scale	Location: region/rural or urban area/ industrial zone	Sales orientation (in 2000)	Technological vintage	Ownership	EST score	Regulatory compliance	Donor assist.	EMS
V1	Wood, kraft pulp, PW paper	Large	Phu Tho, rural	100% D	Modern	100% government	PAT + HTC	Yes	Swedish government	Yes
V2	Wood and AR mechanical pulp, newsprint, packing paper	Large	Dong Nai, urban	100% D	Modern	100% government	PAT + HTC	Yes	–	No
V3*	Wood and AR, kraft pulp, PW paper	Medium	Dong Nai, industrial zone	99.5% D, 0.5% E	Standard	100% government	PAT + MTC	No (has been penalized)	UNIDO	No
V4*	Wood and AR, kraft pulp, PW paper	Small	Viet Tri, urban area	100% D	Standard	100% government	PAT + MTC	No (has been penalized)	UNIDO	No
V5	AR pulp, thermo-mechanical pulp,	Small	Thai Nguyen, urban	100% D	Traditional	100% government	No PAT + LTC	No	UNEP	No

	packing paper and cardboard									
V6	AR pulp, PW paper	Small	Binh Duong, rural area	100% D	Standard	100% government	No PAT + LTC	No	—	No
V7	RP pulp, toilet paper, tissues, cardboard	Small	Ho Chi Minh City, urban	50% D, 50% E	Traditional	100% government	PAT + MTC (municipal treatment)	No (has been penalized)	—	No
V8	AR pulp, PW paper	Small	Khanh Hoa, rural	100% D	Traditional	100% private domestic	PAT + MTC	No (has been penalized)	—	No
V9	RP pulp, cardboard	Small	Binh Duong, rural	100% D	Traditional	100% private domestic	No PAT/ no CT	No (has been penalized)	Japan	No

Notes: printing and writing (PW); agro-residuals (AR); recycled paper (RP); domestic (D); export (E); pollution abatement technology (PAT); higher order technological complexity (HTC); medium order technological complexity (MTC); lower order technological complexity (LTC).
* Kraft process has been stopped and now only chemical soda is used in these mills.

Source: INEST (2002).

were ISO 9001/9002 certified and one was ISO 14001 certified; and four had integrated R&D departments, that engaged mainly in quality control and in the installation and adaptation of new technology.

Process Technology and CT Characterization

Compared with developed countries, the overall technological level and the quality control of Viet Nam's pulp and paper mills were low. From a technological point of view even the leading mills were, in general, 20 to 30 years behind developed countries. This was the underlying reason for the inefficient production, low competitiveness and serious environmental pollution. To improve the technological level comprehensively, many improvements were needed: upgrading raw material input, changing the technological structure, revising products and reforming the management system.

As of the year 2000 the great majority of Viet Nam's mills primarily used one of two processes: the kraft pulping process, commonly used by wood-based mills, or the chemical soda process, most frequently used by agro-residue-based mills. Of the nine mills investigated, four used chemical soda for pulping agro-residuals, three used hydo-pulping for pulping recycled paper, one used kraft for pulping wood and one used chemi-mechanical processes for pulping wood and agro-residuals (Table 10.4).

The mills can be classified into four groups according to their technological level:

- Group 1 – fairly modern technologies: Only two mills, both included in the survey, fell into this category. They accounted for 50 per cent of the pulp production and 36 per cent of the paper production in the country.
- Group 2 – intermediate technologies: Four mills, of which three were included in this survey, fell into this category. These four mills accounted for 24 per cent of pulp production and 25 per cent of paper production.
- Group 3 – below-average technologies: This group was the largest in number; three included in the survey came in this category. These mills used equipment, often second-hand, imported from China or Taiwan Province of China. The technologies used were 30 years or more behind global standards. This group accounted for 32 per cent of pulp production and 22 per cent of paper production.
- Group 4 – old classic technologies: This group included those that had been equipped with locally made equipment copied from the imported outdated technologies used by Group 3. There were a large number of mills in this group, but most had small capacities, normally below 1000 tons per year. One mill included in the survey was

in this category. This group accounted for only 3 per cent of pulp production and 15 per cent of paper production (VNCPC, 2004).

The majority of the mills included in the survey were passing through a transitional stage, with a mixture of traditional and modern equipment. The survey team assigned them to one of three categories, based on the technology vintage of their pulp production equipment: two used modern, three used standard, and four used traditional equipment (Table 10.4). None used best available technology (BAT) at any stage of the production process.

The team also classified the mills into three groups based on the highest order of complexity of the CTs used in each mill (low, medium and high). Eight of the nine mills used CTs of varying degrees of technological complexity: two used CTs of a higher order of complexity; four used CTs of a medium order of complexity; two used CTs of a lower order of complexity; and one mill used no CTs. Only one had an environmental management system. It should be pointed out that the use of CTs in the eight mills was not representative of the pulp and paper sub-sector because five of the nine were in the two groups with relatively more advanced technologies. In total, the six mills in these two groups accounted for a large share of the country's pulp and paper production, 75 and 60 per cent respectively.

The eight mills using CT options used them in all stages of the production process. Some of the CTs used in several process areas and the number of mills using them are identified in Table 10.5. The most extensive CT use was in the recovery of black liquor from the pulping process and the closure of the water system in paper-making. Improvements in other process areas were minor.

Table 10.5   CTs used in the nine mills

Process area	Option	Number of mills using practice/equipment
Pulping	Install cyclone for heat recovery	1
Screening	Upgrade screening system	1
Bleaching	Use of H_2O_2 for reducing chlorine consumption	2
Recovery black liquor	Recovery of black liquor	2
	Improve boiler	1
Paper-making	Improving forming device	1
	Closure water system	4
	Fibre recovery (save all)	1

Source: INEST (2002).

The potential of CTs in pulp and paper mills in Viet Nam to reduce water and chemical use and pollutant discharge into the aquatic environment was documented during a CP project undertaken by the United Nations Environment Program (UNEP). The results achieved by one of the three mills are shown in Box 10.1. Implementation of CT options resulted in measurable reductions at little or no cost to the mill.

BOX 10.1   CLEANER PRODUCTION CASE STUDY: VIET NAM

This SOE, a small traditional enterprise located in the Thai Nguyen urban area, supplies the local market with industrial packing paper. Due to a lack of finance, most of the CT measures implemented were both organizational and managerial. These include: chemical savings: from 400 kg to 270 kg of soda per ton of product; water savings of 100 cubic metres per hour (40 KWh of electricity saved per ton of product from water pumping); recycling of white water from paper machine for diluting pulp (less wastewater volume, pulp loss and suspended solids in wastewater) with savings of 60 000 000 VND per month; increased recovery of black liquor (less pollution load) with savings of 50 000 000 VND per month; and recovery of pulp loss with savings estimated of 72 000 000 VND per month.

Source: INEST (1999).

PAT Characterization

Most mills in the sub-sector lacked secondary ETPs. They had only simple wastewater treatment, such as settling tanks to remove fibre and suspended solids.

Of the nine mills investigated, only four had their own ETP, one discharged into a CEPT and three had yet to construct an ETP and were thus discharging directly into water bodies. The four with their own ETPs used either an aerated lagoon or activated sludge. For the most part, best practices in air emission treatment and solid waste management were not being implemented.

It should be noted that the adoption of PATs was not a result of donor assistance programmes. Only one mill investigated benefited from extensive donor assistance, while four others received limited advice on CTs.

Environmental Performance

MONRE established a national network for ambient environmental monitoring and analysis in 1994, which expanded from five monitoring stations in

1994 to 20 in 40 provinces in 2002. Based on data from this network, BOD and ammonia levels were estimated to exceed national quality standards in the two major water systems, the Red River and Mekong; households and firms were therefore the main river polluters. In addition, only five of the 65 industrial zones had proper operating CETPs, and 90 per cent of the firms established before 1995 did not have ETPs (VEPA, 2002).

Essentially there were no reliable data on the impact of industrial activities on environmental quality in Viet Nam. While VEPA and several DONREs produced environmental reports regularly, this information was not publicly available. Viet Nam did not have even the most basic data on pollutant loadings collected at source from industry (VEPA, 2002).

The only estimate of pollutant release from the manufacturing sector at that time was the one calculated for this study (Table 10.2). The pulp and paper sub-sector was estimated to be responsible for approximately 25 per cent of BOD loadings, making it the second largest industrial source of BOD after the food and beverage sub-sector (58 per cent).

Only a few large- and medium-scale mills complied with the discharge standards for wastewater. Wastewater released from smaller mills was almost completely untreated when discharged into rivers. Of the nine mills investigated, only two were reported to be in compliance with environmental norms in 2002. The other seven were not; provincial authorities penalized some of them, though probably to little avail given the insignificant fines they imposed.

KEY INFORMANTS AND INTERNATIONAL DONORS

Four groups, in addition to governmental environmental regulatory agencies and technology centres, are in a position to influence in different ways the extent to which plants adopt EST: NGOs, business associations, international donors of technical asssistance and chemical and equipment suppliers. Some information on the first three is presented in this section; there is insufficient information to characterize the firms that supplied chemicals and equipment to Viet Nam's pulp and paper sub-sector.

NGOs

With Viet Nam's evolution from a centrally planned to a market-oriented economy, NGOs now played a role in the country, and in the mid-1990s the government issued a directive explicitly supporting their activities (APPC, 2004).

Around 350 international NGOs were active in Viet Nam at the time of this study, the World Wide Fund for Nature and the International Union for Conservation of Nature and Natural Resources being two of the larger organizations addressing environmental protection issues. During the 1990s indigenous NGOs were still in their infancy but, as in other countries, they operated primarily at the grassroots level (UNDP, 1995). One of their priority tasks of NGOs in the country environmental was environmental education and community awareness.

The survey team interviewed one environmental NGO, the Association for Industrial Environmental Protection, founded in 2000. Its aim is to raise public awareness of the harmful effects of industrial pollution and to bring together specialists in many different fields involved with reducing industrial pollution. It lobbies for regulations on the import of obsolete production technologies and the use of economic instruments in environmental management, and publishes a journal, *Environmental Protection*.

Business Associations

Business associations in Viet Nam support private sector growth and represent the interests of the private sector to the government. Two larger associations are the Chamber of Commerce and Industry of Viet Nam (representing firms and associations from all economic sectors) and the Union of Associated Industrialists of Ho Chi Minh City. The survey team interviewed one business association, the Viet Nam Papermaking Association, founded in 1992. Its members consist primarily of the SOEs managed by the Viet Nam Paper Corporation. It represents the pulp and paper industry at governmental and international meetings but, given its limited resources, does not provide technical advice to its members.

International Donors

Between 1985 and 1999 international donors financed 408 environment-related projects, of which 156 were initiated after 1996. Over this entire period, their commitments reached US$1 billion, around 80 per cent of which was for natural resource management and only 20 per cent for urban and industrial pollutant reduction projects. VEPA received only 5 per cent of the funds, while the Ministry of Agriculture and Rural Development received around 80 per cent. The management of the funds was highly centralized, with provincial and local agencies responsible for managing only 11 per cent of the total. Regional allocation was also uneven, focusing mainly on large urban areas (UNDP, 1999).

Multilateral agencies, such as the World Food Programme, the Asian Development Bank and the World Bank, were the largest multilateral donors for environmental projects between 1985 and 1999. The Swedish International Development Agency and the EU were the largest bilateral donors (UNDP, 1999).

At least 14 donor funded projects for the promotion of CP were implemented in the 1990s. At least four undertook CP assessments of pulp and paper mills: the VNCPC, the Network for Industrial Environmental Management, the Industrial Pollution Reduction in Dong Nai project and the Industrial Pollution Reduction in Viet Tri project. The first two did extensive work in the pulp and paper sub-sector, and are described below.

In 1998 the VNCPC programme started with financial assistance of US$2.5 million provided by the government of Switzerland through UNIDO/UNEP (UNIDO, 2003). The programme provided CP services to industry and advised the government on CP strategies. Since 1998 the VNCPC had conducted 71 in-plant CP assessments, of which 15 were in the pulp and paper mills. It assisted VEPA in drafting the CP National Action Plan 2000–2005. As a result, CP had become one of the main activities of the country's National Environmental Protection Strategy up to the year 2010 and its general planning up to the year 2020.

The Network for Industrial Environmental Management, managed by the UNEP regional office in Bangkok, was established in 1987 to support environmental management in the pulp and paper sub-sector in the Asia-Pacific region. Between 1994 and its completion in 2000 it had a special focus on CP, successfully carrying out more than 50 CP assessments of pulp and paper mills in the Asia-Pacific region. In Viet Nam the project's counterpart, the Institute for Environmental Science and Technology (the host institution of the VNCPC), carried out CP assessments of three mills, including one of the mills in this study (Swenningsen, 2001).

SUMMARY

Viet Nam's aggregate economic performance indicators suggest an above-average performance compared to other East Asian countries with economies in transition, whereas its environmental performance indicators show a less satisfactory and partially unknown performance. While GDP increased by almost 140 per cent between 1990 and 2002, MVA increased even more, by almost 250 per cent. As a result, the percentage of MVA in GDP increased from 12.3 to 20.6 per cent. GNI per capita at PPP increased by 150 per cent during the same period. At the same time, energy use in the manufacturing sector surged by 249 per cent due to the large increase in MVA. As a result, energy-use intensity remained approximately the same in spite of the extensive closure of SOEs. Due to the lack of data it is not possible to determine whether total BOD effluent and BOD-effluent intensity increased or decreased during this period.

Overall, Viet Nam's environmental policy for industrial environmental management was maturing in the period from 1990 to 2002, the time of this study, but still lacked plant-level monitoring and sufficiently high penalties for non-compliance. As a result of the latter, there was limited adoption of EST, including even the most basic PATs, and where they were in place, their performance was often not high enough to meet environmental standards. Complementary policy instruments, particularly CP programmes, filled this gap to some extent with advice on both basic and advanced CTs.

The collective impact of three economic policies, industrial, trade and resource pricing, on the adoption of technological modernization in the 1990s was probably limited, despite the many seemingly positive changes. Clearly the 'doi moi' industrial policies, including the four specific policy instruments of FDI, export promotion, privatization and industrial zones, were, as of 2002, in the process of rapidly transforming the economy and bringing about a degree of technological modernization of the manufacturing processes. However, the impact of these four policy instruments on EST adoption was still limited because of their incomplete and ineffective implementation. Trade-related import restrictions remained restrictive and so did not create competitive pressures that would have encouraged domestic producers, especially SOEs, to use more advanced production techniques and technologies. Finally, increases in the price of energy and water resources did not create a sufficient incentive for firms to introduce more resource-efficient technologies that would have reduced their use of energy and water use to levels comparable to those of more advanced developing countries. Indeed, estimates of energy-use intensity in Viet Nam as measured by the EUI index, indicate that the manufacturing sector made little progress in resource-use efficiency during this period.

The influence of technology policy and associated institutional arrangements on the use of more advanced production technologies, many of which would be CTs, was at best ambiguous. Policy changes emphasizing technology over science along with institutional modifications aimed to achieve a better alignment between the needs of firms for technology upgrading and the services provided by the newly designated R&D institutes. However, the extent to which this was achieved is doubtful. The fundamental constraints lay not only in the declining capabilities of R&D

institutes but also in the weaknesses of firms to absorb new capabilities and in limitations in their existing production technology.

The country's pulp and paper sub-sector increased pulp for paper production from 67 000 to 314 000 tons (a 380 per cent increase) and paper and paperboard production from 62 000 to 384 000 tons (a 520 per cent increase) between 1990 and 2002. As of 2002, there were approximately 300 pulp and paper mills in the sub-sector, the vast majority of which were small or micro-sized, with outdated production technology. Large-scale mills accounted for most of the increase in the production of paper and paperboard between 1990 and 2002, benefiting from increasing demand and a relatively inexpensive supply of raw materials. However, improvements in process technology and the adoption of EST were hampered by scarce financial resources and the ineffective enforcement of environmental regulations. The survey team investigated nine of the 300 mills, including five of the six with relatively more advanced production technology and higher production. Two used CTs of a higher order of complexity, four used CTs of a medium order of complexity, two used CTs of a lower order of complexity and one used no CTs. Among the nine mills, only five had installed secondary treatment ETPs; one had installed a pre-treatment system and discharged its effluent into a municipal CETP; and three had yet to construct an ETP. Only two were reported to be in compliance with environmental standards in 2002.

The influence of NGOs and business associations on EST adoption during the 1990s was limited. While NGOs and business associations in many countries play a significant role in awareness-raising and information dissemination, this was not the case with Viet Nam because of financial and human resource constraints. However, large-scale international donor programmes appear to have made an important contribution to the adoption of CTs with their support for CP assessments and associated technical advice.

To conclude, EST adoption in the pulp and paper sub-sector was still at the initial stage at the time of this study. This sub-sector remained one of the most polluting in the country. Few plants adhered to the national environmental standards, even if several improvements were achieved through the adoption of EST. However, some mills in the sub-sector had realized the environmental and financial benefits of EST adoption, primarily CTs, and were working towards their implementation. The key factors that would press plants to adopt additional EST were increased prices for water and energy supplies, enforcement of environmental regulations, and pressure from local communities.

NOTES

1. The WDI CPI only covers the period 1995–2002 for Viet Nam. For all other countries included in this study, it covers the full period of interest, 1990–2002.
2. The World Bank (2004) does not provide internationally comparable data on discharge of BOD for Viet Nam, as for the other countries included in this study. However, it was possible, using World Bank pollutant coefficients and UNIDO employment data, to estimate the BOD discharge in 2000, but it was not possible to estimate BOD discharge in 1990 because of the lack of sub-sector employment data. The estimated BOD intensity was 12.8 tons per million US dollars of MVA. In comparison, China had a BOD intensity of 6.2 tons per million US dollars of MVA, while India had an even lower BOD intensity of 6.1 tons per million US dollars of MVA.
3. While data were not available for estimating BOD-effluent intensity in 1990, as was the case for the other eight countries included in this study, it can be assumed that the government made little effort to compel plants to adopt EST before that time nor even by 2002, at which time BOD-effluent intensity remained reasonably high (12.6 tons per million US dollars of MVA).
4. This presumption is based on the economy-wide average annual growth rate in gross fixed capital formation of 17.2 per cent between 1990 and 2002 (World Bank, 2004).
5. The FDI for 1990 has been taken as the three-year average of 1989–91 and for 2002 as the three-year average of 2001–3, in order to even out fluctuations in FDI flows.

REFERENCES

APCEL (1998a), 'Environmental Protection Law, Decree Guiding Implementation (Government Decree No. 175-CP, 1994)', Asia-Pacific Centre for Environmental Law, Singapore: National University of Singapore.

APCEL (1998b), 'Wastewater, Industrial Discharge Standards (TCVN 5945,1995)', Asia-Pacific Centre for Environmental Law, Singapore: National University of Singapore.

APPC (2004), 'Viet Nam: Third Sector Legal Environment: Taxation', Manila, The Philippines: Asia Pacific Philanthropy Consortium (available on http://www.asianphilanthropy.org/countries/vietnam/taxation).

CIE (1996), 'A Study for a Medium Term Industrial Strategy for Viet Nam', Sydney, Australia: Centre for International Economics (CIE).

CIE (1999a), 'Vietnam: Trade and Industry Policies for Integration', Sydney, Australia: Centre for International Economics (CIE).

CIE (1999b), 'Paper, Prices and Politics: an Evaluation of the Swedish Support to the Bai Bang Project in Vietnam', Sydney, Australia: Centre for International Economics (CIE).

EIU (2004), 'Country Report: Vietnam', London: Economist Intelligence Unit.

FAO (2004), 'FAOSTAT – Forestry Statistics', Rome: Food and Agriculture Organization of the United Nations (available on: http://www.fao.org).

FAO (2005), 'AQUASTAT: FAOSTAT', Rome: Food and Agriculture Organization of the United Nations (available on: http://www.fao.org).

GSO (2005), *Statistical Yearbook*, General Statistics Office, Ha Noi, Viet Nam: The Statistical Publishing House.

IEA (2005), 'Online Data Services', IEA Energy Information Centre, Paris: International Energy Agency (available on: http://www.iea.org).

INEST (1999), 'Mission Report UNEP LOA No MH/1202-94-14-2212', prepared for the United Nations Environment Programme, Ha Noi, Viet Nam: Institute for Environmental Science and Technology, Ha Noi University of Technology.

INEST (2002), 'Assessing the Adoption of EST in the Pulp and Paper Industry in Viet Nam', prepared for UNIDO, Ha Noi, Viet Nam: Institute for Environmental Science and Technology, Ha Noi University of Technology.

ISO (2003), 'The ISO Survey of ISO 9000 and ISO 14001 Certificates', Geneva: International Organization for Standardization (available on: http://www.iso.org).

Leproux, V. and H. Douglas (2004), 'Vietnam: Foreign Direct Investment and Post Crisis Regional Integration', ERD Working Paper No. 56, Manila, The Philippines: Asian Development Bank (available on: http://www.adb.org).

Martin, K. (2002), 'Vietnam: Deepening Reforms for Rapid Export Growth', Working Paper for publication following the WRO accession workshop, Washington, DC: The World Bank Group (available on: http://www.worldbank.org).

Meske, W. and D. Thinh (2000), 'Viet Nam's Research and Development System in the 1990s: Structural and Functional Change', WZB Paper P00-401, Berlin, Germany: Wissenschaftszentrum Berlin für Sozialforschung Gmbh (WZB).

NISTPASS (2002), 'Learning Technological Capability for Viet Nam's Industrial Upgrading: Challenges of the Globalization', Ha Noi, Viet Nam: National Institute for Science and Technology Policy and Strategy Studies.

Swenningsen, N. (2001), 'Network for Industrial Environmental Management – A New Approach to old Challenges in the Asia-Pacific Pulp and Paper Industry', *Paperex Magazine* (Swedish Pulp & Paper Industry Association), April.

Thong, L. and N.A. Ngoc (2004), 'Incentives for Wastewater Management in Industrial Estates in Vietnam', Research Report, Economy and Environmental Program for Southeast Asia (EEPSEA), Singapore: International Development Research Centre.

UNDP (1995), 'Partners in Development, Non-Governmental Organizations', Ha Noi, Viet Nam: United Nations Development Programme (available on: http://www.undp.org.vn).

UNDP (1999), 'A Study on Aid to the Environment Sector in Viet Nam', Ha Noi, Viet Nam: United Nations Development Programme (available on: http://www.undp.org.vn).

UNIDO (2000), 'A Science Technology and Industry Strategy for Vietnam', prepared by Keith Bezanson for the UNDP/UNIDO Project Vietnam – Contribution to the Preparation of the Socio-Economic Development Strategy to the Year 2010, Vienna: UNIDO.

UNIDO (2003), 'Report of the Independent Joint In-depth Evaluation Mission', Viet Nam National Cleaner Production Centre (US/VIE/96/063), Vienna: UNIDO.

UNIDO (2004), *International Yearbook of Industrial Statistics 2004*, Cheltenham, UK and Northampton, MA, US: Edward Elgar Publishing.

UNIDO (2005), 'Technical Assistance to the Revolving Fund and the Industrial Pollution Minimization Fund in Ho Chi Minh City: Further Improvement of Operational Policies and Capitalization of the Funds', Ha Noi, Viet Nam: UNIDO.

VEPA (2002), 'Viet Nam Environment Monitor', Ha Noi, Viet Nam: Viet Nam Environment Protection Agency (available on http://www.nea.gov.vn).

VEPA (2005), 'Environmental Management Organization', Ha Noi, Viet Nam: Viet Nam Environment Protection Agency (VEPA) (available on http://www.nea.gov.vn).

VNCPC (2004), 'An Assessment of the Replacement with Cleaner Technology in Pulp and Paper Industry', Working Paper for workshop 'Promotion of Cleaner Technologies in Vietnam's Environmental Protection Strategy to 2010' in Ha Noi, 8–9 November 2004. Ha Noi, Viet Nam: Viet Nam National Cleaner Production Centre.

World Bank (2004), 'World Bank Development Indicators (WDI) 2004', CD-ROM version, Washington, DC: The World Bank.

World Bank (2005), 'World Integrated Trade Solution (WITS)', Washington, DC: The World Bank (available on: http://wits.worldbank.org).

11. Zimbabwe

INTRODUCTION

A survey team from the Scientific and Industrial Research and Development Centre (SIRDC) in Zimbabwe investigated the specific factors influencing the adoption of environmentally sound technology (EST) in the country's leather processing sub-sector. The team used semi-structured questionnaires provided by UNIDO to interview plant managers at ten of the 13 plants in this sub-sector and key informants in three business associations, two technology centres, two chemical and equipment suppliers, one environmental NGO, and four environmental regulatory agencies. The team also collected background data on the country and the leather processing sub-sector.

This chapter describes the economic and environmental context in Zimbabwe for EST adoption; relevant environmental, economic and technology policies; the leather processing sub-sector and the plants investigated; and key informants and international donors.

THE ECONOMIC AND ENVIRONMENTAL CONTEXT FOR EST ADOPTION

The following selected economic and environmental performance indicators define the context in which manufacturing plants made their technology adoption decisions and, in particular, their decisions to adopt EST during the late 1990s/early 2000s.

Economic Performance Indicators

Zimbabwe's economy had sizeable commercial, agricultural, manufacturing and mining sectors at the time of this study in 2002 and was therefore a more diversified economy than those of many other sub-Saharan countries. However, all the sectors of the economy came under tremendous pressure due to the political and economic crisis that had engulfed the country. During the 1990s the average annual growth of gross domestic product (GDP) was slightly less than one-tenth of 1 per cent. Between 1990 and

2002 GDP increased by slightly more than 1 per cent and GDP per capita decreased by 20 per cent, while the population increased by 38 per cent (Table 11.1). During the same period gross national income (GNI) per capita in purchasing power parity (PPP) – a more accurate indicator of well-being than GDP per capita – increased by only 2 per cent. Based on its GNI per capita, Zimbabwe is classified by the World Bank as a low-income country.

The manufacturing sector performed poorly during the 1990s, with a decrease of 35 per cent of manufacturing value added (MVA). Its share of GDP declined from 22.9 per cent in 1990 to 13.0 per cent in 2002. In 1990 Zimbabwe had had one of the more advanced manufacturing sectors in sub-Saharan Africa, with a share of MVA almost twice that of Kenya (11.8 per cent of GDP).

From the mid-1990s the country experienced a general macroeconomic deterioration. This was partly due to the removal of protective tariffs but could also be attributed to the lack of competitiveness caused by the overvalued exchange rate, the slow depletion of foreign exchange for purchasing production input and, more recently, price controls (EIU, 2003).

Table 11.1   Economic performance indicators for Zimbabwe

Economic indicator	Year	Value	Percentage change
GDP (constant 1995 US$) (billion)	1990	6.7	1.0
	2002	6.8	
GDP per capita (constant 1995 US$)	1990	650.0	−20.0
	2002	520.0	
Population (million)	1990	9.4	38.0
	2002	13.0	
GNI per capita at PPP (current international $)	1990	2140.0	2.0
	2002	2180.0	
MVA (constant 1995 US$) (billion)	1990	1.4	−35.0
	2002	0.9	
MVA (per cent of GDP)	1990	22.9	9.9
	2002	13.0	
CPI (1995=100)	1990	30.0	–
	2002	1990.0	
Interest rate (commercial lending rate)	1990	12.0	204.0
	2002	36.5	
Exchange rate (Z$/US$)	1990	2.5	2100.0
	2002	55.0	

Source: World Bank (2004).

Between 1990 and 2002 the lack of harmonization between fiscal and monetary policies and the government's increased level of borrowing led to increased taxation and higher interest rates, which, with high inflation, had a negative impact on private investment at the enterprise level. In addition, the exchange rate of the Zimbabwe dollar to the US dollar fell by more than 2100 per cent.

Environmental Performance Indicators

Generally speaking, the pollution problems caused by Zimbabwe's manufacturing sector were concentrated in a few areas, mainly because the country was still relatively underdeveloped industrially.

Selected environmental indicators, namely, energy use, carbon dioxide (CO_2) emissions, organic matter effluent measured as biochemical oxygen demand (BOD) and water use, as well as the intensity of use of each of these, provide an insight into the state of industrial environmental performance in Zimbabwe; these are presented in Table 11.2. Energy use in the manufacturing sector, measured in tons of oil equivalent (toe), declined by 40 per cent between 1990 and 2002, which was more than the percentage decrease in MVA. Consequently the energy-use intensity of MVA decreased, in this case by 20 per cent. Associated CO_2 emissions dropped by 65 per cent and CO_2-emission intensity decreased by 47 per cent. Not surprisingly, BOD effluent also decreased by 28 per cent over the same period, though BOD-effluent intensity decreased by only 3 per cent. Finally, information on water use in the manufacturing sector is only available for 2000. In that year 0.3 billion cubic metres of water were used, and water-use intensity was 230 cubic metres per million US dollars of MVA.

The decline in BOD effluent in the manufacturing sector can be attributed primarily to two factors. First, there was a significant decrease in manufacturing activity as measured by MVA. Second, the percentage of MVA produced by the resource-intensive manufacturing sub-sectors, such as chemicals, pulp and paper and iron and steel, decreased slightly. To an unknown but probably lesser extent, major investments, largely donor-driven, in PATs and to a lesser extent in CTs contributed to the improved environmental performance.

In 1996 the distribution of BOD effluent among manufacturing sub-sectors was as follows: food and beverages, 48 per cent; textiles, 15 per cent; iron and steel, 14 per cent; pulp and paper, 11 per cent; chemicals 6 per cent; and others, 3 per cent. The BOD loadings of the leather processing sub-sector, aggregated under the 'other' category, were clearly small compared to those of other sub-sectors (World Bank, 2004).

Table 11.2   Environmental performance indicators for Zimbabwe

Source code	Environmental indicator	Year	Value	Percentage change
1	Total energy use in the manufacturing sector (million toe)	1990 2002	1.5 0.9	−40
1 & 2	Energy-use intensity (toe per million US$ of MVA)	1990 2002	1120.0 900.0	−20
1	CO_2 emissions from the manufacturing sector (million tons)	1990 2002	4.7 1.6	−65
1 & 2	CO_2 intensity (tons per million US$ of MVA)	1990 2002	3340.0 1780.0	−47
2	BOD effluent from the manufacturing sector (thousand tons)	1990 2000	12.2 8.8	−28
2	BOD-effluent intensity (tons per million US$ of MVA)	1990 2000	8.7 8.5	−3
3	Water use in the manufacturing sector (billion m³)	1990 2000	n.a. 0.3	−
2 & 3	Water-use intensity (thousand m³ per million US$ of MVA)	1990 2000	n.a. 230.0	−
4	Per cent of MVA produced by the most pollutant-intensive sub-sectors	1990 1996	19.0 18.0	−1
5	Number of ISO 14001 certificates	1999 2002	4.0 5.0	25

Note: Data shown for 2000 on BOD for Brazil are from the year 1996, which is the latest year available.

Sources: 1. IEA (2005); 2. World Bank (2004); 3. FAO (2005); 3. UNIDO (2005); 4. ISO (2003).

The number of ISO 14001 certificates, five in 2002, was low, probably attributable to Zimbabwe's limited integration into the global economy. Its ratio of 5.5 certificates per billion US dollars of MVA was much higher than Kenya's ratio of 1.2 certificates and lower than South Africa's ratio of 7.8 certificates.

Implications for EST Adoption

During the period investigated for this study, the overall economic and environmental conditions in Zimbabwe were not particularly conducive to the adoption of EST by the country's manufacturing sector. Though a lesser developed country, Zimbabwe had a large manufacturing sector as a percentage of its GDP in 1990 and a relatively low level of BOD-effluent intensity compared to all other lesser developed countries, which suggests that there had been some regulatory and community pressure on plants to comply with environmental norms before 1990. From 1990 to 2002 the manufacturing sector deteriorated, with a 2.0 per cent negative annual average growth rate in MVA. In parallel, the annual average growth rate in new investment was a negative 37.1 per cent, giving little scope for investment in EST and the import of foreign, cleaner technology. This was not surprising, however, given the excessive rate of inflation (more than a 6000 per cent increase in the consumer price index (CPI)) and the steep climb in the interest rate (12 per cent to 36.5 per cent). The 35 per cent decrease in annual MVA between 1990 and 2002 was accompanied by a 44 per cent decrease in energy use and a 14 per cent decrease in energy-use intensity, the outcome of declining MVA and modest investments in energy-efficient technology. BOD effluent also decreased by 28 per cent, and BOD-effluent intensity by 3 per cent, most of which was probably attributable to a shift in the industrial structure away from the more pollutant-intensive sub-sectors rather than to the decline in MVA.[1]

ENVIRONMENTAL POLICY

Zimbabwe did not have a comprehensive environmental policy during the 1990s but had rather fragmented environmental legislation. Of a total of 25 Acts, seven were applied to air, ten to water and eight to soil. The New Water Act, approved in 1999, harmonized those regulations that had a bearing on water. The more recent Environmental Management Act of 2002 was designed to harmonize all the legislative instruments that related to water and the environment. It provided for the establishment of an environmental management agency, a standards enforcement committee and an environmental fund, and made an environmental impact assessment a legal requirement.

The government established the Ministry of Environment and Tourism (MET) in the early 1980s as the central authority for coordinating environmental management. This was at a time, however, when environmental legislation was sufficiently comprehensive to cover a wide range of issues but was so fragmented that responsibilities overlapped and effective enforcement was difficult.

The Department of Natural Resources and its successor, the Environmental Management Agency, drew on several environmental policy instruments for industrial environmental management, classified into four categories. These are command and control regulations, economic and fiscal incentives, voluntary programmes and transparency and disclosure.

The command-and-control regulatory approach, enacted in the 1970s, remained the dominant policy approach to industrial environmental management. Discharge standards were, however, poorly enforced and the fines imposed on violators were too low to be a deterrent. Even if local authorities had made an effort to enforce environmental regulations, the process of imposing fines on an offender was too time-consuming in the absence of an environmental court. Local authorities were required to report the offending plant to the local police, after which a criminal law procedure had to be followed before a fine could be imposed by a court of law.

The water discharge standards were generic ones for all industrial subsectors and were only concentration-based rather than a combination of concentration- and load-based. They were also much less stringent for organic matter than were most countries, allowing 1000 mg/l of BOD. For example, the BOD standard for industrial discharge into water bodies was in the range of 20 to 100 mg/l for many countries and for Kenya in particular it was 20 mg/l. There were no concentration-based standards for BOD discharge into sewers, but there were standards for suspended solids and chemical oxygen discharge.

In contrast to earlier environmental regulations, which had little effect, Zimbabwe's new Water Act of 1999 was structured along the lines of 'the polluter-pays' principle and imposed higher fines and disposal fees (Jaspers, 2001). Local authorities adopted the same principle to deal with plants that discharged into municipal common effluent treatment plants (CETPs), thereby ensuring that excessive pollutant loads did not burden the CETP. The City of Bulawayo, for instance, introduced a trade effluent tariff system based on toxicity and volume of effluent discharged into the CETP and therefore no longer needed to rely on costly bureaucratic policing.

Although an environmental impact assessment policy was formulated in 1996, Bekhechi and Mercier (2002) reported that there had been limited implementation of its recommendations and little compliance with its requirements. However, there were expectations that the Environmental Management Act of 2002, which made an environmental impact assessment a legal requirement for specified projects, would change the situation.

While little use was made of economic incentives in Zimbabwe, two voluntary programmes with industry participating got under way. One was the CP programme run by the Zimbabwe Cleaner Production Centre (ZCPC), described later in this chapter, with several others, in the section on donor programmes. The other was the ISO 14000 certification programme, which was actively promoted by the Standards Association of Zimbabwe.

Global Comparison

In summary, Zimbabwe did not have a comprehensive or effective environmental policy during the 1990s. The environmental regulations in place were difficult to enforce and were eventually replaced by the Environmental Management Act of 2002. There was limited implementation of the environmental impact assessment policy and little use of economic incentives. More recent legislation should correct this situation. Thus it is not surprising that Zimbabwe's ranking on the environmental governance (EG) index declined from forty-sixth among 66 countries in 1990 to sixtieth in 2001. It ranked thirty-fourth among 40 developing countries, and seventh among the eight countries included in this study in 2001.

ECONOMIC POLICY REGIMES

Overviews of Zimbabwe's three economic policy regimes, industrial, trade and resource pricing, the economic policies that most directly influence technological modernization in the manufacturing sector and thereby increase the likelihood of the adoption of EST (see Chapter 3), are presented in this section.

Industrial Policy

Zimbabwe, as all countries included in this study, pursued several policies and strategies supporting its manufacturing sector during the 1990s. The most notable and ambitious of these was the Economic Structural Adjustment Programme (ESAP), which was put into effect between 1990 and 1995. The objective of ESAP was to move away from a highly regulated economy to one where market forces played a more central role. ESAP target areas included (a) macroeconomic and fiscal policy; (b) international trade; (c) foreign investments; (d) price controls; and (e) public sector enterprises.

However, MVA declined during the period in which ESAP was implemented because domestic demand stagnated after severe droughts affected the country, and an increased volume of imported goods resulted in fierce price competition. ESAP did not directly address the issue of the competitiveness of domestic industrial products. As a result, many local producers encountered difficulties in coping with competition from imports. In addition the government responded inadequately to these external pressures while it was implementing its policies. It did not manage ESAP in a fitting manner, nor did it succeed in restoring macroeconomic stability (Mhone and Bond, 2001).

Between 1996 and 2000 the government implemented the Zimbabwe Programme for Economic and Social Transformation, which was based on the same principles as ESAP. While only scattered information is available on its performance, the core themes of the programme regarding economic policy included re-orienting the public sector; investing in human resources; furthering economic empowerment and poverty alleviation; facilitating public and private savings; and restoring macroeconomic stability. However, limited external financial support for the programme impaired the achievement of its goals.

In 1998 the government introduced its Policy Framework for Industrial Development, Trade and Investment, prepared by the National Economic Consultative Forum. This policy proposed a strategy for industrial development, promoting both the expansion of large enterprises and the development of SMEs. The Confederation of Zimbabwe Industries, a private sector association, was given the task of leading the industrialization process. The programme supporting the strategy, funded by the World Bank, was however terminated in May 2000 when the World Bank cancelled all economic aid to Zimbabwe.

These major shifts in industrial policy included changes in three policy instruments, foreign direct investment (FDI), export promotion, and export processing zones, all with the potential for stimulating the modernization of technology.

FDI

Zimbabwe had traditionally welcomed FDI, even more so with reforms in the 1990s that eased the requirements on investment approval and removed many constraints on dividend repatriation. The Zimbabwe Investment Centre was set up in 1989 to promote domestic and foreign investment. Although net capital inflows decreased between 1990 to 2002, FDI inflows actually increased from a negative US$7 million to US$17 million over the same time period; as a share of GDP, FDI inflows increased from –0.08 to 0.2 per cent (World Bank, 2005).[2]

Export promotion

The government relied primarily on ZimTrade, established in 1992, to nurture export-oriented sub-sectors, such as leather. ZimTrade's objective was to help Zimbabwean enterprises explore foreign markets and transform their businesses into permanent, and not just *ad hoc*, operations. A vital component of its entire export development and promotion agenda was marketing support for export start-ups. Overall, however, the increase in exports of manufactured goods, from US$453 million to US$811 million between 1990 and 2002, was a modest 80 per cent, approximately, compared to other countries. The manufacturing sector's share of merchandise exports increased from 31 to 38 per cent (World Bank, 2004).

Export processing zones

The Export Processing Zones Authority approved investments in export processing zones in the 1990s with a 90 per cent local resource utilization requirement of labour, material and facilities, and also encouraged the establishment of industrial clusters. With their requirement that plants build and operate CETPs, these were an encouragement to the increased adoption of EST, in particular of PATs. Two Zimbabwean tanneries came under the Authority and benefited from its assistance.

Global comparison

In summary, industrial policies, in spite of their worthy objectives, do not appear to have offered significant support to the manufacturing sector in the 1990s. The lack of effective public sector support accounted to some extent for the manufacturing sector's deterioration in performance, as measured by the CIP index. Zimbabwe ranked fifty-fifth among 93 countries on this index in 2000, placing it among the countries showing medium low industrial performance. However, this marked a sharp decline in its ranking over the period 1980 to 2000, from thirty-fifth in 1980 to forty-second in 1990, and more steeply to fifty-fifth in 2000. This steep decline is similar to that of Kenya in the period 1990 to 2000. It should be pointed out, however, that 19 sub-Saharan African countries were among the 30 countries that ranked last on the CIP index, although there was a clear break in the ranking between these and the most industrialized economy in the region, South Africa, which ranked thirty-fifth in 2000. Zimbabwe ranked sixth in 2002 among the eight countries included in this study.

Trade Policy

From 1991, as part of ESAP, Zimbabwe substantially liberalized its trade regime. It virtually eliminated its highly restrictive import-licensing regulations, reformed its foreign exchange controls and foreign direct investment restrictions, and moved decisively to reduce tariffs, including surcharges, which were now the most important barrier to trade (GATT, 1995).

It carried out its trade liberalization as a participant in many trade agreements. It actively participated in the Uruguay Round of the General Agreement on Tariffs and Trade (GATT) between 1986 and 1994 and was a founding member of the World Trade Organization (WTO) in 1995. It also became a member of the Common Market for Eastern and Southern Africa (COMESA), which succeeded the Preferential Trade Area for Eastern and Southern African States, and of the Southern African Development Community (SADC). These regional integration efforts were aimed at removing trade barriers and promoting cooperation, notably in technology transfer, to improve the productivity of the manufacturing sector. Zimbabwe had in place, as of 2002, up to 40 bilateral trade agreements designed to eliminate inefficient trade restrictions and provide access to markets and economies on a larger scale.

The cumulative reduction of import restrictions on manufactured goods caused by numerous trade-related agreements was most clearly but only partially reflected in the change in the TMP. Between 1996 and 2001 Zimbabwe reduced its TMP from 41.3 to 20.6, a seemingly large reduction that would have lowered the barrier to adopt EST. However, in spite of its decreased TMP, its ranking deteriorated from forty-third out of 48 countries in about 1990 to fiftieth out of 53 countries in about 2002, and it had the sixth highest TMP in 2002 among the eight countries included in this study, only Tunisia and India being higher (World Bank, 2004).

In fact the import regime was only modestly to highly restrictive, as indicated by Zimbabwe's ranking on the more comprehensive TRI. Zimbabwe received a medium high TRI score (6 out of 10) as of 2004, based on all its restrictions. It ranked sixtieth among 66 countries, which indicates that the combined impact of all tariff and non-tariff measures was still reasonably restrictive.

The relatively small percentage increase of only 38 per cent in the import of manufactured goods from US$1.4 billion in 1990 to US$1.9 billion in 2002 was partially attributable to the generally restrictive tariff and non-tariff regime. Similarly the import of capital goods, one sub-category of manufactured goods, increased only slightly, from US$0.7 billion in 1990 to US$0.8 billion in 2002. As a result, the share of capital-good imports as a percentage of imported manufactured goods decreased from 50 to 44 per cent.

Leather processing sub-sector
However, the TMP and the TRI are misleading in terms of tariff rates and the effects of these on the leather processing sub-sector. Their relevant tariff levels dropped considerably between 1990 and 2002 but, in spite of the elimination of the tariff on equipment, the unfavourable investment climate meant that the import of equipment did not increase (World Bank, 2004). On the other hand, the import of chemicals, for which the tariff rate was substantially reduced, increased in value from US$1.7 million in 1990 to US$2.4 million in 2002. This increase, however, was primarily due to the Export Retention Scheme begun in the late 1990s and not to tariff reductions. The scheme allowed exporting tanneries to retain a fraction of their earnings in foreign currency, which enabled them to import tannery chemicals that had become very expensive in the 1990s.

Although the simple average tariff on hides and skins declined, this did not have a positive effect because there was no demand for imported raw hides and skins by 2002 due to the overall decline in demand for leather products.

As regards finished leather imports, there was also a steep decline in the average tariff, approximately equal to the decrease in the TMP, but it appears that the reduction had little effect because the import of finished leather declined in value from US$2.2 million in 1990 to US$0.6 million in 2002.

Global comparison
In summary, Zimbabwean trade liberalization policies reduced the TMP during the 1990s, but the level remained relatively high compared to other countries. Even with the lowering of the TMP, the import of manufactured products increased only marginally, from US$1.4 billion in 1990 to US$1.9 billion in 2002, primarily because of the overall adverse economic situation in the country. Moreover, due to the overall investment climate, specific tariff reductions made in the leather processing sub-sector were not sufficient to stimulate the import of machinery, although, with policy changes on retained earnings, the import of chemicals was stimulated. Given its relatively high TMP and, more importantly, its level of economic development, it is not surprising to find that Zimbabwe indeed ranked low on the use of foreign technology, based on the TI index. In 2001 it was seventy-second among all 91 countries covered by the TI index and thirty-seventh among 55 developing countries, a significant decline from twenty-fourth among 64 developing countries in 1990. Among the eight countries included in this study, it ranked sixth in 2001, a decline from third in 1990.

Resource Pricing Policy

As with all the other countries included in this study, it was not possible to find information to provide a comprehensive overview of resource pricing policies, including the use of subsidies, for either energy or water; nor to calculate an average change in resource prices over the period 1990 to 2002. Accordingly the presentation in this section consists of only limited information on resource pricing policies, prices *per se* and resource use in response to price changes. Higher resource prices, as described in Chapter 3, are often incentives for adopting EST, particularly CTs.

In Zimbabwe, as elsewhere, the average nominal cost of electricity increased during the 1990s. The average charge per kWh for industrial consumers increased between 1993 and 2000 from Z$0.2 per kWh to Z$1.8 per kWh (ZESA, 2002). However, until 2000 price increases in electricity and water (discussed below) were below the rate of inflation and did not serve as stimuli for energy- and water-saving technologies. Further price increases for electricity and water in 2001 and 2002, though, do appear to have stimulated industry to initiate energy- and water-saving projects.

Between 1990 and 2002 the manufacturing sector's consumption of energy (defined as energy derived from oil, coal, natural gas, nuclear power, renewable sources and electricity) decreased by 40 per cent, as shown in Table 11.2. This sector accounted for 19 per cent of the total energy consumption in 1990 and 11 per cent in 2002.

Energy consumption by the leather processing sub-sector decreased by 50 per cent during the same period, from 4.9 ktoe to 2.5 ktoe per million US dollars of MVA,[3] and energy-use intensity decreased by about the same percentage, from 0.7 to 0.3 ktoe. The sub-sector accounted for 0.29 per cent of the total energy consumption of the manufacturing sector in 1990 and 0.26 per cent in 2002 (IEA, 2005).

Water charges rose steeply during the 1990s. For example, the Harare City Council introduced a two-tier tariff system for water consumption in 1994, charging a lower tariff per cubic metre for the first 300 cubic metres consumed and a higher tariff per cubic metre consumed thereafter. The Council wanted to encourage a culture of recycling and more efficient water use that was just beginning to emerge in industry. In some cases, however, plants avoided having to pay these increased charges by resorting to the use of borehole water instead of tap water.

As a countermeasure to this practice the Water Act of 1999 was introduced, requiring all water users to pay for water, irrespective of whether it was tap water supplied by a local authority or water obtained directly from boreholes. Unfortunately, the Act did not address the variability of water pricing among local authorities. Some local authorities deliberately set low rates for water as a way of attracting investment, thereby undermining the pricing policy effort.

Global comparison

There is no global assessment that one can draw on to compare the relative effectiveness of resource pricing in Zimbabwe; nor were studies found on the effect of pricing on resource use. As an alternative, an EUI score for the manufacturing sector was calculated for use in this study. In the case of Zimbabwe, it appears that there was a reduction in energy-use intensity during the 1990s, from 1050 toe per million US dollars of MVA in 1990 to 870 toe in 2002. However, this improvement was modest in a global comparison, as Zimbabwe's ranking on the EUI index dropped among 93 countries, from seventy-first in 1990 to seventy-second in 2002, and from forty-fourth in 1990 to forty-fifth in 2002 among 65 developing countries. Among the eight countries included in this study, it ranked fifth.

TECHNOLOGY POLICY

The major government technology policy was the Science and Technology Policy issued in 1992. This promoted, among many other things, the adoption and use of CTs, and included several incentives for research and development (R&D). It gave Zimbabwean firms that funded R&D projects with a value up to Z$10 million a tax break of that amount. Zimbabwean legislative representatives hoped that this policy would result in a significant change in the country's R&D efforts, moving from an insignificant percentage of GNP invested in this field to about 1 per cent by 2010.

The government established the Scientific and Industrial Research and Development Centre (SIRDC) in 1993 to implement the Science and Technology Policy. The objectives of SIRDC included: transfer of technology by providing and assessing technological information on process, equipment and products or by demonstrating new technologies; adaptation of technologies to local conditions; development of new technologies by R&D activities; and industrial use of local raw materials and natural resources. SIRDC provided technological services on a 'user-pays' basis and supported start-ups in exchange for equity. In 1997 it initiated a programme to set up several research units, including the Production Engineering Institute, the Environment and Remote Sensing Institute and the Energy Technology Institute, all of which supported, directly and indirectly, the adoption of CTs. These institutes provided a range of support services, including technological advice, to the manufacturing sector.

Besides SIRDC there were several other organizations that provided technical know-how, training and information to the manufacturing sector. These included universities and technical colleges, technical units of business associations, and public service institutions. Of notable importance for the leather processing sub-sector was the Standards Association of Zimbabwe, the organization for quality assurance and standards development for the industrial sector. It was partially financed by an industrial levy that allowed it to expand its services. In spite of its active promotion of standards as important export tools, only 15 per cent of the firms registered with the Confederation of Zimbabwe Industries met the minimum requirements of ISO 9000 quality management standards series by 2000 and, as stated earlier, only a few had adopted ISO 14000 environmental quality management standards.

It must be noted that it was mainly training organizations that formed the technology infrastructure. Very few of them were actually engaged in technology development. They were nevertheless important because they trained most of the key personnel for the manufacturing sector. Furthermore, of all the listed organizations, only the Technology Information Promotion

Services and SIRDC had programmes directed at SMEs, and more than half the leather tanneries in Zimbabwe were in this category. The former disseminated information on technology, research and trade to SMEs while the latter assisted SMEs in improving their production processes through technology assessments and advice.

It is difficult to assess the effectiveness of the formulation of the science and technology policy more than a decade later due to the lack of data. Teitel (2000), in his survey of manufacturing enterprises in Zimbabwe in the mid-1990s, found that 'the proportion of scientists and engineers employed in industry is too low, and the results of their research too concentrated in biology and medicine to the detriment of engineering, technology and related sciences'. Yet it remains to be seen whether the science and technology policy will actually lead to a significant improvement in both R&D and adoption of newer technologies by industry. SIRDC itself recognized that there was only limited technology transfer and development in the 1990s, apart from a few foreign investments and assistance from the international development community. As of 2002 there still remained a lack of cohesion and coordination of efforts supporting science and technology development (Lall and Pietrobelli, 2002).

Global comparison
In summary, the lack of public sector coordination and support for adaptation and diffusion in the period 1990 to 2002 was consistent with Zimbabwe's modest ranking on the TC index. Among 162 countries, its ranking slipped from eighty-sixth in 1990 to ninety-sixth in 2000. Its rank in 2000 placed it in the group of countries with low technology capability. It was forty-ninth among 114 developing countries and fifth among the eight countries included in this study.

LEATHER PROCESSING SUB-SECTOR IN ZIMBABWE

Economic Overview

The production of hides and skins in Zimbabwe was the same in both 1990 and 2000, 11 900 tons, with a slight decrease during the mid-1990s (Table 11.3), while the production of semi-finished and finished leather slowly decreased, falling by 26 per cent over the period to 15.1 million square feet. The country's production of hides and skins accounted for 0.2 per cent of global production in 2000 and of finished leather for almost 0.1 per cent, making it the sixty-fourth largest producer of hides

Table 11.3   Raw hides and skins and semi-finished and finished leather
*   production, import and export*

Year	Raw hides and skins (thousand tons)[a]			Raw hides and skins (US$ million)[b]	
	Production	Import	Export	Import	Export
1990	11.9	0.8	2.2	1.2	6.5
1995	10.1	0.2	1.5	0.2	5.3
2000	11.9	0.8	2.5	1.8	10.3

Year	Semi-finished and finished leather from bovine, sheep and goats (ft² million)[a]			Semi-finished and finished leather from bovine, sheep and goats (US$ million)[b]	
	Production	Import	Export	Import	Export
1990	20.4	–	4.8	2.3	6.1
1995	17.3	–	12.0	5.1	20.6
2000	15.1	–	10.0	n.a.	11.3

Sources: [a] FAO (2004); [b] World Bank (2005).

and skins among 158 countries, and the sixty-fourth largest producer of semi-finished and finished leather among 116 countries (FAO, 2004).

Zimbabwe's leather industry was among the country's most successful exporters. Export of raw hides and skins increased in value by approximately 60 per cent between 1990 and 2000 while export of finished leather increased by approximately 90 per cent, with the bulk of the export going to destinations outside the Southern African region. Many tanneries marketed their own raw hides and skins and semi-finished leather without intermediaries, with some of them having their key personnel in marketing positions. The decline in finished leather production after 1995 was partly due to the effects of the agrarian reform of the late 1990s. Shortages of foreign currency and the subsequent shortages of imported raw materials, such as chemicals, also adversely affected production.

The government put in place a number of licensing requirements, particularly an export ban on hides and skins. Tanneries that wished to export these were required to obtain a special export permit from the Ministry of Lands and Agriculture, under whose jurisdiction raw hides and skins fell. This ban came about as a result of the blanket ban on agricultural commodities, imposed by the government in 2001. Despite the ban, tanneries did not encounter any serious problems in acquiring the licences. Concern, however, was expressed by firms that produced finished leather about the ease with which hides and skins were exported because this left them short of raw materials for finishing.

Since the leather processing sub-sector in Zimbabwe was quite small, there was limited internal competition. Some of the tanneries were small and specialized, which allowed them to serve niche markets, while others were big and produced for larger consumers in foreign markets.

It is also clear from the responses of plant managers to the survey that current environmental regulations did not have a major impact on the competitiveness of firms in spite of the claims that compliance with regulations was costly. Of more importance was the enormous increase in the cost of production inputs and labour as a result of the turbulent macroeconomic environment.

The skills base in the sub-sector was quite broad. Most of the chief operators had international training and experience as there was no leather technology school in Zimbabwe with a high reputation. According to the survey, over 50 per cent of the top managers in the tanneries had international experience, and most of the tanners had been trained in either South Africa or the United Kingdom. Skills were also developed in house, on the job, and through courses organized by the Leather Institute of Zimbabwe. Suppliers of raw material, especially chemical suppliers, who carried out training on new methods whenever these come onto the market, also provided in-house assistance.

Overall, the leather processing sub-sector (ISIC 3231) is thought to have made a small contribution to Zimbabwe's economy during the 1990s, based on data that are available only for leather and leather products (ISIC 323) and only cover the period 1990 to 1996. The value added of the sub-sector increased from US$4.6 million in 1990 to US$5.2 million in 1996, a growth of 13 per cent, while Zimbabwe's MVA declined by almost 35 per cent in the same period. The sub-sector's percentage share of MVA was 0.5 per cent in 1996, and it employed directly some 1200 workers in 2000, about 0.6 per cent of manufacturing employment in the formal workforce.

Sub-sector Profile

In 2001, the leather processing sub-sector consisted of 13 operating tanneries, scattered around the country in four municipal areas and four rural district councils. Of these, seven were set up between 1991 and 2000. Some tanneries only produced semi-finished leather while others covered the whole range of outputs up to finished leather.

Ten of the 13 tanneries were selected for this study based on criteria that included variations in production process, size, location and raw material input. The selected tanneries corresponded to the criteria as follows: three produced only semi-finished leather and seven produced finished leather; five were large-scale and five small-scale operations; six were in urban/industrial and four in rural areas; and five used exclusively bovine hides, three used a mix of bovine hides and animal skins, and two used game skins (Table 11.4).

Other characteristics of the tanneries worth noting are: all were privately owned, eight by Zimbabweans, one by a joint venture and one was a multinational; six exported 50 per cent or more of their production and the remaining four sold almost exclusively to the domestic market; only two were ISO 9001/9002 certified; one was ISO 14001 certified; and four had integrated R&D departments, engaged mainly in quality control and in the installation and adaptation of new technology.

Process Technology and CT Characterization

Technological investments are expensive to make and, not surprising given the financial problems that had always beleaguered the country, the survey team found that most of the equipment declared as new was actually purchased overseas second-hand. This hardly qualified as advanced technology, although it could be an improvement on what was currently being used. The survey team found that plant managers themselves were not satisfied with this technology.

Most plant managers replaced equipment only when repairs were no longer possible, a practice further encouraged by the foreign currency shortages that prevailed in Zimbabwe during the late 1990s. They invested in equipment on the basis of its durability, with no consideration of whether it incorporated CTs. Existing equipment was refurbished and reconditioned and in some cases equipment such as tanning drums were made in house. All of the firms invested in some equipment during the 1990s and also invested in PATs. UNIDO projects alone accounted for more than US$350 000 in PAT investments in three tanneries in 1999 and 2000.

The ten tanneries used all kinds of equipment, ranging from the very old to modern automated equipment in some of the newer plants. The survey team assigned the plants to one of four categories based on the predominant technological vintage of their production processes: two tanneries used mainly traditional processes; two used mainly modern processes; four used a mix of both; and only two used mainly best available technology (BAT) (Table 11.4).

Plant managers gave limited consideration to CTs, not only because of financial constraints but also because of their limited knowledge of CP. However, awareness of the potential of CTs was, in some instances,

Table 11.4 Profile of the ten tanneries investigated

Tannery	Process and product type	Scale	Regional location	Sales orientation (in 2000)	Technology vintage	Ownership	EST score	Regulatory compliance	Donor assist.	EMS
Z1	Bovine, SF and F	Large	Kadoma/urban/industrial	50% D, 50% E	Mixture (modern/BAT)	100% private (foreign)	PAT + MTC	Mostly	UNIDO and DANIDA	No
Z2	Bovine and game, SF and F	Large	Harare/urban/industrial	50% D, 50% E	BAT	100% private (domestic)	PAT + HTC	Mostly	UNIDO and DANIDA	Yes
Z3	Bovine, SF and F	Large	Nyabira/rural	10% D, 90% E	BAT	100% private (domestic)	PAT + HTC	Yes	No	No
Z4	Bovine, sheep and goat, SF and F	Small	BYO/urban/industrial	100% D	Mixture (traditional/BAT)	100% private (domestic)	PAT + MTC	Mostly	No	No
Z5	Bovine and game, SF and F	Large	BYO/urban/industrial	85% D, 15% E	Mixture (traditional/modern)	100% private (domestic)	PAT + MTC	Partially	UNIDO	No
Z6	Bovine, SF and F	Small	Marondera/rural	25% D, 75% E	Modern	100% private (domestic)	PAT + LTC	Mostly	UNIDO and DANIDA	No
Z7	Ostrich and game, SF and F	Small	BYO/urban/industrial	100% E	Mixture (modern/BAT)	100% private (joint venture)	PAT + MTC	Mostly	No	No

278

Z8	Bovine, SF	Small	Banket/rural	100% D	Traditional	100% private (domestic)	No PAT or CT	No inspection	No	No
Z9	Game skins, SF and F	Small	Bromley/rural	50% D, 50% E	Traditional	100% private (domestic)	PAT + LTC	No inspection	No	No
Z10	Bovine, SF	Large	BYO/urban/industrial	100% D	Modern	100% private (domestic)	PAT + MTC	Mostly	No	No

Abbreviations: semi-finished (SF); finished (F); Bulawayo (BYO); domestic (D); export (E); best available technology (BAT); pollution abatement technology (PAT); higher order technological complexity (HTC); medium order technological complexity (MTC); lower order technological complexity (LTC); Danish International Development Agency (DANIDA).

Source: SIRDC (2002).

reasonably high as a result of various training workshops held under donor-funded projects during the latter half of the 1990s. In plants where CP was introduced, some form of in-house training was undertaken for plant-based teams. This not only raised awareness but also helped the plant teams to identify their key problem areas and implement low- and no-cost measures without external assistance.

The survey team classified the tanneries into four groups based on the order of complexity of the CTs used in each (none, low, medium and high). Of those investigated, none were using the most advanced CT but most were implementing or had already implemented some CT measures. According to the survey findings, two tanneries used CTs of a higher order of complexity, five used CTs of a medium order of complexity, two used CTs of a lower order of complexity and one did not use any (Table 11.4). CT options were used in all stages of the production process. Some of those used and the number of tanneries using them are presented in Table 11.5.

Tanneries that adopted CTs benefited financially through savings in raw material input and reductions in effluent charges. Only one tannery, however, was able to provide actual figures on how much was saved (Box 11.1). Other tanneries indicated that they received some financial benefits as a result of implementing process changes but were unable to provide a quantitative estimate of the savings accrued.

Table 11.5   CTs used in the ten tanneries

Process area	Option	Number of tanneries using practice/equipment
Soaking	Green hide fleshing	1
Liming	De-hairing	2
De-liming, bating	Carbon dioxide de-liming	2
Tanning	Recycling of chrome floats	2
	Tanning products and methods that improve exhaustion rate	4
	Wet-white production to reduce chrome	1
	Other material tanning (e.g. vegetable)	2
Wet finishing	Post-tanning products and methods to improve exhaustion rates	4
Finishing	Reduction in solvent-based products	6

Source: SIRDC (2002).

BOX 11.1   CLEANER PRODUCTION CASE STUDY:
ZIMBABWE

A large tannery in Harare invested US$47 000 in a compacting filter for
hair recovery and a change of chemical recipe for the de-hairing process.
These changes reduced the import and use of chemicals by 50 per cent
and the chemical oxygen demand by 50 per cent. It also brought the
tannery into compliance with the municipal discharge limits. The investment generates an annual saving of US$13 500 in effluent treatment cost
and municipal charges.

Source: SIRDC (2002).

PAT Characterization

Effluent treatment was fairly well developed in most of the tanneries
because it was a legal requirement. Nine of the ten tanneries have some type
of treatment technology for modifying their process effluent. The six that
discharged effluent into CEPTs in the cities of Harare, Bulawayo and
Kadoma were required by municipal regulations to pre-treat their effluent
before its discharge. The four that discharged their effluent directly into
rivers were required by the regulations set out by the Zimbabwe National
Water Authority to construct their own effluent treatment plants (ETPs).
Three out of four have built secondary ETPs (aerated lagoons) while one
has yet to comply with the requirement.

The use of PATs by tanneries in Zimbabwe was largely a result of donor
assistance programmes, which provided consultants and financial support
for PAT investments. In the case of one multinational tannery, which was not
included in the survey, its international corporate policy required that the
production process comply with national environmental standards. Some
tanneries invested in PAT upgrades and one built a completely new ETP.

Environmental Performance

The Department of Natural Resources did not collect or publish data on
pollutant discharge by industry. The only available data on environmental
compliance were those collected during the survey for this study. As can be
seen in the column on regulatory compliance in Table 11.3, one tannery
fully complied with the effluent discharge standards, six mostly complied
and one only partially complied. There were no inspection reports for two
of the tanneries.

In those localities with a concentration of tanneries, local authorities had made complaints against the tanneries about odour and wastewater quality. Although their pollutant discharge was significant within the local setting, the environmental impact of the sub-sector overall was, however, not of major significance when compared to other manufacturing sub-sectors in Zimbabwe, as described at the beginning of this chapter in the section on economic and environmental indicators.

KEY INFORMANTS AND INTERNATIONAL DONORS

Four groups, in addition to government environmental regulatory author-ities and technology centres, are able to influence in different ways the extent to which plants adopted EST: NGOs, business associations, inter-national donors of technical assistance, and chemical and equipment sup-pliers. Some information about the first three is presented in this section; there is insufficient information to characterize the firms that supplied chemicals and equipment to Zimbabwe's leather processing sub-sector.

NGOs

NGOs in Zimbabwe at the time of this study saw themselves as playing a complementary role to the government. This role, however, appears to have been minimal in terms of the environmental pressure exerted on industry. A plant was rarely forced to improve its environmental performance as a result of pressure exerted by civil society (Sibanda, 1996).

Most complaints only came to light through media reports. Complaints from members of the public were channelled through the local authority, which then notified the concerned tannery. In Bulawayo and Gweru the local authorities penalized tanneries in their municipality in response to media reports highlighting the problem of odour emanating from the tanneries.

The survey team interviewed Environment Africa, an African NGO with Zimbabwe branches in Harare, Victoria Falls and Mutare. Its mission is to raise the level of environmental awareness of the general public, the busi-ness sector, schools, community groups, the media and governments in Africa. Its activities are designed to work together with all sectors of society, advocating and encouraging action for a better environment that will uplift the general livelihood. One of Environment Africa's major pro-jects at the time of this study was to reduce water pollution in the river that runs through industrial areas in Harare.

The survey team found that the civil society in Zimbabwe exerted very little or no pressure at all on the leather processing sub-sector to comply with environmental regulations. Not a single plant manager mentioned civil society pressure as a key driving force in the adoption of EST. Market pressure, however, was seen as a key factor, especially for those firms that exported their products to international markets. The local market, however, appeared to be little concerned about environmental performance.

Business Associations

The survey team interviewed three business associations, one of which, ZimTrade, is described earlier, in the section on industrial development policy.

The Leather and Allied Industries Federation of Zimbabwe (LIZ), set up in 2001 and supported by the government, is a very active business association that focuses on the technical aspects of the industry, including quality, reliability and service delivery. However, its members seldom use the services it provides.

The Confederation of Zimbabwe Industries, founded in 1923, is the main industrial association in Zimbabwe, with members from both large corporations and SMEs. It is an independent, self-financed, legally constituted association whose functions include, among others, representation and advocacy, policy and economic advice, and information dissemination.

The business associations that participated in the survey attributed the lack of adequate pressure on industry to improve environmental performance to the lack of environmental awareness among the public. ZimTrade organized environmental awareness workshops for exporters and would-be exporters, and the environmental committee of the Confederation of Zimbabwe Industries supported campaigns to improve the environmental performance of firms, including those in the leather processing sub-sector.

INTERNATIONAL DONORS

As of 2002, a number of donor-funded projects had been implemented in Zimbabwe to assist industry in acquiring CTs and improving its environmental management. Most of these programmes targeted the whole manufacturing sector while a few specifically targeted the leather processing sub-sector.

Donor initiatives in industrial environmental management started with the establishment of the ZCPC in 1994. This was a UNIDO/UNEP initiative and, in the initial phase, a total of 19 plants were audited, including two tanneries.

Several bilaterally funded projects complemented this CP programme in the 1990s. The Swedish Industrial Development Agency assisted Zimbabwe's tannery sub-sector in improving the performance of its ETPs under the 'Clean Green and Profitable' project; it assisted four big tanneries. The Norwegian Agency for Development, through the International Labour Organization, funded the Employers' Confederation of Zimbabwe to offer training in CP, and three tanneries were audited as part of the project. The German Agency for Technical Cooperation, working with the Confederation of Zimbabwe Industries, undertook an environmental cost management project. Cost analyses were prepared for several plants, including one at a tannery. Finally, the Danish International Development Agency funded a project to build capacity for CP within SIRDC and ZCPC. More than 30 plants, including four tanneries, were assisted with CP audits, and 12 demonstration projects, including one at a tannery, were undertaken in several industrial sub-sectors.

In 1997, UNIDO initiated a project on tannery pollution control, funded by the government of the Netherlands and aimed at reducing the effluent discharged by the leather processing sub-sector. To meet this objective, it assisted four tanneries to reduce pollutant discharge by upgrading their ETPs. Part of the project supported the Zimbabwe Investment Centre in the promotion of investment and technology transfers from South Africa. The project, however, resulted in very limited levels of technology transfer because of the reluctance of foreign partner firms to invest in a country with problematic macroeconomic conditions.

In 2000, UNEP financed a number of training courses on CP financing. Three tanneries participated in these and generated CP investment proposals. However, only one of the proposals was successfully implemented as a result of securing donor funding.

SUMMARY

Zimbabwe's aggregate economic performance indicators show that the economy performed poorly during the 1990s, whereas its aggregate environmental performance indicators reveal some progress. While GDP increased by only 1 per cent between 1990 and 2002, MVA actually contracted by 35 per cent. As a result, the share of MVA in GDP decreased from 21.0 to 13.5 per cent. GNI per capita at PPI barely held its own, with a 1 per cent increase during the same period. Manufacturing energy use declined by 40 per cent and energy-use intensity declined by 20 per cent. BOD effluent decreased by 28 per cent, but BOD-effluent intensity decreased by only 3 per cent. The reduction in BOD effluent was primarily attributable to the decline in industrial activity.

Zimbabwe did not have a comprehensive or effective environmental policy during the 1990s. The environmental regulations in place at the time were difficult to enforce and were replaced by the Environmental Management Act of 2002. There was limited use of environmental impact assessments and economic incentives. Country-specific data on EST adoption or on compliance with environmental regulations are not available so it is difficult to ascertain the extent to which the manufacturing sector complied with environmental regulations.

The collective impact of three economic policies, industrial, trade and resource pricing, on technology modernization was limited. Industrial policies, in spite of their worthy objectives, do not appear to have offered any significant support to the manufacturing sector, including the leather processing sub-sector, in the 1990s. Trade policies, especially those dealing with tariffs, kept tariff rates relatively high compared to those of other countries, and this discouraged technology import. Resource pricing policies, particularly for water, aimed to encourage the use of CTs, but were effectively undermined by the high rate of inflation, loopholes in regulations and subsidized water pricing by local authorities.

Zimbabwe's technology policy and programmes appear to have done little to enhance domestic capabilities to adopt or to make significant improvements in technology. The government technological infrastructure, which was supportive of SMEs, only started in the late 1990s.

In the leather processing sub-sector there were 13 operational leather tanneries in Zimbabwe in the year 2002. This sub-sector produced the same amount of hides and skins, 11 900 tons, in both 1990 and 2000 and actually produced less finished leather, with production dropping from 20.4 to 15.1 million square feet over the period. The survey team found that the ten tanneries they investigated operated with vastly different process technology. Two used CTs of a higher order of complexity, five used CTs of a medium order of complexity, one used CTs of a lower order of complexity and one used none. Nine had invested in some form of PATs, six using pre-treatment technology before discharging their effluent to CEPTs and three operating their own ETPs. As a result, most of the ten tanneries complied to some extent with the established effluent discharge standards.

The influence of other institutional actors, NGOs, business associations and international donors, on EST adoption was limited primarily to international donors during the 1990s. Several donor organizations supported CP training programmes and demonstration projects and, in some instances, funded the purchase of EST. The business community, including the Environmental Forum of Zimbabwe, which was not interviewed during the survey, attempted to increase environmental awareness. Environmental

NGOs appear to have had very little influence on improving the environmental performance of manufacturing plants.

In conclusion, the leather processing sub-sector in the 1990s responded positively to the double-edged challenge of improving productivity and competitiveness and, at the same time, reducing pollutant discharge. Consequently its contribution to both MVA and exports increased in the 1990s in spite of turbulent economic conditions and limited governmental support. It also invested in PATs, often with some support from international technical cooperation programmes. However, the sub-sector still needed to do more to modernize its production processes, expand the use of CTs, reduce resource consumption and improve its compliance with environmental regulations. Suffice it to say that governmental policies and, more particularly, industrial support and regulatory organizations needed to improve service delivery and credibility if they were to contribute to the much-needed technological modernization of the country.

NOTES

1. This can only be assumed because sub-sector data for Zimbabwe's manufacturing sector are only available for the period 1990 to 1996.
2. The FDI for 1990 has been taken as the three-year average of 1989–99 and for 2002 the three-year average of 2001–3, in order to even out fluctuations in FDI flows.
3. The IEA does not provide exclusive energy consumption data for the leather sub-sector; it was therefore calculated according to the proportion of MVA of the textile and the leather sub-sectors, for which the IEA provides information as one sub-sector.

REFERENCES

Bekhechi, M. and J. Mercier (2002), 'The Legal and Regulatory Framework for Environmental Impact Assessments: a Study of Selected Countries in Sub-Saharan Africa', Law, Justice, and Development Series, Washington, DC: The World Bank.

City of Harare (2001a), 'Price for Tap Water', personal communication with SIRDC survey team, Harare, Zimbabwe: City Treasurers' Department.

City of Harare (2001b), 'Tannery Effluent', personal communication with SIRDC survey team, Harare, Zimbabwe: Trade Waste Inspectorate.

EIU (2003), 'Country Profile: Zimbabwe', London: Economist Intelligence Unit.

FAO (2004), 'World Statistical Compendium for Raw Hides and Skins, Leather and Leather Footwear, 1984–2002', Rome: Food and Agriculture Organization of the United Nations (available on: http://www.fao.org).

FAO (2005), 'AQUASTAT, FAO STAT', Rome: Food and Agriculture Organization of the United Nations (available on: http://www.fao.org).

GATT (1995), 'Trade Policy Review: Zimbabwe', Geneva: General Agreement on Tariffs and Trade.

IEA (2005), 'Online Data Services', IEA Energy Information Centre, Paris: International Energy Agency (available on: http://www.iea.org).

ISO (2003), 'The ISO Survey of ISO 9000 and ISO 14001 Certificates', Geneva: International Organization for Standardization (available on: http://www. iso.org).

Jaspers, F. (2001), 'The new water legislation of Zimbabwe and South Africa – comparison of legal and institutional reform', *International Environmental Agreements: Politics, Law and Economics*, **1** (3), 305–25.

Lall, S. and C. Pietrobelli (2002), *Failing to Compete: Technology Developments and Technology Systems in Africa*, Cheltenham, UK and Northampton, MA, US: Edward Elgar Publishing.

Mhone, G. and P. Bond (2001), 'Botswana and Zimbabwe: Relative Success and Comparative Failure', WIDER Discussion Paper WDP/2001/38, Helsinki, Finland: World Institute for Development Economics Research.

Sibanda, H. (1996), 'NGO Influence on National Policy Formation in Zimbabwe', IDR Reports, Vol. 11, No. 2 (available on: www.jsi.com/idr/web%20reports/html/ 11-2.html).

SIRDC (2002), 'Assessing the Adoption of EST in Zimbabwe's Leather Tanning Sector', Harare, Zimbabwe: Scientific and Industrial Research and Development Centre of Zimbabwe (SIRDC). Report prepared for UNIDO.

Teitel, S. (2000), *Technology and Skills in Zimbabwe's Manufacturing: from Autarky to Competition*, London: Macmillan.

UNIDO (2005), *International Yearbook of Industrial Statistics 2005*, Cheltenham, UK and Northampton, MA, US: Edward Elgar Publishing.

World Bank (2004), 'World Bank Development Indicators (WDI) 2004', CD-ROM version, Washington, DC: The World Bank.

World Bank (2005), 'World Integrated Trade Solution (WITS)', Washington, DC: The World Bank (available on: http://wits.worldbank.org).

ZESA (2002), *Energy Sales Price*, Harare, Zimbabwe: Zimbabwe Electricity Supply Authority.

12. Eight-country assessment of factors influencing EST adoption

INTRODUCTION

The findings from the three different modes of investigation used to identify the factors that influenced EST adoption, described in the heuristic model in Chapter 3, are presented in this chapter. The first mode of investigation examines the relationship between the three policy regimes that created the incentive structure brought to bear on plant-level behaviour via government, markets and civil society, and the actual levels of resource-use and pollutant intensities that might be attributed to these policies. The second describes the perceptions of 98 plant managers and 91 key informants of the relative importance of government, markets and civil society as external drivers for EST adoption (perceived factors). The third analyses the factors observed by the survey teams of this study as having influenced plant-level behaviour at the 98 plants in the eight countries (observed factors). The findings from each of these investigations are presented in the sections that follow, but first the survey data used in the analysis of perceived and observed factors are briefly described.

The findings from the second and third modes of investigation draw on the work of teams of national experts in the eight developing countries who conducted face-to-face interviews with plant managers at 98 plants about EST adoption decisions during the period 1990 to 2002. Each country team collected data on only one manufacturing sub-sector in their country (Table 12.1). In total, the teams collected data on 41 pulp and paper mills in four countries, 38 textile mills in two countries and 19 leather tanneries in two countries. In addition to interviews with plant managers, the teams also interviewed a variety of key informants, namely, representatives of business associations, technology centres, equipment and raw material suppliers, NGOs and environmental regulatory authorities. In total they interviewed 91 key informants, who confirmed or clarified the information provided by the plant managers and expressed their own opinions on drivers for the adoption of EST from an outsider's point of view.

The second mode of investigation, the description of plant managers' and key informants' perceptions of the main drivers for the adoption of

288

Table 12.1 Distribution of the plants and key informants

Country	Sub-sector	By sub-sector	Plants	Business associations	Technology centres	Suppliers	NGOs	Environmental authorities
Brazil	Pulp and paper		7	4	2	3	4	5
China	Pulp and paper	41	11	1	3	3	2	6
India	Pulp and paper		14	1	1	5	1	2
Viet Nam	Pulp and paper		9	1	1	1	1	1
Thailand	Textiles	38	28	1	4	5	1	2
Tunisia	Textiles		10	1	2	1	1	1
Kenya	Leather	19	9	5	1	2	1	3
Zimbabwe	Leather		10	3	2	2	1	4
Total			98	17	16	22	12	24

Source: Chapters 4 through 11.

EST, is largely qualitative; its purpose was to capture the range and heterogeneity of the perceptions of these two groups in different countries and sub-sectors, the richness of which could not be captured in the statistical analysis presented in the third section of this chapter. However, the limitations of this investigation of the perceived factors are that it fails to take into account plant-internal characteristics that influenced EST adoption and to identify which internal and external factors actually influenced adoption. Hence the value of the third mode of investigation is a statistical analysis of the overall impact of factors observed by the survey teams, both internal ones such as plant size and technological capabilities, and external ones such as the regulatory approach and donor assistance. The advantage of using a statistical approach to evaluate the observed factors, in this case an ordered-choice model, is that it identifies factors that influenced the adoption of EST regardless of what plant managers consciously identified as important factors. The findings from the statistical analysis are presented in the third section of this chapter.

POLICY INFLUENCES

The eight country case studies in Chapters 4 to 11 describe three policy regimes, environmental, economic and technology, which largely defined the incentive structure for the adoption of EST in each country. A rigorous comparison of the effectiveness of the different policy regimes on EST adoption is unfortunately not possible, given the difficulties of identifying specific causal pathways of influence, the small number of countries investigated and the absence of national data on EST adoption. However, it is possible to estimate the effect that those regimes had on country-level resource-use and pollutant intensities, such outcomes being consequences of adopting EST.

To begin this analysis, the relationship among levels of economic development, the effectiveness of the three policy regimes, and resource-use and pollutant intensities for all eight countries in 2002 is summarized in Table 12.2. First, the eight countries are ranked on the basis of their level of economic development, defined in terms of either their standard of living (GNI per capita at PPP) or industrial output (MVA per capita), with country names in the third column. Based on either measure, all eight countries fall into three out of four possible groups: lesser-developed countries, accelerating-developing countries, advanced-developing countries and developed countries. Three are classified as advanced-developing countries, three as accelerating-developing countries, and two as lesser-developed countries (UNSTATS, 2005).

Table 12.2 Level of economic development and policy effectiveness and environmental outcome

GNI pc (2002)	MVA pc (2002)	Country (level)*	Policy effectiveness indices/scores					Energy-use intensity (2002)	Water-use intensity (2000)	BOD intensity (2001)	CO₂ intensity (2002)
			CIP (2002)	TI (2001)	EUI (2002)	EG (2001)	TC (2000)				
1 (int$7450)	2 (US$874)	Brazil (adv)	3 (0.324)	3 (0.010)	3 (430)	4 (0.620)	2 (0.330)	3 (430)	3 (72)	1 (1.4)	1 (610)
2 (int$6890)	1 (US$1009)	Thailand (adv)	1 (0.386)	1 (0.023)	2 (350)	2 (0.690)	1 (0.342)	2 (351)	2 (37)	2 (2.0)	2 (700)
3 (int$6440)	3 (US$490)	Tunisia (adv)	5 (0.241)	2 (0.019)	1 (340)	1 (0.760)	4 (0.288)	1 (340)	1 (25)	3 (3.5)	3 (850)
4 (int$4520)	4 (US$357)	China (acc)	2 (0.379)	4 (0.005)	4 (670)	3 (0.660)	3 (0.306)	4 (670)	6 (420)	4 (4.8)	4 (920)
5 (int$2650)	6 (US$78)	India (acc)	4 (0.275)	8 (0.001)	7 (1280)	5 (0.600)	7 (0.225)	7 (1280)	7 (480)	5 (6.7)	8 (2890)
6 (int$2300)	5 (US$82)	Viet Nam (acc)	7 (0.196)	5 (0.004)	6 (910)	6 (0.520)	6 (0.239)	5 (912)	–	7 (12.6)	7 (2570)
7 (int$2180)	7 (US$71)	Zimbabwe (les)	6 (0.213)	6 (0.002)	5 (900)	7 (0.500)	5 (0.279)	6 (970)	5 (230)	6 (8.5)	5 (1780)
8 (int$1010)	8 (US$26)	Kenya (les)	8 (0.134)	7 (0.002)	8 (1520)	8 (0.420)	8 (0.204)	8 (1500)	4 (124)	8 (21.5)	6 (1850)

Note: * acc is accelerating-developing country, adv is advanced-developing country, les is lesser-developed country, and int$ indicates international dollar amount.

Sources: World Bank (2004) and Chapters 4 through 11.

The eight countries are then ranked on the basis of the policy effectiveness indices (scores in the case of EUI) introduced in Chapter 3 and elaborated upon in each of the country chapters. These are CIP for industrial policy, TI for trade policy, EUI for resource policy, EG for environmental policy and TC for technology policy.[1] The index or score on each policy variable is included in parentheses.

The countries in each development group have remarkably similar effectiveness rankings for their policies, most notably for the group of advanced-developing countries (three countries and five policies), which accounts for 12 out of the 15 highest policy effectiveness rankings. There is not such a strong relationship for the group of accelerating-developing counties (three countries and five policies) or the group of lesser-developed countries (two countries and five policies). The former accounts for eight of the 15 mid-range policy rankings and the latter for six of the ten lowest policy rankings. While some inconsistency was expected in the accelerating-development group, given the rate of change in their institutions, it was not expected in the lesser-developed country group, where countries were not experiencing significant changes in their institutions. The lack of correspondence between level of economic development and policy effectiveness for the lesser-developed country group is due to Zimbabwe, which is an atypical lesser-developed country. If another more typical lesser-developed or least-developed country in Africa had been investigated in this study, there would have been a better correspondence.

Finally, the eight countries are ranked on the basis of their resource-use and pollutant intensities, in lieu of national data on EST adoption. The country data on intensities, described in Chapter 2 and used in each country chapter, are included in this table. Not surprisingly there is a degree of consistency between country rankings on policy effectiveness (as well as level of economic development) and lower resource-use and pollutant intensities, but not as much as between levels of economic development and policy effectiveness. The group of advanced-developing countries accounts for all 12 of the lowest resource-use and pollutant intensity measures. However the picture is more mixed for the group of accelerating-developing countries, which accounts for only six out of 12 middle ranked resource-use and pollutant intensity measures, and for the group of lesser-developing countries, which accounts for two of the eight highest resource-use and pollutant intensity measures.[2]

In order to gain some insight into the relationship between policy effectiveness and resource-use and pollutant intensities, a series of equations were calculated using the available data from all countries, which include the eight countries investigated. The data for each of the equations varied since each policy and resource-use and pollutant intensity variable provided information for a different set of countries. In Table 12.3, all 15 valid equations found are shown with an indication of the number of countries on which the equation was estimated, their level of significance together, and the R^2, which describes the amount of variation in the observed response values that is explained by the independent variable.

Table 12.3   Country regression analyses of the impacts of policy effectiveness on resource-use and pollutant intensities

	Equation-dependent and independent variables	Number of countries	Significance levels	R-squared
Energy	$logEI = 2.06 - 1.02\, logCIP$	76	***	0.43
	$logEI = 2.18 - 0.25\, logTI$	65	***	0.31
	$logEI = 2.45 - 1.05\, logEG$	63	***	0.28
	$logEI = 2.34 - 0.74\, logTC$	93	***	0.17
Water	$logWI = 4.34 - 0.77\, logCIP$	40	**	0.12
	$logWI = 3.94 - 0.54\, logTI$	41	***	0.25
	$logWI = 4.75 - 0.79\, logEG$	34	*	0.09
BODI	$BODI = 8.14 - 13.9\, CIP$	77	***	0.49
	$BODI = 6.61 - 24.9\, TI$	71	***	0.55
	$logBOD = 0.0713 - 1.38\, logEG$	66	***	0.30
	$BODI = 12.2 - 17.4\, TC$	102	***	0.45
CO_2	$logCO_2I = 2.31 - 0.98\, logCIP$	79	***	0.33
	$logCO_2I = 2.42 - 0.24\, logTI$	67	***	0.24
	$LogCO_2I = 2.71 - 0.90\, logEG$	65	***	0.17
	$logCO_2I = 2.54 - 0.80\, logTC$	101	***	0.18

Note: Significance notation: *** is significant at the 99% level, ** is significant at the 95% level and * is significant at the 90% level.

This set of equations provides a useful insight into the effect of each policy by itself where everything else remains the same. Given the complexity inherent in each variable, a much more complex analysis would be needed to integrate each policy variable into one equation, with an analysis of the interaction of each policy with each other and probably with other country policies not included here.

Given the negative exponential relation between most corresponding variables (as included in each equation), the data were transformed with logarithms for computing the equations in most cases except for BOD intensity. In that case, a linear relationship rather than an exponential one best fitted the data. Note that in no case did the EUI policy variable have a significant and correctly signed influence on an intensity measure. This variable therefore presented no valid set of equations, which only confirms the earlier stated scepticism about the meaningfulness of that index.

The exponential equations indicate that the initial result of improvements in policy effectiveness leads to a decrease in the resource-use or pollutant intensity. As policy effectiveness reaches its limits, its impact on intensities declines until it has no discernible effect. The linear equations (three for BOD intensity) indicate that the effect of an improvement in effectiveness leads to an even decrease over the full range of performance improvements in BOD intensity.[3]

PERCEIVED FACTORS

The investigation of the perceptions of 98 plant managers and 91 key informants of the relative importance of a number of external drivers for EST adoption in the actions of government, markets and civil society is the second mode of investigation of the factors identified in the heuristic model described in Figure 3.1 in Chapter 3. Whereas the 'new model' of the World Bank (2000) focuses on factors that influence the environmental performance of plants, defined in terms of investments in pollution abatement equipment, pollutant discharge or compliance with environmental regulation, the heuristic model focuses on factors that influence the adoption of EST, the precursor to improved environmental performance.

Definitions of Perceived Factors

The external drivers for EST adoption, which constitute the perceived factors and the hypotheses about their influence on the adoption of different types of EST, are drawn from the literature reviewed in Chapter 3 to the extent that these drivers have been investigated. Grouped in the three categories of government, markets and civil society they are defined as follows:

Government

- *Current environmental regulation*:   Standard command-and-control environmental regulatory programmes aim to ensure that plants comply with environmental standards, achieved in most cases by the use of PATs. Although empirical investigations have confirmed regulatory pressure as a significant determinant of environmental performance – even where regulation is relatively weakly implemented – there is as yet only limited empirical evidence showing the types of technological changes that regulatory pressure may cause at plants.

- *Financial incentives*: Economic incentives, such as loans, grants, and tax exemptions for capital investments, are examples of public policy measures that are often used by governments to encourage plants to adopt EST. Empirical evidence supports the hypothesis that financial incentives, such as tax breaks or duty-free imports, influence the extent to which plants invest in PATs.
- *Future environmental regulation*: While current regulations do not exert much pressure on plants in some countries, an anticipated increase in the stringency of such regulations could motivate plants to start improving their environmental performance.

Markets

- *Environmental reputation*: The better environmental performance of competitors may motivate plant managers to adopt EST in order to achieve a comparable reputation.
- *High cost of production inputs*: The high cost of natural resource inputs, including energy and water, make it difficult to be competitive, particularly in markets characterized by stiff price competition, and motivate managers to adopt more resource-efficient CTs to reduce their use of these inputs. If plant managers are aware of the cost-reducing potential of CTs, they are likely to adopt them to reduce the cost of production and thus improve their competitive position.
- *Product specifications in foreign markets*: Plants in developing countries seeking market access abroad often need to meet stricter product specifications (usually products must be free of certain chemicals) than when they produce for domestic consumption. Case study evidence exists of this factor's influence on developing countries' EST decisions about changing input material.
- *Requirements imposed by owners and investors*: Owners and investors have a legitimate right in market economies to require a plant's management to improve environmental performance. Several studies have confirmed that they influence a plant's management decisions on EST adoption.
- *Supply chain demands*: The environmental requirements of a plant's business partners, primarily supply chain buyers but also customers, increasingly act as drivers for EST adoption in plants that are active in supply chains. Anecdotes tell of the influence of OECD buyer pressure on environmental performance. This pressure increases in product market segments that are close to final consumers.

Civil society

- *Peer pressure*:   Trade and business associations are usually trusted by their members to represent their interests and to give impartial advice on the need to comply with environmental standards. Such advice can encourage EST adoption.
- *Public pressure*:   Local communities, NGOs, the media and the public at large can act as an effective complement to formal regulation. This type of public pressure is documented by a number of recent studies.

It was hypothesized that the influence of these external drivers of EST adoption, as consciously perceived by plant managers, would be positive at the aggregate level of analysis but that there would be significant variations in the relative importance attributed to them when data were disaggregated by sub-sector and country. Indeed, it was expected that important differences in sub-sector technological configuration, market structure, pollutant intensity and scope for implementing EST options would probably result in managers attributing different ratings to different sources of pressure, as would pronounced country-level differences in the perceived importance of the degree of present and future regulatory pressure.

The Importance of Drivers as Perceived by Plant Managers

Plant managers were asked to rate the drivers on a scale of one to five, with five as the most important. The last column of Table 12.4 shows that their perception of the three most important drivers in descending order, aggregated across the eight countries, was the high cost of production inputs (3.8), current environmental regulation (3.7) and anticipated future environmental regulation (3.3). In general their assigning importance to several drivers, particularly those outside traditional environmental regulation, is consistent with the new model of pollution control (World Bank, 2000) and the heuristic model of EST adoption used in this study. Both models show that a mix of drivers influences plant-level behaviour.

Sub-sector differences
Variation in the perceived importance of drivers among the sub-sectors relates significantly to the technological configurations and product markets of each sub-sector. The pulp and paper sub-sector is one of the most energy- and material-consuming and thus pollutant-intensive manufacturing sub-sectors. Not surprisingly, therefore, pulp and paper mill managers gave their highest rating to regulatory pressure (3.9), followed by the

Table 12.4   Perceived drivers for EST adoption by plant managers

Drivers for EST adoption[a]	Pulp and paper[b]				Textile[b]		Leather[b]		Pulp and paper	Textiles	Leather	Total
	Brazil	China	India	Viet Nam	Thailand	Tunisia	Kenya	Zimbabwe				
Government												
Current environmental regulations	**3.7**	3.7	**4.4**	3.6	3.6	4.0	2.8	3.5	**3.9**	3.8	3.2	3.7
Financial incentives for pollution abatement	1.0	3.3	1.5	3.0	2.1	–	2.5	1.1	2.2	2.1	1.8	2.1
Future environmental regulations	2.3	4.1	1.4	3.9	3.8	–	3.9	**4.0**	2.9	3.8	**4.0**	3.3
Markets												
Environmental image	1.8	3.3	1.4	2.7	3.4	–	2.8	2.9	2.3	3.4	2.9	2.6
High costs of production inputs	2.3	**4.4**	3.1	**4.6**	**4.3**	4.4	3.6	3.4	3.6	**4.4**	3.5	**3.8**
Product specifications in foreign markets	2.0	2.8	1.1	3.0	3.3	3.5	2.6	2.0	2.2	3.4	2.3	2.5
Requirement of owners and investors	2.7	2.5	1.1	3.0	3.1	–	**4.4**	3.3	2.3	3.1	3.9	2.9
Civil society												
Supply chain demands	1.3	2.4	1.1	2.1	3.4	**4.5**	3.1	2.6	1.7	3.9	2.9	2.6
Public pressure	2.2	2.8	3.2	3.3	2.3	–	2.9	2.5	2.9	2.3	2.7	2.7
Peer pressure	1.2	2.8	1.4	3.1	2.1	–	1.8	2.0	2.1	2.1	1.9	2.1

Notes: [a] Highest rated driver for each country and sub-sector in bold. [b] Sub-sector average only for business associations, technology centres and suppliers.

Source: Chapters 4 through 11.

need to reduce the use of high-cost production inputs (3.6). Textile mill managers, working in one of the most price-competitive sub-sectors globally, perceived, not surprisingly, the need to reduce costly production inputs (4.4) as the dominant driver. In second place was supply chain demands by buyers/importers (3.9), followed closely by current and future environmental regulations (each 3.8) probably because of developed countries' scrutiny of textile production in developing countries. The leather tannery sub-sector, where managers saw anticipated future environmental regulation (4.0) and requirements imposed by owners/investors (3.9) as the dominant drivers, is not pollutant intensive like the pulp and paper sub-sector, nor is it subject to supply chain demands (at least not for tanned leather) as is the textile sub-sector.

Country differences
Within individual sub-sectors there was considerable variation among countries. The most important driver for pulp and paper mill managers operating in free market economies, in this case Brazil (3.7) and India (4.4), was current environmental regulation, whereas the most important one for mill managers operating in socialist economies, in this case China (4.4) and Viet Nam (4.6), was reduction of the use of high-cost production inputs. Similarly the second most important driver for these managers in China and Viet Nam was anticipated future environmental regulation, which suggests that environmental regulation is just beginning to become effective in these two countries. Different drivers were rated highest by mill managers in the two textile-producing countries; for Thailand it was the high-cost production inputs (4.3) while for Tunisia it was supply chain demands (4.5). This variation is not surprising in that most of the plants surveyed in Tunisia export to Europe, whereas most of those surveyed in Thailand produce for the domestic market or export only to regional markets. The most important drivers for the leather tannery managers in the two African countries also differ, in the case of Kenya the requirements of owners/investors being most highly rated (4.4) and, in the case of Zimbabwe, anticipated future environmental regulation (4.0). The specific response in Kenya is explained by the fact that most tanneries were confronted with community pressure on local owners to reduce pollutant discharge. Hence the low rating assigned to public pressure has a corresponding high rating assigned to the requirements of owners/investors. In any case the survey team confirmed that community pressure was a significant driver for the installation of PATs in Kenya. The highest and second highest ratings given by tannery managers in Zimbabwe, anticipated future environmental regulation and current environmental regulation, respectively, are consistent with the view of the survey team that the cooperative regulatory activities

of local authorities were effective in bringing about pollutant reduction in that country.

In addition, the survey teams asked plant managers to identify the drivers for setting up an environmental management system (EMS) in those cases where plants had one. Only about a third of sampled plants actually had an EMS or were in the process of establishing one. EMS use is very uneven, with plants in Brazil, Thailand and Tunisia representing the lion's share. Supply chain demands were mentioned as by far the most prominent driver for EMS adoption, requirements of owners/investors and current environmental regulation being cited, respectively, as the second and third most important drivers.

The Importance of Drivers as Perceived by Key Informants

The perceptions of key informants, as distinct from those of plant managers described above, are listed in Table 12.5. Aggregated across eight countries, the three most important drivers for key informants were current environmental regulation (4.0), the high cost of production inputs (3.8) and product specifications in foreign markets (3.3). The fact that key informants saw current environmental regulation as the dominant driver is not surprising since about one quarter of them were environmental regulatory authorities.

The most striking difference in perceptions between the key informants and plant managers across all countries and sub-sectors was the importance assigned to product specifications in foreign markets by key informants, particularly in Brazil, Kenya, Thailand, Tunisia, Viet Nam and Zimbabwe. It was only in Tunisia and Thailand that plant managers acknowledged this as a factor, albeit not rating it as highly as did key informants. Another notable divergence in perceptions between the two groups was the influence of anticipated future environmental regulation as a factor affecting plant-level behaviour. Plant managers generally saw it as having an influence, whereas key informants did not.

Looking at sub-sector data, the perceptions of key informants differed in some cases from those of plant managers. In the pulp and paper sub-sector both groups assigned importance first to current environmental regulation and then to the high cost of production inputs. In the textile sub-sector key informants rated current environmental regulation as most important, whereas plant managers rated the high cost of production inputs as most important. Supply chain demands were underscored by both groups and in both countries (Thailand and Tunisia) as an important influence. In the leather processing sub-sector key informants saw product specifications in foreign markets as a real source of pressure, whereas plant managers did not rate it as important.

Table 12.5 *Perceived drivers of EST adoption by key informants*

Drivers for EST adoption[a]	Pulp and paper[b]				Textile[b]		Leather[b]		Pulp and paper	Textiles	Leather	Total
	Brazil	China	India	Viet Nam	Thailand	Tunisia	Kenya	Zimbabwe				
Government												
Current regulations	**4.7**	**4.6**	**3.4**	3.8	**4.5**	**4.4**	3.4	3.1	**4.1**	**4.4**	3.2	**4.0**
Financial incentives	2.0	2.7	1.2	3.0	3.1	2.9	2.8	3.0	2.2	3.0	2.9	2.6
Future regulations	3.6	4.2	1.8	3.8	3.5	1.4	3.1	3.5	3.4	2.5	3.3	3.1
Markets												
Environmental image	4.3	3.0	2.1	3.4	2.8	1.2	2.5	2.9	3.2	2.0	2.7	2.8
High cost of production inputs	3.3	4.4	2.8	**5.0**	3.9	3.5	4.0	3.4	3.9	3.7	3.7	3.8
Product specifications in foreign markets	3.9	3.1	1.0	3.8	3.8	3.6	3.6	**3.8**	3.0	3.7	**3.7**	3.3
Requirement of owners and investors	3.0	2.3	1.2	2.4	3.3	1.1	2.1	2.2	2.2	2.2	2.2	2.2
Supply chain demands	3.0	2.0	1.0	2.0	4.2	3.3	2.4	3.2	2.0	3.8	2.8	2.6
Civil society												
Public pressure	3.3	2.2	3.3	2.8	3.0	2.1	**4.2**	2.2	2.9	2.6	3.2	2.9
Peer pressure	2.0	2.0	1.3	2.0	2.6	1.9	2.7	2.1	1.8	2.3	2.4	2.1

Notes: [a] Highest rated driver for each country and sub-sector in bold. [b] Sub-sector average only for business associations, technology centres and suppliers.

Source: Reports for chapters 4 through 11.

OBSERVED FACTORS

The analysis of the factors observed by the survey teams as having influenced EST adoption at the 98 plants in this study, as distinct from the stated perceptions of plant managers and key informants, is the third mode of investigation of the factors identified in the heuristic model. Not all the factors identified could be analysed in this investigation of observed factors because of data limitations. The observed factors actually analysed are depicted in italics in Figure 3.1 in Chapter 3 in abbreviated form. The first part of this section describes how these factors (variables) were constructed, based on information obtained by the survey teams, while the second part describes the results of the statistical analysis.

Deffnitions of Variables

The dependent variable, EST adoption, and the 13 independent variables are described below. Independent variables are categorized under in-plant characteristics, government, markets and civil society. Hypotheses about how each independent variable might influence EST adoption are included along with the description of the variable.

Dependent variable

EST adoption: As described in Chapter 1, a basic distinction is made within EST between PATs and CTs. Among CTs a variety of categories and options can be distinguished. In Chapter 2 (Appendix 2A) there are brief descriptions of the seven categories used by the survey teams to classify the various CT options.[4] To construct the dependent variable, these seven CT categories were grouped according to their level of technological complexity into 'low', 'medium' and 'high'. The grouping reflects a continuum of technological possibilities.

Thus a plant's EST adoption status is set out on a scale ranging from standard pollutant abatement technology external to the production process to pollutant prevention technology internal to the production process and of the highest order of technological complexity. Assessing a plant's EST adoption status therefore took into account two dimensions: the 'technological complexity' of the EST adopted and the degree to which plants had moved away from pollutant mitigation to prevention measures that reduced the resource-use intensity of production processes. EST adoption, expressed as an ordinal variable, took one of the following values: 0 = no PATs and no CTs; 1 = PATs only; 2 = PATs plus lower order of complexity CTs [(2) input material change and (3) better process control]; 3 = PATs plus medium order of complexity CTs [(4) equipment modification; (5) on-site reuse and (6) useful by-products]; 4 = PATs plus higher order of complexity CTs [(7) major technology change and (8) product modification].

In-plant characteristics

Environmental commitment (ENVCOM): The *ENVCOM* variable reflects the extent to which a plant, or its parent firm, has taken measures to improve its environmental management. The variable is based on whether a plant had an environmental policy and had an EMS; information on the construction of this variable is provided in Appendix 12A. A positive relationship is assumed between the environmental attitude and commitment of plant management and EST adoption, based on several empirical investigations (Kemp, 1997; Dasgupta et al., 2000; Tukker et al., 2000; and Fryxell and Lo, 2003). Adopting an environmental policy and introducing an EMS are considered clear signs of environmental commitment. The introduction of an EMS can help plants identify cost-effective opportunities to improve their environmental performance. However, only limited evidence exists on the influence of an EMS on the type of technological change. In a study of Standard and Poor 500 firms, Anton et al. (2004) found that implementation of an EMS is particularly conducive to the adoption of process-integrated CTs as compared to PATs.

Ownership (OWN): The *OWN* variable shows whether private parties or the government owns a plant. It is a binary measure. Several World Bank studies have found that state ownership is strongly associated with higher levels of pollutant discharge (World Bank, 2000). SOEs are seen as shielded from formal and informal regulatory pressure. In addition, these cited studies show that SOEs have a record of wasteful resource use and financial distress, less investment in PATs and higher pollutant intensity. Accordingly a positive correlation is assumed between private ownership and EST adoption.

Profitability (PROFIT): The *PROFIT* variable relates to company-reported profits as a fraction of sales and is an ordinal variable. Profits as a percentage of sales are assigned to one of five values. According to the technology adoption literature cited in Chapter 3, higher levels of profitability indicate that firms generally have internal financial resources and/or easier access to external financing for productivity-enhancing investments. A positive relationship between profitability and EST adoption is therefore assumed.

Size (SIZE): The *SIZE* variable is based on either the number of employees (textile sub-sector) or production volume (pulp and paper and leather processing sub-sectors). It reflects each country's definition of the cut-off point between large plants and small- and medium-sized plants. A positive relationship is assumed between size and EST adoption because large plants can take advantage of economies of scale in technology use, which is particularly important in the use of PATs. In addition they have better access to capital and information and normally hire employees with greater technological skills.

Technological capabilities (TECHCAP): The *TECHCAP* variable captures a plant's skills (technical, managerial or organizational) that enable it to adopt equipment and information effectively. It reflects the investment, production and linkage capabilities of a plant (or its parent firm), following Lall (1999), and is based on seven different measures of a plant's technological capability. Details of the construction of the variable are to be found in Appendix 12A. In line with the literature on technological capabilities, a plant's technological capabilities are assumed to be a key determinant of a plant manager's decision on EST adoption. The limited empirical evidence on the importance of a skilled workforce for CT adoption (Adeoti, 2002; Blackman and Kildegaard, 2003) lends further support to this hypothesis.

Independent variables: government
International donor assistance (DONOR): The *DONOR* variable indicates whether a plant had or had not participated in a donor funded, government-approved demonstration project through a cleaner production centre. Participation was counted only if there was documentation that the plant had actually invested in PATs and/or CTs as a result of the demonstration project. A positive relationship is assumed between donor assistance and EST adoption based on the investigation by Luken et al. (2003) that reported on the adoption of CTs as a result of the technical assistance provided by eight UNIDO/UNEP National Cleaner Production Centres.

Regulatory implementation strategy (REG): The *REG* variable reflects how a plant perceives the domestic environmental regulatory regime and its own relationship with the regulatory authorities, categorized from 'positive' and 'cooperative' to 'negative', 'arbitrarily imposed' and 'strictly enforced'. Details of the construction of this variable are provided in Annex 12A. Based on the literature reviewed in Chapter 3 and Reijnders (2003), a flexible regulatory approach by a regulatory authority that is positively disposed towards a plant's experimentation with alternative cost-effective solutions and a willingness to accept delays in the realization of pollutant reductions is assumed to be positively correlated with the adoption of more technologically complex CTs.

Technical assistance (ASSIST): The *ASSIST* variable indicates the extent to which a plant has used or has had the opportunity to use external technological support services. Such services can assist plant managers in identifying, negotiating the purchase of, transferring and implementing technology. These external sources include public or semi-public institutions (technology institutes, universities and regulatory agencies). Support from internal sources, such as a parent firm, is not included. Details of the construction of the *ASSIST* variable are provided in Appendix 12A. In light of the pervasive market failures of technology in developing countries, described by the technological capabilities literature, a positive relationship between this variable and EST adoption is expected. Unfortunately none of the empirical studies reviewed in Chapter 3 statistically examined the influence of institutional technological support on a plant's adoption of EST.

Independent variables: markets

Export orientation to OECD markets (EXPORT): The *EXPORT* variable is a proxy for the influence of buyer pressure on a plant's EST adoption. In line with similar studies (Dasgupta et al., 2000), only export sales to OECD markets were taken into account when constructing the measure. *EXPORT* is an ordinal variable based on the percentage shares of plants' exports to OECD markets. The five values of this variable relate to the percentage of production that is exported. A positive influence of export orientation, particularly to OECD countries, on a plant's level of EST adoption is assumed. The reasons advanced are the stricter regulations as well as the greater level of green consumerism in the importing countries, which may impart greater environmental as well as social sensitivity to export-oriented plants (Johnstone et al., 2004). However empirical studies have so far not found any substantial evidence to confirm the widespread anecdotal claims. No studies were found that had examined the impact of a plant's export orientation on the type of technology change taking place at the plant level.

Foreign involvement (FOREIGN): The *FOREIGN* variable, a binary measure, indicates whether foreign investors made new management techniques and new technologies available to a plant. Despite a lack of clear evidence of foreign involvement in a plant's environmental performance (Dasgupta et al., 2000), a positive effect of foreign involvement on the type of technological adjustment can be inferred from the limited empirical evidence available on this effect (Adeoti, 2002).

Water-energy price perception (WEPP): The *WEPP* variable is constructed from a plant's response to a question inquiring in what way developments in the prices for water and energy influenced technological change. Plant managers rated the significance of water and energy price developments separately on a scale from 1 to 5; answers that were then combined into a compound variable with four categories. In general, higher resource prices motivated plant managers to reduce total expenditure on resources by using CTs that lower water and energy use per unit of output (Kemp, 1997; Reijnders, 2003). The price effect prevails however only when plants are required to pay the costs for all energy and water inputs, which is not always the case, and the share of the utility cost in the total manufacturing cost per unit of output is significant.

Independent variables: civil society

Business association influence (ASSOC): The *ASSOC* variable is constructed from a plant's response to a question on whether its principal business association had influenced its decision to adopt EST. The response is scored as a simple yes–no answer. In order for the response to be counted as yes, plant managers had to identify at least one specific example of how their EST adoption was influenced by their principal business association. A positive relationship is assumed between business association assistance and a plant manager's decision to adopt EST. In a business environment characterized by information scarcity and technological uncertainty, particularly with respect to CT, business or trade associations often claim they play a role in information dissemination on the technological options for reducing pollutant discharge and their performance characteristics. Blackman and Banister (1998), for example, found evidence of the influence of trade associations on CT adoption among traditional Mexican brick-makers.

Community pressure (COMPRESS): The *COMPRESS* variable is constructed from a plant manager's response to a question on the extent to which environmental NGOs, citizen groups or media had exerted pressure on the plant to reduce pollution. The complaints from these groups are classified into five categories. A positive relationship is assumed between community pressure and EST adoption, based on the literature reviewed in Chapter 3. Whereas community pressure has been identified by many studies as an important determinant of environmental performance, very few studies have examined the influence of this pressure on the type of technological change. As one of the few to examine this effect, Montalvo (2002) found only a limited impact of community pressure on the willingness of a firm to undertake technology change *per se*.

The percentage distribution of plants over the dependent and independent variables' values is presented in Table 12.6. Since the primary purpose of

Table 12.6 Percentage distribution of plants over variable values

Dep. var.	EST index	%	no PATs 5	only PATs 5	PATs + low CTs 30	PATs + med CTs 42	PATs + high CT 18
In-plant characteristics	Environmental commitment (ENVCOM)	%	(0) 36	(1) 42	(2) 22		
	Ownership (OWN)	%	(public) 17	(private) 83			
	Profitability (PROFIT)	%	(0 or neg.) 6	(0–5%) 42	(5–10%) 23	(10–15%) 8	(15%+) 21
	Size (SIZE)	%	(small) 47	(large) 53			
	Technological capabilities (TECHCAP)	%	(1–3) 7	(4–6) 47	(7–10) 36	(11–13) 10	
Government	International donor assistance (DONOR)	%	(no) 75	(yes) 25			
	Regulatory implementation strategy (REG)	%	(0) 12	(1) 15	(2) 24	(3) 20	(4) 29
	Technical assistance (ASSIST)	%	(0) 16	(1) 38	(2) 26	(3) 20	
Markets	Export orientation (EXPORT)	%	(0%) 59	(0–10%) 11	(10–25%) 4	(25–50%) 14	(>50%) 12
	Foreign involvement (FOREIGN)	%	(no) 92	(yes) 8			
	Water-energy price perception (WEPP)	%	(1–2) 19	(3–5) 33	(6–8) 31	(9–10) 17	
Civil society	Business association influence (ASSOC)	%	(no) 57	(yes) 43			
	Community pressure (COMPRESS)	%	(0) 39	(1–5) 29	(6–10) 11	(11–20) 12	(>20) 9

this study was to examine CT adoption, it is appropriate that the number of plants investigated was heavily weighted to those that had adopted more technologically complex CTs.

The cross-sectional data used in the probit model were pooled for all sub-sectors and all countries because the sample size was too small to run separate regressions for each sub-sector or each country.[5] While acknowledging the diversity among the sub-sectors and countries, it needs to be pointed out that the apparent heterogeneity regarding the topic of the investigation, the adoption of EST, is not nearly as great as it seems and need not cause a problem for the statistical analysis. First, the major pollution problem caused by three sub-sectors is the discharge of water pollutants, and the EST required to abate this type of pollutant is similar for all three. The PATs used in all three sub-sectors are primarily for the abatement of water pollutants, and the CTs used, while differing in their specifics in some cases, could be categorized into similar orders of technological complexity described in Chapter 2 (Appendix 2A). Second, all eight countries, as described in Chapters 4 to 11, have amazingly similar governmental regimes that affect the adoption of EST. They all rely primarily on command-and-control environmental regulatory systems, support technology extension organizations to provide advice to firms and draw on the support of international donors to achieve their environmental objectives. For example, all have international donor-funded cleaner production programmes, and, in all of them, civil society organizations, both local community groups and business associations, are actively engaged, as described in the country chapters, in pressuring plants to comply with environmental standards. Third, the environmental commitment of all plants could be categorized using recognizable measures (written environmental policies and environmental management systems) and their technological capabilities measured using standard variables for technological capabilities (Lall, 1999).

Statistical Analysis of Observed Factors

Two kinds of statistical tools are introduced in this section. First the bilateral relationships between EST adoption and the 13 independent variables are measured. Then a probit model of EST adoption, in which all 13 factors are included as independent variables, is estimated to test the proposed hypotheses about EST adoption. These two procedures should be seen as complementary rather than as alternatives. The first procedure measures the bivariate relationships without any claims to causality. It is useful because it shows the variations in the strength of association of the independent variables among the three sub-sectors, which is lost in the application of the probit model. The latter procedure measures the overall impact of all possible determinants on EST adoption.

Measures of association

A Spearman Rho correlation coefficient is used to measure the strength of bivariate association between EST adoption and the selected factors because all of these are of an ordinal nature. A summary of the results at the aggregate and sub-sectoral levels is found in Table 12.7.

At the aggregate level, eight of the 13 examined variables are significantly correlated with EST adoption. In order of strength of the relationship they are: *ENVCOM, REG, TECHCAP, PROFIT, SIZE, FOREIGN, ASSIST* and *DONOR*. Furthermore, all statistically significant variables are positively correlated with EST adoption. Although the *OWN, ASSOC* and *COMPRESS* variables show no significant correlation with EST adoption at the aggregate level, nonetheless, for one sub-sector, pulp and paper, these three variables are significantly correlated with EST adoption. Whereas the *ASSOC* and *COMPRESS* variables are positively correlated with EST adoption as anticipated, the reverse holds true for the *OWN* variable, a result that was not anticipated.

At the sub-sectoral level, the association with EST largely shows the same tendencies for all variables as at the aggregate level. However, while the values of the associations are mainly similar to those at the aggregate level, their significance is often lacking at the sub-sectoral level. This is mainly due to the limited number of observations and to the lower variations within a sector. Two variables, *ENVCOM* and *REG*, are significant for three sub-sectors, pulp and paper, leather and textiles; *TECHCAP* and *SIZE* are significant for the pulp and paper and leather sub-sectors; *ASSIST* is significant for the pulp and paper and textiles sub-sectors; *PROFIT*, ASSOC and *COMPRESS* are only significant for a single sub-sector, pulp and paper and *DONOR* and *WEPP* are only significant for the leather sub-sector.

The *OWN* variable is significant only for the pulp and paper sub-sector, but not at the aggregate level and is negatively related to EST adoption, which is inconsistent with the assumption about its effect. A possible explanation is the skewed distribution of this variable over the entire sample. The vast majority of plants in the entire sample are privately owned. The only exceptions are most pulp and paper plants in China (70 per cent state-owned) and Viet Nam (80 per cent state-owned), which explains the significant correlation for this sector. The negative relationship, which indicates that state ownership is positively correlated with higher order EST adoption, is best explained by the privileged position enjoyed by SOEs in these two countries, where heavy industry, which includes pulp and paper, faces soft budget constraints and has easier access to modern technologies

Table 12.7 Measures of association

Dep. var.	EST with....	Total sectors	Pulp and paper	Leather	Textile
	N	98	41	19	38
In-plant characteristics	Environmental Commitment	0.526***	0.624***	0.601***	0.433***
	Ownership	−0.136	−0.305*	no variation	−0.24
	Profitability	0.361***	0.579***	0.269	0.187
	Size	0.283***	0.27*	0.607***	0.149
	Technological Capabilities	0.385***	0.706***	0.648***	0.15
Government	International Donor Assistance	0.191*	−0.022	0.516**	0.049
	Regulatory implementation strategy	0.46***	0.577***	0.463**	0.281*
	Technical Assistance	0.23**	0.328**	−0.039	0.286*
Markets	Export Orientation	0.114	0.202	0.233	−0.108
	Foreign Involvement	0.24**	0.26	0.222	0.21
	Water-energy price perception	0.152	−0.003	0.462*	0.212
Civil society	Business association influence	0.164	0.352**	0.112	−0.045
	Community pressure	−0.022	0.465***	−0.176	−0.131

Notes: Significance notation: *** significant at the 99 % level, ** significant at the 95 % level and * significant at the 190 % level. The measure of association for variables is the Spearman Rho except for the export variable, where the Pearson correlation coefficient is used.

because of the need to maintain employment levels. Thus the negative relationship in the case of these two countries is similar to that of private ownership in other countries, where it is assumed that there is a positive relationship between ownership and adoption of EST.

In addition, *ASSOC* and *COMPRESS* are significant only for the pulp and paper sub-sector. One possible explanation is that the pollutant loadings of this sector are often odoriferous, hence the increased concern of the business associations and the increased number of complaints from the public.

Probit model
An ordinal probit model was used to assess the joint impact of the independent variables on a plant's level of EST adoption. The use of this model is appropriate because a plant's level of EST adoption, the dependent variable, satisfies two conditions. These are that the values of a dependent variable must have an order and the differences between the ordered categories must not be equal. The former is the case because the five levels of EST reflect increasingly higher orders of technological complexity and the latter because the differences among the five levels of complexity are not identical. In addition, the reported standard errors obtained using the White estimator of the variance corrected for inter-sector heteroscedasticity.

The preliminary set of independent variables consists of all 13 variables and three sector dummies. The dummies capture generic variations in abatement costs and process technologies across the three sub-sectors covered by the survey. One sub-sector dummy was later dropped due to collinearity. This model is referred to as the 'full' model. It contains several insignificant parameters. This could be caused by the weak effect of these parameters on the adoption of EST, but also by the eventual multi-collinearity among the variables. Correlation between the variables was checked in the course of the analysis. Correlation was present, but not strongly with the highest value being 0.5.

In order to remove multicollinearity and assess a statistically significant model, it was necessary to run several rounds of top-down and bottom-up stepwise estimations. After each round the least significant variable was excluded, base on the t-test. The process was continued until all remaining parameters reached significance. The results based on both approaches were identical. The 'final' model was regarded as statistically correct, making it possible to undertake further calculations and discuss the results (Table 12.8). Whereas 13 variables plus two sector dummies are in the full model, only seven variables (*DONOR, ENVCOM, FOREIGN, OWN, REG, TECHCAP* and *WEPP*) and the two sector dummies are in the final model. Variables from two of the three institutional categories and in-plant

Table 12.8   Summary of the ordinal probit regression for adoption of EST
– final model

Variable	Coefficient	Std. Err.
Environmental commitment (ENVCOM)	0.699***	0.041
Ownership (OWN)	−0.675**	0.24
Technological capabilities (TECHCAP)	0.224***	0.058
International donor assistance (DONOR)	0.570**	0.169
Regulatory implementation strategy (REG)	0.165*	0.071
Foreign involvement (FOREIGN)	0.718*	0.322
Water-energy price perception (WEPP)	0.307***	0.11
Textile dummy	0.932***	0.124
Leather dummy	1.321***	0.076
Number of observations	98	
Pseudo-R^2	0.271	

Notes: Significance notation: *** significant at the 99 % level, ** significant at the 95 %
level and * significant at the 90 % level.

factors are present in the final model. Civil society influence is apparently
not strong enough to influence the adoption of EST.

The interpretation of the estimated parameters based on the final model
is never made directly because the ordinal probit model is non-linear.
Instead the parameters are transformed into predicted probabilities and
then interpreted. This enables an interpretation of the results in terms of
discrete changes in these probabilities as a result of variations in the independent variable (Scott-Long, 1997). The likelihood of a plant appearing
in a particular EST category is indicated by a probability that is based on
the estimated parameter. When the level of a particular variable changes,
there is a corresponding change in these probabilities. For some EST categories the probability will be higher and for others lower because the sum
of the probabilities must be zero. This allows one to observe spillovers
among categories after a change in a variable takes place. The results of
such transformations for each of the variables entering the 'final' model are
presented in Table 12.9. Note that only one variable is changed at a time,
keeping the other variables constant at their means. This is a standard
approach that shows the impact of just one variable while assuming the rest
to be static.

For every independent variable, some magnitude of increase, $\Delta 1$, $\Delta \sigma$, or
$0 \rightarrow 1$, occurs (column 'change').[6] The measure of change depends on the
type of variable. For multinomial variables (*ENVCOM, TECHCAP, REG*
and *WEPP*) there are changes of $\Delta 1$ and $\Delta \sigma$ (standard deviation) around

Table 12.9   Discrete changes in the predicted probabilities of five levels of EST

	Variable	Change	$\bar{\Delta}$	No PATs	PATs only	PATs + low CTs	PATs + med CTs	PATs + high CTs
In-plant characteristics								
	ENVCOM	$\Delta 1$	0.102	−0.011	−0.026	−0.217	0.149	0.105
		$\Delta \sigma$	0.077	−0.008	−0.02	−0.166	0.114	0.079
	OWN	$0 \rightarrow 1$	0.088	0.006	0.017	0.198	−0.087	−0.134
	TECHCAP	$\Delta 1$	0.033	−0.003	−0.008	−0.071	0.049	0.033
		$\Delta \sigma$	0.083	−0.009	−0.021	−0.179	0.123	0.085
Government								
	DONOR	$0 \rightarrow 1$	0.078	−0.006	−0.016	−0.173	0.092	0.103
	REG	$\Delta 1$	0.024	−0.002	−0.006	−0.052	0.036	0.024
		$\Delta \sigma$	0.065	−0.007	−0.016	−0.139	0.096	0.065
Markets								
	FOREIGN	$0 \rightarrow 1$	0.089	−0.005	−0.015	−0.203	0.068	0.156
	WEPP	$\Delta 1$	0.05	−0.005	−0.012	−0.108	0.075	0.05
		$\Delta \sigma$	0.05	−0.005	−0.012	−0.107	0.074	0.05

Notes: The sign $\bar{\Delta}$ stands for average absolute discrete change in predicted probabilities throughout the EST categories. The sign $\Delta \sigma$ is a centred change of one deviation around the mean.

the mean of the variable in the sample, while for binomial variables (*OWN*, *DONOR* and *FOREIGN*) only a change from $0 \rightarrow 1$ is possible. For each increase in a variable, a corresponding change occurs in the predicted probability that a plant will fall into any of the five EST categories. The changes are then shown in the respective cells (no PATs to PATs + high CTs). The $\bar{\Delta}$ column indicates the so-called average absolute discrete change i.e., the overall effect of the variable's increase, regardless of the EST level. Mathematically, this is an average of absolute values of the changes across all the EST categories. Some of the results are discussed below:

- For *ENVCOM, REG, TECHCAP* and *WEPP*, an increase by one point in their value decreases the probability that a plant will appear in the three lower EST categories but increases the probability of its being in the two higher EST categories, mainly variables thought to be influenced by internal management factors, government and market forces.
- If the status of foreign involvement (*FOREIGN*) changes from 0 to 1, it increases the probability of a plant appearing in the highest EST

category by 15 per cent. This percentage change is the largest one in the model. This finding lends support to the description in several country chapters of the impact of FDI on CT transfer.

- *OWN* is the only variable which actually contradicts its assumed hypothesis. If the status of the ownership variable changes from public to private, the probability of a plant appearing in the lower three categories increases, while the probability of it appearing in the upper two EST categories decreases. As already stated, a possible explanation for this finding could be that SOEs in China and Viet Nam have privileged access to finance.

- It is unfortunately not possible to determine which variable has the largest overall impact, given that the independent variables are of a different nature, both multinomial and binomial variables. It is, however, possible to examine the relative impact of variables of the same type on EST level. A comparison is therefore made among the three binomial variables and then among the four multinomial variables.

- In terms of the binomial variables, the impacts of *FOREIGN* and *OWN* are almost identical and clearly higher than *DONOR*. The absolute average change for *FOREIGN* is 1.1 per cent higher than that for *OWN*.

- To examine which multinomial variable has the biggest overall impact on EST level is a little bit trickier. Note that they have different ranges; hence, the $\Delta 1$ change does not necessarily mean comparable units. Therefore, the four multinomial variables are additionally presented as a change of the size of the standard deviation ($\Delta \sigma$). The standard deviation expresses the natural volatility in each variable existing in the sample. The $\Delta \sigma$ change can be regarded as equal change for the different multinomial variables. Comparing the $\bar{\Delta}$ for $\Delta \sigma$ changes shows that *TECHCAP* has the strongest impact, an average of 8.3 percent. The *ENVCOM* does not lag much behind with an average of 7.7 per cent, while *REG* is weaker with an average of 6.5 per cent and *WEPP* is weakest with an average of only 5.0 per cent.

In summary, the statistical analysis reveals that a host of factors influenced EST adoption, particularly higher order complexity CTs. Plant–specific factors, specifically *ENVCOM*, *OWN*, *TECHCAP* and market factors, specifically *FOREIGN* and *WEPP*, mattered significantly in determining the type of technological response and thus in explaining the adoption of higher order EST, that is technologically complex CTs. Two governmental factors, *REG* and *DONOR*, also play a role in the adoption of EST. However, civil society, in particular community pressure that has been identified as an important determinant, did not play a role, most likely because the sample of plants was skewed towards those that use higher order CTs, whose adoption was most influenced by in-plant characteristics.

APPENDIX 12A   INDICES

Environmental Commitment (*ENVCOM*)

This index, which combines responses to three questions, was constructed as follows: (a) did the firm have an environmental policy? (no = 0, yes = 1); (b) did the firm participate in any waste minimization or pollution prevention programme? (no = 0, yes = 1); and (c) does the firm have an EMS? (no = 0, yes = 1).

Regulatory Implementation Strategy (*REG*)

This index, which combines the responses to four questions, was constructed as follows: (a) did forms of cooperation exist between the plant manager and regulators, for example, consultation on regulations, negotiated standards and emissions, and was opportunity given for voluntary compliance by companies? (no = 0, yes = 1); (b) did regulators only penalize or did they additionally offer advice on the EST adopted? (penalize only = 0, offer advice = 1); (c) did the plant management make information on pollutant releases freely available to the public? (no = 0, yes = 1); (d) had national environmental regulations reduced or strengthened the plant's competitiveness? (reduced = 0, strengthened = 1). The index thus captures in essence the relationship a firm had with the principal environmental regulator. At one end of the scale the relationship was primarily antagonistic and at the other end primarily cooperative. The index measures the degree to which either cooperation or compulsion worked.

Technical Assistance (*ASSIST*)

This index, which combines responses to three questions, was constructed as follows: (a) did regulators offer any type of advice or support for the reported EST adopted? (no = 0, yes = 1); (b) did the plant rely on external institutional technical support in identifying, assessing, selecting, negotiating, transferring and/or implementing the reported EST adopted? (no = 0, yes = 1); (c) did the plant have a recognized link with institutions or associations that promoted the diffusion of technology? (if no link = 0, if link = 1).

Technological Capabilities (*TECHCAP*)

Different ways of categorizing technological capabilities are suggested in the literature. The construction of this index is based on a 'technology index', presented in Lall (1999), which in turn draws on Lall's 'Illustrative Matrix of Technological Capabilities' (Lall, 1992). *TECHCAP*, which aggregates seven different aspects of a firm's technological capabilities, was constructed as follows: (a) the (relative) extent of its search for technology (minimal = 0/standard = 1/extensive = 2); (b) the existence of an engineering department (none = 0/basic = 1/well-established = 2); (c) the existence of a quality management system (none = 0/yes = 1/ISO compatible = 2); (d) the (relative) level of process technology (traditional = 0/standard-modern = 1/best available technology (BAT) = 2); (e) the level of technological activity over the period (none = 0/some = 1/a lot = 2); (f) the (relative) level of product quality (low = 0/standard = 1/high = 2); and (g) the extent of its technology linkages with other enterprises, that is, suppliers, buyers, competitors, and technology support institutions, that is, technology centres and universities (none = 0/some = 1/extended = 2). The national technology experts, who participated in each country survey team, validated the results of the scoring.

NOTES

1. Four of the policy effectiveness measures are thought to be reasonable reflections of effectiveness. The measure of policy effectiveness for resource pricing, energy-use intensity is used for the sake of completeness but it is not comparable to the other measures because it is the same as the policy impact measure. It does not reflect the effectiveness of energy or water resource management to the extent of the other measures.
2. This qualitative finding is in line with the mixed empirical investigations of the environmental Kuznets curve that posits a simple relationship between economic development and environmental quality. See Stern (2004) for a discussion of the mixed empirical findings.
3. The finding here about the relationship between environmental governance and resource-use and pollutant intensities is consistent with the findings of Dasguta et al. (2006).
4. The most basic lower order of technological complexity of CT, good housekeeping, was not considered in determination of the EST variable because its use is too difficult to identify and verify. Thus the numbering of CT categories starts with number 2, found in Chapter 2, appendix A.
5. Dummy variables for sub-sectors and countries were added in order to test for fixed effects. The sub-sector dummies were significant and used in the statistical analysis, but the country dummies were not significant and thus not used in the statistical analysis.
6. There are no discrete changes in predicted probabilities for sector dummies because it is obviously not possible to change sectors.

REFERENCES

Adeoti, J. (2002), *Technology and the Environment in Sub-Saharan Africa: Emerging Trends in the Nigerian Manufacturing Industry*, Burlington, US: Ashgate Publishing.

Anton, W., G. Deltas and M. Khanna (2004), 'Incentives for environmental self-regulation and implications for environmental performance', *Journal of Environmental Economics and Management*, **48** (1), 632–54.

Blackman, A. and G. Bannister (1998), 'Community pressure and clean technology in the informal sector: an econometric analysis of the adoption of propane by traditional Mexican brick makers', *Journal of Environmental Economics and Management*, **35** (1), 1–21.

Blackman, A. and A. Kildegaard (2003), 'Clean Technology Change in Developing Country Industrial Clusters: Mexican Leather Tanning', Discussion Paper 03-12, Washington, DC: Resources for the Future.

Dasgupta, S., H. Hettige and D. Wheeler (2000), 'What improves environmental compliance? Evidence from Mexican industry', *Journal of Environmental Economics and Management*, **39** (1), 39–66.

Dasgupta, S., K. Hamilton, K. Pandey and D. Wheeler (2006), 'Environment during growth: accounting for governance and vulnerability', *World Development*, **34** (9), 1595–611.

Fryxell, G.E. and C.W.H. Lo (2003), 'The influence of environmental knowledge and values on managerial behaviours on behalf of the environment: an empirical examination of managers in China', *Journal of Business Ethics*, **46** (1), 45–69.

Hettige, H., M. Huq, S. Pargal and D. Wheeler (1996), 'Determinants of pollution abatement in developing countries: evidence from South and Southeast Asia', *World Development*, **24** (12), 1891–904.

Johnstone, N., P. Scapecchi, B. Ytterhus and R. Wolff (2004), 'The firm, environmental management and environmental measures: lessons from a survey of European manufacturing firms', *Journal of Environmental Planning and Management*, **47** (5), 685–707.

Kemp, R. (1997), *Environmental Policy and Technical Change: A Comparison of the Technological Impact of Policy Instruments*, Cheltenham, UK and Northampton, US: Edward Elgar Publishing.

Lall, S. (1992), 'Technological capabilities and industrialization', *World Development*, **20** (2), 165–86.

Lall, S. (ed.) (1999), *The Technological Response to Import Liberalization in Sub Saharan Africa*, London: Macmillan Press.

Luken, R., J. Navratil and N. Hogsted (2003), 'Technology transfer and the UNIDO/UNEP national cleaner production centres programme', *International Journal of Environmental Technology and Management*, **3** (2), 107–17.

Montalvo, C. (2002), *Environmental Policy and Technological Innovation: Why do Firms Adopt or Reject New Technologies?*, Cheltenham, UK and Northampton, MA, US: Edward Elgar.

Reijnders, L. (2003), 'Policies influencing cleaner production: the role of prices and regulation', *Journal of Cleaner Production*, **11**, 333–8.

Scott-Long, J. (1997), *Regression Models for Categorical and Limited Dependent Variables*, Advanced Quantitative Techniques in the Social Sciences, Vol. 7, Thousand Oaks, CA, US: SAGE Publications.

Stern, D. (2004), 'The rise and fall of the environmental Kuznets curve', *World Development*, **32** (8), 1419–39.

Tukker, A., E. Haag and P. Eder (2000), 'Eco-design: European State of the Art, Institute for Prospective Technological Studies', Joint Research Centre, Brussels: European Commission.

World Bank (2000), *Greening Industry: New Roles for Communities, Markets and Governments*, Oxford, UK: Oxford University Press.

World Bank (2004), 'World Bank Development Indicators (WDI) 2004', CD-ROM version, Washington, DC: The World Bank.

United Nations (UNSTAT) (2005), 'Methods and Classifications: Composition of Macro Geographical (Continental) Regions, Geographical Sub-regions, and Selected Economic and Other Groupings' (available on: http://www. unstats. un.org).

13. Findings, policy implications and programme proposals

INTRODUCTION

This chapter presents a summary of the findings of this study and the policy implications derived from these findings as a basis for identifying proposals for government programmes that have the potential to accelerate EST adoption. The first section, findings, summarizes the findings in Chapters 2 to 12 that are relevant to the discussions of policy implications and programme proposals that follow. This first section is sub-divided into three parts. The first part describes the differences in trends in the decoupling of industrial growth and environmental pressure between 1990 and 2002, and the potential of CTs to reduce these differences, presented in Chapter 2, and the heuristic model for EST adoption, presented in Chapter 3. The second part summarizes the findings from Chapters 4 to 11 about the policy regimes in the eight countries of the study, with the aim of identifying which policies were more favourable to the adoption of EST. The third part highlights the major findings from the policy effectiveness analyses and the data about perceived and observed factors influencing the adoption of EST in the eight-country assessment presented in Chapter 12. The second section, Policy Implications, then examines the policy implications for accelerating EST adoption derived from the preceding analysis of policies and the data about perceived and observed factors. The third and final section, Programme Proposals, describes two government programmes aimed at encouraging the adoption of EST, particularly the use of more complex CTs.

FINDINGS

Chapters 2 and 3: Decoupling and the Role of CTs; the Heuristic Model of EST Adoption

The decoupling of the relative rates of growth of environmental pressure and industrial output, the latter a cause of the former, between 1990 and circa 2002 is documented in Chapter 2 with reference to the four country groupings defined in that chapter, namely, developed countries, transition economies, developing countries and least developed countries. While the relative decoupling achievements of the developing and the least developed country groups were encouraging, there is clearly a need for more to be done to bring the resource-use and pollutant intensities of their manufacturing sectors into line with those of the developed country group. The energy-use intensity of industry remains almost three times higher in developing than in developed countries, water-use intensity more than 11 times higher, water-pollutant intensity six times higher and carbon dioxide intensity four times higher.

The adoption of more technologically complex CTs is thought to have the potential to reduce resource-use and pollutant intensities by between 10 and 30 per cent. This potential was illustrated by plant case studies from three developing countries (taken from the UNIDO CP database). The limited literature published on CT adoption in developing countries suggests that this potential has yet to be exploited because only CTs of a lower order of technological complexity have been extensively used to date.

The heuristic model of EST adoption used to direct this research into the determinants of EST adoption in developing countries, described in Chapter 3, was developed from a review of the more general literature on technology diffusion and upgrading and, especially, from a review of the more specific literature on the adoption of EST in developing countries, in particular the literature related to the World Bank's 'new model' of pollution control. The literature on EST adoption in developing countries documented that manufacturing plants in developing countries were complying with environmental standards more than many had thought. It also found that improved environmental performance was influenced not only by environmental regulation but also by a combination of environmental regulation, market forces and civil society pressures.

This heuristic model was built around the understanding that a plant's incentive structure to adopt EST is created by three policy regimes, environmental, economic (with subdivisions for industrial, trade and resource pricing policies) and technology, and is transmitted to plant managers via the three pathways of government, markets and civil society. In turn, internal plant-level characteristics determine the extent to which plants can respond to these incentives.

Chapters 4 to 11: Environmental, Economic and Technology Policies in the Eight Countries

The eight country case studies presented in Chapters 4 to 11 describe the three policy regimes, environmental, economic and technology, that were most relevant to the adoption of EST. The following three paragraphs briefly appraise the incentive support that these policies provided for the technology upgrading that could lead to greater adoption of EST. The findings of the sub-sector investigations in the country chapters are not included here because these are not relevant to the discussion of policy and programme implications.

First, the environmental policy regimes in most countries were considerably enhanced between 1990 and 2002 with stronger command-and-control regulatory programmes and supplemented with other innovative policy instruments, such as economic incentives and voluntary programmes. In spite of these significant improvements and with some exceptions, such as Brazil and Thailand, the incentive structure did not motivate environmental regulatory agencies to aggressively require plants to adopt EST.

Secondly, changes in economic policy regimes between 1990 and 2002 created incentives for technology upgrading, including greater use of EST, in the eight countries of this study, with varying degrees of success among the countries and the policy regimes. The increased orientation of most countries to global markets required modifications in industrial and trade policies that resulted in effective incentives for technological modernization, except in Kenya and Zimbabwe, which were constrained by economic and political instability. However there was no similar force, such as an energy or water crisis, that would have precipitated changes in energy and water prices and acted as a stimulus for technological modernization. The modernization that did take place and resulted in some cases of significant reductions in industrial energy-use intensity appears to have been an indirect benefit of the overall technology upgrading efforts to achieve the productivity improvements needed to compete in international markets.

Thirdly, as part of their effort to participate in the global economy, most countries enhanced their technology policy regimes in ways that resulted in improved institutional capacities. Unfortunately the incentives created did not focus most technical support organizations on the real technological and skill needs of industry, and thus the organizations were in most cases marginalized supporters of the technological modernization that would have included adoption of CTs.

Chapter 12:   Eight-country Assessment of Factors Influencing EST Adoption

Three different approaches were used to identify the factors that influenced EST adoption in the eight countries of this study. The findings from these were presented in Chapter 12. The first approach compared the relationship between the three policy regimes that created the incentive structure brought to bear on plant-level behaviour via government, markets and civil society, and the actual levels of resource-use and pollutant intensity in these countries. The second approach described the perceptions of 98 plant managers and 91 key informants of the relative importance of government, markets and civil society as external drivers for EST adoption. The third approach analysed the factors observed by the investigating teams in this study that appear to have influenced plant-level behaviour at the 98 plants. The findings from each approach are summarized below.

Policy effectiveness for EST adoption

Policy effectiveness indices listed in Table 3.1 are thought to be the best proxies for quantitatively comparing the relative strength of the incentive structures created by the different policies in the eight countries. Below, a comparison is done separately for the three policy regimes, environmental, economic and technology (and, within economic policy, for the subsets of industrial, trade and resource pricing policies), and is based on the relative rankings and changes in the rankings of the eight countries over the period of this study, except in the case of two policy regimes [environmental and economic (industrial)] for Viet Nam for which there were no data for 1990 to calculate an index.

As shown by the EG index, environmental governance remained comparatively strong in Tunisia and Thailand, improved considerably in China and India, deteriorated in Zimbabwe, and remained weak in Kenya. The relatively stable and strong rankings for Tunisia and Thailand are in line with the qualitative policy reviews in the respective country chapters. The relative strengthening in China and India are also in line with the qualitative policy review in the respective country chapters, which suggests that environmental governance improved but much more needed to be done. The relative deterioration in Zimbabwe is surprising in light of the qualitative findings, while the low relative ranking in Kenya is consistent with the qualitative policy review.

The CIP index shows that the industrial performance of most countries improved considerably over this period (China, Thailand and Tunisia) or held steady (Brazil and India), though in two countries (Kenya and Zimbabwe) it deteriorated compared to the others. The industrial policy changes reviewed contributed to some extent to the improved economic performance, which would have brought considerable technological modernization and with that the likelihood of greater use of CTs.

The TI index shows that technology import was reasonably similar in both 1990 and 2001 for Brazil and China, declined slightly for Thailand,

Tunisia and Viet Nam and declined significantly for India, Kenya and Zimbabwe. The noticeable reductions in tariffs in many countries apparently did not significantly lower the barrier to import newer technologies, many of which would have incorporated CT features even if they were not classified as such. Clearly other factors, particularly changes in demand for final products and domestic capacity to manufacture chemicals and equipment, were more important determinants of the level of technology import.

The EUI score shows that energy-use intensity declined significantly both in an absolute sense and in relative ranking in many countries, most notably in China and Tunisia, and increased significantly both in an absolute sense and in relative ranking in Brazil. It declined slightly in an absolute sense for Kenya, India and Zimbabwe, and increased slightly in Thailand and Viet Nam. As there are no country-specific aggregate prices for energy, it is not possible to say much about changes in the domestic prices for energy use in the manufacturing sector. In the case of China the improvements were primarily due to industrial consolidation and in the case of Tunisia were a by-product of a national technological upgrading programme set in motion by the European Commission technical cooperation programme. In Brazil the absolute decline in energy-use efficiency is baffling, suggesting an error in the data.

As shown by the TC index, seven of the eight countries received low rankings and were classified as latecomers and one, Kenya, received a very low ranking and was classified as marginalized. However the relative rankings of three countries, Thailand, China and Viet Nam, improved considerably though the country descriptions suggest their relevant technical support organizations failed to provide the services needed. The more modest improvements in Brazil and Tunisia are consistent with the qualitative finding that their technical support organizations responded to needs, but the modest improvement in India in the capability of providing services did not meet industry's needs. The decline in the ranking of Zimbabwe and the low ranking given to Kenya are consistent with the qualitative description of the weakness of technology-upgrading organizations in these countries.

In conclusion, the use of comparative policy effectiveness indexes suggests, in some cases, different impressions than a purely qualitative characterization. Their positive feature is that they provide a basis for comparing countries and for showing changes within a country over time. The negative feature is that they are only proxies for the incentive effects of policies on technological modernization and are misleading in some cases. Thus they need to be used in conjunction with qualitative information to gain a good sense of the effects of policy incentives.

Factors perceived by plant managers and key informants as influencing EST adoption

The eight-country comparison of plant managers' perceptions of drivers for adopting EST revealed that the three most important, in descending order aggregated across the eight countries, were (a) high cost of production inputs; (b) current environmental regulation; and (c) anticipated future environmental regulation. The probably higher rating assigned to the need to reduce the high cost of production inputs most likely reflects the managers' judgement of the cost-saving potentials of CTs. This is in contrast to Adeoti (2002), who found that the three most important drivers as perceived by plant managers were environmental policy, prevention of accidents and improvement of environmental reputation. The most important drivers for key informants, in contrast to those of plant managers, were, in descending order of importance aggregated across the eight countries, (a) current environmental regulation, (b) the high cost of production inputs and (c) product specifications in foreign markets (3.3).

The eight-country aggregation of perceived drivers by plant managers, however, masks a number of important sub-sectoral variations. Current regulatory requirements were found to be the most important for a pollutant intensive sub-sector such as pulp and paper, whereas the high cost of production inputs was most important for globally competitive sub-sectors such as textiles, with yet another set of dominant drivers being perceived to influence EST adoption in the leather sub-sector.

There was also considerable variation among countries where the same sub-sector was investigated. The perceived dominant driver differed between pulp and paper mills operating in free market economies (Brazil and India) and those in planned economies (China and Viet Nam), between textile mills exporting primarily to Europe (Tunisia) and those exporting to Asian regional markets (Thailand), and between tanneries where there was a need to be responsive to community pressure on local owners (Kenya) and those where this could be ignored (Zimbabwe). In the case of Brazil the influence of current environmental regulation on the adoption of CTs suggests a shared understanding between plant managers and regulators of the importance of CTs for achieving compliance with environmental standards. In Tunisia the influence of the high cost of production inputs on the adoption of CTs reflects the cost-competitive nature of textile export to European markets.

In summary, the survey teams found that the three most important drivers for plant managers were the high cost of production inputs, current environmental regulation and anticipated future environmental regulation, whereas the three most important for key informants were current environmental regulation, the high cost of production inputs and product specifications in foreign markets. The difference in perceptions of the importance of regulation suggests that there was a gap in the understanding of environmental regulatory requirements between plant managers and key informants, which could be causing a problem for plant managers who need clarification from regulators about future environmental regulation. Thus there appears to be a need to improve communication between the two groups.

The diversity of drivers across government, markets and civil society found in this investigation supports the proposition in the heuristic model of EST adoption that it is the tripartite relationship of government, markets and civil society rather than governmental regulation alone that motivates compliance with environmental standards in developing countries. This finding goes beyond the new model for controlling pollution put forward by the World Bank (2000) by assigning more importance to governmental pressure, either in the form of current or future regulations, and market pressure, particularly cost competition, than to civil society pressure. The only exception is in the leather-tanning sub-sector in Kenya, where community groups put pressure on local owners because of the almost complete absence of governmental regulation due to the low level of development.

Factors observed by the investigating teams
The statistical analysis reveals that a host of factors influenced EST adoption, particularly higher order complexity CTs. Plant-specific factors, specifically *ENVCOM*, *OWN* and *TECHCAP* and market factors, specifically FOREIGN and WEPP, mattered significantly in determining the type of technological response and thus in explaining the adoption of higher order EST, that is technologically complex CTs. Two governmental factors, *REG* and *DONOR*, also played a role in the adoption of EST. However, civil society, in particular *COMPRESS* that has been identified as an important determinant, does not play a role, most likely because the sample of plants was skewed towards those that use higher order CTs, whose adoption is most influenced by in-plant characteristics.

The findings based on perceived and observed factors are consistent with each other. The statistical analysis of observed factors found that plant-internal, government and market factors were significantly related to EST adoption. The drivers identified by the plant managers were in line with the findings of the statistical analysis because of the higher ratings assigned to current and future regulations and high cost of production inputs. Moreover, the drivers identified by the key informants were also in line with the significant observed factors because importance was assigned to two market drivers, high cost of production inputs and product specifications, in addition to current regulation. The only difference was that key informants had a more comprehensive view of market forces.

A comparison of the above findings with the few studies that have so far investigated the adoption of CTs reveals similarities as well as divergences with the findings of the statistical model. First, the probit model findings on the role of in-plant (*TECHCAP*) and market (*FOREIGN*) factors in the adoption of CTs are corroborated by Adeoti (2002) and Blackman and Kildegaard (2003). The former assigned a key role to both a plant's capabilities to innovate and its access to foreign equity, while the latter identified the share of technical personnel as important. Secondly, a noteworthy divergence from Adeoti (2002) and in line with Montalvo (2002) concerns the significance of regulatory pressure, notably the role of a cooperative regulatory implementation strategy (*REG*) for CT adoption found in this investigation to be significantly correlated with EST adoption. Thirdly, Blackman and Kildegaard (2003) found that factors related to information acquisition drive the adoption of CTs. Adeoti (2002), for his part, even though he observed in his correlation analysis that a plant's 'technological-knowledge-related external network' could well be important for CT adoption, found in his statistical analysis, using a logit model, that this factor's importance is significantly reduced in relation to other, more important, determinants of adoption. The same relationship holds for this investigation because one information-related contextual variable, *ASSIST*, was significantly correlated with EST adoption. However, in the probit model it had to give way to other more important determinants in arriving at the 'final' model, which in fact retained one information-related variable, *DONOR*.

The findings in this investigation on the roles of *DONOR*, *ENVCOM* and *OWN* on EST adoption cannot be directly related to other EST adoption studies because these variables were not examined in other studies. Nevertheless, a comparison with the results of some other related studies with an explicit focus on environmental performance rather than EST adoption provides some additional insights. To start with, the finding here that *ENVCOM* played a key role in CT adoption complements the findings of Fryxell and Lo (2003), who find an influence of environmental knowledge and value on managerial behaviour, and of Dasgupta et al. (2000) who assign a key role to EMS in furthering environmental compliance. Combined, these findings suggest that EMSs have the potential to play an important role. Not only are they conducive to improving environmental performance but they also, importantly, induce enterprises to look at technological responses beyond PATs.

A final observation relates to the role of *OWN*, which appears to have an ambiguous impact on EST adoption. Indeed, while state ownership has been consistently found to be negatively associated with actual environmental performance in most studies (Hettige et al., 1996; Dasgupta et al., 2000), the results of this investigation indicate that state ownership is a determinant of PATs and lower order of complexity CTs. This discrepancy results from state-owned plants' privileged access to finance, which allows them to comply with environmental norms by using PATs and lower order of complexity CTs.

POLICY IMPLICATIONS

The findings of this study about policy incentives, the perceptions of plant managers and key informants and the factors observed by the investigating teams need to be taken into account in designing more effective environmental, economic and technological policies for improving the environmental performance of manufacturing plants in developing countries, particularly in regard to their adoption of more complex CTs.

The findings about policy incentives revealed the potentials and failures of various policies in different countries to encourage the adoption of EST. Environmental policy, in spite of significant modifications in its formulation and with some exceptions, was not used by most environmental regulatory agencies to accelerate the adoption of CTs as distinct from PATs. The three economic policy regimes examined, industrial, trade and resource pricing, created positive incentives in varying degrees for technological modernization in all of the eight countries except Kenya and Zimbabwe, which were constrained by economic and political instability. Finally, technology policy did not focus technology-upgrading organizations on the real technological needs of industry in most of the eight countries, and these organizations were thus marginalized supporters of the technological modernization that would have brought about more extensive adoption of CTs.

The findings on the perceptions of the drivers for EST adoption support the view that various drivers across government, markets and civil society are all motivators of compliance with environmental standards in developing countries. Governmental pressure, either in the form of current or future regulations, and market pressure, particularly cost competition, appear to be much more important drivers than civil society pressure. The only exception is in the leather-tanning sub-sector in Kenya. Here, civil society pressure, in the form of community group pressure on local tannery owners, played an important role as described above.

The findings from the observed factors have several implications for the design of policies that could improve environmental management in developing countries. First, the role of in-plant factors in determining CT utilization means that policy makers and regulatory agencies have to take into account plant and firm heterogeneity and target their actions accordingly. Implementing one-size-fits-all measures is unlikely to be effective in regulating a large number of diverse manufacturing plants. This is not to say that general incentives will not work. It rather means that general incentives towards CT adoption have to be complemented by specific measures that target different plant segments.

Second, the importance for EST adoption of in-plant factors, TECHCAP, and market factors, primarily FOREIGN, suggests using economic and technology policies that enhance these factors as ways to encourage EST (in particular CT) adoption by a country's manufacturing sector over the longer term. Improving in-plant capabilities will require specific public intervention, given the pervasive market failures surrounding plant-level technology utilization in developing countries. While technical and engineering skills acquired by formal education are an important component of technological capability building, the capability literature suggests that specific, often informal, technological training is needed for plant personnel to help build up in a cumulative fashion the necessary investment, production and innovation capabilities. Intervention by governments should take a dual approach i.e., creating incentives to stimulate technological effort on the demand side and ensuring the necessary technology-upgrading support on the supply side. In addition to capability building, industrial policies should also encourage openness to foreign involvement in the manufacturing sector as it often brings more advanced management techniques and technologies into a country. However, as there is no evidence that plants with significant foreign involvement are particularly more compliant with environmental standards, regulatory monitoring and enforcement naturally have to complement more openness to foreign involvement.

Third, the key role identified for environmental commitment suggests that policy measures aimed at building up such commitment, particularly in the form of an EMS, can be very effective. As suggested by Dasgupta et al. (2000) and Johnstone et al. (2004), a good case can be made for instituting public programmes which promote more effective environmental management and training within plants because these have the potential to increase plant managers' responsiveness to regulatory pressure. Johnstone et al. (2004) refer to a number of OECD countries that have already adjusted their regulatory system in an effort to increase the incentives for firm-level environmental management initiatives. Initiatives cited are: regulatory relief (reduction of inspection rates for ISO 14001 certified firms), corporate environmental reporting, personnel incentives, accounting procedures and organizational structure. Dasgupta et al. (2000) argue that EMS training might be more cost-effective than the conventional strengthening of regulatory monitoring and enforcement in developing countries because training promotes greater emission reductions without significant countervailing economic distortions. Thus the authors argue that in some cases this may warrant the diversion of substantial resources from conventional regulation to the dissemination of environmental information and training programmes. The fact that firm size, mainly larger size, is a clear determinant of EMS adoption suggests that SMEs should form a particular target group for such programmes.

Fourth, the significant influence of REG on the adoption of EST (in particular CT) suggests that environmental regulatory policy should allow for flexibility in the enforcement of environmental standards. A regulatory policy that is positively disposed towards a plant's experimentation with alternative cost-effective solutions and willing to accept delays in achieving reductions in pollutant discharge contributes to the longer-term environmental sustainability of the country's manufacturing sector.

In summary, there is a high degree of similarity between these findings that EST-related technological decisions are influenced by a diverse set of factors and the findings of the few other investigations reviewed in Chapter 3 into industrial environmental performance in developing countries. This study found, in particular, that a limited set of in-plant factors, market forces and governmental intervention are the most influential determinants of CT adoption. In view of the importance of these factors, public intervention in environmental management should go beyond the traditional domain of environmental policy and its associated implementation strategies to the use of economic and technology policies if its aim is to achieve a reduction in the resource use intensity of production by using CTs in addition to the protection of the environment achieved primarily with PATs.

PROGRAMME PROPOSALS

The findings and policy implications presented in the first two sections support the need for improved programmes for accelerating the adoption of EST in developing countries. Two of the more necessary governmental programmes suggested by this research are described below.

Support Technology-upgrading Programmes

Two findings of this research argue for additional financial support for technology-upgrading programmes. One is that in-plant factors, in particular environmental commitment and technical capability, are of central importance for the adoption of EST, especially of more complex CTs. The other is that environmental regulatory agencies, while gaining strength in developing countries, remain relatively ineffective and under-funded. More governmental political and financial support is still and will continue to be needed for governmental programmes that have the potential to accelerate the technology upgrading that contributes to improved environmental performance.

In most countries there is a need to create and adequately finance sub-sectoral and regionally focused (state and province) technology-upgrading programmes. These programmes would align all the factors, both internal and external to a firm, that could mitigate the more serious environmental pollution problems and reduce the usage of energy, water and material resources, resulting in 'factories for tomorrow'. To be successful, however, the programmes would have to undertake the challenging task of enhancing the technological capabilities of firms to compete in domestic and international markets, in particular their capability to obtain and adapt increasingly sophisticated technology developed elsewhere, not only abroad but also from other firms within their own country. Enhancing this capability would go hand in hand with enhancing their environmental capabilities and commitments because the selection and use of increasingly sophisticated technologies requires taking into account the resource-use intensity of new technologies. Based on the experience of first-tier East Asian new industrialized economies, building these capabilities within firms requires 'substantial investments in engineering education, an incentive system that rewards firms who have learned to upgrade, and providing assistance to indigenous firms when they have difficulty getting their first world joint venture partners to invest in technical upgrading of local firms' (Angel and Rock, 2001: 33).

Using technical extension institutions to build firm-level capabilities that enhance environmental capabilities as well as general capabilities is a long-term effort.[1] This is partially so because the existing technical institutions themselves need to build up sub-sector-specific environmental expertise. In the shorter term, other measures are clearly needed. One such measure could be subsidized programmes for those willing to be the early movers in using CTs. Without these measures, many firms, particularly SMEs, would hesitate to use technically proven CT options. Another and less costly measure would be enhanced information dissemination about the financial as well as environmental benefits of EST, and about the importance of addressing environmental issues.[2]

Exploit Policy Synergies

The findings on policy incentives and the perceptions of plant managers and key informants show that economic and technology policies, as well as environmental policies, and their implementation through pressure from government, markets and civil society can motivate the adoption of EST needed to comply with environmental standards. Yet most countries implement these three policies independently of each other. They fail to take advantage of the potential synergies for achieving technological change, including EST adoption, by a more explicit integration of environmental, economic (primarily industrial), and technology policies (Wallace, 1996; Johnstone, 1997; Rock and Angel, 2005).

A more effective integration of these policies requires improved coordination, cooperation and coherence among the policies (Luken and Hesp, 2003). Coordination among policies, the first and most basic type of integration, is often required by governmental legislation on such matters as foreign involvement, the location of industry, and the choice of technology. The second, cooperation, comes in the form of cooperative projects and programmes among industrial support institutions in such matters as industrial extension services that provide advice on environmental compliance. Coherence among policies, that is, a national vision of a common goal, is the third and most advanced type of integration. It would bring together the cumulative value added from different policies that is crucial for achieving environmental goals.

Although there are some promising examples in developing countries of coordination and cooperation of these three policy regimes, they are clearly not widespread. Promising examples of coordination include the closing of small polluting plants for both financial and environmental reasons in China, the joint determination by industrial and environmental ministries of industrial estate location in Thailand, and conditioning foreign investments with requirements for advanced technologies and transfer of management skills in Tunisia, while promising examples of cooperation are cleaner production programmes in numerous countries (25 countries in the UNIDO/UNEP NCPC programme alone) and joint research programmes that combine industrial and environmental investigations in Brazil. Although planning efforts in a few countries (China in particular) recognize the importance of policy coherence, no country has come forward with a national vision for technological modernization that simultaneously enhances economic productivity and environmental protection.[3]

In summary, supporting technology-upgrading programmes and exploiting potential policy synergies have the potential to encourage input-oriented environmental policies that are distinct from output-oriented (or rather, non-product output-oriented) environmental policies. The former are aimed at improving the resource efficiency of production processes and are increasingly being recognized as necessary. A 1995 European Environment Agency report shows that, with their output-oriented environmental policies, most EU countries did not succeed in reducing the dangers of climate change, dying forests or rapidly decreasing biodiversity (Gorlach et al., n.d.). One of the principal limitations of conventional output-oriented environmental policies is the neglect of material and energy inputs into industrial processes. The highly industrialized economies, in particular, trigger enormous material and energy flows that are relatively soon released back into the environment after short-term consumption. Each exploited resource can only be temporarily dealt with by active countermeasures that require additional energy inputs, which in turn generate wastes. Input environmental policies in contrast are aimed at reducing material flows by focusing on the causes of environmental pressures rather than on their symptoms.[4]

NOTES

1. There is an extensive literature on building technological capabilities in firms in developing countries. No attempt was made to include the findings from this literature in the programme proposals in this chapter. One starting point for reviewing the literature is Romijn (2001).
2. Similar efforts are also needed in the European Union. In a European survey more than 75 per cent of the firms polled requested information about CTs and best available technology (BAT) solutions (EC, 1995).
3. A few other examples of policy integration other than those cited here have been identified in three Asian countries (Singapore, Taiwan Province of China and Malaysia) by Rock and Angel (2005).
4. For a survey of input-oriented environmental policies directed at the manufacturing sector, see Luken and Sedic (2002).

REFERENCES

Adeoti, J. (2002), *Technology and the Environment in Sub-Saharan Africa: Emerging Trends in the Nigerian Manufacturing Industry*, Burlington, US: Ashgate Publishing.

Angel, D. and M. Rock (2001), 'Policy Integration: Environment and Development in Asia', paper prepared for the US Asia Environmental Partnership, Washington, DC: US Asian Environmental Partnership (USAEP).

Blackman, A. and A. Kildegaard (2003), 'Clean Technology Change in Developing Country Industrial Clusters: Mexican Leather Tanning', Discussion Paper 03-12, Washington, DC: Resources for the Future.

Dasgupta, S., H. Hettige and D. Wheeler (2000), 'What improves environmental compliance? Evidence from Mexican industry', *Journal of Environmental Economics and Management*, **39** (1), 39–66.

EC (DG III) (1995), 'Attitude and Strategy of Business Regarding Protection of the Environment: Common Environmental Framework', Brussels: European Commission.

Fryxell, G.E. and C.W.H. Lo (2003), 'The influence of environmental knowledge and values on managerial behaviours on behalf of the environment: an empirical examination of managers in China', *Journal of Business Ethics*, **46** (1), 45–69.

Gorlach, B., F. Hinterberger and P. Scgepelmann (no date), 'From Vienna to Helsinki: The Process of Integration of Environmental Concerns in all Policies of the European Union', Wuppertal Institute for Climate Change, Environment and Energy (available on: http://www.wupperinst.org).

Hettige, H., M. Huq, S. Pargal and D. Wheeler (1996), 'Determinants of pollution abatement in developing countries: evidence from South and Southeast Asia', *World Development*, **24** (12), 1891–904.

Johnstone, N. (1997), 'Globalization, Technology and the Environment', in OECD, Environment Directorate 'Globalization and Environment: Proceedings of the Vienna Workshop', ENV/EPOC/GEEI (97), Paris: Organization for Economic Cooperation and Development, pp. 163–203.

Johnstone, N., P. Scapecchi, B. Ytterhus, and R. Wolff (2004), 'The firm, environmental management and environmental measures: lessons from a survey of European manufacturing firms', *Journal of Environmental Planning and Management*, **47** (23), 685–707.

Luken, R. and A. Sedic (2002), 'National Policies for Efficient Resource Utilization and Protection', in P. Lens, L. Pol, P. Wilderer and T. Asano (eds), *Water Recycling and Resource Recovery in Industry*, London, UK: IWA Publishing, pp. 86–108.

Luken, R. and P. Hesp (eds) (2003), *Sustainable Development and Industry? Reports from Seven Developing and Transition Economies*, Cheltenham, UK and Northampton, MA, US: Edward Elgar Publishing.

Montalvo, C. (2002), *Environmental Policy and Technological Innovation: Why do Firms Adopt or Reject New Technologies?*, Cheltenham, UK and Northampton, MA, US: Edward Elgar Publishing.

Rock, M. and D. Angel (2005), *Industrial Transformation in the Developing World*, Oxford: Oxford University Press.

Romijn, H. (2001), 'Technology support for small-scale industry in developing countries: a review of concepts and project practices', *Oxford Development Studies*, **29** (1), 57–76.

Wallace, D. (1996), *Sustainable Industrialization*, London, UK: Earthscan and James and James.

World Bank (2000), *Greening Industry: New Roles for Communities, Markets and Governments*, Oxford, UK: Oxford University Press.

Index

abatement technologies (PATs) 3,
  14–15, 17, 33, 57
  see also individual countries
absolute decoupling 7–8
activated sludge 73, 135, 196, 224, 252
Aden, J. 31, 32
aerated lagoons 73, 135, 165, 252, 281
air pollution 15, 34, 83, 205
Albaladejo, M. 43, 44
Amigos do Meio Ambiente (Friends of
  the Environment) 74
anti-dumping measures 61, 124
Archibugi, D. 45
Arundel, A. 15
ASEAN (Association of South East
  Asian Nations) 181–2, 240
ASEAN Environmental Improvement
  Programme (ASEAN–EIP) 198
Asian Development Bank 108, 198,
  255
Association for Industrial
  Environmental Protection 254
Association of Thai Bleaching,
  Dyeing, Printing and Finishing
  Industries 197

Bannister, G. 34
Bekhechi, M. 266
biochemical oxygen demand (BOD)
  effluent, decoupling trends 9, 10,
  11–12
Blackman, A. 29, 34
bleaching process 69, 104, 131, 225
BOD effluent *see* biochemical oxygen
  demand (BOD) effluent
BRACELPA (Brazilian Association of
  Pulp and Paper Manufacturers)
  75
Brazil
  business associations 75
  command-and-control regulatory
    programme 57

competitive industrial performance
  (CIP) index 39, 60–61
economic incentives 57
economic policy regimes 58–65
energy consumption 63–4
energy-use intensity (EUI) index
  64–5
environmental governance (EG)
  index 39, 58
environmental labelling 58
environmental management study
  32–3
environmental management system
  (EMS) 69
environmental policy 56–8
EST adoption, context for decisions
  economic performance indicators
    52–4
  environmental performance
    indicators 54–5
  implications for adoption 55–6
export promotion 59–60
foreign direct investment (FDI) 59
import regime 61–2, 63, 67
industrial policy 58–61
international donors 75–6
ISO 14001 certification programme
  54–5, 69
key informants 74–6
NGOs 74–5
privatization 60
pulp and paper sub-sector
  cleaner production case study
    73
  economic overview 66–8
  environmental performance 73–4
  PAT characterization 73
  process technology and CT
    characterization 69–73
  profile 68–9, 70–71
  trade policy 62–3
resource pricing policy 63–5

technological capabilities (TC) index
39, 66
technology import (TI) index 39, 63
technology policy 65–6
trade policy 61–3
transparency and disclosure
programmes 58
wastewater management 73
water management 64
Brazilian Association of Pulp and
Paper Manufacturers
(BRACELPA) 75
Brazilian Pulp and Paper Technical
Association 75
business associations
Brazil 75
China 107
India 137
Kenya 166–7
Thailand 197
Tunisia 226
Viet Nam 254
Zimbabwe 283

capital goods imports 43
Brazil 61
China 92–3
India 124–5
Kenya 149, 154
Thailand 182
Tunisia 213
Viet Nam 240–41
Zimbabwe 270
carbon dioxide (CO_2) emissions,
decoupling trends 9, 10, 12
Carl Duisberg Gesellschaft (CDG) 198
chemical mechanical pulping process
247
chemical soda pulping process 104,
131, 247, 250
China
air pollution 83, 86
business associations 107
command-and-control regulatory
programme 86
competitive industrial performance
(CIP) index 39, 91
economic policy regimes 88–95
electricity costs 94
energy consumption 94

energy-use intensity (EUI) index 95
environmental governance (EG)
index 88
environmental labelling 87
environmental policy 85–8
EST adoption, context for decisions
economic performance indicators
81–3
environmental performance
indicators 83–4
implications for adoption 84–5
export promotion 90, 91–2
foreign direct investment (FDI)
89–90
General Agreement on Tariffs and
Trade (GATT) 91–2
import regime 92–3
industrial policy 88–91
international donors 107–8
ISO 14001 certification programme
84, 100
key informants 106–8
NGOs 107
pollution levies 86–7
privatization 90–91
pulp and paper sub-sector
cleaner production case study
105
CT applications 22, 23–4
economic overview 98–9
environmental performance 86,
106
PAT characterization 105–6
process technology and CT
characterization 100, 104
profile 99–100, 101–3
research and development (R&D)
97
trade policy 93
research and development (R&D)
96–7
resource pricing policy 93–5
technological capabilities (TC) index
39, 98
technology import (TI) index 39, 93
technology policy 95–8
trade policy 91–3
transparency and disclosure
programmes 87
voluntary programmes 87

wastewater management 83, 86, 95, 106, 107, 109
water management 94–5
water pollution 83, 86
World Trade Organization (WTO), entry into 89, 92
China Paper Industry Association 107
CIP index 39, 43, 321
civil society, influence on EST adoption 35, 36, 37, 41, 166, 296
cleaner production case studies
　Brazil 73
　China 105
　India 135
　Kenya 165
　Thailand 196
　Tunisia 224
　Viet Nam 252
　Zimbabwe 281
cleaner production (CP) strategy 18
cleaner technologies (CTs) 1, 3, 17–18, 22, 24, 33
　applications
　　leather processing sub-sector 22, 25
　　pulp and paper sub-sector 22, 23–4
　　textile sub-sector 20, 21
　categories 18, 19–20
　see also individual countries
CO_2 emissions, decoupling trends 9, 10, 12
Coco, A. 45
command-and-control regulatory programmes 41, 294, 320
　Brazil 57
　China 86
　India 118
　Kenya 148–9
　Thailand 177
　Tunisia 208
　Viet Nam 236
　Zimbabwe 265–6
community pressure as regulation 31, 34, 166, 296, 298
competitive industrial performance (CIP) index 39, 43, 321
computer-assisted dyeing 223
Confederation of Zimbabwe Industries 268, 283, 284

Copeland, B. 16
CP (cleaner production) strategy 18
CTs (cleaner technologies) 1, 3, 17–18, 22, 24, 33
　applications
　　leather processing sub-sector 22, 25
　　pulp and paper sub-sector 22, 23–4
　　textile sub-sector 20, 21
　categories 18, 19–20
　see also individual countries

Danish Cooperation for Environment and Development (DANCED) 198
Danish International Development Agency 284
Dasgupta, S. 37, 327
de Bruyn, S. 15
decoupling of environmental pressure from industrial growth 7–8
　CTs, role of 318–19
　factors affecting 12–16
　global trends 8–12
developing countries, EST adoption, empirical studies 30–35
drivers of EST adoption
　civil society 296
　country differences 298–9
　government 294–5
　markets 295
　as perceived by key informants 299, 300
　as perceived by plant managers 296–9
　sub-sector differences 296–8

Eco-mark 119
economic incentives for EST adoption 295, 320
　Brazil 57
　India 118–19
　Kenya 149
　Thailand 177–8
　Tunisia 208
　Viet Nam 236
economic performance indicators
　Brazil 52–4
　China 81–3

India 113–15
Kenya 143–5
Thailand 172–4
Tunisia 203–4
Viet Nam 231–3
Zimbabwe 261–3
economic policy regimes 35, 42–5,
    319–20
Brazil 58–65
China 88–95
effectiveness assessment 42–5
India 120–27
Kenya 150–57
rankings and indices 39–40
Thailand 179–85
Tunisia 209–15
Viet Nam 237–43
Zimbabwe 267–72
EG (environmental governance) index
    39, 41–2, 321
energy use, decoupling trends 9, 10,
    11
energy-use intensity (EUI) index 39,
    40, 45, 322
ENORME–CETIME Initiative 227
Environment Africa 282
environmental governance (EG) index
    39, 41–2, 321
environmental labelling
Brazil 58
China 87
India 119
environmental management 32–3
environmental management systems
    (EMSs) 32
Brazil 69
drivers for 299
India 131
Kenya 149
training 327–8
Tunisia 227
Viet Nam 251
Zimbabwe 266
environmental performance indicators
Brazil 54–5
China 83–4
India 115–16
Kenya 145–7
Thailand 174–5
Tunisia 205–6

Viet Nam 233, 234
Zimbabwe 263–4
environmental policies 35, 319–20, 326
Brazil 56–8
China 85–8
effectiveness assessment 41–2
India 117–20
Kenya 147–50
rankings and indices 39–40
Thailand 176–9
Tunisia 207–9
Viet Nam 235–7
Zimbabwe 265–7
Environmental Protection 254
environmental releases 8
environmental reputation 295
environmental withdrawals 8
environmentally sound technology
    (EST) 3, 17
environmentally sound technology
    (EST) adoption
empirical studies, developing
    countries 30–34
government policies, effectiveness
    assessment 38–46, 290–94,
    320–26
heuristic model 35–7, 319
modes of investigation 38–48
observed factors 47–8, 324–6
dependent variable 301–2
independent variables 302–7
indices 314–15
measures of association 308–10
probit model 310–13
statistical analysis 307–14
perceived factors 46, 294–300,
    323–4
programme proposals 328–31
technology capabilities, literature
    review 28, 29–30
technology diffusion, literature
    review 28–9
see also individual countries
equipment modification 19
EST *see* environmentally sound
    technology
ETE (Euro-Tunisie-Entreprise)
    Programme 212
EUI (energy-use intensity) index 39,
    40, 45, 322

Euro-Tunisie-Entreprise (ETE)
  Programme 212
European Union (EU)
  environmental policies 330–31
  and Tunisia, free trade zone 212, 226
  Viet Nam, bilateral donor 255
Export Financing Programme
  (PROEX) 60
export processing zones
  Kenya 152
  Tunisia 211
  Viet Nam 239
  Zimbabwe 269
export promotion
  Brazil 59–60
  China 90, 91–2
  India 121–2
  Kenya 152
  Thailand 180
  Tunisia 210
  Viet Nam 238
  Zimbabwe 268
external drivers of EST adoption
  civil society 296
  country differences 298–9
  government 294–5
  markets 295
  as perceived by key informants 299,
    300
  as perceived by plant managers
    296–9
  sub-sector differences 296–8

Federation of Kenyan Employers 167
Federation of Thai Industries 186–7
financial incentives for EST adoption
  295
Fonds d'Accès aux Marchés 210
foreign direct investment (FDI) 42
  Brazil 59
  China 89–90
  India 120–21
  Kenya 151–2
  Thailand 180
  Tunisia 210
  Viet Nam 238
  Zimbabwe 268
foreign markets, production
  specifications 295, 299
Friends of the Earth 75

Friends of the Environment 74
Fundacao Gaia (Gaia Foundation) 74
future environmental regulation 295,
  299

Gaia Foundation 74
General Agreement on Tariffs and
  Trade (GATT)
  China 91–2
  Zimbabwe 269
German Technical Cooperation
  Agency 226–7, 284
global trends in decoupling 8–12
good housekeeping 19
government policies, effectiveness
    assessment 38–41
  economic policy 42–5
  environmental policy 41–2
  technology policy 45–6

Hettige, H. 16, 31
hydro-pulping process 131, 247

IARPMA (India Agro and Recycled
  Paper Mills Association) 137
ICICI (Industrial Credit and
  Investment Corporation of India)
  138
Ikiara, G. 154
import regimes
  Brazil 61–2, 63, 67
  China 92–3
  India 123–5
  Kenya 153–4
  Thailand 182–3
  Tunisia 212–13
  Viet Nam 240–41
  Zimbabwe 269, 270
import restriction policies 43–4
incentives for EST adoption 35–7
India
  business associations 137
  cleaner production programme 119
  command-and-control regulatory
    programme 118
  competitive industrial performance
    (CIP) index 39, 123
  eco-labelling scheme 119
  economic incentives 118–19
  economic policy regimes 120–27

energy consumption 126
environmental governance (EG)
    index 39, 119–20
environmental impact assessments
    118
environmental management system
    (EMS) 131
environmental policy 117–20
EST adoption, context for decisions
    economic performance indicators
        113–15
    environmental performance
        indicators 115–16
    implications for adoption 116–17
Export–Import Policy 121, 124
export promotion 121–2
foreign direct investment (FDI)
    120–21
import regime 123–5
industrial policy 120–23
international donors 137–8
ISO 14001 certification programme
    115, 116, 131
key informants 136–8
NGOs 136–7
privatization 122–3
pulp and paper sub-sector
    cleaner production case study 135
    economic overview 129–30
    environmental performance 135–6
    PAT characterization 135
    process technology and CT
        characterization 131–5
    profile 130–31
    trade policy 125
research and development (R&D)
    127, 128
resource pricing policy 126–7
technological capabilities (TC) index
    40, 128–9
technology import (TI) index 40,
    125–6
technology policy 127–9
trade policy 123–6
transparency and disclosure
    programmes 119
voluntary programmes 119
water management 126–7
Water Pollution Act 118
water-use charges 118

India Agro and Recycled Paper Mills
    Association (IARPMA) 137
India Brand Equity Fund 121–2
Industrial Credit and Investment
    Corporation of India (ICICI)
    138
Industrial Development Bank of India
    138
industrial policies
    Brazil 58–61
    China 88–91
    effectiveness assessment 42–3
    India 120–23
    Kenya 150–53
    Thailand 179–81
    Tunisia 209–11
    Viet Nam 237–9
    Zimbabwe 267–9
informal regulation 31
    see also community pressure as
        regulation
input environmental policies 331
input material change 19
international donors
    Brazil 75–6
    China 107–8
    India 137–8
    Kenya 167–8
    Thailand 198
    Tunisia 226–7
    Viet Nam 254–5
    Zimbabwe 283–4
International Energy Agency (IEA)
    8
International Union for Conservation
    of Nature and Natural Resources
    254
Investe Brasil 59
ISO 14001 certification programmes
    Brazil 54–5, 69
    China 84, 100
    India 115, 116, 131
    Kenya 146, 147, 161
    Thailand 175, 178, 190
    Tunisia 205, 206
    Viet Nam 233, 234
    Zimbabwe 264, 277

Japanese Bank for International
    Cooperation 137

Japanese Overseas Economic
  Cooperation Fund 198
Johnstone, N. 15

Kemp, R. 15, 29
Kenya
  business associations 166–7
  civil society, influence on EST
    adoption 166
  command-and-control regulatory
    programme 148–9
  competitive industrial performance
    (CIP) index 39, 152–3
  economic incentives 149
  economic policy regimes 150–57
  electricity costs 155
  energy consumption 155
  energy-use intensity (EUI) index 157
  environmental governance (EG)
    index 39, 150
  environmental impact assessments
    149
  environmental management system
    (EMS) 149
  environmental policy 147–50
  EST adoption, context for decisions
    economic performance indicators
      143–5
    environmental performance
      indicators 145–7
    implications for adoption 147
  export processing zones 152
  export promotion 152
  foreign direct investment (FDI)
    151–2
  import regime 153–4
  industrial policy 150–53
  international donors 167–8
  ISO 14001 certification programme
    146, 147, 161
  key informants 165–8
  leather processing sub-sector 154–5
    cleaner production case study 165
    economic overview 159–61
    environmental performance 165
    PAT characterization 164–5
    process technology and CT
      characterization 161–4
    profile 161, 162–3
  NGOs 166

research and development (R&D)
    157, 158
  resource pricing policy 155–7
  technological capabilities (TC) index
    40, 159
  technology import (TI) index 40,
    154–5
  technology policy 157–9
  trade policy 153–5
  voluntary programmes 149
  wastewater management 165, 169
  water management 156–7
Kenya Association of Manufacturers
    167
Kenya National Chamber of
    Commerce and Industry 166–7
Kenyan Tanners' Association 167
Kildegaard, A. 34
kraft pulping process 69, 77, 104, 131,
    247, 250

Lall, S. 43, 44, 95
Leather and Allied Industries
    Federation of Zimbabwe (LIZ)
    283
leather processing sub-sector, EST
    adoption
  Kenya 154–5
    cleaner production case study
      165
    CT application 22, 25
    economic overview 159–61
    environmental performance 165
    PAT characterization 164–5
    process technology and CT
      characterization 161–4
    profile 161, 162–3
  perceived drivers 298, 299, 300
  Zimbabwe
    cleaner production case study 281
    economic overview 274–6
    energy consumption 272
    environmental performance 281–2
    PAT characterization 281
    process technology and CT
      characterization 277, 280–81
    profile 276–7, 278–9
    trade policy 270–71
local communities *see* community
    pressure as regulation

manufacturing value added (MVA) 2,
7–8, 13–14
markets, role in EST adoption 35–7
Martin, P. 34, 38
Mercier, J. 266
MERCOSUR 61
Mexico 32, 33–4
Montalvo, C. 33–4
MVA (manufacturing value added) 2,
7–8, 13–14

National Cleaner Production Centres
Brazil 76
China 87, 107–8
India 138
Tunisia 208, 226
Viet Nam 20, 237, 255
National Federation of Thai Textile
Industries 197
NGOs, influence on EST adoption
Brazil 74–5
China 107
India 136–7
Kenya 166
Thailand 197
Tunisia 225–6
Viet Nam 253–4
Zimbabwe 282–3
Nigeria, EST adoption study 33
Norwegian Agency for Development
284
Norwegian World Cleaner Production
Society 226
Nucleo Amigos da Terra (Friends of
the Earth) 75

observed factors determining EST
adoption 47–8, 324–6
dependent variable 301–2
independent variables 302–7
indices 314–15
measures of association 308–10
probit model 310–13
statistical analysis 307–14
off-site recycling 18
on-site recovery and reuse 19
organic matter effluent *see* biochemical
oxygen demand (BOD) effluent
output-oriented environmental policies
330–31

Paper Environmental Protection 107
Parana Association of Pulp and Paper
Manufacturers (SINPACEL) 75
PATs (pollutant abatement
technologies) 3, 14–15, 17, 33, 57
see also individual countries
peer pressure as external driver for
EST adoption 296
perceived factors for EST adoption 46,
294–300, 323–4
pollutant abatement technologies
(PATs) 3, 14–15, 17, 33, 57
see also individual countries
pollutant discharge *see* biochemical
oxygen demand (BOD) effluent;
carbon dioxide (CO_2) emissions
polluter pays principle 119, 266
prevention technologies *see* CTs
product modification 19–20
PROEX (Export Financing
Programme) 60
public pressure as regulation 31, 34,
166, 296, 298
pulp and paper sub-sector, EST
adoption
Brazil
cleaner production case study 73
economic overview 66–8
environmental performance 73–4
PAT characterization 73
process technology and CT
characterization 69–73
profile 68–9, 70–71
trade policy 62–3
China
cleaner production case study 105
CT applications 22, 23–4
economic overview 98–9
environmental performance 86,
106
PAT characterization 105–6
process technology and CT
characterization 100–105
profile 99–100, 101–3
research and development (R&D)
97
trade policy 93
India
cleaner production case study 135
economic overview 129–30

environmental performance 135–6
PAT characterization 135
process technology and CT
characterization 131–5
profile 130–31
trade policy 125
perceived drivers 296–8, 299, 300
Viet Nam
cleaner production case study 252
economic overview 245–7
energy consumption 242
environmental performance 252–3
PAT characterization 252
process technology and CT
characterization 250–52
profile 247–50
trade policy 241

relative decoupling 7
Reppelin-Hill, V. 34, 38
resource pricing policies
Brazil 63–5
China 93–5
effectiveness assessment 44–5
India 126–7
Kenya 155–7
Thailand 183–5
Tunisia 214–15
Viet Nam 242–3
Zimbabwe 271–2
Rio Grande do Sul Association of
Pulp, Paper and Cork
Manufacturers 75
Rock, M. 32

Samutpraken Environment Society 197
Seroa da Motta, R. 32–3
SINPACEL (Parana Association of
Pulp and Paper Manufacturers) 75
skills *see* technological capabilities
South Asian Association for Regional
Cooperation 124
South China University of Technology
97
Standards Association of Zimbabwe
273
sulphate pulping process 104, 131
supply chain demands 295, 299
Swedish Industrial Development
Agency 284

Taylor, M.S. 16
technological capabilities, literature
review 28, 29–30
technological capabilities (TC) index
39–40, 45–6, 322
Brazil 66
China 98
India 128–9
Kenya 159
Thailand 187
Tunisia 217
Viet Nam 245
Zimbabwe 274
technological capability building 327
technological configuration, effect on
decoupling 14–16
technology diffusion, literature review
28–9
technology effort (TE) index 49
technology import (TI) index 30–40,
43–4, 321–2
technology licensing 43–4
technology modification 19
technology policies 35, 319–20, 326
Brazil 65–6
China 95–8
effectiveness assessment 45–6
India 127–9
Kenya 157–9
rankings and indices 39–40
Thailand 185–7
Tunisia 215–17
Viet Nam 243–5
Zimbabwe 273–4
technology-upgrading programmes
328–9
Teitel, S. 274
textile sub-sector, EST adoption
CT applications 20, 21
perceived drivers 298, 299, 300
Thailand
cleaner production case study 196
economic overview 187–9
environmental performance 196
PAT characterization 195–6
process technology and CT
characterization 190–95
profile 189–90
Tunisia
cleaner production case study 224

economic overview 218
energy consumption 213
environmental performance 224–5
PAT characterization 223–4
process technology and CT
    characterization 222–3
profile 219–22
trade policy 213
Thai Productivity Institute 186
Thai Textile Institute 186
Thai Textile Manufacturing
    Association 197
Thailand
business associations 197
command-and-control regulatory
    programme 177
competitive industrial performance
    (CIP) index 39, 181
economic incentives 177–8
economic policy regimes 179–85
electricity costs 184
energy consumption 184
energy management 184
environmental governance (EG)
    index 39, 179
environmental policy 176–9
EST adoption, context for decisions
    economic performance indicators
        172–4
    environmental performance
        indicators 174–5
    implications for adoption 175–6
export promotion 180
foreign direct investment (FDI) 180
import regime 182–3
industrial estates 181
industrial policy 179–81
international donors 198
ISO 14001 certification programme
    175, 178, 190
key informants 197–8
NGOs 197
pollutant discharge 177–8
research and development (R&D)
    185–6
resource pricing policy 183–5
technological capabilities (TC) index
    39, 187
technology import (TI) index 39, 183
technology policy 185–7

textile sub-sector 182–3
    cleaner production case study 196
    economic overview 187–9
    environmental performance 196
    PAT characterization 195–6
    process technology and CT
        characterization 190–95
    profile 189–90
trade policy 181–3
transparency and disclosure
    programmes 178
voluntary programmes 178
wastewater management 174, 178,
    196, 199
water management 184–5
water-use intensity 174
TI (technology import) index 43–4,
    321–2
trade policies
Brazil 61–3
China 91–3
effectiveness assessment 43–4
India 123–6
Kenya 153–5
Thailand 181–3
Tunisia 211–13
Viet Nam 240–42
Zimbabwe 269–71
transparency and disclosure
    programmes
Brazil 58
China 87
India 119
Thailand 178
Tunisia 209
Tunisia
business associations 226
command-and-control regulatory
    programme 208
competitive industrial performance
    (CIP) index 39, 211
economic incentives 208
economic policy regimes 209–15
effluent standards 208
energy consumption 213
energy-use intensity 215
environmental governance (EG)
    index 39, 209
environmental management system
    (EMS) 227

environmental policy 207–9
EST adoption, context for decisions
  economic performance indicators
    203–4
  environmental performance
    indicators 205–6
  implications for adoption 39
export promotion 210
foreign direct investment (FDI) 210
import regime 212–13
industrial estates 211
industrial policy 209–11
international donors 226–7
ISO 14001 certification programme
  205, 206
key informants 225–7
NGOs 225–6
research and development (R&D)
  215–16
resource pricing policy 214–15
technological capabilities (TC) index
  39, 217
technology import (TI) index 39, 213
technology policy 215–17
textile sub-sector
  cleaner production case study 224
  economic overview 218
  energy consumption 213
  environmental performance 224–5
  PAT characterization 223–4
  process technology and CT
    characterization 222–3
  profile 219–22
  trade policy 213
trade policy 211–13
transparency and disclosure
  programmes 209
voluntary programmes 208–9
wastewater management 207, 208,
  211, 222, 224, 225
water management 214–15
water regulations 207
Tunisian Association for Protection of
  Nature and the Environment
  225–6
Tunisian Centre for Export Promotion
  210

UNEP (United Nations Environment
  Programme) 8, 104, 108

UNIDO/UNEP National Cleaner
  Production Centres
  Brazil 76
  China 87, 107–8
  India 138
  Tunisia 208, 226
  Viet Nam 20, 237, 255
UNIDO (United Nations Industrial
  Development Organization) 8, 43,
  167–8, 284
United States Agency for International
  Development (USAID) 198, 208,
  226
United States–Viet Nam Bilateral
  Trade Agreement 240

Viet Nam
  business associations 254
  Cleaner Production Centre 20, 237,
    255
  command-and-control regulatory
    programme 236
  competitive industrial performance
    (CIP) index 39, 239
  consumer price index (CPI) 232–3
  economic incentives 236
  economic policy regimes 237–43
  electricity costs 242
  energy consumption 242
  energy-use intensity 40, 243
  environmental governance (EG)
    index 39, 237
  environmental management system
    (EMS) 251
  environmental policy 235–7
  EST adoption, context for decisions
    economic performance indicators
      231–3
    environmental performance
      indicators 233, 234
    implications for adoption 233–5
  export processing zones 239
  export promotion 238
  foreign direct investment (FDI) 238
  import regime 240–41
  industrial environmental
    management 237
  industrial estates 239
  industrial policy 237–9
  international donors 254–5

ISO 14001 certification programme
    233, 234
key informants 253–5
Law on Environmental Protection
    235
NGOs 253–4
privatization 239
pulp and paper sub-sector
    cleaner production case study 252
    economic overview 245–7
    energy consumption 242
    environmental performance 252–3
    PAT characterization 252
    process technology and CT
        characterization 250–52
    profile 247–50
    trade policy 241
research and development (R&D)
    244
resource pricing policy 242–3
science and technology policy 243,
    244, 245
technological capabilities (TC) index
    40, 245
technology import (TI) index 40,
    241–2
technology policy 243–5
textile sub-sector, CT applications
    20, 21
trade policy 240–42
voluntary programmes 237
wastewater management 239, 243,
    252, 253
water management 242–3
Viet Nam Paper Corporation 247, 254
Viet Nam Papermaking Association
    254
voluntary programmes
    Brazil 57–8
    China 87
    India 119
    Kenya 149
    Thailand 178
    Tunisia 208–9
    Viet Nam 237
    Zimbabwe 266

Wang, H. 34, 95
wastewater management 15, 20
    Brazil 73

China 83, 86, 95, 106, 107, 109
Kenya 165, 169
Thailand 174, 178, 196, 199
Tunisia 207, 208, 211, 222, 224, 225
Viet Nam 239, 243, 252, 253
water management
    Brazil 64
    China 94–5
    India 126–7
    Kenya 156–7
    Thailand 184–5
    Tunisia 214–15
    Viet Nam 242–3
water pollution 34, 83, 205
water use, decoupling trends 11
Wheeler, D. 34, 38
Wignaraja, G. 154
wood pulp production, adoption of
    CTs 34
World Bank
    Brazil, pollution control funding 75
    India, assistance to 137, 138
    industrial pollution survey 136
    'new model' of pollution control 35
    Zimbabwe, cancellation of aid to
        268
World Food Programme 255
World Trade Organization (WTO),
    China's entry 89, 92
World Wide Fund for Nature 166, 254

Zhang, X. 91
Zimbabwe
    business associations 283
    command-and-control regulatory
        programme 265–6
    competitive industrial performance
        (CIP) index 39, 269
    economic policy regimes 267–72
    Economic Structural Adjustment
        Programme (ESAP) 267
    electricity costs 271–2
    energy consumption 272
    energy-use intensity 40, 272
    environmental governance (EG)
        index 267
    environmental management system
        (EMS) 266
    environmental policy 265–7
    EST adoption, context for decisions

economic performance indicators 261–3
environmental performance indicators 263–4
implications for adoption 264–5
export processing zones 269
export promotion 268
foreign direct investment (FDI) 268
import regime 269, 270
industrial policy 267–9
international donors 283–4
ISO 14001 certification programme 264, 277
key informants 282–4
leather processing sub-sector
cleaner production case study 281
economic overview 274–6
energy consumption 272
environmental performance 281–2

PAT characterization 281
process technology and CT characterization 277, 280–81
profile 276–7, 278–9
trade policy 270–71
NGOs 282–3
research and development (R&D) 273, 277
resource pricing policy 271–2
science and technology policy 273, 274
technological capabilities (TC) index 40, 274
technology import (TI) index 40, 271
technology policy 273–4
trade policy 269–71
voluntary programmes 266
water charges 272
ZimTrade 268, 283